LEE'S ENDANGERED LEFT

LEE'S ENDANGERED LEFT

The Civil War in Western Virginia
Spring of 1864

RICHARD R. DUNCAN

LOUISIANA STATE UNIVERSITY PRESS   *Baton Rouge*

Copyright © 1998 by Louisiana State University Press
All rights reserved
Manufactured in the United States of America
First printing
07 06 05 04 03 02 01 00 99 98 5 4 3 2 1

Designer: Michele Myatt Quinn
Typeface: Goudy Old Style
Typesetter: Coghill Composition Co.
Printer and binder: Edwards Brothers, Inc.

Library of Congress Cataloging-in-Publication Data:
Duncan, Richard R.
    Lee's endangered left : the Civil War in western Virginia, spring
of 1864 / Richard R. Duncan.
      p. cm.
    Includes bibliographical references and index.
    ISBN 0-8071-2291-2 (alk. paper)
      1. Virginia—History—Civil War, 1861–1865. 2. West
Virginia—History—Civil War, 1861–1865. 3. Lee, Robert E.
(Robert Edward), 1807–1870. I. Title.
E581.D86 1998
973.7'455—dc21   98-33689
                                            CIP

In Memory
Emma Swing Duncan
and
Ray Howard Duncan

Contents

ILLUSTRATIONS

PHOTOGRAPHS AND ART

MAPS

PREFACE

On May 4, 1864, a determined Ulysses S. Grant wired Major General Henry W. Halleck from Germanna Ford, "Forty Eight hours now will demonstrate whether the enemy intends giving battle this side of Richmond." Earlier that morning cavalry units of the Army of the Potomac crossed the Rapidan River and began pushing in Southern pickets.[1] Once again the opening of a new spring campaign reverberated throughout the Virginia countryside. With the renewal of campaigning, Grant, using concerted moves, struck at Lee's Army of Northern Virginia and General Joseph Johnston's army in Georgia, but also high on his priority list was western Virginia. If Grant could destroy Lee's base of support, then the Army of Northern Virginia would be forced to retreat into North Carolina. If Lee's army were deprived of the agriculturally rich Shenandoah Valley, Confederate operations in Virginia, including the defense of Richmond, would be doomed. In addition, the destruction of the saltworks and lead mines in southwestern Virginia would strike a serious blow at the Confederate war effort. A key element in Grant's strategy was in targeting Lee's western transportation system. Destruction of the Virginia and Tennessee and Virginia Central Railroads and the James River and Kanawha Canal would not only wreck those supply links but, in the case of the Virginia and Tennessee Railroad, prevent the Confederacy from using interior lines to move troops between Virginia and Tennessee.

Initially, Federal operations in western Virginia proved only partially successful. Despite a victory at the Battle of Cloyds Mountain and the destruction of the New River bridge, Grant's pincer movements faltered in the Shenandoah Valley at the Battle of New Market. Yet a renewal of the initiative, now focused on the Valley, briefly secured dominance over western Virginia in early June as the Army of West Virginia drove to the

1. John Y. Simon, ed., *The Papers of Ulysses S. Grant* (Carbondale, 1982), X, 397.

gates of Lynchburg in central Virginia before being stopped. Confederate forces, now seizing the initiative, swept down the Shenandoah Valley to threaten Washington in July.

For the civilian population the renewal of campaigning in that spring posed an ominous threat. The drive of Federal forces beyond their vulnerable supply lines forced them to live off the countryside. War-weariness, the need to feed an army and secure fresh horses for the cavalry, and Union objectives designed to cripple the South's ability to sustain the war inflicted serious losses on Confederates and Unionists alike. Hostile acts were accorded little toleration, and past ones of disloyalty exacted a price. The ruins of the Virginia Military Institute and the home of former Governor John Letcher bore witness to the changing nature of warfare. The destruction of both private and public property would dot the route of the Army of West Virginia up the Shenandoah Valley and across the Blue Ridge Mountains to Lynchburg.

Grant's strategy for western Virginia in 1864 set into motion a series of movements for control over the Shenandoah Valley. Some of the most dramatic moments of that campaign would come in September and October in the engagements between Generals Jubal Early and Philip Sheridan, capturing the imagination of both historians and readers. However, the focus on Early's raid on Washington and Sheridan's countermove obscures earlier Federal objectives in western Virginia and distorts the full scope of the Valley campaign, which consisted of four distinct phases. Union movements dominated the first two until the middle of June, whereas in the second half Southern forces seized the initiative in reasserting their control over the Shenandoah until Sheridan's stunning victories at Winchester and Cedar Creek ended any effective Confederate presence in western Virginia.

A number of recent works attest to the continuing interest in the second half of the Valley campaign, and they provide a fine scholarly coverage for the period from late June through October. However, examinations of the earlier months have focused primarily on individual battles without integrating them into an extended coverage of operations during that period. Edward Raymond Turner's classic work *The New Market Campaign, May 1864*, made a major contribution in 1912, and more recently William C. Davis' *Battle of New Market* (1975) provides a model for military historians and undoubtedly a definitive coverage of that engagement. Importantly,

Marshall M. Brice in *Conquest of a Valley* (1965) and more recently Scott C. Patchan in his excellent study *The Forgotten Fury: The Battle of Piedmont, Virginia* (1996) call attention to the often ignored but significant Battle of Piedmont. Howard Rollins McManus' fine article "Cloyd's Mountain," in the *Civil War Times Illustrated* (1980), and his book *The Battle of Cloyds Mountain: The Virginia and Tennessee Railroad Raid, April 29–May 19, 1864* (1989) helped to rescue it from neglect and obscurity. For military movements around Lynchburg, both Frank Vandiver's *Jubal's Raid* (1960) and B. F. Cooling's *Jubal Early's Raid on Washington, 1864* (1989) begin their narratives with the defense of that city. Older works, such as Milton W. Humphreys' *History of the Lynchburg Campaign* (1924) and Henry A. Du Pont's *Campaign of 1864 in the Valley of Virginia and the Expedition to Lynchburg* (1925), provide a broader but limited coverage. Since George E. Pond's *Shenandoah Valley in 1864* (1883), Jed Hotchkiss' *Virginia* (1899) in the Confederate Military History series, and Sanford Cobb Kellogg's *Shenandoah Valley and Virginia, 1861 to 1865* (1903), no treatment integrating the military operations in western Virginia prior to Early's dramatic attack on Washington has been written. With a substantial body of fine scholarship already existing on the details of the various battles, I have covered them in only a cursory manner in this book. A reader should refer to the works of Davis, McManus, and Patchan for their extensive treatments. Instead, this study focuses primarily on the strategy, its implementation, and the impact on the civilian population.

The author is indebted to numerous librarians and archivists for their assistance and patience in seeking out material for this book. Special debts of gratitude are owed to Nathan E. Bender, head of Special Collections at West Virginia University; John M. Coski, historian of the Museum of the Confederacy; Rebecca A. Ebert, archivist of the John Handley Library in Winchester, Virginia; H. E. Howard, Inc. of Lynchburg, Virginia; Diane B. Jacobs, archivist, Virginia Military Institute, Lexington, Virginia; Cora P. Teel of the James E. Morrow Library, Marshall University, Huntington, West Virginia; Richard Shrader of the Manuscript Department of the University of North Carolina, Chapel Hill; Richard J. Sommers, archivist-historian at the United States Military History Institute, Carlisle, Pennsylvania; and Robert Tolar of Washington, D.C. Special recognition goes to Jonathan Lawrence of Columbus, Ohio, for his patience, advice, and wisdom.

ABBREVIATIONS

B&L   Robert Underwood Johnson and Clarence Clough Buel, eds., *Battles and Leaders of the Civil War*. 4 Vols. New York, 1884–88

CWH   *Civil War History*

CWT   *Civil War Times Illustrated*

CV   *Confederate Veteran*

DU   William R. Perkins Library, Duke University, Durham, North Carolina

JML   Jones Memorial Library, Lynchburg, Virginia

JSH   *Journal of Southern History*

LC   Manuscript Division, Library of Congress

MC   Eleanor S. Brockenbrough Library, Museum of the Confederacy, Richmond

MHS   Maryland Historical Society, Baltimore

NA   National Archives

OHS   Ohio Historical Society, Columbus

OR   *The War of the Rebellion: A Compilation of the Official Records of the Union and Confederate Armies*. 130 Vols. Washington, D.C., 1880–1901, All references to Series I unless noted.

PMHSM *Papers of the Military Historical Society of Massachusetts*. 14 Vols. Boston, 1881–1918

RBHPCL   Rutherford B. Hayes Presidential Center Library, Fremont, Ohio

RR   Frank Moore, ed., *Rebellion Record: A Diary of American Events with Documents, Narratives, Illustrative Incidents, Poetry, etc.* 11 Vols. New York, 1861–68

SCCP   Southern Claims Commission Papers

SHC   Southern Historical Collection, University of North Carolina, Chapel Hill

SHSP   *Southern Historical Society Papers.* 49 Vols. Richmond, 1876–1944

USMHI   U.S. Army Military History Institute, Carlisle, Pennsylvania

UV   Alderman Library, University of Virginia, Charlottesville

VHS   Virginia Historical Society, Richmond

VMH&B   *Virginia Magazine of History and Biography*

VMI   Virginia Military Institute, Lexington

W&L   Washington and Lee University, Lexington, Virginia

W-FCHS   Winchester–Frederick County Historical Society and Handley Archives, Archives Room, Handley Regional Library, Winchester, Virginia

WVA&HL   West Virginia Archives and History Library, Charleston

WVH   *West Virginia History*

WVR   *West Virginia Review*

WVU   West Virginia University, Morgantown

LEE'S ENDANGERED LEFT

I

Preparations for Battle

As day broke on the morning of April 28, 1864, a galvanized Federal army shattered the calm of the West Virginia countryside. "The fluttering of a hundred banners, the gleaming of bayonets, the flashing sabers, . . . the booming of cannon and the sweet strains of music from a score of bands" echoed from the surrounding hills of Martinsburg. The call to formation announced the readiness of the Army of the Shenandoah to undertake another spring campaign. As a thrilled Dr. Alexander Neil of the 12th West Virginia Regiment watched, Major General Franz Sigel and his staff rode up and down the line inspecting the troops. "The heavens were almost rent with cheers" as once again a Federal army prepared to march up the war-torn Shenandoah Valley.[1]

The climactic battles of 1863, despite stunning Union victories, had failed to resolve the outcome of the Civil War. The fall of Vicksburg in the west delivered a devastating blow to the Confederacy in that region and enhanced Major General Ulysses S. Grant's growing reputation and stature. Lincoln had watched Grant's campaign unfold with both approval and reservations. The more Grant's plans unfolded, however, the more impressed Lincoln became, asserting in May that the general's strategy was "one of the most brilliant in the world." Despite mounting pressure from critics to remove Grant for the protracted siege of Vicksburg, he re-

1. Alexander Neil to Father and Mother, April 28, 1864, Alexander Neil Letters, UV.

fused. Later, on July 5, 1863, Lincoln told one officer that if the general were to take the city, "Grant is my man and I am his the rest of the War."[2] That hope soon materialized. On July 7 an exuberant Secretary of the Navy Gideon Welles rushed to the White House and handed Lincoln the dispatch announcing the fall of Vicksburg. Lincoln took Welles's hand and put his arm around him, exclaiming, "I cannot, in words, tell you my joy over this result."[3] At last he had an aggressive general who would fight. Grant was indeed his man.

Less impressive was the Union victory in the east. The Confederate defeat at Gettysburg in early July had nearly shattered General Robert E. Lee's Army of Northern Virginia. Yet General George Meade failed to grasp the opportunity for a crushing victory. A disappointed Lincoln, though thankful for Meade's success, feared that he would merely force the Southerners "to evacuate Cumberland Valley" and allow them to get "across the river again without a further collision"—and, worse, without destroying Lee's army.[4]

The president's concerns proved justified. Despite his prodding "not to let the enemy escape" and Meade's desire to attack the retreating army, wariness ruled. Three days' fighting had left the Army of the Potomac badly worn, and energetic pursuits were never its strong point. The scarcity of reliable intelligence added to the hesitancy and crippled decision making, while probes near Williamsport found the Southern army in strong positions. Newly appointed to command, Meade, despite Lincoln's entreaties, consulted his corps commanders, the majority of whom advised against an attack. Yet, after more reflection that night, he decided to confront Lee. The following morning, however, he learned that during the night and early morning the Army of Northern Virginia had successfully crossed the Potomac on an improvised pontoon bridge. The golden opportunity of trapping the Southern army quietly slipped away with the floodwaters of the river. Lee's escape, as John Hay remembered, caused the president to suffer "one of the deepest and bitterest disappointments of the war." In a letter intended for Meade but never sent, he unburdened his frustration: "I do not believe you appreciate the magnitude of the misfor-

2. Lincoln to Isaac N. Arnold, May 26, 1863, in Roy P. Basler, ed., *The Collected Works of Abraham Lincoln* (New Brunswick, N.J., 1953), VI, 230–31; T. Harry Williams, *Lincoln and His Generals* (New York, 1952), 230, 272.

3. Howard K. Beale, ed., *Diary of Gideon Welles* (New York, 1960), I, 364.

4. *OR*, Vol. XXXVII, Pt. 3, pp. 519, 567; Basler, ed., *Works of Lincoln*, VI, 318.

tune involved in Lee's escape." Meade, aware of the criticism, offered his resignation, but Major General H. W. Halleck placated him. A few days later, when Noah Brooks, a reporter for the Sacramento *Daily Union*, reported to the president on his return from western Maryland, he found that Lincoln's "grief and anger were something sorrowful to behold."[5]

Badly bruised but still a dangerous adversary, the Army of Northern Virginia moved safely back into the Shenandoah Valley. While Lee temporarily entrenched in the Winchester vicinity and waited for flooded streams to subside, Meade sent cavalry units to secure the mountain passes and watched for Confederate activity from his defensive positions on the north side of the Potomac. Instead of pursuing, Meade toyed with another idea. He proposed a movement into the Valley to destroy the summer crops there. The administration, however, remained focused on obliterating the Southern army. Halleck discounted Meade's proposal, wiring him on July 27, "Lee's army is the objective point."[6] Yet administration policy in requiring approval of movements produced a frustrated Meade and limited his maneuverability in protecting Washington. A proposed advance on Culpeper received disapproval from Lincoln. Further complicating any potential moves, draft riots in New York distracted Washington's attention and necessitated a diversion of men from the Army of the Potomac. In addition, the expiration of enlistments, plus the dispatch of a division from the XII Corps to South Carolina, left Meade with only some two-thirds of his army by early August. Despite some minor troop additions, the Army of the Potomac remained below strength. Occupying the fords of the Rappahannock, Meade temporarily remained on the defensive.[7]

Despite the loss at Gettysburg, Lee hoped to regain the initiative as he moved south. Yet complicating factors—the loss of more than twenty thousand men, the necessity of resupplying and refitting his troops, and the need for an infusion of men—demanded restraint and slowed any immediate advance on Meade. Developing threats at two other points further constrained his actions. Wilmington seemed threatened, while the movements by Major General William S. Rosecrans in eastern Tennessee

5. John G. Nicolay and John Hay, *Abraham Lincoln: A History* (New York, 1914), VII, 277–78; Basler, ed., *Works of Lincoln*, VI, 327–28; Freeman Cleaves, *Meade of Gettysburg* (Norman, Okla., 1960), 184–85; Noah Brooks, *Washington, D.C., in Lincoln's Time*, ed. Herbert Mitgang (New York, 1962), 94.

6. *OR*, Vol. XXVII, Pt. 1, p. 101.

7. Cleaves, *Meade*, 189–91.

captured Richmond's attention. General Braxton Bragg's retreat to Chattanooga threatened to uncover the rail line between the lower South and Virginia. For Lee the choice, as Douglas Southall Freeman writes, was between "attacking Meade and attacking Rosecrans."[8] He regarded a potential Federal assault on Wilmington as less serious. Despite Lee's desire to strike the Army of the Potomac, as well as the apparent sympathy of Jefferson Davis, the fall of Knoxville on September 2 changed Confederate strategy. Richmond decided to reinforce Bragg instead. Lee acquiesced. Reluctantly, he sent two brigades to Charleston and dispatched Lieutenant General James Longstreet's corps to join Bragg.

Weakened by the departures, Lee temporarily maintained a defensive bluff of strength. As a precautionary move, he sent his surplus supplies back to Gordonsville in case of a forced withdrawal. Bragg's initial victory at Chickamauga augured well for Longstreet's return to the Army of Northern Virginia. In Washington, meanwhile, discussions and limitations had turned offensive planning into defensive caution. Reports of the detachment of the XI and XII Corps from Meade's army to reinforce Rosecrans encouraged Lee to preempt the Federals in taking the initiative again. With the odds now more favorable, he began a turning movement in early October by crossing the upper Rapidan River. The maneuver began a series of movements in what soon became a game of chess with his opponent but only led to a stalemate.

At Bristoe Station, a Federal surprise for General Harry Heth's division, combined with Southern mismanagement, checked the Confederate flanking attack. Some 1,360 Confederate dead, wounded, and missing to fewer than 350 for Meade underscored the Southern loss and embarrassment. Logistics, lack of army strength, and the coming of cold weather caused Lee to reconsider his offensive and withdraw toward the Rappahannock. Major General James Ewell Brown "Jeb" Stuart provided some comic relief in what became known as the "Buckland Races." Turning the tables on General Hugh Judson Kilpatrick's cavalry, Stuart's troopers chased them northeastward from Chestnut Hill to Buckland. As the Army of Northern Virginia moved into a defensive mode, Lee fully realized the hazards of assuming the offensive without first solving the dilemma of manpower and supplies.[9]

8. Douglas Southall Freeman, *R. E. Lee: A Biography* (New York, 1935), III, 165.
9. Ibid., Chap. 10; Cleaves, *Meade*, Chap. 15.

After a short respite—though not from administration pressures—Meade picked up the offensive. Lincoln, analyzing Lee's withdrawal and the reinforcement of eastern Tennessee from his army, suggested to Halleck on October 24 that unless "you have a plan matured" Meade should prepare the Army of the Potomac for an attack on Lee "with all possible expedition." [10]

Soon Federal units began probing toward the southwest. Advancing to Warrenton, Meade sent them slowly toward Kelley's Ford and the Rappahannock Bridge. Lee, aware of the movements, intended to allow the Federals to cross at the ford and then strike them in force, while at the bridge he assumed a defensive posture. However, the sudden storming of the bridgehead at the river and capture of part of Generals Robert F. Hoke's and Harry T. Hays's brigades and four guns on the northern side of the Rappahannock, coupled with the capture of parts of two regiments at Kelley's Ford, changed the military configuration for Lee. By late November, Meade's army was crossing the fords of the Rapidan. Lee, in turn, withdrew to the west bank of Mine Run and entrenched in a formidable position. Prepared to meet the Federal assault, he soon became puzzled by their lack of aggressiveness and anticipated taking the offensive himself. Yet as his army readied to advance, much to the surprise of Lee's pickets on the morning of December 2, they discovered Meade's army gone and on its way back to the Rapidan. With the cessation of operations for the winter, the two armies once again faced each other along the Rappahannock-Rapidan line waiting for spring. [11]

A new and critical factor emerged in the planning for the renewal of campaigning in 1864. Grant, now a focal point of attention, gave renewed hope to a thankful administration. The early promise he had shown at Fort Donelson seemed fulfilled. Lincoln liked success and admired generals who fought. Grant demonstrated both. As a reward for his achievement at Vicksburg, Lincoln appointed Grant to overall command in the west. Further recognition came in September with his handling of the army at Chattanooga in the wake of Rosecrans' disaster at Chickamauga. The reverse not only shook the confidence of the administration in "Old Rosy" but placed the Army of the Cumberland in peril of having its supply

---

10. Basler, ed., *Works of Lincoln*, VI, 534.

11. Freeman, *Lee*, III, Chap. 11; Cleaves, *Meade*, Chap. 16; Clifford Dowdey and Louis H. Manarin, eds., *The Wartime Papers of R. E. Lee* (Boston, 1961), 619–20, 628.

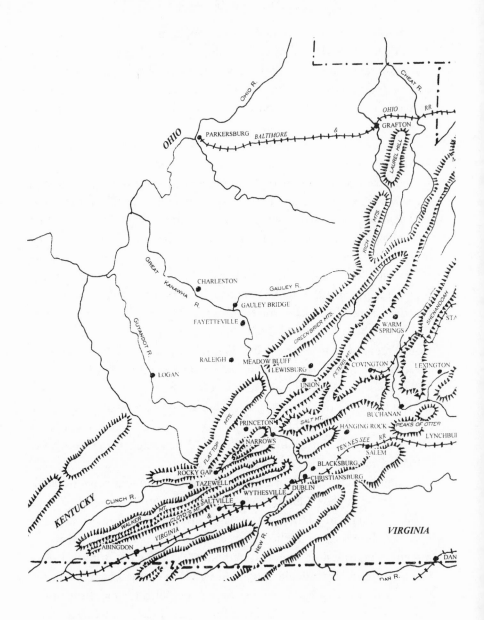

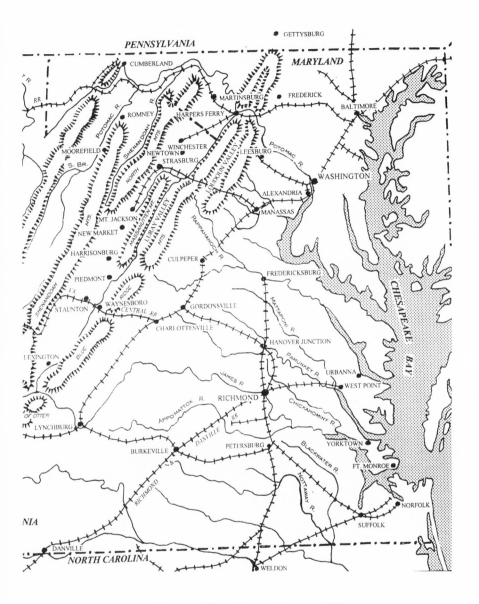

Virginia–West Virginia Theater of War
Map by Robert Tolar

lines cut. Grant left for Tennessee to investigate the predicament and with full authority to remove Rosecrans, if warranted. Even before arriving in Chattanooga, he made his decision and appointed Major General George Thomas to command the Army of the Cumberland. Then at Lookout Mountain–Missionary Ridge the army scored a stunning victory over Bragg under Grant's supervision. Lincoln wired his congratulations.[12] A jubilant Congress, with Grant in mind, revived the rank of lieutenant general. The president, more than pleased, readily appointed him to the position.

As general-in-chief, Grant bore responsibility for the 1864 campaign season. Following Chattanooga, he began making proposals, ranging from an offensive against Mobile to the replacement of Meade in the east. In response to an invitation from Halleck in early January, he presented his evolving ideas on strategy. Hasty and faulty at first, his recommendations grew sharper after he corresponded and conversed with Halleck and Lincoln. In March, Grant traveled to Washington to accept his new commission and conferred briefly with Lincoln on the day of its presentation. He asked the president what he expected of him; Lincoln merely replied that "the country wanted him to take Richmond." Other than reassuring him that he would have sufficient troops, Lincoln left the specifics to Grant.[13]

The next day Grant left for Brandy Station to visit Meade and the Army of the Potomac and to evaluate the situation there personally. Satisfied with retaining Meade, he then set out for Cincinnati to consult with Major General William Tecumseh Sherman. Together they worked out a preliminary plan for the forthcoming campaign, deciding to make in essence "a simultaneous movement all along the line." The new approach infused a new aggressiveness, long missing in the east, into the operations there. Attack, apply pressure, and hold the enemy simultaneously in a tightening vise—this became the new military theme. Destroy the enemy's armies and capacity to fight, and then the war would end. Lincoln, reminded of his own ideas and suggestions, liked Grant's intention "to move at once upon the enemy's whole line so as to bring into action to our advantage our greater superiority in numbers." Such a policy would, he believed, prevent the South from using interior lines to its advantage. In a final interview with the president, Grant remarked that "those not

12. Basler, ed., *Works of Lincoln*, VII, 53.
13. Nicolay and Hay, *Abraham Lincoln*, VIII, 343.

fighting could help the fighting." Lincoln quickly added, "Those not skinning can hold a leg."[14] The most troublesome area for Grant would be
western Virginia—a leg that refused to be held down.

Grant proposed primarily to strike at the Confederacy's two major armies, one under General Joseph B. Johnston in the lower South and the
other under Lee in Virginia. A concerted movement, he hoped, would
prevent the Confederacy from using interior lines to shift troops to fortify
the most threatened point. In Virginia he intended to apply pressure at
three points. The objective for the Army of the Potomac, under the
watchful eye of Grant, would be Lee's Army of Northern Virginia. Major
General Benjamin F. Butler, commanding the Army of the James, would
move in concert with Meade on Richmond from the southeast. After taking City Point, Butler would advance up the south side of the James River
to invest Richmond and anchor his left flank on the river above the city.
If Meade were able to force Lee back into Richmond's defenses, then the
two armies would unite and act as one.[15]

Simultaneously, in western Virginia, Grant intended to use raids to
cripple Lee by striking at his support system. The region, rich in minerals
and agricultural produce, helped to sustain the Southern presence in Virginia, and its continued security remained a matter of the utmost importance to the Army of Northern Virginia. The Virginia and Tennessee
Railroad—running from Bristol, where it joined with the East Tennessee
and Virginia Railroad, to Lynchburg, where it connected with the South
Side Railroad and the Orange and Alexandria Railroad—linked Richmond to important salt and lead mines in the southwestern region. Not
only did the road carry critical products for the war effort, but it allowed
Confederates to shift military units back and forth along interior lines between Virginia and eastern Tennessee. Lincoln called the rail line "the gut
of the Confederacy." Late in 1863 a Union expedition under Brigadier
General William W. Averell had succeeded in reaching the railroad at
Salem to destroy its depot and a quantity of stores. Yet the raid had only
temporarily disrupted the line's flow of traffic. Rapidly repaired, the road

14. U. S. Grant, *Personal Memoirs of U. S. Grant* (New York, 1886), II, 129–37; Simon,
ed., *Papers of Grant*, X, 253–54n; *OR*, Vol. XXXII, Pt. 3, pp. 312–14; Nicolay and Hay,
Abraham Lincoln, VIII, 347 n. 1; Tyler Dennett, ed., *Lincoln and the Civil War in the Diaries
and Letters of John Hay* (New York, 1939), 178–79. See Grant's version in his *Memoirs*, II,
142–43.

15. *OR*, XXXIII, 795, 904–905.

remained a vital link between the interior and Richmond. For Grant the destruction of that tie became a high priority. In addition to breaking the rail link, Federal authorities wanted to destroy the important salt and lead centers at Saltville and Wytheville.

To the northeast lay the Shenandoah Valley. Stretching some 170 miles northeastward along the Allegheny Mountains to the west and enclosed by the Blue Ridge Mountains on the east, the Valley ran from the James River at Buchanan to the Potomac River. The Shenandoah's fertile fields provided a breadbasket for Lee's army, while the mountainous areas in the upper reaches of the Valley contained sizable quantities of iron ore which fed the region's furnaces and forges. The James River and Kanawha Canal, nearly 148 miles long, with its western terminus at Buchanan and a branch line to Lexington, linked the area to Lynchburg and Richmond.[16] Further to the north, the Valley plain of rolling rich limestone soil produced an abundance of wheat, corn, and barley as well as cattle and sheep. The Virginia Central Railroad, tunneling through the Blue Ridge to tap agriculturally rich Augusta County and the region just across the first ridge of the Alleghenies, tied the area to Charlottesville, Lynchburg, and the Confederate capital. Connecting the various towns in the Shenandoah, the Valley Pike, a well-engineered and macadamized road, stretched from Martinsburg to Staunton with a network of roads feeding into it.

Militarily, the Valley with its pike served as a natural avenue for Confederate incursions into western Maryland and southern Pennsylvania. Quite early, the Shenandoah became a battleground and problem for Union authorities. In the spring of 1862 General Thomas "Stonewall" Jackson effectively tied up two Federal armies there and deflected General Irvin McDowell's move toward Richmond to cooperate with Major General George B. McClellan on the Peninsula. In September of that year a victorious Southern army, following its victory at Second Manassas, moved northward on both sides of the Blue Ridge into western Maryland. Ten months later, Lee's army, in the aftermath of success at Chancellorsville, used the Valley as a route into Pennsylvania. Union authorities longed for control over the disconcerting and threatening Valley. The frequency of Federal disasters embarrassingly earned the Shenandoah its reputation as the "Valley of Humiliation."

16. U.S. House of Representatives, *Preliminary Report of the Eighth Census, 1860* (Washington, D.C., 1862), 240.

Up until 1864, Union penetrations of the Shenandoah remained confined to the lower Valley, thus sparing the upper region and southwestern Virginia from the destruction of earlier military operations. Saltville and Wytheville continued to supply the Confederacy with salt and lead in relative safety. Staunton, an important supply depot on the Virginia Central Railroad, remained untouched. Lee, well aware of the area's importance to his military presence in Virginia, realized the necessity of defending it. He warned Richmond early in January that he considered the region's defense so vital "to the successful conduct of the war" that he would relinquish one of his own commanders to head the department. Confederate authorities agreed, and in early 1864, unhappy with the performance of Major General Samuel Jones as commander of the Department of Western Virginia, they replaced him with a more capable general. In April, Lee warned Davis that "any derangement in their [supplies'] arrival or disaster to the railroad would render it impossible for me to keep the army together, and might force a retreat into North Carolina."[17]

Conversely, the series of Federal embarrassments there intensified Washington's chagrin over the conduct of affairs in the Department of West Virginia. A change seemed to be demanded. The department embraced an extensive region of mountainous terrain and valleys that included all of the state of West Virginia, the Shenandoah Valley and part of Loudoun County in Virginia, and all of western Maryland west of the Monocacy River. Union forces in the department were hardly adequate. A primary concern for its commander was protecting the Baltimore and Ohio Railroad. Extending from Parkersburg through the northern part of West Virginia to Cumberland, Maryland, and then back into Virginia and on to Harpers Ferry before crossing back into Maryland, the rail line remained a constant target for Confederate raids from Grafton to Harpers Ferry. Union authorities, increasingly critical of the purported lack of energetic leadership there, wanted change. Growing pressure demanded the replacement of Brigadier General Benjamin F. Kelley with someone who would be more aggressive.

Kelley, a native of New Hampshire, had settled in the Wheeling vicinity in 1826 at the age of nineteen. Employed as a freight agent there by the Baltimore and Ohio Railroad but subsequently transferred to Philadel-

17. OR, Vol. XXXIII, Pt. 1, pp. 1124, 1275; Dowdey and Manarin, eds., *Papers of Lee,* 662–63, 698.

phia, he returned to Wheeling at the outbreak of the war to organize the
1st Virginia Regiment. After he defeated Colonel George A. Porterfield's
forces at Philippi, the War Department promoted him to brigadier general. While recovering from a wound sustained in the battle, he briefly
headed the Railroad Division. Then, as a reward for the capture of Romney, he was appointed commander of the Department of Harper's Ferry
and Cumberland. Still suffering from his wound, he relinquished his post
until recalled to command the 1st Division of the Middle Department.
However, with Major General Robert M. Milroy's debacle at Winchester
the War Department assigned him to head the Department of West Virginia.[18]

Kelley's assignment was an impossible one. Though he had an extended rail line to protect and troops in short supply, he came under censure for his failure to secure the state against Confederate raids. Critics regarded the "terse, laconic, modest" general as a disappointment.[19]
Pressure for his removal came from a variety of sources. Antagonists complained that the army in his department was inefficient in protecting the
country against raids and guerrillas. Dr. Neil of the 12th West Virginia
noted, "All along the Potomac and all along the Baltimore & Ohio Rail
Road there is a feeling of uncertainty and insecurity which ought not to
exist." Critics attributed Southern successes to Kelley's presumed negligence and dubbed him "the Rebel Quartermaster."[20] They further
charged that Kelley allowed the enemy "to escape when he might overtake and defeat them." His spirit of liberality and determination to resist
harsh measures against Southern sympathizers angered many, leading to
the accusation that he was not "severe enough with the home rebels."
Point Pleasant's *Weekly Register* even questioned the loyalty of Kelley's
family, charging that his "wife and other family connexions were undis-
guised rebel sympathizers."[21]

18. Theodore F. Lang, *Loyal West Virginia from 1863 to 1865* (Baltimore, 1895),
320–22; James Grant Wilson and John Fiske, eds., *Appleton's Cyclopaedia of American Biography* (New York, 1888), III, 504.

19. John W. Elwood, *Elwood's Stories of the Old Ringgold Cavalry* (Coal Center, Pa.,
1914), 163–64.

20. Neil to Father and Mother, Feb. 28, 1864, Neil Letters.

21. Wheeling (W. Va.) *Daily Intelligencer*, Jan. 11, 13, 14, 18, 19, 1864; Wellsburg (W.
Va.) *Herald*, Feb. 12, 1864; Point Pleasant (W. Va.) *Weekly Register*, March 10, 1864; Cecil
D. Eby, Jr., *"Porte Crayon": The Life of David Hunter Strother* (Chapel Hill, 1960), 135.

Unfortunately for Kelley, politics became enmeshed in the conduct of affairs in the department. In February 1864, in an embarrassing guerrilla raid, the Confederates captured Brigadier General Eliakim P. Scammon, then in command of the District of Kanawha, along with two of his aides and some forty soldiers on the steamer *B. C. Levi.* A furor ensued among West Virginia politicians, and when the state legislature met, Kelley quickly became a target. One senator called upon Washington to replace him with a major general, while another condemned the general's administration as being "evil and evil continually." Despite Kelley's endorsement by Governor Arthur I. Boreman, the senate passed a resolution asking "the President to give the command to Gen. Sigel or Gen. Milroy." House members, after considering the measure by a special committee, agreed, but only after amending it to ask merely for "some major general," deleting any mention of Sigel or Milroy. The senate concurred. Colonel David H. Strother, a member of Kelley's staff, scoffed at the resolution, confiding to his diary that the "Senate could not have made a more ridiculous exhibition of itself."[22]

Unworried about the actions of the legislature, Kelley knew his removal would come instead from "outside influences."[23] And indeed, Major General Franz Sigel's subsequent appointment had little to do with the issue of competency. Politics underlay the choice. Two touchy and entwined problems aided in his selection. First, Sigel was an inactive major general with seniority. Second, his standing in the German-American community demanded political care. As a sizable ethnic group with their own schools, newspapers, and leaders, German Americans wielded formidable influence in the Republican (now Union) Party. Ambitious to promote their own, German-American leaders did not hesitate to apply pressure, and 1864 was a presidential election year. Later the Wheeling *Daily Intelligencer* would charge that Sigel's selection came "from a mistaken expectation of . . . strengthening the government with the German element" rather than "from a proper confidence in his abilities to discharge the duties of command." The Wellsburg *Herald*, initially equivocal over Kelley's removal, would agree, declaring that the appointment "seems to have been on the pernicious principle of trying to flatter and conciliate

22. Wheeling *Daily Intelligencer,* Feb. 6, 8, 10, 12–13, 1864; Wellsburg (W. Va.) *Herald,* Feb. 12, 1864; Cecil D. Eby, Jr., ed., *A Virginia Yankee in the Civil War: The Diaries of David Hunter Strother* (Chapel Hill, 1961), 212.

23. Eby, ed., *Virginia Yankee,* 213.

the German element, and on this principle, it should never have been made."[24]

Sigel, a German expatriate, was a darling of the German-American community. Born in 1824 in Sinsheim, Baden, he attended the military academy in Karlsruhe and entered the army as a lieutenant. His liberal and revolutionary ideas often clashed with those of his fellow officers, and a duel in 1847 led to his resignation. Republican uprisings ended his pursuit of a legal education. Instead, he organized a *Freikorps* and led an expedition against Württemberg. Lacking combat experience and a seasoned army, he failed and fled to Switzerland. In a second uprising, he returned to Karlsruhe. Unfortunately, his performance again demonstrated more political acumen than it did a mastery of military leadership. With the defeat of the Republican army, Sigel, by his declaration, assumed the title of commander in chief but soon fled into Switzerland with a remnant of the army. Yet in defeat the myth of the "great general" emerged. Americans never forgot his reputed opposition to eighty thousand government troops with his thirty thousand in making his escape. Sigel never made such a claim, but the legend gained status for him. Defeat, however, offered him only exile. After brief stays in Paris and Great Britain, he emigrated to the United States in 1852.[25] In New York City he became involved in revolutionary circles and the Republican Party. But with an offer of a professorship by Dr. Adam Hammer of the Deutsches Institut he left for St. Louis, Missouri. There he played an increasingly visible role in the Union clubs and in the German-American community. Recognition of Sigel's stature came with his appointment as superintendent of city schools. He further enhanced his prestige in campaigning for Lincoln in the 1860 election.[26]

At the outbreak of the Civil War, the German-American community became a critical factor in holding Missouri in the Union. Overwhelm-

24. William C. Davis, *The Battle of New Market* (Garden City, N.Y., 1975), 7–8; Ella Lonn, "The Forty-Eighters in the Civil War," in A. E. Zucker, ed., *The Forty-Eighters* (New York, 1967), 185–87; Carl Wittke, *Refugees of the Revolution* (Westport, Conn., 1970), 222–23; Wheeling *Daily Intelligencer*, May 28, 1864; Wellsburg (W. Va.) *Herald*, May 27, 1864.

25. Lonn, "Forty-Eighters," 186–87.

26. Stephen D. Engle, *Yankee Dutchman: The Life of Franz Sigel* (Fayetteville, Ark., 1993), Chaps. 1–2; Lonn, "Forty-Eighters," 186–87; "Franz Sigel, U.S.A., 1824–1902," in Walton Rawls, ed., *Great Civil War Heroes and Their Battles* (New York, 1985), 149–50; Davis, *New Market*, 8.

ingly Unionist, Germans enthusiastically volunteered for Federal service. Resigning his superintendency, Sigel volunteered as a second lieutenant in February 1861, but because of his military and political background his regiment elected him as its colonel. Initially he demonstrated considerable promise in helping to secure the state for the Union. As a hero, especially to the Forty-eighters (Germans who had emigrated following the political turmoil of 1848 in Europe), he possessed symbolic value, and the administration recommended his appointment as a brigadier general. Yet Sigel's limitations as a commander showed themselves quite early. Noting his performance at Carthage on July 5, 1861, Stephen Engle writes, "He was not a particularly good strategist and not a born military leader."[27] His defeat at the Battle of Wilson's Creek in August 1861 further tarnished his reputation, except within the German-American community. Reviewing his performance, General Halleck, commander of the Department of Missouri, wired Washington that Sigel was "unfit for the rank he now holds,"[28] and the controversy created an outpouring of support for Sigel. Concurrently, the clamor for the appointment of a German American to a high rank grew, and a number of political leaders in Illinois and Indiana pressured Lincoln to make such a selection.[29] Soon, what military ability failed to achieve, politics accomplished. In March 1862, Sigel received the promotion to major general.

The Battle of Pea Ridge, in March 1862, partially redeemed his reputation, although in reality the victory belonged to Brigadier General Samuel R. Curtis. Transferred to the east to serve under Major General John Pope, Sigel commanded the I Corps. His military performance continued to remain poor. Yet his defenders, in turn, attributed such criticism to the prejudice of West Pointers. Controversy seemed to be second nature to him. In a letter to his father-in-law, Dr. Rudolf Dulon, Sigel lashed out at Halleck as a "slick lawyer." The letter, published in the *New Yorker Volkszeitung*, created a political storm and made the conflict "the affair of the Germans at large." Clashes with generals continued to mark his career. Angered over General Joseph Hooker's reorganization of the army and his assignment to the XI Corps, Sigel asked to be relieved. In February 1863 the War Department complied for "medical reasons."[30]

27. Engle, *Yankee Dutchman*, 66.
28. OR, III, 93–94, and VIII, 626.
29. Wittke, *Refugees of Revolution*, 239.
30. Point Pleasant (W. Va.) *Weekly Register*, June 2, 1864; Engle, *Yankee Dutchman*,

Yet his popularity remained high among German Americans, and political pressure for his military advancement persisted. A St. Louis delegation pressured Lincoln to give him an active command. Lobbying on his own behalf, Sigel corresponded with a number of congressional leaders, including the Speaker of the House, Schuyler Colfax. In early 1864, angry West Virginia legislators petitioned Washington for Kelley's removal. Adding to the clamor, a war correspondent noted that as Congress considered a bill to purge all brigadier and major generals then without a command from army rolls, a group of Sigel's supporters went to Washington to apply pressure on his behalf.[31] A receptive Lincoln knew that such an appointment would be politically popular. Command of the Department of West Virginia also solved the other problem, Sigel's status as a shelved major general.

Colonel Strother cynically recorded in his diary that "the Dutch vote must be secured at all hazards for the Government and the sacrifice of West Virginia is a small matter."[32] A war correspondent noted that the fear in not appointing Sigel was of losing, "in the next Presidential contest, no small portion of the German vote."[33] However, a number of officers expressed dismay. Halleck, an old adversary, was "indignant." Railroad officials did "not favor the change." Even Grant harbored doubts. Miffed at Sigel's use of political connections in attempting to circumvent the chain of command to secure two cavalry regiments for his department, Grant wrote to Halleck in March 1864 that it was time for Sigel to "learn to carry on his official correspondence through proper channels and not through members of Congress."[34] Yet, writing to Sherman on April 4, he adopted a cautiously optimistic attitude. Paraphrasing Lincoln, he summed up his one hope: "If Sigel cant skin himself he can hold a leg whilst some one else skins."[35]

chaps. 3–7; Basler, ed., *Works of Lincoln*, VI, 93, 93n; Allan G. Bogue, *The Congressman's Civil War* (New York, 1989), 36–37; Davis, *New Market*, 8–10; Carl Schurz, *Reminiscences of Carl Schurz* (New York, 1907), II, 348–49, 384, 403–404; Earl J. Hess, "Sigel's Resignation: A Study in German-Americanism and the Civil War," *CWH*, XXVI (1980), 5–17.

31. Wheeling *Daily Intelligencer*, March 1, 1864.

32. Eby, ed., *Virginia Yankee*, 213.

33. Wheeling *Daily Intelligencer*, March 1, 1864.

34. OR, XXXIII, 734; Simon, ed., *Papers of Grant*, X, 222.

35. Wheeling *Daily Intelligencer*, Feb. 26, March 1, 1864; Wittke, *Refugees of Revolution*, 239–40; Engle, *Yankee Dutchman*, 213–14; Simon, ed., *Papers of Grant*, X, 251–53.

With much fanfare, Sigel arrived in Cumberland on the evening of March 11. As thirteen guns saluted the new commander's arrival, Kelley met him at the station. The following day Sigel received the staff. On their meeting, Strother saw a man "small in stature and ungraceful," dressed in a major general's uniform yet wearing "a plain slouch hat." Strother observed that "his hair and beard are tawny, his jaws and cheek bones square and angular, his eyes light blue, forehead narrow, and too small for his face."[36] Others saw his terse and overbearing nature as a "block of ice." Major General Carl Schurz, an ardent supporter, acknowledged that Sigel "possessed in a small degree that amiability of humor which will disarm ill-will."[37] Wilhelm Kaufmann noted that "on horseback the small, thin man with the fixed death-like expression gave no impression of the heroic. . . . One needed to be a German really to know and appreciate him."[38] Speaking to his staff in broken English, Sigel expressed his hope that they would assist him in the arduous duties the post demanded, responsibilities he undertook with "great self distrust." He closed by asking for their cooperation "more as a brother officer than as a commander."[39]

Others saw the appointment in more positive terms. In a letter to the Wheeling *Daily Intelligencer*, one writer commented that the appointment was "generally acceded to, except by a few radical favorites of Gen. Kelly." In April, the men of the 15th West Virginia, despite being "warmly attached to General Kelley," informed the paper that "Sigel and Milroy are regarded as earnest and faithful commanders, in whose skill and judgment the utmost reliance can be placed, so the change produces no dissatisfaction."[40]

In acquainting himself with his department, Sigel hastened to strengthen his political ties in Washington as well. He assured Representative Kellian V. Whaley of West Virginia that he would "take the necessary measures to have justice done to Mr. McConn." He confided to Whaley that organizing his staff "has many difficulties and causes me a great deal to do." Since he "was unacquainted with the military ability and the prac-

36. Eby, ed., *Virginia Yankee*, 213.

37. Schurz, *Reminiscences*, II, 350.

38. Quoted in Lonn, "Forty-Eighters," 188–89.

39. Wheeling *Daily Intelligencer*, March 16, 1864; Eby, ed., *Virginia Yankee*, 213–14; Engle, *Yankee Dutchman*, xviii.

40. Wheeling *Daily Intelligencer*, March 14, April 30, 1864.

tical sentiments of the officers . . . I therefore have to be careful in my selection and appointments." But he hastened to add that he would give him their names "as soon as I have made my positive arrangements." He then asked Whaley to provide him with "as many *names* as you can, of reliable and influential men, as that I may know, how to treat them."[41]

Sigel then outlined for Whaley his intended approach in the state. He wanted to clear West Virginia "from the enemy *as soon as possible*, so that the people can till their fields." He announced that not only did he intend to protect and treat loyal individuals well but that he would provide disloyal elements "no protection, make them responsible for every horse and cow stolen. . . . West Va is a loyal state," he proclaimed, and he had no intention of giving "protection to abbettors of treason and sympathizers with rebellion. . . . Let the Government understand, that West Va is just as important as Richmond and, that we must have the *means* to reconquer the State, of which we possess only one *fourth* or fifth." Underscoring his point, he charged that the forces in the state "are not much stronger than *one* Corps of the army of the Potomac but scattered over a line of more than 400 miles."[42]

To familiarize himself with the department, he asked Strother, whom he retained as an aide-de-camp, to prepare a description of it for his own use and for Secretary of War Edwin Stanton.[43] Immediately he began inspecting the troops and raising their morale, but he soon developed serious reservations about their disposition and poor condition. "Brave as the soldiers may be individually," Sigel attributed their "loose and degenerated [condition] to inactivity and garrison life . . . at this moment they are very far from understanding their duties."[44] As William C. Davis notes, Sigel's efforts put the army in its best condition "since its creation."[45]

Despite Sigel's energy and good intentions, aspects of poor judgment began to appear. Fears that he would surround himself with fellow German Americans were increasingly justified. A correspondent to the Baltimore *American and Commercial Advertiser* warned about his preference "exclusively to men of *his own nativity*," which gave "occasion for heart-

41. Franz Sigel to Kellian V. Whaley, March 15, 1864, James E. Morrow Library, Marshall University, Huntington, West Virginia.
42. Ibid.
43. Eby, ed., *Virginia Yankee*, 216.
44. OR, XXXIII, 764.
45. Davis, *New Market*, 13.

burnings among native-born officers." The writer cautioned against those "who cannot speak our language fluently," as "their orders when issued on the field of battle may not be understood, and thus our cause *suffer harm*."[46] Worse, when Strother caught up with the army at Bunker Hill on May 1, he found the general "surrounded by a set of low scouts, spies, detectives, and speculators" while his staff remained outside. The sight accented his fear of "some disaster in this campaign."[47]

Kelley, relieved of command, asked for a thirty-day leave of absence. Sigel believed that Kelley was "a *good* soldier . . . and I do not believe he will act unfairly towards me . . . and I could not refuse it to him."[48] Kelley's old staff soon felt estranged, while Sigel began making a number of questionable decisions. He failed to appoint a chief of artillery or to create a separate unit to ensure its effective use. He appointed Major General Julius Stahel, a Hungarian expatriate from the Kossuth uprising, as chief of cavalry. Then he made Stahel chief of staff while retaining him in command of the 1st Cavalry Division. On the eve of moving up the Valley, Sigel relieved him as chief of cavalry and assigned him to command the 1st Infantry Division as well as his own 1st Cavalry. Strother confided in his diary that although Stahel "is a very good fancy cavalry officer," he "has never done anything in the field and never will do anything." He believed that Stahel was "too mild and amiable for any such position," yet he felt that he was an honorable and sensible officer and "in no way mixed up in politics or speculations."[49]

Grant expected Sigel's role in West Virginia to complement Meade's and Butler's advances on Richmond. He wanted him "to inflict great damage on the enemy" in western Virginia or to force Lee to detach a large force from his army to prevent him from doing so. In that region Grant conceived of using pincer movements in applying pressure in two strategic areas. Initially he wanted to employ two columns from the Kanawha Valley to strike into southwestern Virginia. The principal one targeted the

46. Wheeling *Daily Intelligencer*, March 31, 1864.

47. Eby, ed., *Virginia Yankee*, 221.

48. Sigel to Whaley, March 15, 1864, Morrow Library.

49. *OR*, XXXIII, 739, 764, 965, 987; William Hewitt, *History of the Twelfth West Virginia Volunteer Infantry* (Twelfth West Virginia Infantry Association, 1892), 99; Eby, ed., *Virginia Yankee*, 222–23; Schurz, *Reminiscences*, 350; Henry A. Du Pont, *The Campaign of 1864 in the Valley of Virginia* (New York, 1925), 6–7; Wittke, *Refugees of Revolution*, 228; Ezra J. Warner, *Generals in Blue* (Baton Rouge, 1964), 469.

important Virginia and Tennessee Railroad "so that it can be of no further use to the enemy," while the other one, a lesser and subordinate cavalry raid, he expected to take Saltville and then move northeastward to form a junction with the main column. Once the columns joined, the objective for the combined expedition would be the capture of Lynchburg and, if possible, the establishment of a supply base on the James River. He designed a third column, advancing up the Shenandoah Valley, merely to threaten Staunton. Such a move would, if necessary, secure an avenue of retreat for the Kanawha force by meeting and reinforcing it with a large supply train.

Initially, Grant did not contemplate the move up the Valley as a major thrust. It remained secondary to the raids from West Virginia. In a dispatch to Sigel on April 13 he wrote that the Valley column "will not require much more than an escort for the wagon train." For Grant the major objectives were in southwestern Virginia: the destruction of the Virginia and Tennessee Railroad, the bridge over the New River, and the salt and lead mines—and, if circumstances permitted, a move on Lynchburg. [50] Such a plan accorded with Lincoln's earlier thoughts. Putting forth his ideas to Halleck on October 24, 1863, the president had suggested not only that Meade should prepare to attack but "that in the mean time, a raid shall, at all hazards, break the Railroad at or near Lynchburg." [51]

In Grant's plan, Sigel commanded the Department of West Virginia. Yet it quickly became obvious that he was not to be the principal commander in the field. Without consulting Sigel, Grant chose Major General E. O. C. Ord to supervise the Kanawha expeditions. Ord's performance at Iuka and Hatchie had earned him Grant's respect and praise. However, his Southern background and wife's family connections with a number of high-ranking Confederate officers, including General Jubal Early, made him suspect for many. Ord was a conservative Democrat, and his Southern views on slavery antagonized Radicals, who questioned his loyalty. Grant did not, and on March 23 he wired Ord at Louisville to report for assignment. Five days later he directed him to come in person "without delay." Leaving Louisville, Ord met and conferred with Brigadier General George Crook, and the two traveled together to Grant's head-

50. OR, XXXIII, 758, 798–99, 827–28, 858; Simon, ed., *Papers of Grant*, X, 233–34, 257–58.
51. Basler, ed., *Works of Lincoln*, VI, 534.

quarters at Culpeper. There Grant gave Ord a confidential memorandum informing him of his appointment and outlining his strategy. He cautioned that "this is not given as positive official instructions, not having been given through the Dept. Commander." But he quickly added that until Ord received those orders, he should familiarize himself with the country. For Ord the problem was not in understanding the countryside but in coping with Sigel's jealousy and perverse determination to command his department fully. [52]

Several days earlier, Crook had already tasted Sigel's hostility. When Crook received instructions on March 24 to report to Grant's headquarters, Sigel balked. Finally admitting that the general could be spared from the department, he reluctantly consented to the trip, though he countered by offering to send Major William P. Rucker instead. He argued that it would take Crook five days to reach Culpeper from Charleston, whereas Rucker was "thoroughly acquainted with that Country and can give you [Grant] valuable information." Lieutenant Colonel Cyrus Comstock replied: "Lt. Genl Grant requests that Gen Crook report to him without delay." In relaying the instructions, Sigel ordered Crook to stop at Cumberland to see him, for "I have some papers for you." [53]

Apprehensive about his reception at Cumberland, Ord wired Grant on March 30 that he was leaving for Sigel's headquarters that day and, unless directed otherwise, would present Grant's instructions to Sigel. Grant replied that as long as Sigel commanded the department, "he will have to be treated with confidence," and directed Ord to deliver the letter. [54]

In the confidential instructions, Grant outlined the Kanawha operations. He specified that Ord's command should move from Beverly by way of Covington to strike and destroy the Virginia and Tennessee Railroad. Crook, in turn, was to advance from Charleston toward Saltville and then turn eastward to form a junction with Ord. Since it would be impossible for Crook to remain in contact with their headquarters, Grant advised him to use his judgment if he was forced to fall back from the rail line as a result of difficulties in securing supplies or from a threat from Longstreet

52. Bernarr Cresap, *Appomattox Commander* (San Diego, 1981), 92, 115–16; OR, XXXIII, 750, 758; Simon, ed., *Papers of Grant*, X, 233–34, 234n; Martin F. Schmitt, ed., *General George Crook: His Autobiography* (Norman, Okla., 1986), 114.

53. OR, XXXIII, 725–26, 734, 740; Simon, ed., *Papers of Grant*, X, 237–38n.

54. OR, XXXIII, 765–66, 770, 778; Simon, ed., *Papers of Grant*, X, 235n, 236–37, 237–38n.

or Breckinridge. If, however, Crook was successful, Grant expected him to move eastward on Lynchburg and establish a base of supplies on the James River. "In case of this much success you will make no backward movement, at least not without further orders." He warned Ord that the instructions were "not given through the Dept. Commander." Yet he indicated that they were the "substance of what I now think."[55]

Grant, attempting to mollify Sigel over Crook's visit, explained that he wanted to learn "the character of the country and roads in West Virginia." He expressed his desire "to determine the practicability of ordering a cooperative movement from your Department, in connection with other movements." Ord, he informed Sigel, would command the expedition, and Sigel was to provide him with every facility "to accumulate at Beverly all the supplies and equipments needed by him." Grant further suggested that Averell should personally direct the cavalry's part in striking toward the railroad, while the infantry under Crook should be held in a state of readiness to advance while Ord's column moved to safeguard the mountain passes.[56]

After reporting to Sigel, Ord left for Martinsburg, where Averell asked to accompany him on a return visit to confer with Grant in Washington. Ord, wiring Halleck for permission, informed him that "It is important."[57] Irritated, Sigel within two days fired off a wire to Washington requesting their immediate return to duty in the Department of West Virginia. Ord felt increasingly frustrated by the general's refusal to cooperate. To him the reason was obvious: "Sigel is as jealous as the devil at my having come here."[58]

Sigel fully intended to command the department. He resented the fact that "all dispositions *were made in such a manner as if I did not exist at all.*"[59] Concerned over his communication with Washington, he asked Grant on April 2, "To whom shall I send my letters and telegrams?" He wanted "the name of the officer at Washington" who would receive his confidential dispatches "so that there may be no delay and confusion." On the previous day, he had wired Crook asking if he had received any requests for in-

55. Simon, ed., *Papers of Grant*, X, 233–34.
56. OR, XXXIII, 765–66; Simon, ed., *Papers of Grant*, X, 236–37.
57. OR, XXXIII, 787 (emphasis added).
58. *Ibid.*, 797; Simon, *Papers of Grant*, X, 235n.
59. Quoted in Davis, *New Market*, 22.

formation or instructions from Grant. From the dispatches, Grant did not suspect the intense hostility between Sigel and Ord. After conferring with Ord and Averell on the evening of April 7, Sigel wired Grant, "All preparations are going on according to your wishes." Yet to Ord it became obvious; Sigel intended to undertake "the entire management of the organization upon himself."[60]

The final blow came with Sigel's decision on April 12 to abandon the move from Beverly. With that Ord believed "my presence there ceased to be necessary." He told Grant that he was not needed and that Averell with a brigade could manage the raid "*better* than I can." Finding it impossible to cooperate with Sigel, he asked to be relieved. Later, fearing possible accusations in the aftermath of the debacle at New Market, he explained to Secretary of State William Seward the reason for his departure—that being the general's subordinate "mortified me and caused the step."[61]

On the very day that Grant delivered Ord his confidential orders, Sigel provided the War Department with an insight into his temperament which foretold much of his caution. In outlining the disposition of his troops, his tenor accented a defensive role. If the department mandated an offensive advance, he asserted, "such plans would principally depend on the movements in other quarters." A clearer understanding of his role came with Grant's conciliatory wire over Crook's visit. Sigel now knew the general outline of the projected Kanawha expeditions, though he lacked specific knowledge of Ord's instructions. In designating Beverly as the principal point for concentrating troops, Grant directed him to amass there "not less than 8,000 infantry, three batteries of artillery, and 1,500 picked cavalry," exclusive of Crook's troops. He informed him of Ord's role and further suggested that since Averell knew the countryside well, he should personally command the cavalry component. At the commencement of operations, Ord should hold the mountain passes against any possible Southern incursions, while Crook and his troopers would strike toward the Virginia and Tennessee Railroad. Crook's "route probably should be left to himself." Once Crook accomplished his objective, he

60. *OR*, XXXIII, 789, 791–92, 823.

61. Cresap, *Appomattox Commander*, 116; *OR*, XXXIII, 844–45, 911, and Vol. XXXVII, Pt. 1, pp. 526–27.

was to join Ord. Then, as Grant noted to Sigel, "This force will be sufficient to choose their own route and time for returning to their base, or for executing such orders as may hereafter be given."[62]

Despite the delineation of responsibilities, Sigel began to assert himself and to modify and refine the plan. In a dispatch on April 2 he complained to Grant that he could assemble only 5,635 infantrymen at Beverly, which, he pointed out, would leave only six regiments to guard the railroad from Parkersburg to the Monocacy River.[63] In reply, Grant explained that he based the projected movement from Beverly through Covington on his limited knowledge of the region and "on examination of your last returns." If the route was not "the best and most accessible," he did not insist on it, "only upon the work to be done." He then asked Sigel to consult with Averell as to the most practical routes to accomplish his objectives.[64]

Four days later, on April 6, in an effort to alleviate Sigel's fears of a concentrated Confederate move against a point on his line, Grant reassured him that his deployments were sufficient "to meet them successfully." He stressed that Sigel's forces "would be accomplishing at home the greatest advantage expected from them by moving south if the enemy do attack you in force, that is they would divide him." Still worried, Sigel requested that the War Department send a heavy artillery unit, then at Baltimore, to Harpers Ferry in order to release the infantry there for use elsewhere. He asked Governor Boreman to call out part of the state's militia for guard duty.[65]

By April 8, after interviews with Ord and Averell, Sigel raised a number of objections to the plan of dividing his forces into three columns. Four days later he suggested more specific modifications. He proposed using a Charleston–Gauley Bridge–Lewisburg route, reasoning that if an advance by Beverly stalled, Ord's column would be "lost power, as it can neither assist us in the Shenandoah nor co-operate with General Crook." Thus he recommended shifting two to three thousand infantry to Crook. Believing that the Confederates were aware of the concentration at Beverly, he suggested using that force merely as a feint.[66]

62. OR, XXXIII, 762–66; Simon, ed., *Papers of Grant*, X, 236–37.

63. OR, XXXIII, 791–92.

64. *Ibid.*, 798–99; Simon, ed., *Papers of Grant*, X, 256–57n, 257–58.

65. OR, XXXIII, 812–13; Simon, ed., *Papers of Grant*, 264–65.

66. OR, XXXIII, 823, 844–45; Simon, ed., *Papers of Grant*, X, 265–66n.

His recommendation of using Gauley Bridge as a point of departure pleased Grant. As he informed Sigel, it confirmed his initial instincts, and he fully agreed. He also added that since the late rains had forced a delay in beginning the campaign, other changes were possible, if necessary. Grant also began to expand his vision of operations in western Virginia. He now thought not only in terms of destroying the Virginia and Tennessee Railroad but also of using Ord's cavalry "to cut the main lines of road connecting Richmond with all the south & southwest."[67]

Curious about preparations in West Virginia, on April 15 Grant sent Lieutenant Colonel Orville E. Babcock to consult with Sigel. To explain the visit, he underscored that Babcock's mission was merely to confer with Sigel and not to give orders. He again stressed his flexibility on routes. But Grant also gave Sigel some pointed advice: "From the extended line you have to guard no troops can be taken from you except to act directly from your line toward the enemy. In this way you must occupy the attention of a large force, and thereby hold them from re-enforcing elsewhere, or must inflict a blow upon the enemy's resources, which will materially aid us."[68]

Ord's request to be relieved precipitated another change. Grant suggested Averell as a replacement, or Sigel could "go yourself, as you deem most advisable."[69] Then, on April 18, Sigel asked permission to give up the Beverly route and leave only a cavalry regiment there. He also proposed restructuring the movement to involve only two columns, the major one under Crook with approximately 10,000 men and a second one under himself with a lesser figure of 7,000 in the Valley. He envisioned Averell's role as commanding the cavalry under Crook, which he expected to number some 2,500. Still thinking in terms of the Charleston–Gauley Bridge–Lewisburg route, he proposed that Crook, after occupying Lewisburg, should strike toward the railroad to destroy as much of it as possible, especially "the New River bridge or the salt-works, which are two real objects." With his own column, Sigel planned to advance up the Shenandoah to Cedar Creek and thereby threaten Southern forces in that region. Babcock agreed and wired Grant's chief of staff, Brigadier General John A. Rawlins, his approval. Babcock believed that the plan offered was the only practical one that would "not uncover the Baltimore and Ohio Railroad"

67. OR, XXXIII, 845; Simon, ed., *Papers of Grant*, X, 282.
68. OR, XXXIII, 874; Simon, ed., *Papers of Grant*, X, 286–87.
69. OR, XXXIII, 893.

to Confederate raids. Grant accepted it and wired Sigel, "Make your prep-arations for executing it with all dispatch."[70]

With Ord's departure, Crook assumed command of the Kanawha cam-paign. Born near Dayton, Ohio, in 1829, Crook graduated from West Point in 1852, then served in California until the outbreak of the war, when he left for New York. Initially appointed as a captain, he preferred instead to go to Columbus, Ohio, where the governor appointed him colo-nel of the 36th Ohio Regiment, then at Summersville, (West) Virginia. Whipping his raw recruits into shape, he defeated a Southern force under General Henry Heth at Lewisburg on May 23, 1862. His performance in the Antietam campaign earned him a lieutenant colonel's commission in the regular army. In October he received a promotion to brigadier general of volunteers and command of the Kanawha Division.[71] In June 1863 the War Department assigned him to the Army of the Cumberland. During the Chickamauga campaign, Crook earned Rosecrans' praise for driving General Joseph Wheeler "in confusion across the Tennessee River" and for "inaugurating the new practice of coming to close quarters without delay." In January 1864 the War Department ordered him to Kelley.[72]

Grant, too, admired Crook for his performance in the Chickamauga campaign, and informed him that he "would like to have me East."[73] His return to West Virginia pleased civilians and veterans alike, both of whom expected that he "will accomplish something."[74] Grant agreed, and before Crook's departure he briefed the general on his desire to have the Virginia and Tennessee Railroad destroyed in order to secure eastern Tennessee. Crook, in turn, "expressed a strong conviction that he could accom-plished [sic] all I asked." In an earlier dispatch to Major General John M. Schofield, lamenting on past difficulties in securing cooperation from troops in West Virginia, Grant had exuded more confidence, believing that Crook "may undertake to strike the road about need [New] river."[75]

70. *Ibid.*, 900–901; Simon, ed., *Papers of Grant*, X, 310–12n.

71. Schmitt, ed., *George Crook*, xx–xxiii, 83–85, 114; Lang, *Loyal West Virginia*, 327–28; OR, Vol. LI, Pt. 1, pp. 874.

72. OR, Vol. XXX, Pt. 2, p. 667, and Vol. LI, Pt. 1, pp. 874, 1146: Simon, ed., *Papers of Grant*, X, 32.

73. Schmitt, ed., *George Crook*, 114.

74. William S. Newton to wife, Feb. 15, 1864, Civil War Letters of William S. Newton, MIC 17, Roll 11, OHS.

75. Simon, ed., *Papers of Grant*, X, 113, 157.

Crook was a highly respected military commander. Physically imposing, he stood slightly over six feet tall. Despite an athletic build, a blond
beard, and "keen, blue-gray eyes," he shunned the military dash that
caught the public eye.[76] A correspondent traveling with Crook during the
raid on Dublin characterized him as "a man of modest unobtrusiveness,
and one, also, who is decidedly adverse to newspaper puffings."[77] Captain
John G. Bourke, who served with him on the frontier, described Crook as
"singularly averse to the least semblance of notoriety, . . . as retiring as a
girl." Independent and at times stubborn, he could be sharp in his judgment of subordinates, but with his "genial and sunny" personality and
courteous manner he also demonstrated strong interest in his junior officers, which gained their respect.[78] His laconic manner of speaking caused
General Jacob Dolson Cox and others to suspect that he "had been so
long fighting Indians on the frontier that he had acquired some of their
traits and habits." Cox also surmised that "his system of discipline was
based on these peculiarities."[79]

According to Captain Bourke, Crook possessed the "ability to learn all
that his informant had to supply, without yielding in return the slightest
suggestion of his own plans and purposes."[80] He preferred to lead rather
than indulge in written orders. His men regarded him as "a fighting General" and knew that in battle he "would be found in the skirmish line, not
in the telegraph office."[81] At the outset of the West Virginia expedition,
Colonel Rutherford B. Hayes expressed "great confidence in his skill and
good judgment,"[82] commenting to his adjutant, Captain Russell Hastings,
that "with Genl. Crook to lead us we shall surely win."[83] A correspondent
for the Cincinnati *Daily Commercial* observed that "General Crook is
younger by many years, than any officer who has heretofore [had] this stu-

76. John G. Bourke, *On the Border with Crook* (New York, 1902), 110–11; John F. Finerty, *War-Path and Bivouac: The Big Horn and Yellowstone Expedition*, ed. Milo Milton Quaife
(1890; rpr. Chicago, 1955), 7.

77. Wheeling *Daily Intelligencer*, May 27, 1864.

78. Bourke, *On Border with Crook*, 109.

79. Jacob Dolson Cox, *Military Reminiscences of the Civil War* (New York, 1900), I, 205.

80. Bourke, *On Border with Crook*, 109.

81. Evelyn Abraham Benson, comp., *With the Army of West Virginia, 1861–1864: Reminiscences and Letters of Lt. James Abraham* (typescript; Lancaster, Pa., 1974), 96.

82. Charles Richard Williams, ed., *Diary and Letters of Rutherford Birchard Hayes* (Columbus, Ohio, 1922), II, 455.

83. Genealogy and Autobiography of Russell Hastings, May 2, 1864, XI, 4, RBHPCL.

pendous job," but hastened to add, "we predict for him a glorious success."[84]

Now in command, on April 18 Crook expressed his concern to Sigel that "I don't know whether I can accomplish all General Grant expects or not by my acting as you suggest, but will do my best."[85] His immediate worry was the weather. Rain brought high water, destroying bridges and leaving roads impassable. Colonel Augustus Moor, in command at Beverly, wired Sigel that twenty-five miles of the road from that point to Baker was "one continued canal of mud." The 12th West Virginia, marching to Beverly, left their artillery behind since "the roads were impassable." In early April, Dr. Neil jested to his family that "a great portion of the time we could only see, as the wagon train passed, the mules ears sticking from beneath the mud." Late snows added to the problem in the mountain passes. Private James W. Mulligan of the 15th New York Cavalry complained to his wife in mid-April that "it is very Cold here at Night last night was very cold in our Cloth Houses." Dr. Neil apprised his family that "the bad & stormy weather has materially changed our original programme."[86]

Satisfied with his artillery and provisions, Crook asked Sigel for 3,500 additional infantry, horses, and mules and a hundred yards of pontoons. But by April 21 he had begun to entertain doubts about the raid on Saltville. With only some 2,500 effective troopers, he feared he did not have sufficient cavalry. Reassuring Sigel on the following day, he affirmed that the projected route of occupying Lewisburg and then turning toward the railroad remained the same. He also informed him that in "keeping a sharp lookout for my left flank" he might make the move on Lynchburg. If so, he hoped to remain in that region, doing as much damage as he could "until it is prudent to retreat." He then asked Sigel if he wanted him to withdraw toward Lewisburg or Staunton after accomplishing his mission.[87]

Two days later, anticipating the order to advance but still unprepared to

84. Cincinnati *Daily Commercial*, May 17, 1864.

85. OR, XXXIII, 910.

86. *Ibid.*, 910–11; Simon, ed., *Papers of Grant*, X, 311n; Neil to Father and Mother, April 5, 8, 17, 1864, Neil Letters; Handwritten memorandum, n.d., n.p., William B. Curtis Papers, WVU; James W. Mulligan to Sarah E. Mulligan, April 18, 1864, James Mulligan Letters, USMHI; E. C. Arthur, "The Dublin Raid," *Ohio Soldier*, Jan. 5, 1889.

87. OR, XXXIII, 910–11, 938, 945; Simon, ed., *Papers of Grant*, X, 311–12n.

move for two or three days, Crook asked permission to engage in a ploy of sending a small force from Beverly toward Marlin's Bottom to spread rumors that a large contingent of infantry and artillery followed them. Sigel approved. Assigning the 21st New Yorkers, Crook ordered them to go only as far as Sulphur Springs, remain there for two or three days, and then return. But by April 25 he was rethinking the entire expedition. While reporting the arrival of five regiments, he informed Sigel that their numbers fell short of his expectations and would cause him to change his plans. As soon as all the troops arrived, he advised, he would submit the details. He reassured him, however, that all would be ready by Grant's mandate of May 2 for beginning the campaign. Sigel, arriving in Martinsburg on April 26, felt confident. He believed that since Crook would "be stronger than any force the enemy can concentrate between Lewisburg and the railroad," he would be successful. [88]

Crook waited until April 30, virtually the eve of the campaign's commencement, to reveal his modified plan. Instead of using two columns, he informed Sigel, he intended to use only one and a secondary cavalry force of 2,000 under Averell. The troopers would advance through Logan Court House to strike toward Saltville. Only a feint would now be made toward Lewisburg, while the main column of infantry, some 6,155, would march from Fayetteville toward the New River bridge. If circumstances militated against attacking Saltville, then Averell's troopers would destroy the Virginia and Tennessee Railroad up to the bridge in order to prevent Southern forces in eastern Tennessee from reinforcing those in western Virginia. There the cavalry would join his column. After capturing the bridge, Crook would advance along the railroad, destroying it as far as prudent toward Lynchburg. Then he expected to retreat toward Lewisburg. [89]

Stunned by the radical changes, Sigel, then advancing up the Valley, immediately wired Grant from Winchester. Prefacing his comments with the hope that the strategy might "prove successful and may have very important results," he complained that Averell's cavalry would be too far west to cooperate with Crook and would consequently be "used up" in future deployments. He feared that the plan allowed Confederate forces spread between Lewisburg and Staunton to concentrate at the latter

88. OR, XXXIII, 964, 975–76, 978–79, 986, 997–98.

89. *Ibid.*, 1027–28, and Vol. XXXVII, Pt. 1, pp. 9–10; Simon, ed., *Papers of Grant*, X, 389–90, 390, 393n.

point. Sigel also objected that the changes prevented any cooperation between his column and Crook's. His understanding, he maintained, was
that Crook's forces were supposed to operate between the New River and
the James with the ultimate objective of undertaking a combined move
against Staunton. Admitting that he might be wrong on the change of
plans but aware that it was too late to interfere, Sigel told Grant, "I will
therefore say nothing to General Crook, but wish his success."[90]

Having distanced himself from the expedition's possible failure, Sigel
now asked Grant what was expected of his column. Grant directed Sigel
not to advance beyond Cedar Creek and to watch for any Confederate
movement that might utilize the Valley. But he also took the opportunity
to remind him of the original plan, which, though modified by Sigel, specified a movement from Beverly and an advance "easterly to Lynchburg and
return to Staunton." There, he pointed out, he was "to meet them with a
train loaded with supplies." He expressed hope that efforts then under way
to raise additional troops would allow him to send reinforcements if a
Southern force attempted to move down the Valley. In closing, Grant underscored his central objective in western Virginia: "To cut New River
bridge and the road ten or twenty miles east from there would be the most
important work Crook could do."[91]

Confederate authorities, acutely aware of Federal objectives, realized their
vulnerability in western Virginia. The Virginia and Tennessee Railroad,
the Virginia Central Railroad, and the James River and Kanawha Canal
formed critical arteries connecting Richmond with the salt of Saltville,
the lead mines of Wytheville, the iron ore region of Buchanan, and the
rich agricultural backcountry so necessary to feed Lee's army. They were
also crucial for transporting forces between Virginia and eastern Tennessee. Underscoring their vulnerability, a cavalry raid by Averell on December 16, 1863, had inflicted considerable damage on the Virginia and Tennessee at Salem. The Confederates could not afford a repetition, since a
crippled transportation system in western Virginia might well mean the
abandonment of Virginia. On April 14, 1864, Lee, anxious over the pau-
city of stores, warned Davis that "any derangement in their arrival or disaster to the railroad would render it impossible for me to keep the army

90. *OR*, Vol. XXXVII, Pt. 1, pp. 368–69.
91. *Ibid.*; Simon, ed., *Papers of Grant*, X, 389–90, 393n.

together, & might force a retreat into North Carolina." Four days later, complaining again of shortages to Bragg in Richmond, he warned that if the Federals forced him back from "our present line the [Virginia] Central Railroad, Charlottesville, & all the upper country will be exposed, and I fear great injury inflicted on us."[92]

The area of most immediate concern for Richmond was southwestern Virginia. Worry over the safety of the Virginia and Tennessee Railroad and of salt and lead mines in the region raised sharp questions concerning the area's security and especially the leadership in the Department of Western Virginia. Major General Samuel Jones, a native Virginian and an 1841 graduate of West Point, had increasingly given the Confederate War Department cause for anxiety. Complaints and charges of poor leadership caused Richmond and Lee to subject Jones to increasing scrutiny. As early as January 1864, Lee had expressed strong reservations about him, writing Davis that "I have been disappointed in my expectations" of Jones. He believed that a reorganization of the department was needed. With Union forces in eastern Tennessee threatening the region, he saw the necessity of appointing "a man of judgment and energy, whose discretion can be depended upon without always awaiting orders," an officer who would bring to bear "able, intelligent, and vigorous management." Davis asked for the general's advice on a replacement.[93]

Adding to this pressure for Jones's removal, twenty-five Virginia legislators from the southwest and upper Valley petitioned Davis to send more troops to the region. They reminded him that the southwestern counties produced large surpluses of "horses, cattle, hogs, grain and hay" and that "nearly all the iron, salt, and lead manufactured in the Confederate States is made in that section." A raid would cause "a considerable part of the population" to flee to other areas of the Confederacy. The legislators especially dreaded the possibility of the destruction of the Virginia and Tennessee Railroad. For Lee, however, leadership remained the critical factor, not manpower.[94]

Incoming intelligence accentuated Southern anxieties. Jones reported that Averell occupied the same base from which he had conducted his previous raid on Salem and that scouts reported a buildup for another one.

92. OR, XXXIII, 1275, 1284–85; Dowdey and Manarin, eds., *Papers of Lee*, 698, 701.
93. OR, XXXIII, 1086, 1107; Dowdey and Manarin, eds., *Papers of Lee*, 651.
94. OR, XXXIII, 1106–1107.

He informed Secretary of War James Seddon that reports pointed to another attempt to destroy the railroad as well as "the iron and lead mines and the saltworks." He maintained that if the Federals did not attempt a raid that winter, Averell, knowing the inadequacy of the Confederate force, certainly would strike in the spring. News of a shift of Federal cavalry from eastern Tennessee to Kentucky on the Virginia border alarmed Jones, and on December 26, 1863, he asked the War Department to assign Major General Robert Ransom's infantry and part of his artillery to protect the mines and the railroad. He wanted the men moved to Bristol, from where they could be easily moved to wherever they might be needed along the rail line. However, Longstreet, Ransom's commander, refused. Jones further requested that since one regiment of Brigadier General Gabriel Wharton's brigade was then at Saltville, the remainder of it should be moved to the vicinity of Glade Springs. Five days later he repeated his request for Wharton's brigade. [95]

On December 29, Jones again reminded the War Department of the December raid on Salem to emphasize the importance of security for the railroad. In stressing his intention to maintain an adequate force "directly on this road," he nevertheless complained that the department had "obliged [him] to send [the 54th and 63rd Virginia Regiments] away, and [he had] not been able since then to replace it." He asked for their return, believing they belonged "properly to my command" and could "render most valuable aid in protecting this section of country." The War Department declined. Samuel Cooper, the adjutant and inspector general, opposed separating them from Johnston's army, for "experience has shown that where regiments are stationed in sections where they are enlisted military discipline is apt to be loose . . . and this has proven to be the case to some extent in Western Virginia." [96]

In reply to a January 31 dispatch from Jones, Lee responded on February 2 that he could not spare any troops and that "the facts had better be reported to the Secretary of War, as your department is beyond the limits of my command." He agreed that the Federals would attempt another raid when the weather permitted, but added that Averell's "success appears . . . to be owing to the terror with which he has inspired the troops. As soon as his approach is announced his progress is neither retarded nor

95. *Ibid.*, 1107–1109, 1135.
96. *Ibid.*, 1109–10.

watched." Lee, realizing Jones's problem of defending a long line and his inability of maintaining a force at every vulnerable point, suggested fortifying the various mountain passes where small units could "greatly embarrass their passage," as well as organizing the local citizenry to aid in the region's defense. He also recommended that if Jones could attack an exposed point in the enemy line and "throw them on the defensive it would lighten your labor exceedingly."[97]

Eight days later, Jones assured Lee that he had no intention of asking for any units from his army. Instead, he offered his comments only as a warning that any movement from the Kanawha Valley might be a feint for another one "east of but near my department." Though admitting that his department was "beyond your command," he did not understand "why you should not give me a little temporary aid in protecting a very long and important line, if you could do so without endangering your own command." In his own defense, he maintained that his numbers would be greater if he had earlier refused to allow some of his own units to go beyond his department. Stung by Lee's comments on Averell's achievements and purported terrorizing of his troops, Jones retorted that Lee "overestimate[d] the success which has heretofore attended General Averell's expeditions." Pointing to three such raids, he charged that on the first one, near White Sulphur Springs, he whipped Averell and drove him back "with heavy losses." On the second one, at Droop Mountain, Averell "suffered so severely." For the Salem raid, Jones charged, Federals penetrated the area between commands and did not come within his department. He denied that Averell created terror in his men. In deference, Jones noted his appreciation for Lee's advice on taking the offensive, but he quickly briefed him on the problems of such a course of action. If Lee fully knew the strength of Jones's forces, he asserted, "you would not advise me to make an aggressive movement at this time."[98]

Meanwhile, Lee had responded to Davis' query on a change in commanders. Apologetic for his delay, he admitted that the challenge in proposing the right commander caused his silence. Though there were a number of excellent candidates, he hesitated, for sending them "to a new and difficult field would be an experiment." Yet he regarded the region as so important "that I will relinquish any of them you may select for its

97. *Ibid.*, 1141–42.
98. *Ibid.*, 1155–56.

command." Without recommending a particular candidate, except to indicate that "Ransom is the most prominent," he urged the appointment of "an energetic active commander." Lee, thinking in regional rather than departmental terms, further proposed that if a proper one could be found, the Valley District should be included in his jurisdiction so that "he might concentrate the troops where most necessary." In addition, he suggested that "their local character should be abolished by law" to achieve better discipline. "In a word, the system should be such as to organize the men of the country for its defense, and not for their convenience or the benefit of certain individuals." But for Lee the first step remained the appointment of a commander with energy, and "no time should be lost in his selection."[99]

Jones, aware of the rumors of his pending removal, wrote to the War Department on February 14 for reassurance. He denied ever making a request to be relieved. Seddon replied diplomatically, telling him that he was misinformed about any such announcement. Yet he advised him that after fully reviewing the issue, "the best interests of service require a change of command." Though praising the general's zeal, he wrote that Jones "had ceased to command the general confidence of the people, and discontent and apprehensions of hurtful nature were prevailing in regard to the security of your department." His successor, the secretary of war apprised him, was Major General John C. Breckinridge.[100]

Davis wanted to choose not only a competent officer but one who would also restore the confidence of the region's inhabitants. Initially a number of his advisers suggested his aide, Brigadier General Custis Lee. Davis offered Lee the post, but his inexperience militated against him. Even his father, Robert E. Lee, agreed and believed that the appointment would be a liability. However, Breckinridge offered more telling qualifications. As a member of a prominent Kentucky family with roots and connections in Virginia, a politician of no small achievements, and an officer with considerable military experience and skill, he easily filled all requirements. To his admirers he was "the handsomest man in the Confederate army."

Born near Lexington, Kentucky, in 1821, Breckinridge graduated from Centre College and studied law at Transylvania College. As a major in the

99. *Ibid.*, 1124.

100. *Ibid.*, 1172–73, 1198, and Vol. LI, Pt. 2, pp. 816, 820.

3rd Kentucky Regiment, he served in the Mexican War but saw no action. Returning home, he won a seat in the state legislature in 1849. Two years later his district elected him to Congress. He became identified with Southern interests but not as a "fire-eater." In the 1856 presidential campaign he was James Buchanan's running mate and won election as vice president of the United States. However, in 1860 schisms rent the Democratic Party, and the bolting Southern wing nominated him as its presidential candidate. With his defeat, the Kentucky legislature sent him back to the Senate. Unionists in the special session of Congress doubted his loyalty, and his opposition to administration policies seemed to confirm their suspicion. Fearing arrest, he fled south to cast his lot with the Confederacy.

With ties to a number of prominent families, the "hard-drinking" and "tobacco-chewing" Breckinridge rose to the rank of major general by late 1863. Quarrels with Bragg during the siege of Chattanooga, however, alienated the two, and this antagonism destroyed Breckinridge's effectiveness in the Army of Tennessee. His transfer to the western Virginia post became a means of resolving that conflict. The appointment also provided the region with a competent commander and a publicly well-received one. No other general received such popular support. As the editor of the Staunton *Spectator* enthusiastically commented, "Everyone is favorably impressed."[101]

Breckinridge's new assignment as commander of the Department of Western Virginia, with its headquarters in Dublin, was an almost impossible one. Covering a vast region of rugged mountainous terrain, the department included all of Virginia west of the Blue Ridge Mountains and south of Staunton, the southern portion of West Virginia, and parts of eastern Tennessee. Worse, the department lacked adequate troops to protect its three-hundred-mile-long frontier. For this vast territory, forces in

101. See William C. Davis, *John C. Breckinridge* (Baton Rouge, 1974) for definitive biography; William C. Davis, *Jefferson Davis: The Man and His Hour* (New York, 1991), 550; Davis, *New Market*, 16–17; Steven E. Woodworth, *Jefferson Davis and His Generals: The Failure of Confederate Command in the West* (Lawrence, Kans., 1990), 117–20, 191–94, 196, 245, 250–52, 360–61 n. 192; Thomas Lawrence Connelly and Archer Jones, *The Politics of Command* (Baton Rouge, 1973), 52, 55, 62–71, 73–75, 78; "John Cabell Breckinridge," CV, XIII (1906), 257–60; Staunton (Va.) *Spectator*, March 22, 1864, quoted in Everhard H. Smith III, "The General and the Valley: Union Leadership During the Threat to Washington in 1864" (Ph.D. dissertation, University of North Carolina, Chapel Hill, 1977), 32.

February 1864 numbered only 445 officers, 5,175 men, and fourteen pieces of artillery. In the aggregate he could count on a potential of 10,885, present and on leave.[102] With his manpower spread so thin, any Federal incursion posed a serious threat. Chronic problems of poor discipline and other abuses plagued the army. Military reverses invariably cast blame on the commander, and the department came to have the reputation of being "the graveyard of Confederate generals."[103] The Lynchburg *Virginian* noted that "Gen. Breckinridge has a most difficult and important command—one in which no officer has ever yet given entire satisfaction."[104]

Before assuming the post, Breckinridge spent two weeks in Richmond conferring with Davis and the War Department. Arriving at Dublin on March 4, he took up his duties the following day. His immediate concern centered on putting his men in a state of combat readiness. In order to tighten discipline, see to the construction of key defenses, collect intelligence on Federal activity, and prepare his troops for the spring campaign, he undertook an arduous four-hundred-mile tour of inspection of his three brigades from Warm Springs to Abingdon.[105] At Narrows, after reviewing his troops before a large crowd, a pleased and politically savvy Breckinridge complimented the men on "their high state of efficiency and discipline." Prevailed upon to make a brief address, he called attention to his Virginia ties and remarked that "it had never been his fortune heretofore to command Virginia troops." On visiting Colonel William "Mudwall" Jackson's brigade, he exhorted the men: "You have enlisted for the war—So have I. Let us not become faint or weary, and in due time we shall reap the rich fruit of independence."[106]

Breckinridge's striking appearance, "frank manly bearing, and . . . courteous and affable manners" acted as a much-needed tonic for his men. One soldier complimented his new commander by inference: "I am like Genl Breckenridge [sic], I think the time for speeches has passed that the

102. J. Stoddard Johnston, "Sketches of Operations of General John C. Breckinridge," *SHSP*, VII (1879), 257–58; *OR*, XXXIII, 1203.

103. J. Stoddard Johnston, *Kentucky*, Vol. X of *Confederate Military History*, ed. Clement A. Evans (Atlanta, 1899), 184.

104. Lynchburg *Virginian*, March 23, 1864.

105. Johnston, "Sketches of Operations of Breckinridge," 257–58; Johnston, *Kentucky*, 185; August Moor to Franz Sigel, March 21, 1864, Franz Sigel Papers, Western Reserve Historical Society, Cleveland, Ohio; Davis, *New Market*, 17–18.

106. Staunton (Va.) *Spectator*, March 29, 1864.

hour for action has arrived."[107] Not only did he instill greater confidence, but his energetic presence increased his force by 10 percent. By the end of March he reported 443 officers and 5,667 effectives for an aggregate of 11,027 present and absent, plus four additional fieldpieces.[108] The Lynchburg *Virginian* relished reports that "the people of South-western Virginia are greatly pleased with the administration of affairs, and he is winning golden opinions."[109]

Quickly demonstrating a knowledge of the region's various strategic points, Breckinridge began making troop dispositions and constructing fortifications to thwart potential raids. Flexibility became the key to his planning. His activity, especially the fortification of defenses for the railroad, pleased Lee, who did, however, suggest that Breckinridge connect his line of defense to the Valley District. In terms of Federal strategy, Lee warned that the enemy generally attempted to threaten several points and then concentrated on one. He recommended that Breckinridge's line should be far enough in advance to allow him to fall back to a point where he could consolidate his forces "in the retired positions."[110]

Breckinridge carefully scrutinized Federal activity in West Virginia. He noted Jones's earlier admonition of another raid. The day after Breckinridge assumed command, Brigadier General John Echols, relaying intelligence from "Mudwall" Jackson at Warm Springs, advised him that Federal operations would begin "on this end of your line." Five days later, on March 10, Brigadier General John D. Imboden, in the Valley District, suspecting that there would be "a big raid here," suggested to Lee that he should inform Breckinridge. Since he had 350 men building fortifications in various passes, Imboden urged "Mudwall" to do the same at Millborough and for Breckinridge to secure the area south of that point. He warned that if Averell made a raid with five to six thousand men and threatened two or three places, "we shall be sorely put to meet him unless these works are finished and other troops sent to the district."[111]

Previously Lee had sent Breckinridge a report and map on the defenses of western Virginia used by Early. Though appreciative of the map, Breckinridge found flaws in the defensive line when it entered his department,

107. J. Z. McChesney to Lucy, April 12, 1864, H. E. Matheny Collection, WVU.
108. *OR*, XXXIII, 1250.
109. Lynchburg *Virginian*, March 23, 1864.
110. *OR*, XXXIII, 1231, 1239.
111. *Ibid.*, 1135, 1210–11, 1215.

observing that it left undefended Greenbrier and Monroe Counties and a portion of Alleghany County through which the last raid had penetrated. He reported to Lee that his men now occupied positions fifty miles in advance of that line. To mask and guard the "main roads leading to the Virginia and Tennessee Railroad, the lead mines of Wythe, and the saltworks," he intended to construct "a large self-sustaining work" at Princeton. He saw that point as "the salient or key point . . . lying west of New River." Lee approved. The further advanced the positions were, he advised, the better, provided "they cannot be turned and the garrisons cut off."[112]

In reply to Seddon's March 21 warning of a Federal raid, Breckinridge acknowledged having received similar reports. He apprised the secretary that he had alerted Jackson to watch the railroad bridges over Jackson's and Cow Pasture Rivers. Since Jackson's unit was small, he hoped to support him with troops from Rockbridge and Augusta Counties, but he warned that because of a threat from the Kanawha Valley, Echols could not "leave the line of Greenbrier." At the end of March, Jackson informed Echols of the presence of ten regiments at Clarksburg. He was not worried, believing the Federals would not advance "during this bad weather."[113]

On April 1, Echols sent Breckinridge an analysis of Union intentions. Citing the reputed buildup of some four thousand cavalry and an equal number of infantry in the Kanawha Valley, he pointed to their likely routes and tactics. Among the various configurations, he suspected that part of the Federal infantry might strike toward Princeton while the remainder moved on him to keep both himself and Colonel John McCausland occupied. Or they might send all of their infantry toward Princeton and a cavalry force against him in the Warm Springs region. Cautioning that "they know the location and strength of our different forces" and of those protecting the New River bridge, he warned that "it has been an earnest desire upon their part to destroy this bridge."[114]

By the middle of April, Jackson's reports heightened Echols' awareness of increasing Federal activity in the Kanawha Valley, New Creek, Beverly, Clarksburg, and Buckhannon areas. Yet McCausland reported to Breckin-

112. *Ibid.*, 1231.
113. *Ibid.*, 1236, 1243.
114. *Ibid.*, 1253–54.

ridge that the force in the Kanawha "has neither been diminished nor increased." He did note Crook's return from his visit to Washington, while scouts soon detected the westward movement of Averell's cavalry along the Baltimore and Ohio Railroad. Lee believed, as he informed Davis, that this presaged a raid on the Virginia and Tennessee Railroad or Staunton "at the time of the general movement upon Richmond." Relaying the information to Imboden on April 18, he warned that Averell would probably move on the railroad from a "point beyond the North Mountain," though he hastened to add, "I see no indications of a movement up the Valley." Lee hoped Imboden and Breckinridge could unite to "beat him back," for "I shall be so occupied, in all probability, that I shall be unable to aid you." Reiterating much of what he told Imboden, Lee urged Breckinridge to have Jackson's scouts probe the Beverly area for intelligence.[115]

Incoming reports to Echols from "Mudwall" and Imboden kept accenting the buildup in West Virginia. Imboden alerted Jackson to a possible threat from Beverly, citing concentrations at Grafton, New Creek, Cumberland, and Martinsburg. "Another raid brewing," he warned. Informed by sources that "nearly all the force in Northwestern Virginia is at Beverly," Jackson assumed they "either intend a raid or are preparing to resist one." Four days later Imboden's scouts reaffirmed the report of April 18 that Averell's entire command had left Martinsburg for the west, while Brigadier General Jeremiah Sullivan reputedly concentrated eight thousand men at Beverly. Scouts reported to McCausland at Narrows that citizens on the Kanawha River said "the Yankees make no secret of it, and say that they will move when Grant is ready." Showered with such reports, Breckinridge wired Major C. S. Stringfellow at Dublin to order Echols and McCausland to "be ready to move any moment."[116]

In reply to a dispatch from Echols, Breckinridge laid out his thinking. Because of the extended territory covered by the department and the size of his force, he counseled against separating the "troops too far." Reflecting Lee's own advice, he recommended that if forced back, Echols should retire toward McCausland, "who would advance." He suggested keeping Jackson's men and scouts as far in advance as possible in order to provide an early warning. Anxious over the activity around Beverly, he wanted

115. *Ibid.*, 1284, 1287–88, 1291, 1295.
116. *Ibid.*, 1296–97, 1301–1302, 1306.

Echols to determine Federal strength there. Meanwhile, the War Department, increasingly sensitive to the vulnerability of the southwest, ordered Wharton's brigade to Dublin to augment the troops there.[117]

While digesting the array of intelligence, Breckinridge diligently readied his troops, reporting to Bragg on April 27 that his infantry was now "respectably armed" and the cavalry, "hardly armed" on his arrival, now "nearly supplied."[118] To ensure sufficient ammunition, he issued a circular in May ordering officers to prevent any waste of ordnance, especially .54 caliber, which was especially scarce.[119] Despite continuing shortages of forage, grain, and foodstuffs, he believed his department was in a much better state of readiness to challenge a raid. In a line stretching for almost 140 miles, his troops held strategic points. "Mudwall" Jackson, with approximately one thousand cavalry and mounted scouts, anchored the northeast, south of Warm Springs, and operated as a screen toward Huntersville and Beverly. Echols' brigade, poised seven miles from Lewisburg, covered the routes to Covington and Salem. Further to the southwest, Breckinridge posted McCausland's brigade at Narrows and Princeton. On the southern end of the line, in Tazewell County, he deployed some cavalry to cover the approaches to Wytheville and the lead mines, while a regiment and fourteen pieces of "tolerable" artillery protected Saltville. Major General S. B. Buckner's troops in the Abingdon region could, if needed, provide additional support. Even though his troops were spread thinly, Breckinridge, undoubtedly remembering Lee's advice of March 23, believed they would provide him with an early alarm system as to which route a Federal advance would take. Their disposition also gave him the necessary time and ability to concentrate once that threat developed. "We must trust to the earliest intelligence and then to the promptest movements," he told Echols and McCausland.[120]

The following day, one of Brigadier General John Morgan's scouts confirmed Averell's presence in the Kanawha Valley. Information earlier forwarded to Lee from Imboden had placed him at New Creek, and Lee had advised Breckinridge that "he cannot, therefore, as reported, have gone to Kanawha." The new intelligence changed that assumption. Buckner informed both Breckinridge and the War Department that Averell was at

117. *Ibid.*, 1310–12.
118. *Ibid.*, 1318.
119. Circular, May 12, 1864, Clarke Papers, MHS.
120. *OR*, XXXIII, 1318–19.

Point Pleasant on April 20 with 2,500 troopers and was "expecting to start on a raid in a very few days." He told Breckinridge that he was moving a portion of his men to cover Saltville and wanted a directive from Richmond as "to what extent I am expected or authorized to move troops out of this department to co-operate with you."[121]

Unburdening his frustration to Echols, Breckinridge lamented, "It is hard work with the troops we have to defend the salt-works, the lead-mines, the railroad, the iron-works, &c. dotted over an extended country accessible to attack from many quarters." But he quickly added, "Yet I will do all I can short of entire and fatal separation of the troops." Again he warned Echols and McCausland against dividing their forces. For Breckinridge the key in fending off a raid or general advance became concentration of his forces. Expressing his confidence in both McCausland and Echols, he asserted that either one could "whip a raiding party," but he cautioned against allowing their two brigades to move "too far apart." To Echols he reiterated his advice that scouts should be sufficiently advanced to provide him with an early warning, for as he pointed out to McCausland, "The enemy occupies a position from which roads lead in every direction to our numerous assailable points, each of which is expected to be defended." Exhorting increased readiness, he warned Echols that "matters look too imminent for delay."[122]

Finally, on May 1, Lee sounded the tocsin. Alerting Breckinridge to incoming intelligence that pointed to the beginning of a movement by Averell to strike at either the Virginia and Tennessee Railroad or Staunton, he concluded that the Federals would follow the same route as on the previous raid. He recommended cooperation to both Breckinridge and Imboden in destroying him. Yet Lee mistakenly believed that Staunton was Averell's principal target, cautioning Breckinridge against being deceived by feints in the Kanawha Valley. If Imboden could hold his front, Lee suggested a move on Averell's line of communication, or Breckinridge might "concoct some other plan of defeating him." Since any such move would undoubtedly be made in concert with an offensive by Grant, Lee forewarned that it would "be impossible to send any reinforcements to the Valley from this army."[123]

121. *Ibid.*, 1322–23.

122. *Ibid.*, 1323–25.

123. *Ibid.*, Vol. XXXVII, Pt. 1, p. 707; Dowdey and Manarin, eds., *Papers of Lee*, 716–17.

Galvanized, Breckinridge alerted Echols and McCausland to probe Federal intentions. He directed Brigadier General William E. "Grumble" Jones, then at Saltville, to move his men to Jeffersonville (present-day Tazewell). McCausland temporarily shifted to Princeton, while Wharton's brigade headed toward Giles Court House. Jones soon confirmed the presence of some four hundred Federal troopers in Logan County, with seven regiments following them. Southern sympathizers in the area, he informed Breckinridge, reported that "everything . . . indicate[s] a raid in this direction." Echols' scouts also confirmed Averell's presence in the Kanawha Valley, reporting that "this force is called on the Kanawha River the right wing of Grant's army." The enemy's intention, Echols related, was "to strike the salt-works and New River Bridge."[124]

With Federal arms in motion on May 2, Lee's and Breckinridge's strategy would soon be tested by combat in southwestern Virginia and the Shenandoah Valley.

124. OR, Vol. XXXVII, Pt. 1, pp. 709–11.

2

The Dublin Raid

On the morning of May 3, a "thunderous applause from the throats of 7,000 Union soldiers" greeted the sound of the long roll as it resounded through General Crook's camp at Fayetteville. Captain J. H. Prather of the 91st Ohio knew the sound as the beginning of the spring campaign.[1] Preparations for the West Virginia expedition had become increasingly obvious in the Charleston area during the latter part of April, and military operations in the Kanawha Valley had transformed the town of some fifteen hundred into a bustling center. Already a virtual army base by 1864, Charleston and its neighboring camps now teemed with soldiers and excitement. This concentration of troops, especially cavalry, signaled impending combat and the city was "agog for many days" with increasing activity. "Something certainly is intended to be done," Dr. William Newton wrote to his wife.[2] Private William A. Tall of the 2nd West Virginia Cavalry Regiment informed his mother and sisters, "There is more troops now in the vicinity of the Kanawa (River) than ever I saw together before and I should not wonder if somebody got hurt before we see the fair Charles-

1. Tim McKinney, *The Civil War in Fayette County, West Virginia* (Charleston, 1988), 190–91; Mary Elizabeth Kincaid, "Fayetteville, West Virginia, During the Civil War," *WVH*, XIV (1953), 364.

2. Roy Bird Cook, "Charleston and the Civil War, " *WVR*, XI (1934), 322; Roy Bird Cook, "The Civil War Comes to Charleston," *WVH*, XXIII (1962), 153; William S. Newton to wife, April 27, 1864, Newton Papers, OHS.

town again."[3] As Averell assembled his troopers, a pleased Colonel Hayes, commander of the 1st Infantry Brigade, relished the commotion, knowing that "all things point to early action." Among the officers, all the talk was of the forthcoming campaign. Confidence, especially in Crook, ran high. "We all feel great confidence in his skill and good judgment," wrote Hayes.[4]

In late March, Grant had conferred with Crook and Ord at Culpeper, explaining his objectives in making a forward movement with all of his forces. He emphasized his desire to see the Virginia and Tennessee Railroad destroyed at different points, for he regarded it as "one of the most important lines connecting the confederate armies." After concluding their discussions, both generals speedily returned to Washington by special train. With little delay, Crook hurried back to Charleston. His objectives were clear: destroy the Virginia and Tennessee Railroad and its bridge over the New River, form a juncture with Sigel, who would move on Staunton from the lower Shenandoah Valley, and then jointly march on Lynchburg.[5]

Upon his return, Crook began trimming down the army. Cavalry units under Averell and Brigadier General A. N. Duffié sent all their extra baggage to the rear. He allowed an infantry regiment only six wagons for the officers' mess and some luggage and a wagon for brigade headquarters. The troops would carry their own, plus rations for two or three days. He allowed no tents, except for some of the officers.[6] By the end of April, Crook's troops were assembled in the Fayetteville area, and he wired Sigel his readiness to begin the movement on May 2. Much to Sigel's distress, he now told the general of his radical change of strategy. Crook intended to use only one main column to strike at the New River bridge while Averell's cavalry headed toward Saltville. The projected advance on Lewisburg

3. W. A. Tall to Mother and Sisters, April 29, 1864, Wm. Allen Tall Letters, Civil War Miscellaneous Collection, USMHI.

4. Cincinnati *Daily Commercial*, May 14, 1864; Cincinnati *Daily Gazette*, May 17, 1864; Williams, ed., *Diary and Letters of Hayes*, II, 454; Extracts from Rutherford B. Hayes Diary, May 10, 1864, Rutherford B. Hayes Papers, RBHPCL; Extracts from the Diary of James M. Comly, April 23, 1864, James M. Comly Papers, RBHPCL; Diary of Andrew Stiarwalt, Sr., 13, RBHPCL; Diary of James F. Ellis, April 25–May 2, 1864, Roy Bird Cook Collection, WVU; Arthur, "Dublin Raid," Jan. 5, 1889.

5. Schmitt, ed., *George Crook*, 114–15; Simon, ed., *Papers of Grant*, X, 236–37.

6. Hastings Autobiography, April 29, 1864, XI, 4.

he had changed merely to a feint. By May 2 his column of some 6,155 was in motion. Rumors among the troops suggested that the Virginia rail line was the target, but it was not until the next day that, as Captain Hastings noted, "the column turned its head to the gorge leading up Cotton Mountain [and] all knew that Newbern Bridge was to be burned and the Va. and Tenn. R.R. destroyed."[7]

As Crook's infantry, "with colors flying and bands playing," turned southward toward Raleigh Court House, cheers rang out from the men. The weather, however, suddenly turned, and what had begun as a warm spring day gave way to "a cold, chilly rain" by noon and then a "blinding storm of sleet and rain" which turned to snow. Many in the 3rd Pennsylvania Reserve had discarded their overcoats and blankets that morning, and with temperatures that night plunging to below freezing and producing "ice 1/2 inch thick," the troops suffered severely. The snow and cold dampened the mood of the troops, silencing, as Hastings noted, "that rollicking humor of the previous day." That night the Pennsylvanians, "wet to the skin, and shivering with the cold, presented a pitiable sight." Hayes found the weather "a rough opening of our campaign."[8]

As they advanced toward Princeton, Crook's infantry, following a route through Beckley and Wyoming Court House, encountered little resistance except for felled trees designed to block the way. The army's pioneers easily cleared the route, which wound through a sparsely populated region and over rough wilderness terrain. Corporal James F. Ellis of the 15th West Virginia Regiment observed, "From the Kanawha Falls to Princeton is nothing but mountains and wilderness. There is not 12 inhabited houses on the road. Nearly a hundred Miles."[9] The country and

7. Sigel to Crook and Crook to Sigel, April 27, 1864, Crook to Sigel, April 30, 1864, Sigel Papers; *OR*, XXXIII, 964, 997–98; Extracts from Comly Diary, April 30, May 2, 1864; Hastings Autobiography, April 30–May 2, 1864, XI, 4; Diary of John McNulty Clugston, April 27–May 2, 1864, RBHPCL; Diary of John T. Booth, May 2, 1864, John Booth Papers, OHS; Albert G. Wright Diary, May 2–3, 1864, George A. Fluhr Collection, USMHI; R. B. Wilson, "The Dublin Raid," in *G.A.R. War Papers* (Cincinnati, n.d.), I, 99.

8. Hastings Autobiography, May 2–3, 1864, XI, 4–6; Journal of the 23rd Regiment, Ohio Volunteer Infantry, 15, RBHPCL; Extracts from Comly Diary, May 2–4, 1864; Extracts from Hayes Diary, May 2, 1864; Journal of George W. Baggs, May 2, 1864, Charles Austin Goddard Papers, VHS; Edward Davis Diary, May 2, 1864, USMHI; Arthur, "Dublin Raid," Jan. 5, 1889; Wilson, "Dublin Raid," 99–100; E. M. Woodward, *History of the Third Pennsylvania Reserve* (Trenton, 1883), 240.

9. Ellis Diary, May 6, 1864.

its mountains appeared breathtaking in their beauty, but as Captain R. B. Wilson of the 12th Ohio noted, "To the soldier who had to march up and down their interminable ascents and descents, they were a great weariness to the flesh." [10]

Crook took no chance of being surprised. He allowed no army calls which might alert the local populace or bushwhackers to their presence. A small force of cavalry moved well in advance of the infantry to screen its location and prevent any concentrated attack on it at any point. He deployed videttes on the left and right of the column to guard against being fired upon from distant heights. For additional concealment the men fired scrub oak trees, especially as the army passed over mountains, to provide a smoke screen and cloak the army's route and strength. Yet the blazes became a dangerous tactic, with the fire and its residue making both horses and men nervous, especially those guarding ammunition wagons. [11]

Initially Crook's encountered few bushwhackers. Captain Hastings attributed it to actions taken earlier in the war, believing that "the burning of houses in this neighborhood in 1862 had a lingering effect." [12] As a diversionary tactic, Crook at the outset of the expedition sent Lieutenant R. R. Blazer's scouts and the 5th West Virginia Cavalry under Colonel A. A. Tomlinson toward Lewisburg, hoping the stratagem would "keep the enemy from leaving there." The move achieved some success. Captain Thomas A. Bryan's battery at first believed that the Federals intended to advance on Princeton, but by midafternoon, after receiving reports of Federal movements, they thought the enemy "had gone by way of Lewisburg." [13]

Hoping to slow the Federal advance, Echols ordered the cutting of trees to block the road to Lewisburg. With orders from Breckinridge to take his brigade to Staunton, he became nervous about pulling his troops out of

10. Wilson, "Dublin Raid," 95; Hastings Autobiography, May 5, 1864, XI, 6–7; Stiarwalt Diary, 14; Clugston Diary, May 5, 1864; Baggs Journal, May 4–5, 1864; Davis Diary, May 5, 1864; New York *Herald*, May 29, 1864; Extracts from Hayes Diary, May 5, 1864; Arthur, "Dublin Raid," Jan. 5, 1889.

11. Woodward, *Third Pennsylvania Reserve*, 241–42.

12. Hastings Autobiography, May 6, 1864, XI, 7.

13. OR, Vol. XXXVII, Pt. 1, p. 10; Crook to Sigel, April 30, 1864, Sigel Papers; Asbe Montgomery, *An Account of R. R. Blazer and His Scouts* (Marietta, Ohio, 1865), 11; Milton W. Humphreys, *A History of the Lynchburg Campaign* (Charlottesville, 1924), 6; Petre Jenning Diary, April 1864–July 1864, May 5, 1864, W-FCHS.

the region, especially when a scout reported that Federal trains "staid at foot of Big Sewell" on the night of May 4. But the more pressing need for his brigade was to join Breckinridge, and by the time Blazer's scouts approached Lewisburg the Confederates were on their way to the Shenandoah Valley. Yet Crook regarded the maneuver as a success, believing it had drawn bushwhackers away from their route so effectively that "not a hostile gun was fired at us until we reached the vicinity of Princeton."[14]

At Princeton on May 6, the Federals encountered their first significant opposition. Crook fully expected to find Colonel McCausland there. Instead, his brigade, which had arrived there from Narrows on May 4, left the following day under orders from Breckinridge to proceed to Staunton. Only a small cavalry company, commanded by Captain J. S. A. Crawford, remained. Using three companies of the 12th Ohio as skirmishers, Major Rucker, at the head of a contingent of 2nd West Virginia troopers, charged them. Crawford's men offered only a token resistance, and after a short skirmish they "precipitately" retreated toward Tazewell. The affair provided a tonic for Crook's men and provoked "prolonged cheers." At Princeton the general found a handful of dilapidated houses, a log jail, the remnants of a brick courthouse, abandoned Confederate tents, and an unfinished fort. Two years earlier, Confederates under the command of Colonel W. H. Jenifer had burned Princeton before Hayes and his men could occupy it. Jenifer had saved six or eight homes, but the public buildings lay in ruin. The unfinished fort, named for Breckinridge, delighted the Federals. They rearranged the sod on its side and now designated it Fort Crook. One wit remarked, "The name is changed as easily as the fort was captured."[15] Before leaving, they burned the Southerners' winter quarters.

From Princeton, Crook had the choice of two roads in moving on the railroad. The better one was the Narrows-Pearisburg Pike, where McCaus-

14. OR, Vol. XXXVII, Pt. 1, pp. 10, 717–18; Montgomery, *Blazer*, 11–15; Cincinnati *Daily Gazette*, June 2, 1864.

15. OR, Vol. XXXVII, Pt. 1, pp. 717–18, 721–22; Hastings Autobiography, May 6, 1864, XI, 7; Autobiography of Milton Humphreys, May 5, 1864, UV; Jenning Diary, May 3–5, 1864, W-FCHS; Booth Diary, May 6, 1864; Clugston Diary, May 6, 1864; Stiarwalt Diary, 14; Extracts from Comly Diary, May 6, 1864; Ellis Diary, May 6, 1864; B. F. Williams Journal: Crook's Raid, May 6, 1864, p. 2, #3733, M612, UV; New York *Herald*, May 29, 1864; Cincinnati *Daily Gazette*, June 2, 1864; Woodward, *Third Pennsylvania Reserve*, 243; A. H. Windsor, *History of the Ninety-First Regiment, O.V.I.* (Cincinnati, 1865), 44; Arthur, "Dublin Raid," Jan. 5, 1889.

land might be waiting. The other was a rougher road crossing over the Alleghenies and through Rocky Gap. Though "a little out of his way," that route would be more unexpected and thus less likely to provide the Confederates with opportunities to obstruct the army's movement. Crook decided on the second one, and at 4 A.M. the army, "all in fine spirits & ankous for a fight," was up and moving toward the Gap.[16]

The Union capture of Princeton struck a blow to the Confederate defense of the region. Breckinridge regarded the town as the salient point west of the New River, since it guarded "all the main roads leading to the Virginia and Tennessee Railroad, the lead mines of Wythe, and the saltworks." The size and direction of the Federal advance also worried Brigadier General Albert Gallatin Jenkins, then temporarily commanding the Department of Western Virginia. In a dispatch to Breckinridge on May 6 he confessed his "inability to defend this country" if the estimates of Federal strength were correct. He complained that he had heard nothing from Jones. Worse, Crawford's retreat down the Tazewell Road toward Rocky Gap, rather than toward Narrows, alarmed him. Crawford's route deprived Jenkins of scouts, and without cavalry he was now forced to rely on infantry for pickets. The greater worry was Crook's route through Rocky Gap, which exposed Jenkins' rear. Warning Breckinridge that he possessed only two hundred men "to defend this section of country, including Dublin Depot and the New River bridge," he then asked if he could keep McCausland's brigade for a few days. Reluctantly, Breckinridge consented. The following day Jenkins apprised Breckinridge that the Federals were aiming at the saltworks but would probably strike at a number of points, especially Dublin with its government stores. He suggested that Major Charles Stringfellow, Breckinridge's assistant adjutant general there, secure two freight trains for potential use. Stringfellow could use these, Jenkins argued, to concentrate his army at a threatened point or, in case of emergency, to evacuate the stores at Dublin.[17]

Crook, delaying at Princeton only overnight, pushed ahead the next morning, May 7. The 3rd Pennsylvania Reserves, acting as skirmishers, led the way. Intermittent fighting marked their progress. Crawford's men would fire at them from long distances and then fall back. Tired of playing games, the Pennsylvanians finally drove them, "at the point of the

---

16. Arthur, "Dublin Raid," Jan. 5, 1889; Hastings Autobiography, May 6, 1864, XI, 7.
17. OR, Vol. XXXVII, Pt. 1, pp. 721–23.

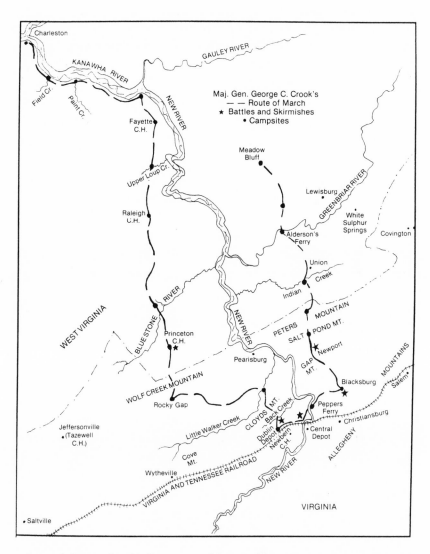

General George Crook's Route to and from Dublin, Virginia, Spring of 1864
From Howard Rollins McManus, The Battle of Cloyds Mountain: The Virginia and
Tennessee Railroad Rail, *April 29–May 19, 1864 (Lynchburg, 1989).*
Courtesy of H. E. Howard, Inc.

bayonet, about a mile off." Crook, expecting a challenge at the narrow pass at Rocky Gap, sent the 4th Pennsylvania on a flanking movement while the 3rd Pennsylvania rested and ate. Much to their surprise, they met little resistance, easily driving Southern sharpshooters off the mountaintop and marching through the Gap.[18]

That night they camped on Wolf Creek. "Suddenly" it appeared to the men "as if the gates of heaven had opened to this weary band, thousands of camp-fires burst into view, lighting up the gently rolling meadows and fields . . . their joy could scarcely have been greater."[19] As E. C. Arthur of the 23rd Ohio recalled, scavengers began to scour the countryside, stealing from area residents "nearly every thing good to eat, and for that matter things that weren't including beef of the hoof, chickens, sheep, contrabands and horses, followed the boys to camp."[20]

The next day, after marching twenty-four miles along the creek, the army reached Shannon's Bridge at the juncture of the Giles Court House, Princeton, and Dublin Roads, some ten miles from their objective, Dublin Depot. There they were joined by Colonel J. H. Oley's four hundred mounted troopers of the 7th West Virginia Cavalry, moving along a route by way of Logan Court House but delayed in reaching Crook at Princeton. Crook's telegraph operator, G. K. Smith, tapped the telegraph line between Dublin and Giles Court House. After an exchange of messages, the Southern operator discovered the tapping. Greeting Smith with "Hello, Yank," he then graciously invited Crook to supper at Dublin. The general accepted, but for the following evening.[21] As his troops rested, Crook realized that the Confederates were concentrating north of Dublin on the southern side of Cloyds Mountain. Incoming reports also indicated that they occupied the summit of the mountain. Crook's men, pausing that night, knew a battle was imminent the next day.[22]

Grant's pincer movement created a serious crisis for Southern leaders. Despite the Federal threat, their principal concern remained the security of Staunton and the Virginia Central Railroad, the southwest remaining

---

18. *Ibid.*, 719–20; Woodward, *Third Pennsylvania Reserve*, 243; Journal of 23rd Regiment, 16; B. F. Williams Journal, May 7, 1864, pp. 2–3; Wright Diary, May 8, 1864.

19. Wilson, "Dublin Raid," 103.

20. Arthur, "Dublin Raid," Jan. 5, 1889.

21. *Ibid.*

22. OR, Vol. XXXVII, Pt. 1, p. 10; Davis Diary, May 8, 1864; Woodward, *Third Pennsylvania Reserve*, 244; New York *Herald*, May 29, 1864; Arthur, "Dublin Raid," Jan. 5, 1889.

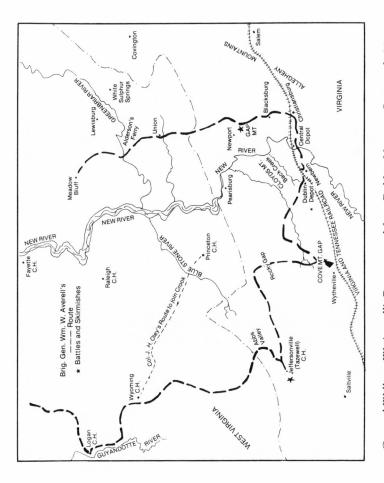

General William W. Averell's Route to and from Dublin, Virginia, Spring of 1864
From McManus, Battle of Cloyd's Mountain. *Courtesy of H. E. Howard, Inc.*

secondary. Stringfellow, at Dublin, informed Breckinridge on May 7 that Crook had occupied Rocky Gap that morning, and notified Jones at Glade Spring of the maneuver and his expectation of a cavalry attack on the New River bridge. Jones wired back that he was sending four hundred infantry to help protect the bridge. Despite concerns over protecting Saltville and the lead mines in the Wytheville region, he believed the town possessed sufficient forces to fend off an attack on the mines. In meeting any potential threats, he informed Stringfellow, he planned to deploy his men in such a way as to defend either Saltville or the bridge. Meanwhile, Jenkins hurried from Narrows to Dublin, where he telegraphed Bragg for reinforcements and asked for authority to temporarily retain McCausland's brigade, which was then on its way to join Breckinridge. Reporting that he possessed only two regiments, Jenkins apprised Bragg of his request for aid from Jones, who, he complained, boasted of having twice as many men as he needed to defeat Averell. "[I] cannot hold this place or New River bridge with my present force," he warned.[23]

Despite grave reservations, Albert Gallatin Jenkins, a planter-politician turned soldier, decided to challenge the Federals on the Dublin-Pearisburg Pike at Cloyd Farm on Back Creek. As an ardent Virginian and popular politician from Cabell County on the Ohio River, he had earlier served two terms in the U.S. House of Representatives. A slaveholder and "Southern man," in 1861 he had joined in signing a letter to Lincoln warning against coercion of the South. Choosing to follow his state, he resigned his congressional seat in April of that year. Back home, Jenkins converted a local militia unit known as the Border Rangers, armed mainly with shotguns, into a cavalry company. A commanding figure, standing five feet, eleven inches tall with dark hair, a brown beard, blue eyes, and a fine physique, Jenkins was elected as the company's captain, and in May 1861 the unit became Company E in the 8th Virginia Cavalry.

Jenkins' early military performance demonstrated promise. For his critical role in the Battle of Scarey Creek in July 1861 he received a promotion to lieutenant colonel, and he soon led a number of raids in the area. Briefly he returned to politics and represented his district in the first Confederate Congress. Yet, preferring military service, he resigned at the end of the first session to return to active duty. Promoted to brigadier general

23. OR, Vol. XXXVII, Pt. 1, pp. 723–25, and Vol. LI, Pt. 2, p. 905; Milton W. Humphreys, "The Battle of Cloyd's Farm," CV, XVII (1909), 598.

in August 1862, Jenkins commanded the 8th and 14th Virginia Cavalry regiments and soon earned considerable praise in conducting a raid into northwestern Virginia. During the Gettysburg campaign he sustained a slight wound, but later in 1863 he returned to his command at Narrows.[24]

To confront Crook, Jenkins chose a strong position at the foot of Cloyds Mountain. The mountain's slope, as it descended toward Back Creek, was wooded and serrated with numerous ridges. Toward its bottom the land became more open, with thickets of pine and a meadow stretching to the creek. The stream, varying from ten to twenty feet in width and one to four feet in depth, lay some three hundred yards from the mountain's base. Its eastern bank on the right of the turnpike was a steep bluff, somewhat less severe on the left, which ended the rolling countryside stretching from Dublin to the mountain. The turnpike, descending through a hollow, ran along the left side of the bluff and across the creek. The terrain on the left, approaching Back Creek from Dublin, was open, while on the right the bluff was bare until it reached a wooded ridge and ran parallel to the creek until it turned northward.[25]

When McCausland reached Dublin, Jenkins detained him to augment his army. He also pressed into service the Ringgold battery, just arriving at the depot on its way to join Lee. Jenkins ordered both units to move out on the Dublin-Pearisburg Pike to Cloyd Farm. McCausland, galloping up to Bryan's battery, stopped them as they were putting their pieces on flatcars for transport to Staunton. Shouting that Crook was advancing by way of Shannon's Bridge, he exclaimed, "These damned people are following right on our heels." Already irritated, McCausland disliked Jenkins'

24. James D. Sedinger, Diary of a Border Ranger, Co. E, 8th Va. Cavalry, 1, WVA&HL; Lynchburg *Virginian*, May 30, 1864; Roy Bird Cook, "Albert Gallatin Jenkins—A Confederate Portrait," *WVR*, XI (1934), 225–27; Ezra J. Warner and W. Buck Yearns, *Biographical Register of the Confederate Congress* (Baton Rouge, 1975), 130–31; "Ben: Perley Poore," comp., *The Political Register and Congressional Directory* (Boston, 1878), 468; Flora Smith Johnson, "The Civil War Record of Albert Gallatin Jenkins, C.S.A.," *WVH*, VIII (1947), 392–400; Richmond *Daily Dispatch*, May 25, 1864; Baltimore (Md.) *Sun*, June 10, 1864; Wellsburg (W. Va.) *Herald*, June 17, 1864; Robert White, *West Virginia*, Vol. II of *Confederate Military History*, ed. Clement A. Evans (Atlanta, 1899), 133–35; Terry Lowry, *The Battle of Scary Creek* (Charleston, 1982), 13–14; "Proceedings of the First Confederate Congress," *SHSP*, XXXXV (1925), 176; Ezra J. Warner, *Generals in Gray: Lives of the Confederate Commanders* (Baton Rouge, 1965), 154–55. See Jack L. Dickinson, *Jenkins of Greenbottom: A Civil War Saga* (Charleston, 1988).

25. Humphreys, *Lynchburg Campaign*, 9.

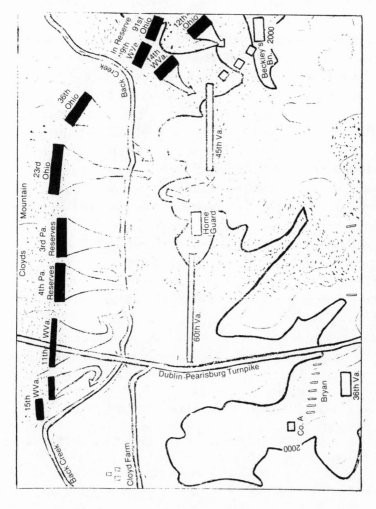

Disposition of Forces at the Battle of Cloyds Mountain
From McManus, Battle of Cloyds Mountain. Courtesy of H. E. Howard, Inc.

choice of Cloyd Farm as well, yet he believed the position offered the best choice under the circumstances. Despite reservations, he began deploying his men. [26]

That evening Jenkins and his staff rode out to confer with McCausland and determine the best strategy to use against Crook. Lieutenant A. Whitlocke Hoge of the Ringgold battery wanted to fortify the top of the mountain with a gun. The home militia forces also favored taking positions there to block the pass, arguing that it would be more difficult for the Federals to handle their men and make use of their artillery there. The position, they asserted, would buy time for additional reinforcements to arrive. First Lieutenant W. P. Robinson, fearing the possibility of the Federals' flanking and enveloping the fieldpiece, disagreed and persuaded Captain Crispin Dickinson to deny the request. Others also opposed the plan. "Let the enemy come down the mountain and into the valley," they maintained, "and we can defeat and capture his entire army." [27] Jenkins agreed. "Should the battle be lost, he would give up the ghost." Pleased with the deployment, he returned to Dublin, where he could keep in contact with Richmond and Wytheville. With the Federals now camped some six miles over the mountain at Shannon's Bridge, McCausland's men spent the night in battle formation awaiting the Federal advance. That night Bryan's gunners saw the reflection of the enemy campfires illuminating the sky. [28]

At sunrise McCausland's men began constructing fortifications "of logs, rails, stumps and sticks." Lieutenant Colonel Edwin H. Harman's 45th Virginia Regiment, arriving early that morning from Saltville, joined in the work. When Jenkins returned with his staff, he sent Major Stringfellow back to Dublin to wire General Morgan at Wytheville to hurry additional reinforcements. After placing the 45th Virginia on the right of the line, Jenkins surveyed the disposition of his troops. Not fully satisfied with McCausland's deployment along the edge of the woods, back from the creek's bluff, he began making minor refinements. Though McCausland protested sharply, Jenkins rejected most of his arguments. He re-

26. Humphreys Autobiography, II, 311, UV; Humphreys, *Lynchburg Campaign*, 7–8.

27. W. P. Robinson, "The Battle of Cloyd's Farm," CV, XXXIII (1925), 97.

28. OR, Vol. XXXVII, Pt. 1, pp. 46–47; Milton Wylie Humphreys, Diary from March 1862 to End of the War, May 8, 1864, UV; Jenning Diary, May 8, 1864; Humphreys, *Lynchburg Campaign*, 8; Staunton (Va.) *Spectator*, May 17, 1864; Arthur, "Dublin Raid," Jan. 5, 1889.

tained the 36th Virginia, supporting Bryan's battery, which occupied a rise in the regiment's immediate front on the extreme left of the road. He placed one gun of the Ringgold battery in front of Bryan's battery, while he positioned two others across the road on its right with another one some four hundred yards to their right and to the right of the 60th Virginia. In that position the guns covered the road for twelve hundred yards to the base of the mountain. The 12-pound Napoleon, commanded by Hoge and occupying the extreme right slightly in advance of the 60th Virginia, remained in a much more exposed position. Lieutenant William H. Lipscomb with twenty-nine men acted as support for the gun.[29]

Jenkins made further alterations to the remainder of the line. He moved the 60th Virginia and the 45th Virginia Battalion to new positions on the right. He advanced the 60th Virginia three hundred yards and anchored its right with Hoge's 12-pound Napoleon. To its right he placed a small unit of Home Guards from Pulaski and Montgomery Counties under Captain White G. Ryan, and then Colonel W. H. Browne's 45th Virginia, its left occupying the highest point. Finally, the 45th Virginia Battalion, with only 183 men and officers under Lieutenant Colonel Henry M. Beckley, a little to the rear, anchored the extreme right in an area covered by dense undergrowth, trees, rhododendron, and shrubs. Both Browne and Jenkins felt confident that the right flank would remain secure. All totaled, Jenkins small army numbered approximately 2,350 men with ten pieces of artillery, against an approaching Federal force of slightly over 6,500 with twelve guns.[30]

At sunrise Crook's army, in high spirits with "the bands playing, the troops cheering and the battle flags floating in the breeze," moved toward Cloyds Mountain. The atmosphere took on a festive note; one soldier thought it seemed like a "holiday parade, rather than . . . going forth to do battle."[31] The 2nd Brigade, with the 11th West Virginia in the advance, led the way. As they approached Walker Mountain Gap, Southern skirmishers fired, and Crook quickly sent several companies ahead to drive

---

29. OR, Vol. XXXVII, Pt. 1, pp. 46–47, 60.

30. Ibid., 8–10; Humphreys, "Battle of Cloyd's Farm," 598; Arthur, "Dublin Raid," Jan. 5, 1889; Davis Diary, May 9, 1864; Howard R. McManus, "Cloyd's Mountain," CWT, XVIII (1980), 24; Howard Rollins McManus, The Battle of Cloyds Mountain: The Virginia and Tennessee Railroad Raid April 29–May 19, 1864 (Lynchburg, 1989), 21–23; Michael Cavanaugh, The Otey, Ringgold, and Davidson Virginia Artillery (Lynchburg, 1993), 48–50.

31. Arthur, "Dublin Raid," Jan. 19, 1889.

them in. On reaching the base of Cloyds Mountain, Crook, aware of the Confederates positioned on the summit, sent the 15th West Virginia and the 4th Pennsylvania of the 3rd Brigade, followed by the 1st Brigade, up the steep and rocky slope directly toward the summit. Crook dismounted and, guided by a local black, led the 2nd Brigade and two regiments from the 3rd Brigade to the left of the road, crossing the mountain some half a mile east of the road. As Colonel Horatio G. Sickel with his West Virginians and Pennsylvanians approached the summit, they encountered a detachment of forty men from the 36th Virginia covering the road. Briefly halted by the "dogged resistance" of the Southerners, Sickel decided to flank their position. Sending Captain Michael Egan and his company of the 15th West Virginia to their right, Sickel with his remaining men then flanked them on the left. The enfilading fire was telling and forced the Virginians to flee in disorder. Meanwhile, three-quarters of a mile away, Crook's column crossed the summit around 9 A.M. There with his field glasses he observed the Confederate army laid out before him. Lowering his glasses, he noted that they were "in force and in strong position," but turning to Colonel Carr B. White, he commented, "They may whip us, but I guess not."[32]

Watching the mountain, Jenkins' men could hear the skirmishing, and then they saw the Virginians retreat. Finally a gunner of Bryan's battery called McCausland's attention to their appearance. Observing them through his field glasses, he ordered the firing of the long-range guns. With the distance so great and their fuses too short, the gunners used solid shot. The first discharge went over the mountain. McCausland merely remarked, "Ah, boys, you are shooting too high," and then rode away. Getting the range of the Federals, the battery continued to fire. The gunners "kept up a grave-yard whistle with their artillery everywhere,"[33] and as E. C. Arthur remembered, "the screaming, bursting shells were soon crashing through the tree tops, over our heads."[34]

32. OR, Vol. XXXVII, Pt. 1, p. 10; McManus, "Cloyd's Mountain," 24; Cincinnati *Daily Gazette*, May 24, 28, June 2, 1864; Wellsburg (W. Va.) *Herald*, June 3, 1864; Humphreys, *Lynchburg Campaign*, 11; Arthur, "Dublin Raid," Jan. 19, 1889; Michael Egan, *The Flying, Gray-Haired Yank* (1888), 159–61; Woodward, *Third Pennsylvania Reserve*, 245–46; Frank S. Reader, *History of the Fifth West Virginia Cavalry* (New Brighton, Pa., 1890), 242.

33. Milton W. Humphreys, *Military Operations, 1861–1864: Fayetteville, West Virginia, and the Lynchburg Campaigns* (Fayetteville, W. Va., 1926), 11–12.

34. Arthur, "Dublin Raid," Jan. 19, 1889.

Crook now sent the 3rd Brigade toward Jenkins' left to form a battle line in the woods straddling the Dublin Road. His 1st Brigade, led by Hayes and accompanied by Crook, became his center. Reaching the bottom, the brigade formed into three columns with the 23rd Ohio in the lead. With orders to wait until he heard rifle fire coming from the 2nd Brigade on his left, Hayes readied his men for the charge. Crook sent White's brigade to the left to anchor and extend that flank beyond Jenkins' right. The concealed movements proved highly successful. A number of Southern officers began to believe that the Federals had retreated. One optimistically declared that when Crook saw their position, he "had better sense than to attack it." But other Southerners saw Crook's men descending the slopes. As a long line of soldiers, two abreast, to the right of the pass came down the mountain, Milton Humphreys called McCausland's attention to them. Eyeing them with his field glasses, the colonel remarked, "Yes, and a damned lot of people."[35]

The sudden descent of Captain James R. McMullin with four pieces and Captain Daniel W. Glassie's battery destroyed whatever complacency remained. Charging down the road, they temporarily halted at an unsuitable site. Then Glassie charged into an open field. McMullin, under a "galling fire" from Bryan's battery, followed. Now Glassie's and McMullin's ten guns began dividing their fire between the Southern fortifications and artillery to rake their line.[36] As the batteries dueled, skirmishing erupted on the Southern right. Confederates began probing Federal positions but quickly retired to their line. Meanwhile, Southerners noticed a movement toward their extreme left and opened fire with a single howitzer, killing and wounding several. On the Union left, Crook ordered White's 2nd Brigade to find Jenkins' right and "strike hard." He told White that three quick cannon volleys would signify the beginning of the attack. After waiting sufficiently and with the noise from the artillery duel obscuring such a signal, White ordered the charge. Suddenly, around

35. OR, Vol. XXXVII, Pt. 1, pp. 10–11, 16; Hastings Autobiography, May 9, 1864, XI, 8–9; Arthur, "Dublin Raid," Jan. 19, 1889; Wellsburg (W. Va.) *Herald*, June 3, 1864; Humphreys, *Military Operations*, 12–13; J. L. Scott, *Lowry's, Bryan's, and Chapman's Batteries of Virginia Artillery* (Lynchburg, 1988), 44. For E. C. Arthur's pencil sketch of a map of the beginning of the battle, see Cloyd Family Papers of Montgomery County and Pulaski County, VHS.

36. OR, Vol. XXXVII, Pt. 1, p. 10; Arthur, "Dublin Raid," Jan. 19, 1889; Jenning Diary, May 9, 1864.

10:30 A.M., the intensity of gunfire announced the onset of the battle in earnest.[37] As a correspondent to the New York *Herald* wrote, "The harvest of death had begun."[38]

On the left the 12th Ohio and 14th West Virginia Regiments charged the surprised but prepared Virginians. Colonel Beckley suspected an attempt to turn his right. Yet the Ohioans wavered. Jenkins, riding to that point, now ordered Beckley's battalion and two companies of the 45th Virginia Regiment to countercharge, and they rapidly drove the Ohioans back to a ridge toward the woods. Meanwhile the 14th West Virginia, on Beckley's left, charged toward the left and center of the 45th Virginia Regiment. Driving to within twenty yards of their entrenchments, their push also stalled. The severity of the fire forced them to withdraw behind the 9th West Virginia. Jenkins, attempting to bolster his right, ordered two pieces of artillery to move there from the left. As the Confederates countercharged the 12th Ohio, but unknown to Jenkins, a ridge of brush concealed the 91st Ohio and 9th West Virginia Regiments, waiting in a prone position. Once Colonel Jonathan D. Hines's men retreated past them, Colonel Isaac H. Duval ordered his West Virginians to charge the oncoming Confederates. Then Colonel John A. Turley, shouting to fix bayonets, sent his 91st Ohio Regiment surging to threaten the Confederate right flank. Only the propitious arrival of the Southern guns blunted the charge.[39]

Hearing the firing, the 3rd Brigade advanced across the meadow toward the 60th Virginia where the real strength of the Southern army lay. As Sickles' Pennsylvania regiments approached, Bryan's battery delivered a "terrific volley of canister." The meadow quickly became "thickly strewn with their killed and wounded" and panic nearly gripped the Federals. Sickles, realizing the futility of the charge in the face of "this most withering fire," ordered a retreat. Exhilarated, the Virginians, cheering enthusiastically, believed "the victory won." Their jubilation was brief, for to their right a "dense column" of Federals began to flank them.[40]

---

37. OR, Vol. XXXVII, Pt. 1, p. 56; Wilson, "Dublin Raid," 105; Cincinnati *Daily Gazette*, May 28, 1864; Wellsburg (W. Va.) *Herald*, June 3, 1864.

38. New York *Herald*, May 27, 1864.

39. Windsor, *Ninety-First Regiment*, 45; Robinson, "Battle of Cloyd's Farm," 98; McManus, *Cloyds Mountain*, 35–37.

40. OR, Vol. XXXVII, Pt. 1, pp. 30, 36, 56–57; J. R. Sypher, *History of the Pennsylvania Reserve Corps* (Lancaster, Pa., 1865), 556; Woodward, *Third Pennsylvania Reserve*, 245–46.

A more effective blow came with the charge of the 1st Brigade to the 3rd Brigade's left. On Hayes's command the brigade moved, presenting a "slow double-quick" in "a splendid line crossing the green." As they advanced, the 60th Virginia and Captain Ryan's two companies of reserves left their fortifications and moved rapidly toward the bluff. When the 23rd Ohio reached the middle of the meadow, they came "under a galling fire of Grape and Canister." Still, they swept toward the creek at double-quick. Rapidly wading it, they briefly fell to the ground to rest and close up their ranks. Despite the fire, they rose as the bugle sounded and made "a furious assault" up the steep slope. The Virginians "poured volley after volley into their ranks." The impact broke the Confederate line, which fled in confusion to the wooded crest behind them. Company G overran one of the two guns facing them. Private John Kosht exuberantly cried out with "an Indian war-whoop" as he rammed his hat into the piece.[41]

Final disaster came with the collapse of Jenkins' vulnerable right flank. Unfortunately for the 60th Virginia, timber concealed the developing action on their right flank. Jenkins, his vision blocked and unaware of the movement of Hayes's left wing in uniting with the 9th West Virginia, failed to realize the danger. Major Alexander Davis, sending two companies to the left, attempted to stop the Federal advance, but the collapse of the extreme Confederate right forced him to recall them. There the 91st Ohio drove past the right flank of the 45th Virginia and began firing a "a very destructive and murderous fire" into their rear. Jenkins, attempting to rally his men, suffered a mortal wound in his left arm, which later required amputation. He quickly sent word to McCausland to take command. Immediately the colonel ordered the 36th to move to support the right and directed Lieutenant Robinson to follow him with his gun. Once in position, Robinson began firing as fast as the gun could be loaded. The 36th Virginia, double-quicking, reached the right in poor formation and formed two lines some two hundred yards behind Beckley's battalion and the 45th Virginia. Their appearance produced a brief boost for Southern morale. McCausland now ordered them to charge the 91st Ohio. In good alignment they moved down the slope to stop them, but with the developing threat to his left flank, the colonel countermanded the order and di-

41. Autobiography of Hastings, May 9, 1864, XI, 9–10; Journal of 23rd Regiment, 16; Stiarwalt Diary, 15; Extracts from Hayes Diary, May 9, 1864; OR, Vol. XXXVII, Pt. 1, p. 15; Arthur, "Dublin Raid," Jan. 19, 1889; Robinson, "Cloyd's Farm," 98.

rected Smith to return to the left. However, as he began pulling back his Virginians, Smith fell wounded and ended that possibility. When his troops began breaking in disorder Major William E. Fife attempted to rally them, but the regiment continued to retreat some two hundred yards behind their original position. Beckley's battalion, after attempting to rally, joined them. The 45th Virginia now aligned themselves with the 60th Virginia, but the 36th Virginia's movement left Colonel Harman's men exposed. As the 9th West Virginia and 91st Ohio threatened to surround him, Harman attempted to rally his men in front of Lieutenant Aminett White's gun. However, a shot through his lungs silenced him. Major Thomas Broun managed to stop a fleeing artillery company. Using their gun to fire left and right, the 45th Virginia escaped encirclement. Then, abandoning the gun, they broke. Exhilarated, the Federals rushed after the Southerners. Taking them by surprise, Lieutenant Robinson, waiting until the Federals were within fifty yards, opened fire with double canister, "mowing them down with great slaughter, shooting grape and canister at them until there was no enemy seen to shoot at." Then he too joined the retreat toward Dublin.[42]

The Confederate center crumbled rapidly. There Hoge, with his 12-pound Napoleon, fell mortally wounded. The remaining men of the Ringgold battery, along with a few of the Home Guards, tried to stay the attack, but after a fierce struggle they too fled. The position of Bryan's battery provided the Confederates with little help in stemming the Union advance. Despite a change of front to the right, any attempt to fire endangered their own men. Compounding their difficulties, Crook's artillery now enfiladed Bryan's position. Without sufficient infantry support, the site became untenable as the Federals, concealed by the terrain of the hill, began to envelop Bryan's left. Threatened by the 15th West Virginia in their front and on the right, Bryan had little choice but to withdraw and cover McCausland's retreat toward Dublin.[43]

As a delaying tactic, McCausland re-formed the 36th Virginia and other remnants on one of Lieutenant White's guns on a small crest to cover the army's retreat. Fortunately for him, the victory had spent much of Crook's army, and his cavalry, consisting of "odds and ends of several

42. Humphreys, *Lynchburg Campaign*, 16–18; Arthur, "Dublin Raid," Jan. 19, Feb. 2, 1889; Thomas L. Broun, "Cloyd's Mountain Battle," *SHSP*, XXXVII (1909), 349–50; McManus, *Cloyds Mountain*, 37–40.

43. McManus, *Cloyds Mountain*, 39; Humphreys, *Lynchburg Campaign*, 18–19.

regiments, many broken down horses," was in poor shape to undertake a pursuit. "Had I but 1,000 effective cavalry," Crook later lamented, "none of the enemy could have escaped."[44] Oley's cavalry attacked, but the Southerners sharply repulsed them "with considerable loss." Crook ordered a section of Glassie's battery forward, but the gunners, soon dangerously in advance, found the enemy force too formidable. McCausland's men, realizing the section's vulnerability, charged and came close to capturing the guns. Only the quick action of Hayes and a wing of the 23rd Ohio and part of the 34th Ohio saved them and sent the Southerners reeling back in disorder.[45]

Crook had much to be pleased about. His concealment of his army's size and route had made Southerners cautious in concentrating their forces in the region. Confederate intelligence had failed badly. As Milton Humphreys points out, Southerners' miscalculation in believing that Crook intended to use the James River and Kanawha Pike caused them to retain forces in Greenbrier and Monroe Counties.[46] As a result, Jenkins mustered a force of only some 2,350 in contrast to the overwhelming Federal army of some 6,555. However, Captain Wilson of the 12th Ohio undoubtedly identified the most marked ingredient of the battle: "General Crook had the nerve, the skill and the confidence in his army requisite to the undertaking, and his army had the training, the endurance and, above all, the confidence in its leader that left no question of success."[47] The general's aggressive tactics in striking at Jenkins' vulnerable right offset any Southern advantages of terrain.

Even though the battle lasted less than an hour, the fighting was bloody. The Federals, according to Howard Rollins McManus' calculations, suffered a total of 688 casualties, almost 10 percent of Crook's force. Of that number 108 paid with their lives, while 508 suffered wounds and another 72 were missing. Southerners sustained proportionately heavier losses. Some 23 percent were casualties, with 76 dead, 262 wounded, and an additional 200 missing—although many of these were probably

---

44. OR, Vol. XXXVII, Pt. 1, p. 11; Cincinnati *Daily Commercial*, May 21, 1864; Cincinnati *Daily Gazette*, June 2, 1864; New York *Herald*, May 24, 1864; McManus, *Cloyds Mountain*, 40.

45. OR, Vol. XXXVII, Pt. 1, pp. 39, 45; Arthur, "Dublin Raid," Jan. 19, 1864.

46. Humphreys, *Lynchburg Campaign*, 21.

47. Wilson, "Dublin Raid," 107.

wounded—for an aggregate of 538.[48] Sergeant Edward Davis of the 9th West Virginia Infantry noted in his diary, "There dead & wunded lay strewed over the ground very thick. O what a sight a battlefield is, I never want to see it again."[49] Captain John Young observed "wounded and dead as far as I could see." Remembering cries for water from wounded Confederates, he wrote to his wife, "Poor fellows, they have their rights."[50]

Crook did not achieve the complete victory he desired. Lack of sufficient cavalry, Confederate resistance, and the arrival of a fresh contingent of Morgan's men frustrated the pursuit of McCausland's shattered army. The Southern countercharge against Glassie's guns, however, provided only a brief respite, for soon a contingent of the 5th West Virginia Cavalry began chasing the Confederates "on the dead run." The Southerners, rallying in the woods alongside the road, briefly stopped them by pouring "a heavy volley" into them, but after flushing them out of the woods, the West Virginians continued to drive until the remainder of their regiment came up. Passing the others, they ran into a surprise. Colonel D. Howard Smith with his newly arrived 5th Kentucky Cavalry of Morgan's command waited for them. Those left behind shortly witnessed their compatriots retreating with "many riderless horses" and the Kentuckians now pursuing them.[51]

Smith's arrival at Dublin with some four hundred men had come at a propitious moment. Ordered by Morgan to go to the aid of Jenkins, the colonel had left Saltville near midnight by train. Delayed by insufficient cars and a locomotive derailment, he finally arrived around 1 P.M. with only a little over half of his men. At Dublin he learned of the engagement and McCausland's assumption of command and immediately headed his men toward Cloyd Farm at double-quick. Shortly he encountered McCausland's routed troops and located the colonel. McCausland immediately directed him to form his men in a woods to cover his retreat. When the West Virginians appeared, the 5th Kentucky poured "a most destructive fire" into them and drove them back. Suddenly, for the second time, Glassie's gunners found themselves without proper support. Unlimbering their guns, they pushed them, loaded with grape and canister, ahead of

48. McManus, *Cloyds Mountain*, 41.

49. Davis Diary, May 9, 1864.

50. John Young to Wife, May 21, 1864, John Valley Young Papers in Roy Bird Cook Collection, WVU.

51. Reader, *Fifth West Virginia Cavalry*, 243.

their horses and fired at the oncoming Confederates. The recognition by Morgan's men of Glassie's section as the 1st Kentucky Battery acted as a tonic for them. Now more determined, they shouted "Capture the renegade" and "Kill the ——— Southern Yankee." Only the arrival of Crook and some fifteen officers saved the section until the men of the 1st Brigade, double-quicking for several miles, reached the guns. Crook, exhausted, fell to the ground from "nervous prostration and exhaustion." Reviving, he rose, picked up a bowie knife, handed it to a soldier, and quipped, "Go in, boys." Hayes directed them to "yell like devils." Smith, fearing the possibility of a flanking movement, fell back to Dublin, where he found the depot already evacuated and McCausland retreating toward the New River bridge.[52]

The skirmishing provided McCausland with valuable time to remove some of the more important supplies at Dublin and to get his men across the New River, some eight miles to the northeast. At the river he decided against attempting to defend the bridge on the Dublin side. With the defensive works there incomplete and untenable, he feared that such an endeavor would risk trapping his command. As the infantry crossed the bridge, Captain Henry C. Douthat's Botetourt Artillery covered the movement. Then, at around 7 P.M., the battery began transporting their six light pieces across the river by flatboat. With only one boat, the process became an exhausting one. Unable to transport the two 3,000-pound cast-iron 12-pounders positioned at the bridge, they spiked them. Meanwhile, gunners carried their ammunition across the bridge. Douthat's men were fatigued, and only one of their guns was ready for action by the next morning. Following another route, Bryan's battery moved to Newbern and crossed over the Ingles Bridge. By midnight they were moving back toward the railroad bridge. Meanwhile, a local resident guided Smith and his Kentuckians to the bridge, which they crossed shortly before sunset. Determined to obstruct any possible use of it by the Federals, McCausland on

52. *OR*, Vol. XXXVII, Pt. 1, pp. 66–67; James Thomson to Frank (Fannie) Nelson, May 21, 1864, James Thomson Papers, Cincinnati Historical Society; Russell Hastings, Memoirs, II, 10, Russell Hastings Papers, RBHPCL; Account of "John Fields," in Adam R. Johnson, *The Partisan Rangers of the Confederate States Army* (Louisville, 1904), 294; Basil W. Duke, *History of Morgan's Cavalry* (Cincinnati, 1867), 517–18; Arthur, "Dublin Raid," Feb. 2, 1889; Conway Howard Smith, *Land That Is Pulaski County* (Pulaski, Va., 1981), 280–81.

the following morning sent the 60th Virginia Regiment to destroy it. After filling the covered bridge with hay at one end, they ignited it.[53]

At the bridge that evening, McCausland carefully deployed his men. He positioned the artillery under Bryan on a hilltop that ran parallel to the river. Using some of Morgan's men as skirmishers, he sent a few sharpshooters to a blockhouse near the bridge. Beckley's battalion remained some fifty yards behind the artillery in an open field, with the 36th Virginia in a woods behind them. The remaining infantry rested in a woods on the left. Fully realizing the untenable nature of his position, he waited, determined to delay the oncoming Federals.[54]

Meanwhile, with the collapse of any serious resistance, Dublin had easily fallen to Crook. For the first time, Federals overran the town. The depot had once been the smallest one between Bristol and Lynchburg on the Virginia and Tennessee Railroad, but the war had radically changed that. Now, as a military headquarters and supply center, Dublin had become an important prize for the Federals. On entering the town, Crook discovered a number of "significant" Confederate dispatches, possibly bogus and certainly inaccurate, indicating that "Grant had been repulsed and was retreating." Crook decided to use the telegraph to engage in a ruse that might secure additional intelligence. His operator began an exchange of messages with Lynchburg. But from the replies Crook grew concerned about the results of Sigel's movement, and hearing nothing from the general himself, he feared for the security of his own army in its exposed position. He worried that if Grant was unable to maintain pressure on Lee, the Confederates could and would detach a force to cut off his retreat. Since he was then at a considerable distance—some 150 miles— from his base and his rations and ammunition were running short, he decided to retire toward Lewisburg "as rapidly as possible." From his base at Meadow Bluff, some fifteen miles to the northwest, Crook believed he would be well positioned to join Sigel's army at any time to carry out his original instructions.[55] Yet there was an unknown irony for Crook in his

53. OR, Vol. XXXVII, Pt. 1, pp. 45, 58, 67; Humphreys Autobiography, II, 315–16; Humphreys, *Lynchburg Campaign*, 22–23; Jerald H. Markham, *The Botetourt Artillery* (Lynchburg, 1986), 56–57; Smith, *Pulaski County*, 221–22, 281–82.

54. OR, Vol. XXXVII, Pt. 1, p. 45; Humphreys, *Lynchburg Campaign*, 23–24.

55. OR, Vol. XXXVII, Pt. 1, p. 2; Schmitt, ed., *George Crook*, 115–16; Cincinnati *Daily Gazette*, June 2, 1864; Wilson, "Dublin Raid," 108; Woodward, *Third Pennsylvania Reserve*,

decision. Two days later, at Christiansburg, McCausland wired Richmond of his forced retreat from the New River, reporting that "my force is inadequate to keep them back" and asking for reinforcements. The War Department's terse reply offered no hope.[56]

Dispatches were not the only thing the Federals found at Dublin. Large warehouses filled with foodstuffs, wooden-soled shoes, and military equipment fell into their hands. To the delight of the men, the depot was a principal shipping point for tobacco. Soldiers eagerly looted the sheds containing plug and smoking tobacco and stuffed their haversacks with it. They even allowed local blacks to share in the bacon, corn, and other items found in the warehouses. Some fifteen hundred pounds of bacon fell into Federal hands. On the following morning, before pulling out, the army began destroying military property in earnest. In "a scene of the wildest excitement," residents, thronging the street, watched as flames consumed the depot, adjoining railroad property, and warehouses, as well as a magazine containing damaged ammunition. Any building suspected of use by the Confederates, including one or two private houses and the hotel, which had served as headquarters for the Department of Western Virginia, met a similar fate. The railroad received special attention. As the soldiers moved along the line they piled up the wooden ties, placed the iron rails on top, and then set the heap ablaze. For six miles, twisted and warped rails marked their advance.[57] Yet despite all of the destruction, Albert Davidson, a clerk at the depot and a participant in the battle, noted that Crook "seemed to be very much of a gentleman."[58]

As the Federals approached the bridge the next morning, they came under fire from Confederate skirmishers. Crook began deploying his men, and rode out into the open to reconnoiter the enemy positions. A cannonball striking close to him caused the general to dismount momentarily. As he retired into the woods, McCausland's men cheered. Crook then ordered Sickel to clear the sharpshooters from the east bank and to

248–49; Humphreys, *Lynchburg Campaign*, 28–29; T. Harry Williams, *Hayes of the Twenty-Third: The Civil War Volunteer Officer* (New York, 1965), 182.

56. *OR*, Vol. XXXVII, Pt. 1, p. 728.

57. Arthur, "Dublin Raid," March 2, 1889; Journal of 23rd Regiment, 17; B. F. Williams Journal, May 10, 1864; Booth Diary, May 9, 1864; Clugston Diary, May 10, 1864; J. W. Cracraft Journal, June 9, 1864, in Roy Bird Cook Collection, WVU; Woodward, *Third Pennsylvania Reserve*, 249.

58. Albert Davidson to Mother, May 17, 1864, Albert Davidson Correspondence, W&L.

burn the bridge. The 15th West Virginia and the 3rd Pennsylvania, drawing Southern fire away from two companies moving toward the bridge, advanced toward the riverbank. They rapidly drove the Southerners out of their fortifications to the other side of the river. As an act of bravado, the 23rd Ohio regimental band, playing "Yankee Doodle" and escorting two guns from Glassie's battery, marched toward the bridge.[59]

Suddenly and simultaneously around 9:30 A.M. the Federals opened "a furious cannonade." Southern guns immediately replied in kind. The duel, lasting some three hours, blazed between the two sides with apparently no direction given by either. The officer of each gun seemed to determine the target of his own choice. Meanwhile, two guns of Glassie's battery shelled the roundhouse at the Central Depot, a mile in the distance, with telling effect, while McMullin's pieces effectively silenced two Southern guns. Casualties among artillerists on both sides were few, although Captain Bryan barely escaped death when a shell killed his horse underneath him. By noon diminishing ammunition caused considerable concern for the Confederates. Worse, Crook's artillery, with the advantage of a higher elevation, demonstrated its superiority by driving Southern pieces off the field. McCausland, after being informed that a large Union force of infantry was crossing the river some seven miles below at Pepper's Ferry, feared the flanking movement and ordered a withdrawal toward Christiansburg.[60]

The bridge was indeed a prize. A trestlework structure of an old "weatherboarded wooden pattern" with a tin-covered roof, some 780 feet long and 56 feet high, spanned the wide and deep New River on the Virginia and Tennessee Railroad. Despite intense fire, Sickel's men took the bridge. The West Virginians climbed onto the structure and ignited its sides of dry pine. In addition, they loaded several freight cars with combustibles, set them on fire, and then pushed them out onto the bridge. Flames rapidly spread throughout the structure, and as Captain Wilson remembered, smoke poured from every crack "like a boiler under heavy pressure of steam, until suddenly the flames burst through, and the bridge

59. OR, Vol. XXXVII, Pt. 1, p. 26; Ellis Diary, May 10, 1864; Arthur, "Dublin Raid," March 2, 1864; Clugston Diary, May 10, 1864; Woodward, *Third Pennsylvania Reserve*, 249–50; Egan, *Flying, Gray-Haired Yank*, 167.

60. OR, Vol. XXXVII, Pt. 1, pp. 45, 55; Arthur, "Dublin Raid," March 2, 1889; Humphreys Autobiography, 316–17; Humphreys Diary, May 10, 1864; Humphreys, *Lynchburg Campaign*, 25–28; Baggs Journal, May 10, 1864; Egan, *Flying, Gray-Haired Yank*, 168–69.

seemed to leap into the air from its piers, and plunge, a mass of ruins, into the river below."[61] Within two hours the bridge lay in smoldering ruins, with only its piers remaining. A pleased Hayes enjoyed the "fine scene" while his band played "and all the troops hurrahing on the river bank." Lacking explosives, the artillery attempted to destroy the piers by firing solid shot at them, but with little success.[62]

The destruction of the New River bridge—"the most important railroad connection and telegraphic communication in all the rebel territory"—drew high praise from the Northern press.[63] Rebuilding the bridge and rail line cost the Confederates valuable time. Work began on May 16 and consumed nearly a month at a cost of $61,200. By June 1 repairs restored the line to use, and finally, ten days later, a rebuilt bridge was ready.[64]

At Christiansburg, nervous residents prepared to collect their valuables and evacuate the town—a precaution already taken by banks on the previous day. Soon approaching wagon trains told citizens the tale of defeat. Wounded began filling the houses on the town's main street. That evening, McCausland rode into Christiansburg and told frightened citizens that he would probably fight Crook the next morning and that the Federals would probably shell the town. As the wounded left for Liberty, public anxiety sharpened, especially when they received a report of the approaching "Yankees." Then, with McCausland's departure toward Shawsville, despondent residents merely watched and awaited their fate.[65]

Meanwhile, Crook's men celebrated in high fashion. Troops cheered and bands played against the backdrop of the smoldering bridge. At Pepper's Ferry the infantry laboriously crossed the river on a small ferry, while the trains crossed with great difficulty at Rocky Ford.[66] It was not until late

61. Wilson, "Dublin Raid," 111.

62. Hastings Autobiography, May 10, 1864, XI, 14; Humphreys Diary, June 10, 1864; Williams, ed., *Diary and Letters of Hayes*, II, 457; Egan, *Flying, Gray-Haired Yank*, 169–70.

63. *Herald*, May 29, 1864.

64. Report of Superintendent of August 8 to Board of Directors of Virginia and Tennessee Railroad, Minutes of August 10 Meeting of Board of Directors, Virginia Polytechnic Institute and State University, Blacksburg; Davidson to Mother, June 1, 10, 1864, Davidson Correspondence; Richmond *Sentinel*, Sept. 7, 1864.

65. Lula Porterfield Givens, *Christiansburg, Montgomery County, Virginia: In the Heart of the Alleghenies* (Christiansburg, Va., 1981), 97; Patricia Givens Johnson, *The United States Army Invades the New River Valley, May 1864* (Christiansburg, Va., 1986), 32.

66. Journal of 23rd Regiment, 17.

that night that they completed the transit. Large numbers of blacks, taking advantage of their presence, greeted the 1st Brigade as it went into bivouac. By the light of a large bonfire, they celebrated well into the night with music and dancing "in high carnival under the willows." They fully intended "to follow him [Crook] 'out of slavery.' "[67] The loss of black labor to the region dealt a serious blow to area farmers. One plantation owner, James R. Kent, initially lost fifty-two slaves.[68] Albert Davidson estimated that some twelve hundred left Pulaski County with the army.[69] When the army departed the next day, blacks also took up the march. As troops moved northward through Montgomery County, the area with the largest number of slaves,[70] blacks continued to flock to the army. As Captain Wilson later remembered, "They came on foot, on horseback, on muleback, in wagons, in carriages, and in every conceivable grotesque turnout."[71] Their numbers, in turn, slowed down the army. In addition, the ordeal of their trek through treacherous mountain terrain soon tested their determination for freedom.[72]

The following morning, May 11, as the army prepared to move toward Blacksburg, Crook received his first news from Averell. Along with the arrival of fifty prisoners came news of the general's failure to reach Saltville and his subsequent move toward Wytheville. Later in the day, a courier brought word of Averell's defeat at Cove Gap and told the general that the cavalry expected to reach Dublin that evening. Immediately Crook sent back an order directing Averell to advance and destroy the rail line toward Lynchburg.[73] Resting briefly at Blacksburg, Crook's men picked up the march on the morning of May 12 over terrible roads soaked by a drenching rain. As they crossed Gap Mountain and approached the junction near Newport, they ran into the combined forces of Colonels William French and "Mudwall" Jackson. Three days earlier, Jackson had joined French at Narrows. Then, on the morning of May 11, French received or-

67. Arthur, "Dublin Raid," March 2, 1889.

68. Smith, *Pulaski County*, 287.

69. Davidson to Mother, May 17, 1864, Davidson Correspondence.

70. Joseph C. G. Kennedy, comp., *Population of the United States in 1860: Compiled from the Original Returns of the Eighth Census* (Washington, D.C., 1864), 513.

71. Wilson, "Dublin Raid," 113; John Young Diary, May 10, 1864, Young Papers.

72. Arthur, "Dublin Raid," March 16, 1889; Wilson, "Dublin Raid," 114; Stiarwalt Diary, 17.

73. OR, Vol. XXXVII, Pt. 1, pp. 12, 42; Arthur, "Dublin Raid," March 16, 1889.

ders from McCausland, instructing him, if possible, to join him at Christiansburg by way of Blacksburg. Instead, on learning of the Federal movement toward West Virginia, the two decided to block the Union route at Gap Mountain. However, delays slowed their progress, and when they came within two miles of the mountain, scouts informed French that the Federals occupied the Gap. He decided to strike at part of Crook's army at the junction of the roads leading to Narrows and Union with his combined force of 1,425 and four guns. The skirmish was brief and futile. Fearing envelopment, the Southerners "precipitately" fled toward Brown's Ferry before Crook's main force could come up.[74]

Despite the rebuff, the Confederates continued to snip at Crook's train. Jackson with the main contingent fell back to the residence of J. H. Hoge, near the road over Salt Pond Mountain. Unknown to Crook, as his army moved toward the mountain he passed close by the Southerners. A low-hanging cloud obscured their presence, and Jackson made no effort to reveal himself. Soon Crook's advanced units began the climb. Symbolically, bands struck up the tune of the old hymn "When the Swallows Homeward Fly."[75] The journey proved to be a "long and weary march through the darkness, rain and mud." Captain Young estimated that the column of men and trains stretched for nearly eight miles. Fortunately for Crook, a local guide, Lewis Flavius Porterfield, knew the region well and led the way. By morning the next day the rain had changed into "spitting snow," turning the narrow mountain road into a "muddy and slippery" and quite dangerous one by the time they reached Peters Mountain. With mud up "to the wagon's hub," Young dubbed it "Mud Mountain."[76] "Never did I see roads so bad," Lieutenant J. W. Cracraft recorded in his journal.[77] Frustrated with their slow progress, Captain Hastings redistributed food and supplies among the wagons, then instructed his men to push the empty ones off the road to tumble down the mountainside. In this way they jettisoned some one hundred wagons and reduced the train by half. Then he added the freed mules to the remaining ones to make up teams of twelve. The route soon became littered "with blankets shoes & everything you

74. OR, Vol. XXXVII, Pt. 1, pp. 12, 62–65; Ellis Diary, May 11, 1864; Journal of 23rd Regiment, 17; Wright Diary, May 13, 1864; Arthur, "Dublin Raid," March 30, 1889; Cincinnati *Daily Commercial*, May 23, 1864; Cincinnati *Daily Gazette*, June 2, 1864.

75. Wilson, "Dublin Raid," 115.

76. Young Diary, May 14, 1864.

77. Cracraft Journal, May 14, 1864.

could mention."[78] Reflecting back on that night, Hastings remembered it as "one of the very miserable ones of my war experience."[79] The teamsters, however, won Crook's high praise for their work. He regarded their accomplishment as one of "the most remarkable features of the expedition."[80]

French and Jackson, determined to continue harassing the Federals, sent a detachment of some 325 to 350 men to torment them as they crossed Salt Pond Mountain. The remainder hastened back to Gap Mountain to intercept Averell's efforts to catch up with Crook. The harassers achieved little except losses. In a brief skirmish the following day they lost a brass cannon, a caisson, and fifteen wagons. Crook's men easily scattered them. The annoyance, Hastings observed, "only caused fun for the boys."[81]

Far more dangerous was the weather and the shortage of food. The slowness of the march under extremely difficult conditions wore on the army. Rations ran short, and the men increasingly depended on a bleak countryside. According to David Kiester, a Montgomery County farmer, Crook's "command passed so hurriedly that [he] did not know what Regiment or company" took his horse.[82] John Shell, another farmer, lost four horses, twenty gallons of molasses, eight hundred pounds of bacon, and twenty pounds each of sugar and coffee.[83] Captain Young summed up the plight of the local populace in a letter to his daughter: "You may guess what would be left when ten or twelve thousand hungry men and horses would pass through the country." He had observed "the hungry soldier take the last bite from families on the road and leave the women crying— saying their children must starve while all the men are in the Rebel service." Unionist families in Giles County suffered equally with their Con-

78. Hastings Autobiography, May 12, 1864, XI, 16; B. F. Williams Journal, May 13, 1864.

79. Hastings Autobiography, May 12, 1864, XI, 16.

80. OR, Vol. XXXVII, Pt. 1, p. 12; Clugston Diary, May 12, 1864; Davis Diary, May 13, 1864; Booth Diary, May 12–13, 1864; Journal of 23rd Regiment, 17–18.

81. OR, Vol. XXXVII, Pt. 1, pp. 63–66; Ellis Diary, May 13, 1864; Hastings Autobiography, May 13, 1864, XI, 16–17; Journal of 23rd Regiment, 18; Baggs Journal, May 15, 1864.

82. David Kiester, Sr., file 13896, microfiche 1816, and John Carden, file 13889 microfiche 943, Record Group [hereinafter abbreviated as RG] 223, SCCP.

83. John Shell, file 13894, microfiche 1497, RG 223, SCCP.

federate neighbors. As Young noted, "A hungry soldier knows no man."[84] More frequently than not, foraging parties secured scanty results, for as J. W. Cracraft complained, "most everything had been taken to the mountains and hid."[85] By the time the troops passed Union, they were "getting very hungry." As the army approached Alderson's Ferry, Young observed that with the intense foraging "there will not be anything left for the citizens in Monroe [County]."[86]

At Union, Crook immediately wired Charleston to send a supply train to Lewisburg.[87] There Averell's hard-worn and beleaguered cavalry, destitute of supplies and with their ammunition almost exhausted, finally caught up with Crook on May 15. As the army picked up its march toward Lewisburg, Averell's troopers now served as a rear guard to prevent sniping. Crook had succeeded admirably in accomplishing exactly what Grant wanted: the destruction of the New River bridge and ten to twenty miles of the Virginia and Tennessee Railroad. As the general-in-chief had informed Sigel on May 2, it "would be the most important work Crook could do."[88] The Washington *Star* remarked that "the balance of his [Sigel's] force under Averell and Crooks [*sic*], is more than making up for Sigel's short-comings."[89]

Averell's movement achieved little. Yet he succeeded in preventing a concentration of Confederate military resources in southwestern Virginia. The threat against the important saltworks and lead mines demanded protection and thereby divided Southern attention. The choice of Averell for the expedition, considering his background and familiarity with West Virginia, was a good one. As an experienced cavalry officer, he had first come to West Virginia in May 1863 when the War Department assigned him to the Middle Department. His first raid, directed toward Staunton, followed a little over two months later.

As a West Point graduate in the class of 1855, Averell initially served in the West. He participated in a number of campaigns and engaged in some

84. Young Diary, May 17, 1864, and Young to Emma, May 24, 1864, Young Papers.

85. Cracraft Journal, May 15, 1864.

86. Young Diary, May 17, 1864.

87. E. A. Brown to Almyra, May 18, 1864, Box 9, Brown Family Collection, Ohio University, Athens, Ohio.

88. *OR*, Vol. XXXVII, Pt. 1, p. 369; Simon, ed., *Papers of Grant*, X, 390.

89. Washington *Star*, quoted in Cincinnati *Daily Gazette*, May 24, 1864.

twenty-five skirmishes with the Navajo before the Civil War. At the outbreak of war he served in a number of minor roles, but in October 1861 he seized the opportunity to take command of an unruly Kentucky cavalry regiment, newly designated the 3rd Pennsylvania Cavalry. During the Peninsula campaign he earned praise and a promotion to acting brigadier general for his performance. Under General Joseph Hooker's command of the Army of the Potomac, he headed a separate cavalry corps under Major General George Stoneman. A major setback in March 1863 at Kelley's Ford spawned suspicions of incompetence, and his performance ultimately incurred the wrath of Hooker, who relieved him of command. Fortunately, Major General Robert Schenck of the Middle Department, needing an officer to organize a cavalry force in West Virginia, saved his career. The War Department reassigned him there to organize a unit to combat partisan rangers. Yet the appointment represented a serious demotion, as Federal authorities regarded the area as one of secondary importance for offensive operations. They viewed service in the department as garrison duty principally to defend the Baltimore and Ohio Railroad. Banishment left its scar, but it provided an excellent opportunity for Averell to redeem his career and reputation.[90]

Averell's early experience in West Virginia, hampered by shortages of matériel and other factors, allowed for only limited successes. His men, as Major Theodore F. Lang described them, were "loyal, courageous fighters, scattered through have [half] a dozen counties, but who know little of discipline, or of regimental or brigade maneuvers." In drilling, rearming, and equipping his men, he whipped them into shape. Many regarded him as a martinet, yet his reputation "as a gallant and successful cavalry fighter" inspired his men, and he shortly proved to be the "master of the situation."[91] He conducted three raids directed with varying success in 1863. In August he destroyed a saltpeter works at Franklin. Then, in November he decisively defeated Confederate forces under Echols at Droop Mountain. But failure to capitalize on the victory created questions. More successful, but less important, in December he briefly captured Salem and destroyed its

---

90. Edward K. Eckert and Nicholas J. Amato, eds., *Ten Years in the Saddle: Memoir of William Woods Averell, 1851–1862* (San Rafael, Calif., 1978), 3–7; Reader, *Fifth West Virginia Cavalry*, 197–200; Stephen Z. Starr, *The Union Cavalry in the Civil War* (Baton Rouge, 1979–85), I, 278, 343–50, II, 156–57.

91. Lang, *Loyal West Virginia*, 108–109.

depot with a large quantity of stores, five bridges, and stretches of track on the Virginia and Tennessee Railroad.[92]

His skill as an antagonist won the respect of Southerners. He became a master in keeping them off balance. In early January 1864, Lee, commenting to Jefferson Davis on affairs in Hardy and New Hampshire Counties, made reference to "cavalry worn down by their pursuit of Averell."[93] Shortly thereafter, complaining to General Jones, Lee attributed Averell's success to "the terror with which he has inspired the [Southern] troops. As soon as his approach is announced his progress is neither retarded nor watched."[94] Jones sharply disagreed, though Confederate deserters and refugees confirmed Lee's opinion.[95] Yet Averell had earned the admiration of many in western Virginia. Characterizing him as "a dashing cavalry officer" the editor of the Charlottesville *Daily Chronicle* praised him as being "particularly averse to conducting [the war] otherwise than as an officer and a gentleman should do."[96]

Sigel wisely placed Averell in charge of the newly created 2nd Cavalry Division, consisting of the 1st West Virginia, 14th Pennsylvania, 5th West Virginia, 7th West Virginia, 8th Ohio, and Duffié's brigade. He expected him to repeat his earlier success at Salem in operating with Crook, except this time the objective would be Saltville and the railroad in that region. On April 19 Averell left Martinsburg for the Kanawha Valley to take command. There he eagerly began making preparations, which proved extremely taxing for such an extensive raid. He held serious reservations about his brigade commanders, doubting whether they possessed either the experience or the rank their duties required, deficits which he believed resulted in a "want of discipline, neglect of duty, and waste of precious time." He feared "more serious results in the future." His most immediate need concerned the lack of sufficient horses. He wired Stahel that he needed 3,500, for he presumed that "1000 will be required to mount those to return." A worried Crook agreed and telegraphed Sigel on April 12 that unless his command secured the necessary horses soon, "they will be too late for this expedition." In transmitting Crook's comments to Grant, Sigel explained that everything was being done to secure them. In turn he

92. Starr, *Union Cavalry in the Civil War*, II, 157–75.
93. *OR*, XXXIII, 1061.
94. *Ibid.*, 1141.
95. *Ibid.*, 446, 1156.
96. Charlottesville (Va.) *Daily Chronicle*, June 19, 1864.

complained that one-third of the cavalry in the department remained dismounted and that it seemed impossible to "buy as many horses and as fast as we want them." He lamented that the 20th Pennsylvania Cavalry arrived at Cumberland "with 1,000 men, but only 150 horses and no arms except sabers."[97]

Crook, learning that the War Department intended to send the 8th Ohio Cavalry to West Virginia to be mounted and equipped, protested. He told Grant that if the regiment reached the state without first being mounted, it would take a month to ready them for service. Why, he asked, could they not be fitted out at Camp Dennison in Ohio before being sent to Averell? Through Lieutenant Colonel Babcock, Sigel informed Grant's headquarters that he needed at least 2,500 horses at once, just for the old regiments, and an additional 4,000 "for the new and veteran regiments." He warned that if the 2,500 were not forthcoming, "it will materially cripple the anticipated movement."[98]

A frustrated Crook also forewarned Grant of the impossibility of acquiring the necessary horses "within the proper time with the present facilities in this department." He asked for permission to purchase them in Ohio. The following day, April 18, he wired Sigel to "send all the horses and mules you can at once by water." Still dissatisfied with the size of his cavalry, Crook complained that he would not have more than 2,500 in time for the movement. "The demonstration on Saltville will have to be abandoned for want of sufficient mounted force," he threatened. Despite his misgivings, Crook wired Sigel on April 27 that he would be ready to move on May 2. Yet as Sigel found out three days later, it would be in accordance with Crook's revised plan. Accordingly he informed Sigel that "Averell with 2,000 mounted men" would strike toward Saltville.[99]

Finally, on May 1, Averell's troopers advanced up the Kanawha River. He divided his division, totaling 2,079 officers and men, into two brigades, one under Duffié and the other under Colonel J. M. Schoonmaker. Once on the move, 400 of the 5th and 7th West Virginia Cavalries under Colonel Oley left the column near Wyoming Court House with the intent of joining Crook at Princeton. Averell, expecting his wagon train to carry six days' rations and four of forage from Logan Court House, found that the

97. OR, XXXIII, 701, 840–41, 844–45, 986; Sigel to Averell, April 12, 1864, Sigel Papers.

98. OR, XXXIII, 876, 894.

99. Ibid., 900, 910, 938, 1027–28.

miserable condition of the teams, wagons, and roads forced him to reduce his supplies to four days and one and a half for forage. He was finally forced to send the wagons and teams back to Logan on May 5. At Logan the 3rd Virginia Cavalry, stationed there, joined the column.[100] Averell's route, similar to the one used by Colonel John Toland for his raid on Wytheville the previous July, severely taxed his men as they found their way "over pathless mountains and up tortuous streams to Abb's Valley."[101]

As the Federals approached Wyoming Court House, they confronted their first Confederate unit. Brigadier General John S. Williams, commanding the Southern force at Saltville and learning of Averell's advance, sent the 8th Virginia Cavalry under Colonel Abe Cook to determine their strength and, if Saltville was their intended target, to delay them. At the head of Abb's Valley, the Federals surprised two companies on picket duty and captured twenty Southerners. On resuming the march the next morning, they encountered a larger body of Kentuckians near Tazewell Court House, whom they successfully drove back toward Tazewell. That evening Duffié explained to his officers the plan of attack for the following morning. Believing that their situation was critical, he told them that "stubborn hard fighting" would be necessary to "relieve us or secure the object of the expedition." The plan called for Schoonmaker's brigade to attack the Confederate right at sunrise, while Duffié's brigade, except for one regiment, would strike the enemy's left flank. Once the fight was engaged, the remaining regiment would make a saber charge through the center and attack the Southern rear.[102]

Much to his surprise, Averell found only a thin skirmish line facing him the following morning. He easily pushed it in, but as he approached Saltville, reports of Confederate entrenchments and concentration made him increasingly cautious. He learned that both Morgan and Jones were there. Deserters and captured letters revealed that the Southerners knew his strength and objective. From various pieces of intelligence he estimated that Jones's force consisted of 4,500 men. The northern approaches to Saltville were fortified with artillery. With the element of surprise gone, he believed that an attack without infantry and artillery was impractical. Abandoning the attempt, he now decided to strike at Wytheville, reason-

100. Ibid., Vol. XXXVII, Pt. 1, p. 41.
101. Lang, Loyal West Virginia, 374.
102. Benson, comp., With the Army, 42.

ing that such a move would prevent the Confederates from concentrating against Crook. [103]

Both Jones, commanding the Department of East Tennessee, and the War Department knew what Averell intended. As early as May 2, intelligence had indicated a sizable Federal force on its way toward Logan Court House. To counter the threat, Secretary of War Seddon temporarily relieved General Morgan from duty in the Department of East Tennessee and ordered his brigade to report to Breckinridge's department. Jones also readied his troops. He wired Breckinridge of his intention to move to Tazewell, and if the Federals advanced he intended to keep Morgan's command. As a precaution, he immediately ordered Brigadier General A. E. Jackson to put his brigade in a position "to cover the approaches on Saltville" and, if necessary, to render any service to Breckinridge. To guard his flank he ordered the 64th Virginia Regiment to scout the Pond Gap area and report any moves directed toward Abingdon or Saltville. [104]

Surprisingly, a far more serious threat to the security of southwest Virginia came from Richmond. Bragg thought he could make more effective use of Jones's force in the Department of East Tennessee than by helping Breckinridge. On May 3 he ordered Jones to move his cavalry into eastern Tennessee to pursue withdrawing Federals there. However, Jones quickly informed Bragg that he was then expecting a raid from the Kanawha River and that Breckinridge, possessing very little cavalry in that area, had requested his cooperation in covering Saltville. He asked Bragg, "Will this suffice for the movement you ordered yesterday, or must I withdraw support from General Breckinridge?" Then he warned, "In that case Saltville will be in danger." Jones also informed Breckinridge of the order and the "state of affairs here," noting that he asked Bragg "if I must withdraw my support to you." He reassured Breckinridge that both Morgan and his brigade "are to move to you if needed." [105]

Breckinridge reacted sharply, wiring Bragg that he "was going to the front [the Valley] to-morrow." He asked, "Shall he [Jones] change present

103. *OR*, Vol. XXXVII, Pt. 1, pp. 41, 461–62; Cincinnati *Daily Commercial*, June 2, 1864; Cincinnati *Daily Gazette*, June 3, 1864; Joseph J. Sutton, *History of the Second Regiment: West Virginia Cavalry Volunteers* (Portsmouth, Ohio, 1892), 113–14; Wm. C. Pendleton, *The History of Tazewell County and Southwest Virginia, 1782–1920* (Richmond, 1920), 624–25.

104. *OR*, Vol. XXXVII, Pt. 1, pp. 709, 711, and Vol. XXXIX, Pt. 2, p. 567.

105. *Ibid.*, Vol. XXXIX, Pt. 2, p. 577, and Vol. LI, Pt. 2, p. 889.

dispositions?" Then he suggested that a small party might be sent into Tennessee to scout instead. He knew, of course, what the outcome would be. He told Jones that he expected a dispatch from Bragg and Lee that evening "which may produce an entire change of action. Please wait till you hear from me." Bragg reluctantly acquiesced in Jones's retaining his position to defend the "iron or saltworks" but warned that the "enemy is pressing on Johnston from Knoxville, and nothing short of sternest necessity should keep Jones from following." The following day Breckinridge in effect laid the issue to rest. He wired Bragg that Lee had directed him to move to Staunton, and "if General Jones moves into Tennessee, this whole country will be at mercy of force now threatening from Kanawha." To Jones he wrote, "I have telegraphed General Bragg to direct you, in cooperation with General Jenkins, to cover front from Monroe County to salt-works." [106]

With its salt and lead mines, the southwest could hardly be ignored or lightly defended. Both Virginia and the Confederacy depended heavily on the production of both commodities. On the eve of the Civil War, only New York exceeded Virginia in salt production. [107] In the era before refrigeration, salt was essential in the preservation of pork—a major staple of the Southern diet—beef, and mutton, as well as in the production of leather. Salt reserves in Smyth and Washington Counties ranked in a preeminent position in the South. The works of that region, as Ella Lonn points out, "lacked only labor to supply the whole confederacy." [108] Some 2,600 kettles in various kilns in the region attempted to meet Southern demand. [109] Concerned over any interruption of supply, the War Department as early as 1861 had begun to exercise increasing control over production there.

The importance of salt became so fixed in the minds of both Federal and Confederate authorities that their focus became riveted on Saltville. In March 1864, Governor William Smith requisitioned sixty slaves between the ages of eighteen and fifty-five to assist in building fortifications

106. *Ibid.*, Vol. XXXVII, Pt. 1, pp. 713–14, 716, 718–20, and Vol. XXXIX, Pt. 2, pp. 576–79.

107. *Preliminary Report of Eighth Census*, 70, 188.

108. Ella Lonn, *Salt As a Factor in the Confederacy* (University, Ala., 1965), 16–18, 20, 25–26.

109. William Marvel, *Southwest Virginia in the Civil War: The Battles for Saltville* (Lynchburg, 1992), 99.

for the works there. Additional anxiety centered over the scarcity of wood and labor for use in building the defenses.[110] The problem of protecting the branch rail line of the Virginia and Tennessee Railroad from Saltville to the main line at Glade Spring created even greater fears. When Crook destroyed the New River bridge and damaged the rail line, salt production halted for more than ten days. One observer noted that "from a daily furnace, with the capacity to manufacture 9000 bushels of salt, there has not been one bushel made in that time."[111]

Yet the lead works in Wythe County held far more immediate value in the manufacture of ammunition for the Confederacy. Ralph W. Donnelly estimates that the mines "supplied roughly one-fourth to one-third of the lead used by the Confederacy."[112] Production there remained less precarious than blockade-running, and the Union Lead Mining Company became the principal domestic source for the South. Despite the metal's obvious importance in sustaining the Southern war effort, both Union and Confederate authorities failed fully to appreciate Wytheville's production. Apparently the only Union commander who comprehended its importance was Averell. Otherwise, the focus remained on salt.[113]

Fortunately for the defense of both Saltville and Wytheville, the efforts of Breckinridge, Jones, and Morgan proved most effective. By the time Averell's cavalry approached Saltville, Confederates had managed to assemble a force sufficient to challenge any attack. Fearful of attacking the town, Averell decided to strike at Wytheville instead. Morgan, relying on intelligence from his scouts, realized that the town would undoubtedly be his next objective. Leaving the 45th Virginia temporarily at Saltville, he followed the Federals, but when he reached the junction of the Jeffersonville, Wytheville, and Crab Orchard Roads, Morgan broke off his pursuit. He suspected that Averell, in taking the Crab Orchard Road, was actually baiting him to follow. He knew that the mountainous route could allow the Federals to hold him in check, while Averell then could easily turn on

110. Smith, *Pulaski County*, 272; Rho. W. Hughes to Governor William Smith, Aug. 8, 1864, Letters Received, Governor's Office Executive Department, Virginia State Library and Archives, Richmond.

111. Joan Tracy Armstrong, *History of Smyth County, Virginia* (Marion, Va., 1968), II, 143.

112. Ralph W. Donnelly, "The Confederate Lead Mines of Wythe County, Va.," *CWH*, V (1959), 403.

113. Ibid., 402–404, 406–409.

Wytheville, capture its provost guard, and destroy the mines, stores, and railroad there. Morgan decided to use a shorter route through Burke's Garden to beat him to the town.[114]

Marching rapidly, he managed to arrive first. His appearance immediately raised the sagging spirits of alarmed residents. Still remembering Colonel Toland's successful raid the previous July, townspeople feared their troops were insufficient to protect Wytheville. Already many had fled with their movable property on the first alarm. Now somewhat relieved, citizens greeted Morgan's troops enthusiastically. Cheering ladies "waved hankichiefs and flags." Meanwhile a group of citizens, hoping to assist in the defense, readied the town's old 6-pounder for use. Their clumsy efforts provoked "a good deal of laughter," but Morgan took charge and assigned two gunners to man the ceremonial piece. Lacking ammunition but possessing some powder, a blacksmith cut up horseshoes and other iron for use as canister. Fortunately, the 16th Virginia Cavalry under Colonel William L. Graham had just arrived from the Rocky Gap area. Morgan sent them along with the local militia to occupy a long and narrow pass through the mountains on the road between Crocket's Cove and Wytheville. If Averell intended to attack the town, he would have to either use the pass or else make a long detour.[115]

By midafternoon both Graham's men and Averell's cavalry reached Rocky Gap. The 14th Pennsylvania and 1st West Virginia Regiments quickly attacked the Confederate advanced guard. In the opening probe the troopers easily pushed in Southern skirmishers, but as they hastily withdrew Graham ordered his men to dismount. As the Federals approached, the waiting Virginians, deployed on both sides of the Gap and with the artillery piece in their front, "poured a withering fire into the charging Yanks, emptying many saddles, and sending the rest scurrying to cover." As Duffié soon discovered, the Confederates had chosen the position well "for defense or attack," and the Federals found it "impossible to turn with cavalry." Initially Duffié intended to use a column of the 2nd

114. *OR*, Vol. XXXVIII, Pt. 1, p. 41; Benson, comp., *With the Army*, 42; Duke, *Morgan's Cavalry*, 516–17.

115. C. A. Withers, "Humor and Pathos of Four Years in Active Service: Confederate Reminiscences," 37–38, SHC; Edward O. Guerrant Diary, May 10, 1864, SHC; Duke, *Morgan's Cavalry*, 516; George Dallas Mosgrove, *Kentucky Cavaliers*, ed. Bell Irvin Wiley (Jackson, Tenn., 1957), 134; Pendleton, *Tazewell County*, 626; B. F. Nelson, "A Boy in the Confederate Cavalry," *CV*, XXXVI (1928), 375.

West Virginia to charge through the Gap. With drawn sabers they waited for the order. Meanwhile a member of his bodyguard dismounted, reconnoitered, and discovered Morgan's men concentrating in a nearby woods. Immediately he relayed the information to the general, who fully agreed with Colonel W. H. Powell's assessment that such a charge would be "suicidal." Quickly abandoning the idea, he ordered the West Virginians to fall back into the forming Federal line.[116]

Hearing gunfire, Morgan pushed his men rapidly toward the Gap. He directed his brigade to the left, around the mountain and through a woods, to threaten Averell's right and rear. They succeeded in dismounting without discovery, but suddenly Federal sharpshooters spotted them. Meanwhile, Averell's troopers fell back to a ridge commanding a large open field. Morgan, smarting from having his preparations for another raid into Kentucky interrupted, preferred to assume the offensive. Jones agreed and ordered a frontal assault. With a tremendous yell the Southerners charged. The Federals also surged forward but soon fell back behind another hill. Schoonmaker's 1st West Virginia and the 14th Pennsylvania sustained the shock, while Duffié's 2nd and 3rd West Virginia Regiments and the 34th Ohio Mounted Infantry formed "a line" behind them, as Averell would later note, "which the enemy had reason to respect and remember."[117]

As the Federals fell back some five hundred yards, Morgan attempted to turn the Union flank. Despite suffering a minor injury across his forehead, Averell continued to direct his men. Colonel Powell's 2nd West Virginia Regiment, despite being nearly surrounded three or four times, helped to stave off a potentially disastrous rout, and the colonel won high praise from Averell for his troopers' "steady and skillful evolutions" and for "retreating under a galling fire" without breaking ranks. Their maneuvers, Duffié observed, "saved the left of the division." The Federals kept falling back under pressure until sunset, when Jones ordered a halt. For Averell's men, after some four hours of skirmishing and at a cost of some 114 wounded and dead, the cessation brought a sense of relief. As one trooper

116. Pendleton, *Tazewell County,* 626–27; Sutton, *Second Regiment,* 115; Tall to Mother and Sisters, May 21, 1864, Tall Letters; Withers, "Humor and Pathos," 37–38; Benson, *With the Army,* 42–43; Duke, *Morgan's Cavalry,* 516–17; Gary C. Walker, *The War in Southwest Virginia* (Roanoke, 1985), 99; Nelson, "Boy in Confederate Cavalry," 375.

117. Pendleton, *Tazewell County,* 626–27; Guerrant Diary, May 10, 1864; OR, Vol. XXXVII, Pt. 1, p. 43.

in Captain James Abraham's company remarked, the Southerners "sawed off more than we could bring away."[118]

Morgan wrote to his wife that "if we had 2 more hours of daylight [we] would have captured the entire force." Captain Edward O. Guerrant agreed, regretting the lost opportunity to seize "five hundred horses (to say nothing of Yankees) which would have mounted all our dismounted boys." A proud Morgan wrote that his men "fought magnificently driving them from hill to hill, it was certainly the grandest sight I ever witnessed." Impressed with Federal skill, Morgan graciously paid a compliment to his opponent, even if it was a backhanded one: "Averell fought his men elegantly, tried time & time again to get them to charge, but our boys gave them no time." Averell saw his reversal quite differently: "At dark there was some prospect of our being able to drive him, but after dark he retired."[119] Yet he wisely exhibited no intention of resuming the engagement on the following day. In Wytheville an elderly lady gleefully told her neighbor that she "heered the Yankees wus 'vancin' backwards."[120]

Under the cover of darkness, Averell's troopers, with a local black to guide them, moved hurriedly toward Dublin to join Crook. After following a steep trail for hours, he rested his exhausted men and horses for half a day at Crab Orchard before picking up the march again. Moving rapidly, they reached Dublin the following evening, May 11, and spent "a disagreeable" night, soaked by heavy rain. Luckily his timing secured his safety. When he reached the New River on the next morning, Averell found the river swollen by the heavy rains. Despite its "extremely perilous" condition, the river remained passable. The main column began crossing on a flatboat, but his rear guard, feeling the pressure of Morgan's pursuit, risked crossing the rapid current. A number failed to make the transit, but bold actions by some saved others. By the time the pursuing Confederates reached its banks, the river had become impassable. "Had their designs been accomplished in reaching the river before me," Averell reported, "the success of the expedition might have been varied." Instead,

118. Benson, comp., *With the Army*, 43; Pendleton, *Tazewell County*, 626–27; Mary B. Kegley, *Wythe County, Virginia: A Bicentennial History* (Wytheville, 1989), 198.

119. Quoted in James A. Ramage, *Rebel Raider: The Life of General John Hunt Morgan* (Lexington, Va., 1986), 212, Cecil Fletcher Holland, *Morgan and His Raiders* (New York, 1942), 317, and Shelby Foote, *The Civil War: A Narrative* (New York, 1974), III, 246; Guerrant Diary, May 10, 1864; OR, Vol. XXXVII, Pt. 1, p. 42.

120. George F. Robertson, *A Small Boy's Recollections of the Civil War* (Charlotte, 1932), 75.

"The enemy had leisure to observe the ruins of the railroad and bridges."[121]

Temporarily safe, Averell sent a courier to Crook asking for instructions. Initially complying with the order to tear up the Virginia and Tennessee Railroad toward Lynchburg, he sent a pioneer party of twenty men with axes and turpentine along the line to devastate some twenty-six bridges and large sections of track between New River and Christiansburg.[122] In the meantime, needing fresh horses, his troopers scoured their route for new ones. One angry local farmer, Strother Heavenner, complaining over the loss of his horse, was told by an officer that "he could do nothing for me" except provide him with an introduction to Colonel Oley.[123] Edmund Otey, a slave whose master allowed him to work at his trade of carpentry and to earn money and own property, learned that need did not discriminate. Troopers took his horse, telling him that "their horses were broken down & they must have him, but that I should be rewarded for him."[124]

Reaching Christiansburg on May 12, they easily dispersed the small force there and captured two 3-inch guns abandoned by the Southerners. Earlier Crook had bypassed the town, so they now destroyed the railway depot and remaining military supplies, while other units tore up track for four miles beyond the town. Yet they made no effort to burn the courthouse or its records. Occupying the telegraph office, Averell's operator managed to communicate with Salem and Lynchburg. By a ruse he learned that "heavy reinforcements" were on their way west by rail. That information, along with the almost exhausted state of his ammunition and other supplies, caused Averell to reconsider Crook's directive to tear up the railroad. Believing it inexpedient, he aborted the plan and moved to join the main column instead.[125] As one resident, Mrs. John Wade, observed, "They left in a great hurry."[126]

121. *OR*, Vol. XXXVII, Pt. 1, p. 42; Cincinnati *Daily Gazette*, June 2, 1864; Lang, *Loyal West Virginia*, 375; Sutton, *Second Regiment: West Virginia*, 116; Benson, comp., *With the Army*, 45; Kegley, *Wythe County*, 198; Joseph Crockett Kelley, Sr., "Cove Brick Presbyterian Church," *Wythe County Historical Review* (1979), no. 15, 32.

122. *OR*, Vol. XXXVII, Pt. 1, pp. 42, 462.

123. Strother Heavenner file #14705, microfiche 1468, and Davidson Tabor file 1790, microfiche 3220, both in RG 233, SCCP.

124. Edmund Otey file, 19019, RG 217, SCCP.

125. *OR*, Vol. XXXVII, Pt. 1, pp. 42, 462; Cincinnati *Daily Gazette*, June 3, 1864; Davidson to Mother, May 17, 1864, Davidson Correspondence; Sutton, *Second Regiment: West Virginia Cavalry*, 117.

126. Quoted in Givens, *Christiansburg, Montgomery County, Virginia*, 99.

As Averell turned north to follow Crook's route, French and "Mud-wall" Jackson moved to block him. Occupying Gap Mountain, they spot-ted the Federals crossing Brush Mountain. French began deploying his men and placed a battery on a crest to cover the road. Alerted as they ap-proached, Averell's troopers charged "to cut their way through." Although driving the Southerners back, they failed to turn French's left flank. Frus-trated, Averell moved back across Brush Mountain to use the "Hunter's path," leading a wit to remark that the general "always carried a cow path or two in his haversack for emergencies of this kind."[127] Just as the Federals were disengaging from French's men, McCausland and a small cavalry unit approached, their arrival delayed by high water. It was too late for the col-onel, who could merely watch as the enemy escaped.[128]

Meanwhile, McCausland's infantry, having marched twenty-seven miles that day, remained halted near Blacksburg. With the roads in bad shape and local streams swollen from heavy rains, he made no effort to pursue the Federals, except to order Jackson to follow them into Monroe County. Waiting on Salt Pond Mountain, Jackson's men again skirmished with the enemy, only to retreat.[129] Far more dangerous for Averell, the constant rainstorms made the mountainous route extremely treacherous. At times his "men were compelled to dismount, and leading their horses by the bit with one hand, and holding on to the tail of the advance horses with the other in order to keep together."[130] Private Tall recalled for his family the excruciating experience of marching "through mountain paths most of the way. You would think them inaccessible to anything except the goat."[131] Finally, worn out and hungry, the cavalry caught up with Crook on May 15 at Union. In a letter to the Cincinnati *Commercial*, one cavalryman summed up the ordeal for many of his compatriots: "'Riding a raid' might read well on paper, the riding itself was anything but pleasant, and especially so when short of grub."[132]

127. Benson, comp., *With the Army*, 46.

128. Arthur, "Dublin Raid," April 13, 1889; Humphreys Autobiography, II, 317; Jen-ning Diary, May 13, 1864; OR, Vol. XXXVII, Pt. 1, pp. 48, 64–65, 735–36.

129. OR, Vol. XXXVII, Pt. 1, p. 48.

130. Arthur, "Dublin Raid," April 13, 1889.

131. W. A. Tall to Mother and Sisters, May 21, 1864, Tall Letters.

132. Cincinnati *Commercial*, quoted in Washington *Daily Morning Chronicle*, June 6, 1864.

3

The Valley

After completing all the arrangements for Crook's and Averell's expeditions, Sigel had left Cumberland for Martinsburg on April 25 to take personal charge of the drive up the Shenandoah Valley. Pleased with the preparations, he informed Grant from Martinsburg that his forces were "stronger than any force the enemy can concentrate between Lewisburg and the railroad at this moment." By April 28 he was ready. In a wire to Grant he announced his intention to start on the following day. [1]

Before leaving Martinsburg, Sigel decided to hold a grand review. Portending ill for the general, the exercise almost ended in a debacle. As Sigel reviewed the cavalry, regimental commanders managed to form a line only with considerable difficulty. Once formed, however, the display impressed Dr. Neil, who confided to his family, "Our line of Battle extended about 5 miles, and in the fluttering of a hundred banners, the gleaming of bayonets, the flashing of sabers, and on 'all the pomp and circumstance of war,' the bright April sun shone down clear and beautiful, the booming of cannon and the sweet strains of music from a score of bands, lending additional enchantment to the scene, rendering it magnificent beyond description." As Sigel and his staff inspected the lines, "the heavens were almost rent with cheers." [2] The next day, Sigel, with his

---

1. OR, XXXIII, 986, 1006–1007.
2. Neil to Parents, April 28, 1864, Neil Letters.

generals at the column's head, advanced up the Valley to Bunker Hill. The imposing column stretched for over six miles as it moved south. As Dr. Neil observed, "Every body is in good spirits and confident of a successful campaign." As they headed for Winchester, the 12th West Virginia Regiment joyfully sang "We Fights Mit Sigel."[3]

Federal brass bands echoing down the Valley ended the period of Southern speculation over Union intentions in the lower Shenandoah. For Lee and the authorities in Richmond, the Federal move in southwestern Virginia posed a serious threat, but activities in the lower Valley offered conceivably a more immediate danger. A movement there offered a threat to Lee's left flank, as well as to Staunton and the Virginia Central Railroad, and could determine the outcome of the spring campaign in Virginia. Federal activity at Martinsburg and then Sigel's advance on April 29 accentuated these anxieties in Richmond. For over a month various Southern units had closely watched enemy movements and provided the Confederate War Department with a variety of reports and rumors. Imboden kept Breckinridge apprised with incoming intelligence and his speculations on their meaning. Breckinridge, lacking jurisdiction over the Valley District but cooperating with Imboden, busied himself with his more immediate concern, the safety of his own department.

However, on May 4 Breckinridge's focus suddenly shifted to the Valley when Davis wired from Richmond that Sigel's moves "indicated the propriety of your making a junction with General Imboden to meet the enemy on his movements towards Staunton." He directed Breckinridge to communicate with Lee and Imboden. On the same day, Davis ordered Lee, who had earlier suggested concentrating all troops in western Virginia under a single commander, to "direct all operations" there and to regard it as "your left flank." Wiring Breckinridge, Davis directed him to report to Lee, who immediately authorized Breckinridge to "take the general direction of affairs and to use General Imboden's force as you think best."[4]

Sigel's advance significantly diverted Southern attention to the Valley. In the aftermath of the Gettysburg campaign, military activities there had been minimal, and Confederate forces under Imboden remained meager.

3. *Ibid.*, April 30, 1864; William S. Lincoln, *Life with the Thirty-Fourth Massachusetts Infantry in the War of the Rebellion* (Worcester, Mass., 1879), 257–58; Hewitt, *Twelfth West Virginia*, 10.

4. *OR*, Vol. XXXVII, Pt. 1, p. 712, and Vol. LI, Pt. 2, p. 887.

By the general's own estimates, his troops—consisting of his own brigade of cavalry and mounted infantry, Wharton's infantry brigade, two small cavalry battalions under Major Harry Gilmor and Captain T. Sturgis Davis, McClanahan's battery, and Captain John McNeill's rangers—did not exceed 3,000 men. With the continuing inactivity there, the War Department had ordered Wharton's brigade to Lee's army in late 1863. By late April, as Imboden concentrated the main body of his troops some twenty miles north of Staunton in Rockingham County, his force was hardly sufficient to sustain nominal control over the Valley. Now, with Sigel's advance, as Imboden moved his men northwards toward Mount Crawford, he counted only a force of 1,492, plus an additional 100 scouts for a total effective veteran force of some 1,600. He hoped to utilize the reserves from Rockingham and Augusta Counties under Colonel William H. Harman, but as Imboden well knew, they were "undisciplined and armed mostly with hunting-rifles and shot guns."[5]

Imboden had taken command of the Valley District following Gettysburg. As a native of Augusta County and a prominent local politician, he was the logical choice for the post. During the John Brown crisis he had organized the Staunton Artillery, a light battery. With secession he led his men to Harpers Ferry to aid in securing that point, but with General Irvin McDowell's advance on Manassas, Richmond shifted his battery there. After the battle, Imboden received Stonewall Jackson's praise for his performance as a "dauntless leader." Transferred to regular service, he became commander of the Northwestern Virginia Brigade, and in the spring of 1863 Imboden, in concert with "Grumble" Jones, conducted a fairly successful raid into central West Virginia against the Baltimore and Ohio Railroad.

Praise, however, turned to sharp criticism following the Gettysburg campaign, for when Lee needed him, Imboden was resting his men at Hancock, Maryland, some fifty miles southwest of the city. Imboden partially quieted Lee's fury by holding off an attack on the army's wagon trains until additional support arrived, and in October, Lee commended him for capturing a force at Charlestown. Yet Lee undoubtedly remembered the Hancock incident when he learned of Early's remark that

---

5. *Ibid.*, XXXIII, 1332; John D. Imboden, "The Battle of New Market, Va., May 15th, 1864," *B&L*, IV, 480; Edward Raymond Turner, "The Battle of New Market," *CV* (1912), 71.

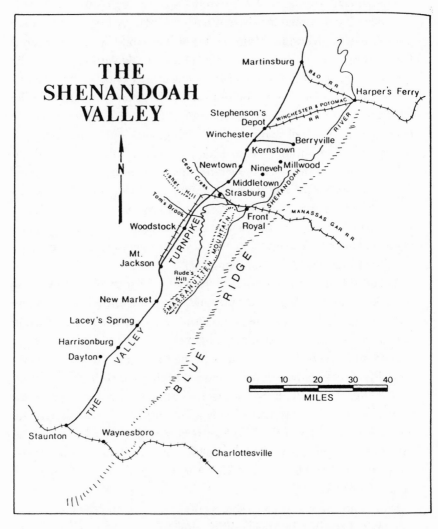

Prominent Civil War Sites in the Shenandoah Valley
From Stephen Z. Starr, The Union Cavalry in the Civil War, *3 vols. (Baton Rouge,*
1979–85). Courtesy of Louisiana State University Press.

Imboden's command was "generally in a very bad state of discipline . . . [and he] should feel great reluctance to have to rely on it in any emergency." A bristling Imboden demanded a court of inquiry, but Lee, not wanting such a divisive hearing, refused the request.[6] The damage was done, however, and Lee harbored serious doubts about Imboden's ability. In early January 1864 he pointedly expressed them to Davis: "My own opportunities of observations have not impressed me favorably with regard to the discipline and efficiency of General Imboden's troops."[7]

Initially, Imboden focused primarily on southwestern Virginia and the southern part of his own district. On March 10 he had prematurely informed Lee that there would be a "big raid here some time this month." To counter it he began constructing a line of fortifications in the mountain passes. But he feared they would not be completed in time, warning Lee that "if Averell comes with 5,000 to 6,000 men and threatens two or three places at once, say Staunton, Lexington, and the Virginia and Tennessee Railroad, we shall be sorely put to meet him unless these works are finished and other troops sent to the district." He further suggested that Breckinridge should undertake a similar project.[8] General Francis H. Smith, superintendent of the Virginia Military Institute, agreed and wrote to Bragg on the importance of these fortifications in blocking incursions into Rockbridge County. Bragg fully agreed.[9]

Yet the most taxing problem for Imboden remained the lack of sufficient troops. With a district stretching from Staunton to the Potomac River and with less than two thousand men, he was strapped for manpower to combat any serious raid. To augment his force, in March 1864 he proposed a plan to the War Department for the creation "of an organization of minutemen," envisaging that it would net him five companies. Lee approved and urged the plan's adoption, arguing that "these regiments . . . ought to be able to protect the valley and punish severely raiding parties

6. John D. Imboden to Major (McCue), Feb. 3, 1864, John D. Imboden Papers, UV; *OR*, XXXIII, 1167–68, 1174; Douglas Southall Freeman, *Lee's Lieutenants* (New York, 1946), III, 48; Davis, *New Market*, 18–19; Hariland Harris Abbot, "General John D. Imboden," *WVH*, XXI (1960), 88–111; J. D. Imboden, "Fire, Sword, and the Halter," in *Annals of the War* (Philadelphia, 1879), 170; "Lee's High Estimate of General Imboden," *CV*, XXIX (1921), 420–21.

7. *OR*, XXXIII, 1086.

8. *Ibid.*, 1215.

9. William Couper, *One Hundred Years at V.M.I.* (Richmond, 1939), II, 256.

of the enemy." After a month's consideration, Richmond granted authorization. On April 30 a pleased Imboden reported that he possessed over a thousand reservists in three counties. In its reply, the department authorized him to call them out on his own judgment. Imboden informed Richmond that he hoped to complete organizing and arming his reserves in Augusta, Rockingham, Shenandoah, and Page Counties by May 2, estimating their numbers at twelve hundred to fifteen hundred.[10] Yet even though the tapping of the area's manpower helped, they hardly substituted for seasoned regulars.

An additional source of manpower remained the Virginia Military Institute in Lexington. Earlier, on March 14, VMI superintendent Smith had proposed allowing cadets to enter regular service, but the governor wanted the cadets to cooperate with the reserves and preferred "to hold them for home defense."[11] On April 22, Imboden diplomatically warned the superintendent that the next raid on the Valley would come "from Kanawha and Beverly" and require their use.[12] He also suggested recruiting local seventeen- and eighteen-year-old boys for garrison duty. Lee preferred using the cadets "in defending our western frontier," holding them "in readiness . . . in case of necessity." On May 4, Breckinridge alerted Smith to the possible necessity of using them to defend various points on the Virginia Central Railroad.[13]

Despite Southern preoccupation with the southwest and upper Valley, scouts and spies continually scrutinized Federal activity in the lower Shenandoah. Imboden fully realized his vulnerability there. Yet rumors of a movement up the Valley received mixed reactions. In late March, Lieutenant Colonel John S. Mosby had noticed the tightening picket lines and the laying of rails on the decimated Winchester and Potomac Railroad again. He warned Jeb Stuart that "the impression among citizens is that a

10. *OR*, XXXIII, 1212–15, 1217, 1333, and Vol. LI, Pt. 2, pp. 885.

11. Couper, *One Hundred Years*, II, 257.

12. Ibid., 259.

13. *OR*, Vol. XXXVII, Pt. 1, pp. 707–708; J. D. Imboden to Francis Smith, April 22, 1864, R. E. Lee to Maj. Gen. Richardson, April 25, 1864, Superintendent's Correspondence: Letter Received, VMI; Francis Smith to Maj. Gen. W. H. Richardson, April 19, 1864, Francis Smith to Brig. Gen. J. D. Imboden, April 28, 1864, Francis Smith to Maj. Gen. John C. Breckinridge, May 2, 1864, Superintendent's Letter Book: Outgoing Correspondence, VMI; *Report of the Board of Visitors of the Virginia Military Institute* (1864), 38–39; Couper, *One Hundred Years*, II, 256–61; Francis H. Smith, *The Virginia Military Institute: Its Building and Rebuilding* (Lynchburg, 1912), 193–94.

movement up the Valley is contemplated." Relaying the information to Davis, Lee interpreted the activity to mean the Federals intended to reoccupy Winchester, but as he cautioned, enemy designs were "not sufficiently developed to discover them." Grant "will concentrate a large force on one or more lines, and prudence dictates that we should make such preparations as are in our power," he warned.[14]

On March 30, Lee suggested making an aggressive diversionary move to disrupt Federal plans "in the West" and "oblige them to conform to ours." Failing this, Longstreet "should be held in readiness to be thrown rapidly into the valley, if necessary to counteract any movement in that quarter." Then, depending on circumstances, Lee and Longstreet could unite on the Rapidan. Three days later, Lee, noting the undetermined activity on the Baltimore and Ohio, confided to Davis that Virginia would likely be "the theater of Grant's campaign" and that a "column may also be pushed up the Shenandoah Valley." With reports in late April indicating a diminished Federal presence in the lower Shenandoah, he reconsidered the possibility of a diversion and directed Imboden to make a demonstration, if practical, against the Baltimore and Ohio Railroad.[15]

Yet Lee remained somewhat complacent about a threat in the lower Valley. On April 11 he wrote Imboden that he concluded from various reports that the Federals were concentrating on the Rappahannock River and in the Chesapeake Bay region and planning a concerted move on Richmond from those positions. To accomplish such an action, Lee pointed out, Grant would have to weaken his forces in other areas. Lee then suggested that if Imboden could complete his fortifications in time, he should seize any opportunity to strike at vulnerable points along the Federal line. And if conditions allowed, he should prepare to cross the Blue Ridge Mountains and operate on the flank and rear of the Army of the Potomac. However, Lee preferred that Imboden gain possession of the rail line in order to disrupt travel and force Grant to detach troops from his army. He strongly suggested that Imboden maintain contact with Breckinridge and cooperate with him. Warning him about feints, he exhorted Imboden "not to be deceived by them, but repulse them boldly."[16]

Continuing reports confirmed the pullout of Federal troops. On April

14. OR, XXXIII, 1240–41, 1244–45, 1260–61.
15. *Ibid.*, 1244–45, 1254–55; 1307; Dowdey and Manarin, eds., *Papers of Lee*, 687–88.
16. OR, XXXIII, 1272–73.

18, Lee informed Davis that the westward movement of Averell's cavalry along the Baltimore and Ohio left only a garrison at Martinsburg and none at Harpers Ferry. He judged that the shift meant the preparation for a raid on the Virginia and Tennessee Railroad or Staunton "at the time of the general movement upon Richmond." Relaying much of that dispatch to Imboden and Breckinridge, he concluded, "I see no indications of a movement up the Valley." He discounted the reconstruction of the Winchester and Potomac Railroad as a feint. However, if the Federals did advance there, he hoped his generals "will be prepared to unite and beat him back . . . and drive him across the Potomac." [17]

Three days later, Stuart confirmed Lee's assessment. Relying on a scout, he reported that "the whole line is very weak since Averell's departure, pickets have fallen back considerably, and the line is now near the railroad." He too suspected that Averell had left for Romney for a "big raid," and noted that a large force then concentrating at New Creek appeared to be aimed at Petersburg, West Virginia. As late as April 30, Lee remained focused on Averell and the potential for an incursion from the Kanawha Valley, confiding to Davis that "Averell and Sigel will move against the Virginia and Tennessee Railroad or Staunton." Breckinridge and Imboden "should act in concert," he suggested. The following day he again urged Breckinridge to prepare and to cooperate with Imboden in destroying Averell "if possible." From intelligence reports, Lee suspected the route would be the same as the December one. Regarding Sigel's presumed presence at Martinsburg, he merely commented that "this conflicts with former reports." [18]

Imboden also discounted rumors of Sigel's presence at Martinsburg. As late as April 30, he concluded that the advance would come from New Creek and Cumberland to cooperate with movements from the Kanawha Valley and Beverly. Reporting to Breckinridge, he estimated the force in his front as "small, guarding the railroad, and apparently meditating no advance up this valley." However, he did recognize the possibility of a force coming from Martinsburg. [19] Although three days earlier he had

17. Lee to Davis and Lee to Imboden, April 18, 1864, Lee's Headquarters Papers, Letter Book, VHS; OR, XXXIII, 1276, 1290–91.

18. OR, XXXIII, 1331–32, Vol. XXXVII, Pt. 1, p. 707, and Vol. LI, Pt. 2, pp. 871–72; Lee to Davis, April 23, 30, 1864, Lee to Imboden and Lee to Breckinridge, April 27, 1864, Lee's Headquarters Papers, VHS.

19. OR, XXXIII, 1332–33.

alerted General Thomas Lafayette Rosser at Waynesboro that "the enemy was advancing up the Valley,"[20] as late as May 2 he still focused on West Virginia. Fearful of the dangers in dividing his small army, Imboden concentrated it in Rockingham County to give it greater flexibility. Alerted by reports of a possible thrust into the Valley from the Lost River region, he shifted his command toward Timberville on May 2.[21]

Sigel's sudden advance on April 29 shattered Southern complacency as Grant's plan of concerted moves in western Virginia became increasingly obvious. Scouts informed Stuart on May 3 that Sigel occupied Winchester. That same day, Imboden wired the news to Breckinridge. Echols also telegraphed to confirm that Averell was on the Kanawha, informing Breckinridge, "This force is called on the Kanawha River the right wing of Grant's army." Their objective, he believed, was the New River bridge and the saltworks. "There is no mistake about this information," he hastened to add. Now convinced, Lee informed Davis, "It may be that they now intend to move up the Valley towards Staunton." Aroused, Davis wired Breckinridge at Dublin that propriety suggested his making a junction with Imboden to block any move on Staunton and that he should contact Lee. Immediately, Breckinridge informed Lee of the distribution of his troops and said he would "wait to hear from you, and act upon your views of the emergency." Davis, informing Lee of the contents of his dispatch to Breckinridge, expressed his "desire that you should direct all operations in Western Virginia, regarding it as your left flank." Lee immediately directed Breckinridge to "use General Imboden's force as you think best."[22]

An anxious Breckinridge, needing clarification of Lee's intended strategy, wired Lee on May 4 for instructions, asking, "Is Staunton the point threatened?" He also queried if he should move Echols in Monroe County, Wharton at Narrows, and McCausland at Princeton to Jackson River depot to board trains for Staunton. If needed, as he told Lee, he could add "Mudwall" Jackson's small unit to his army at that point. That would leave Jenkins and "Grumble" Jones with some four thousand cavalry and six hundred infantry and "a good supply of artillery" to combat

20. Andrew Gatewood to Mother, April 27, 1864, Andrew Gatewood Collection, VMI.

21. *OR*, Vol. LI, Pt. 2, p. 885.

22. *Ibid.*, Vol. XXXVII, Pt. 1, pp. 710, 712–13; Dowdey and Manarin, eds., *Papers of Lee*, 718–19; Lee to Davis, May 3, 1864, Lee's Headquarters Papers; Johnston, "Sketches of Breckinridge," 258.

Crook's advance. In response, Lee candidly admitted not knowing if Staunton was the threatened point. However, his anxiety extended beyond the Valley itself. He feared that all the forces that had gone west "seem to have returned east" and that Sigel might advance only a short distance and then cross over the Blue Ridge to "get on my left." Reports from Imboden, estimating Sigel's strength at seven thousand and his movement as toward Front Royal, alarmed Lee. It seemed to confirm his fear of their crossing the mountains at Chester Gap. Therefore, he wanted Breckinridge to challenge Sigel or cause him to fall back "before they get on my left." He wanted to know the validity of the reports.[23]

Immediately, Breckinridge on May 5 ordered Echols, McCausland, and Wharton to leave for Staunton and sent "Mudwall" Jackson to Narrows to assist General Jenkins. Informing Bragg of his compliance with Lee's orders, Breckinridge asked him to countermand his directive for "Grumble" Jones to move into Tennessee. Instead, he wanted Jones to cooperate with Jenkins in defending southwestern Virginia. In outlining the deployment of his troops there, he told Jones, "You see that the whole country west of New River is uncovered, and depends on you." Later that day, Breckinridge hurried to Narrows to consult with Wharton before he left for Jackson River Depot.[24]

As Breckinridge rode circuitously toward Staunton, reports delineated the bleakness of the situation. Princeton had fallen; Jenkins, yet to concentrate his brigade, possessed only two hundred men at Narrows. An alarmed Stringfellow at Dublin sent word on May 7 that Crook was at Rocky Gap and warned that with "several columns to strike different points," the Federals could easily threaten the stores there. However, he assured Breckinridge, "We will give them a warm reception here." Mixed reports from the lower Valley further confused the picture. Initially, Imboden reported Averell's presence in Winchester with three thousand cavalry. Yet Sigel with some four thousand infantry still remained there. However, for Breckinridge any hesitancy ended with Lee's wire on May 7: "The movements proposed in the Valley, if made, must be made at once." Spurred by the telegram, Breckinridge, covering 145 miles in three days, reached Staunton on the evening of May 9.[25]

23. OR, Vol. XXXVII, Pt. 1, pp. 712–13; Johnston, Kentucky, 185.
24. OR, Vol. XXXVII, Pt. 1, pp. 716–20; Johnston, "Sketches of Breckinridge," 258.
25. OR, Vol. XXXVII, Pt. 1, pp. 721–23, 725; Davis, New Market, 32.

Concentrating his troops posed difficulties for Breckinridge, and it would not be until May 11 that all of them would arrive. He anxiously pressured railroad authorities to ensure sufficient trains and supplies for them once they reached Staunton. However, Echols, on reaching Jackson River depot, found no cars. There he met Breckinridge, who, after delivering a rousing speech, marched with the troops to the Covington-Lexington Pike. The brigade continued a grueling march to Goshen. Echols on May 9 wired that his "men and horses are a good deal broken down," complaining that they could not even obtain "a grain of corn" on the route. He asked Breckinridge to send them a train with supplies and transport to Staunton. He warned, "Our transportation and artillery horses will be used up unless we get some forage."[26]

For Wharton the distance was even greater, stretching some sixty miles from Narrows over mountainous terrain. His brigade reached Jackson River depot by May 9 "very sore footed." He also found no rail transportation or forage. Informed of the unavailability of transport, Wharton wired Breckinridge, "We will reach Staunton," and assured him that they would "come on as fast as possible."[27] Fortunately, a train arrived that evening, and the 51st Virginia and the 30th Virginia Battalion, with four guns, boarded it, the remainder continuing on foot.[28]

With reports estimating Sigel's army at seven to ten thousand, Breckinridge desperately needed additional manpower. Some help came from the five hundred reservists in Augusta and Rockingham Counties under Colonel Harman. In Rockbridge County, VMI superintendent Smith called out the companies there and tendered the services of the cadets. Meanwhile, on May 11, the day Sigel reached Woodstock, Breckinridge sent a courier to the institute. At 9:00 P.M. he handed Smith the request for the cadets to come to Staunton at once. Soon the reverberations of the long drumroll echoing through the barracks roused the cadets from their sleep. By the light of a lantern, Smith read the order "amid breathless silence." On dismissal, as Cadet John S. Wise later remembered, "the air was rent with wild cheering at the thought that our hour was come at last." In the

26. OR, Vol. XXXVII, Pt. 1, pp. 725–26; John Mastin Diary, May 6–11, 1864, in Roy Bird Cook Collection, WVU; Davis, *New Market*, 31; Terry Lowry, *26th Battalion Virginia Infantry* (Lynchburg, 1991), 36.

27. OR, Vol. XXXVII, Pt. 1, p. 727; Davis, *New Market*, 40.

28. Louis H. Manarin, ed., "Civil War Diary of Rufus J. Woolwine," *VMH&B*, LXXI (1963), 435–36.

morning, around 8:30, four infantry companies of 209 cadets and an artillery section of 32 departed for Staunton. An excited local populace watched with mixed emotions. With the cadets and the Home Guard gone, an anxious Mrs. Margaret Junkin Preston complained that "Lexington is left without men."[29]

In response to the Federal move in the lower Valley, Imboden shifted his command to Rude's Hill, near Mount Jackson. With reports of Sigel's advance toward Front Royal, he became apprehensive of Sigel's crossing the Blue Ridge to join Grant. Remembering Lee's entreaties to prevent such a move, he proposed to Breckinridge an attack on Cumberland and possibly a threat to Grafton as well. He also apprised him of Lee's instructions for him to move to Orange if Sigel left the Valley. Imboden urged a "combined movement" that would "bring him back."[30] Undoubtedly remembering his concerted raid into West Virginia with "Grumble" Jones during the spring of 1863, he hoped to repeat that success and create a diversion.[31] Breckinridge, however, merely replied that he was heading for Staunton and that four thousand men were en route there, failing to comment on Imboden's suggestion. Two days later, on May 7, Imboden, reporting Sigel's lack of movement and, incorrectly, Averell's arrival in Winchester, asked to confer with Breckinridge "on important matters." Convinced that a diversionary move would deflect a Federal advance on the following day, he now suggested undertaking an expedition into Hampshire County against the railroad, arguing that Sigel would have to withdraw from Winchester to protect the line. If Breckinridge then advanced into the lower Valley, "we can clear this border in five days, destroy

29. OR, Vol. XXXVII, Pt. 1, pp. 707–708, 730; Nelson Nolan to Father, April 29, May 3, 1864, Nelson Nolan to Mother, May 11, 1864, Nolan Family Papers, UV; Francis Smith to Maj. Gen. J. C. Breckinridge, May 11, 1864, Francis Smith to Maj. Gen. W. H. Richardson, May 12, 1864, Superintendent's Letter Book, 402–403; Lexington (Va.) *Gazette*, May 25, 1864; *Report of Board of Visitors*, 33, 40; Couper, *One Hundred Years*, II, 229–46, 263–64; John G. Barrett and Robert K. Turner, Jr., eds., *Letters of a New Market Cadet: Beverly Standard* (Chapel Hill, 1961), xvi–xvii; John S. Wise, *Battle of New Market, Va.: An Address* (1882), 33–35; Jennings Cropper Wise, *The Military History of the Virginia Military Institute from 1839 to 1865* (Lynchburg, 1915), 285–93; John S. Wise, *The End of an Era* (Boston, 1899), 287–89; John S. Wise, "The West Point of the Confederacy," *Century Illustrated Monthly Magazine*, XXXVII (1888–89), 464–65; Elizabeth Preston Allan, ed., *The Life and Letters of Margaret Junkin Preston* (Boston, 1903), 179.

30. OR, Vol. XXXVII, Pt. 1, pp. 715–17.

31. See Festus P. Summers, "The Jones-Imboden Raid," *WVH*, XLVII (1988), 53–62.

railroad, canal, and coal mines from New Creek to Martinsburg." In a follow-up telegram he reported a "re-enforced" buildup of cavalry and now expected that the enemy would move "eastward in a day or two." Offering reassurance, he wrote, "Staunton will not be endangered by my proposal."[32]

Consideration of Imboden's proposal died with Captain John Hanson "Hanse" McNeill's daring and independent attack on the railroad at Piedmont, a small but important rail depot in central West Virginia near New Creek. McNeill and his rangers, operating as a partisan unit in northeastern West Virginia, presented a ubiquitous threat to Union attempts to control that region. As a native of Hardy County, McNeill was familiar with the region. Nearly forty-nine, he was, as Simeon Miller Bright described him, "a brave, sharp-witted, kindhearted man."[33] Lee regarded him as "bold and intelligent."[34]

As Sigel rested at Winchester, McNeill seized the initiative. Leaving his base at Indian Old Field in Hardy County on the evening of May 3 with sixty rangers, McNeill struck toward Piedmont. On the South Branch of the Potomac, Captain John T. Peerce, then on detached duty, joined McNeill. Crossing Knobly Mountain at Doll's Gap and the summit of the Alleghenies by the Elk Garden Road, they reached the Piedmont-Bloomington Road at daybreak. Quickly they captured Bloomington. Leaving Peerce and ten men there, McNeill and his remaining rangers penetrated Piedmont before they were discovered. Immediately the captain demanded the garrison's surrender. After a brief exchange of shots, the ten-man provost guard from the 6th Virginia Infantry capitulated. McNeill secured for himself a major prize: seven railroad shops (including two roundhouses), nine locomotives, and twenty-two loaded freight cars. The rangers burned the machine and paint shops and the sand and oil houses, then partially wrecked an enginehouse. Within an hour they destroyed property worth an estimated $250,000 to $1 million. In addition, they tore up some two thousand feet of track. Adding insult to injury, McNeill sent six engines at full steam down the line toward the Federal garrison at New Creek.[35]

32. OR, Vol. XXXVII, Pt. 1, pp. 722, 724.

33. Simeon Miller Bright, "The McNeill Rangers: A Study in Confederate Guerrilla Warfare," *WVH*, XII (1951), 341.

34. OR, XXXIII, 1067.

35. *Ibid.*, Vol. XXXVII, Pt. 1, p. 69; *Thirty-Eighth Annual Report of the President and Di-*

Meanwhile, in Bloomington a local man informed Peerce that he had noticed a resident heading toward Frankville on horseback. He warned that the next train, an eastbound mail and passenger one, would be filled with soldiers. Though skeptical, Peerce nevertheless prepared a trap and succeeded in capturing the train and some one hundred soldiers without a struggle. Yet impending exposure threatened McNeill's rangers with capture. He had failed to cut the telegraph wire at Piedmont, and Federal garrisons eastward were quickly alerted to his presence. Initial disbelief, then Federal bungling gave the rangers the time they needed to escape. Despite the presence of a readied train, Lieutenant Charles Bagley, with a Parrott gun and a detachment of seventy-five men, left New Creek on foot to capture McNeill. On reaching the Bloomington vicinity, Bagley positioned his gun on a bluff on the Maryland side overlooking the North Branch of the Potomac River. His firing at the Southerners had little effect. Meanwhile, after paroling Peerce's prisoners and destroying the train, the rangers slipped back into the mountains and to safety. Unwilling to undertake a pursuit, the Federals merely watched them disappear.[36]

McNeill's boldness surprised, embarrassed, and angered Union and West Virginia authorities. On May 5, Governor Boreman wired Secretary of War Stanton the news that Confederate forces "are on the railroad at New Creek and Piedmont."[37] On receiving a telegram from Piedmont at 7 A.M., an alarmed John W. Garrett, president of the Baltimore and Ohio Railroad, had also wired the War Department of the impending attack, warning that unless the government sent additional troops, "great destruc-

---

rectors to the Stockholders of the Baltimore and Ohio Railroad Co. (Baltimore), 54; Baltimore American, May 9, 1864; Cincinnati Daily Commercial, May 13, 1864; Wheeling Daily Intelligencer, May 7, 9, 1864; Morgantown (W. Va.) Weekly Post, May 14, 1864; Edward B. Williams, ed., Rebel Brothers: The Civil War Letters of the Truehearts (College Station, Tex., 1995), 190, 192–93; Virgil Carrington Jones, Gray Ghosts and Rebel Raiders (McLean, Va., 1984), 233, 235–36; Bright, "McNeill Rangers," 353–56.

36. OR, Vol. XXXVII, Pt. 1, pp. 68–69; John Peerce, "Capture of a Railroad Train," Southern Bivouac (Louisville, 1884), II, 352–55; Cincinnati Daily Commercial, May 13, 1864; Wheeling Daily Intelligencer, May 9–10, 1864; Cumberland (Md.) Alleganian, May 10, 1864; "McNeill Wrecks Piedmont Depot," in Valley News Echo: Monthly Civil War Newspaper (Hagerstown, Md., 1965), V, 2, 4; Hu Maxwell and H. L. Swisher, History of Hampshire County, West Virginia: From Its Earliest Settlement to the Present (Morgantown, W. Va., 1897), 667; Jones, Gray Ghosts, 234; Roger U. Delauter, Jr., McNeill's Rangers (Lynchburg, 1986), 66–67; Bright, "McNeill Rangers," 353–56; Williams, Rebel Brothers, 194.

37. OR, XXXVII, Pt. 1, 381.

tion of railroad property and works will probably take place." He urged the sending of the first readied regiment in Ohio to protect the line, underscoring that "rapidity of movement is probably vital to prevent great disasters." He complained to Stanton that during the previous week he had informed Sigel "of the great importance of Piedmont . . . and of the urgent necessity to protect [it], but a few or no troops were left in that vicinity."[38]

Both Halleck and Stanton responded quickly. Halleck authorized Governor Boreman to utilize the 4th West Virginia Infantry Veterans. The secretary wired Garrett that two Ohio regiments, already in a state of readiness, would be sent.[39] To his embarrassment, Garrett later discovered that Sigel had received his warning only after he had begun his movement toward Winchester. On April 28, Garrett had asked W. P. Smith, master of transportation for the Baltimore and Ohio, to contact Sigel "promptly upon the subject" of Piedmont's security. Unfortunately, Smith delayed for two days, and then caused a further holdup by directing the dispatch to Cumberland rather than to Martinsburg. On discovering the fact, Garrett chastised Smith for what "may have proven the origin of the terrible disaster which the company has recently suffered."[40]

The sting galvanized the War Department. Without consulting Sigel, Stanton placed Kelley in charge of the rail line from Wheeling to Monocacy Junction in Maryland. Sigel's friends regarded the move with great suspicion. Brigadier General Max Weber at Harpers Ferry wired the news to Sigel, saying he intended to refuse "to give up the command without orders from you." Sigel, however, counseled caution. Since the order came through the secretary of war, "You have to accept it and act in accordance with it until further orders."[41] Another informant, Ira Cole, fueled suspicions further on May 8 when he reminded Sigel that "Gen. Kelley and his faction would do all in their power to hurt you." He asserted that Kelley "has begun his work."[42] Meanwhile, Kelley, sensitive about his position, asked Halleck to clarify it. Halleck replied that Kelley "remained under

38. *Ibid.*, 382; John W. Garrett to E. B. Stanton, May 5, 1864, #1151, 203, Letter Book VIII, Letters Sent by the Baltimore & Ohio Railroad, 1859–1867, MS 1816, MHS.

39. *OR*, Vol. XXXVII, Pt. 1, p. 382.

40. Garrett to W. P. Smith, April 28, 1864, #1120, 182, and May 7, 1864, #1168, 221–22, Garrett to Kelley, May 7, 1864, #1173, 226, Letter Book VIII; Cecil D. Eby, Jr., "With Sigel at New Market: The Diary of Colonel D. H. Strother," *CWH*, VI (1960), 77.

41. *OR*, Vol. XXXVII, Pt. 1, pp. 395–96, 403.

42. Ira Cole to Sigel, May 8, 1864, Sigel Papers.

General Sigel's orders." Sigel, also seeking clarification, wired Kelley, who reassured him that Kelley's command was "not an independent one."[43]

Surprisingly, Sigel accepted—ostensibly, at least—"full responsibility" for Piedmont. He had recognized the potential for a raid into West Virginia, and a number of informants and politicians had forewarned him. As early as April 29, Governor Boreman had expressed his alarm over local excitement caused by the draining of troops from the mountain areas.[44] On May 1, Weber at Harpers Ferry had alerted Sigel to expect an attack on Romney.[45] In his own defense, Sigel asserted that the raid became insignificant when compared to his achievement in concentrating his scattered units into "two little armies . . . now doing duty in the field." Further mitigating his responsibility, he wrote to the adjutant general of the army that he could not obey Grant's order to consolidate his troops and at the same time ensure the safety of the railroad between Wheeling and Monocacy Junction. In a barb aimed at Governor Boreman, he noted that he had given the governor "timely notice" of some three weeks to utilize the state militia in filling the void. Despite Boreman's promises to do so, Sigel wrote, "I suppose he was not able to bring out the militia." Obviously stung by the raid, Sigel expected to recoup by intercepting the raiders. He decided to send a five-hundred-man cavalry expedition, composed of the 22nd "Ringgold" Pennsylvania and the 15th New York Cavalries under Colonel Jacob Higgins, to trap McNeill. The detachment, he hoped, would also secure his right flank.[46]

Meanwhile, Southern scouts had heard of McNeill's successful strike at Piedmont. Then, on May 8, Imboden learned of Sigel's intent to capture the raiders. The signal station on top of Massanutten Mountain flashed the news that two cavalry detachments left Winchester. Captain Bartlett overestimated their strength at a thousand. He warned that one headed westward on the Moorefield Road toward North Mountain, while the other one, under Colonel William H. Boyd, went toward Front Royal and Chester Gap. Imboden interpreted the moves as an attempt to probe his flanks. The westward one especially interested him. Aware of the potential

43. *OR*, Vol. XXXVII, Pt. 1, pp. 414, 421.

44. Boreman to Sigel, April 29, 1864, Sigel Papers.

45. Weber to Sigel, May 1, 1864, Sigel Papers.

46. *OR*, Vol. XXXVII, Pt. 1, pp. 401–402; Sigel to Adjutant General, May 7, 1864, Sigel Papers; Franz Sigel, "Sigel in the Shenandoah Valley in 1864," *B&L*, IV, 488; William H. Beach, *The First New York (Lincoln) Cavalry* (New York, 1902), 345.

danger to McNeill, he wired Breckinridge that Sigel had detached "thirteen hundred Yankee cavalry" to intercept the raiders and that "McNeill's safety requires me to dash on his pursuers."[47] With two regiments and a section of artillery, he quietly headed west through "Devil's Hole" pass to intercept Higgins. Fearing informers might disclose his plan, he circulated rumors that he was moving his camp five or six miles toward North Mountain to secure better grazing land.[48]

Sigel's plan almost succeeded. At Moorefield, Higgins caught up with McNeill. The rangers had just left the town and were unaware of the approaching Federals. Unfortunately for Higgins, a sergeant in the advanced unit destroyed any element of surprise. Charging into the town, he fired on a remaining Southerner and sounded the alarm of their presence. McNeill moved rapidly to escape but had to wait for a lieutenant and eleven men posted on Toll Gate hill. As the galloping Federals charged, the rangers fired a volley, then hastily retreated by a different road. Riding tired horses, several Confederates fell captive to the Old Ringgold Cavalry. Initially, Higgins had intended to camp outside Moorefield, but after hearing that Imboden with "forty-five hundred men" was on his way to the town, he decided against it. Worried, he now started back toward Winchester by way of the gap at Lost River.[49]

There Imboden waited for his prey. Arriving before dawn, he prepared to ambush Higgins. As the Federals moved toward Wardensville, they ran into pickets. Not realizing Southern strength, the Ringgold troopers charged. After driving them in, suddenly they found Imboden's entire force lying in wait in a large field. Lieutenant Colonel Charles O'Ferrall and his 23rd Virginia Cavalry now charged. Overwhelmed, the Pennsylvanians hastily retreated on the Grassy Lick Road toward Romney. As Sergeant John W. Elwood vividly remembered, "Here began a ride for life."[50] The Pennsylvanians attempted to retard them with rear-guard skirmishes, but only their successful maneuvering under Captains James P. Hart and

47. OR, Vol. XXXVII, Pt. 1, p. 726.

48. *Ibid.*; Imboden, "Battle of New Market," 481; Roger U. Delauter, Jr., *18th Virginia Cavalry* (Lynchburg, 1985), 17.

49. Elwood, *Old Ringgold Cavalry,* 187–88; Ralph Haas, *Dear Esther: The Civil War Letters of Private Aungier Dobbs,* ed. Philip Ensley (Apollo, Pa., 1991), 208–209; Chauncey S. Norton, *"The Red Neck Ties"; or, History of the Fifteenth New York Volunteer Cavalry* (Ithaca, 1891), 32.

50. Elwood, *Old Ringgold Cavalry,* 89.

James Y. Chessrown saved them from capture. Within five miles of Romney, Imboden managed to get on Higgins' flank, then struck him with his
main column to drive him through Romney and across the Potomac River
at Green Spring. "Badly broken down," Higgins' force finally reached
Cumberland on the morning of May 12. Meanwhile, the Southerners
began moving back to the Valley.[51] By the time Higgins reached Cumberland late that night, Imboden rested in the Shenandoah. The following
morning, at Mount Jackson, Imboden wired Breckinridge, "I thrashed part
of three regiments cavalry in Hardy yesterday, ran them twenty-four miles,
killed 5, wounded a number, captured only 13, as they fled to the mountains."[52]

The disaster and rumors of another raid raised Federal concerns over
the security of central West Virginia. Incoming reports gave color to the
fears. Kelley hoped that Grant's and Sigel's movements would "frustrate
their plans," yet he took the precaution of sending a section of artillery to
Beverly. He also wired Captain Thayer Melvin, Sigel's assistant adjutant
general, of the necessity in securing more cavalry, stressing that "We must
kill, capture, or drive McNeill out of the country before we can expect
quiet or safety along line of road."[53] With a report that Imboden intended
to attack either Cumberland or New Creek, Kelley shifted his attention to
his own immediate security. Relaying the news of Higgins' rout to Sigel,
he indicated that with the arrival of the 134th Ohio Regiment he no
longer feared defending Cumberland, but unless one of the Ohio regiments arrived in time, New Creek was a different matter. Alarmed at that
point's vulnerability, he directed Colonel N. Wilkinson to "put your post
in order for defense at once, and defend it at all hazards." Nevertheless, he
reassured Sigel and the War Department that with the pending arrival of
the Ohio unit at New Creek, both points would be safe. Interestingly, he
asked for Grant's consideration in sending another expedition "toward
Moorefield to cut these marauders off."[54]

Kelley, reacting to Higgins' estimate of Imboden's force at between two

51. *OR*, Vol. XXXVII, Pt. 1, pp. 70–71, 421, 427–28, 430–31, 438; G. Julian Pratt to B.
Allison Colonna, Nov. 19, 1910, New Market Battle File, VMI; Higgins to Stahel, May 11,
1864, Sigel Papers; New York *Herald*, June 9, 1864; Norton, "*Red Neck Ties*," 32–33; Elwood, *Old Ringgold Cavalry*, 188–90; Haas, *Dear Esther*, 209–10.

52. *OR*, Vol. XXXVII, Pt. 1, p. 71.

53. *Ibid.*, 415.

54. *Ibid.*, 410, 414–15, 421, 424.

and three thousand, feared the Southerners might operate in the Romney area. In a wire to Halleck he cautioned that if that happened, the Confederates could not only cut the telegraph and railroad lines but would "have flanked General Sigel and got in his rear." Incoming intelligence soon lessened his fears for New Creek and Cumberland. Replying to an offer of aid from Weber at Harpers Ferry, Kelley struck a more confident mood. If he was not attacked the following morning, he wired Weber, the Southerners "will fall back or go round me and to west of the mountain into West Virginia." Any aid from him, he replied, would not arrive in time. With this new assessment, he asserted, "I think I can take care of myself." By the next day, Kelley knew the crisis was over. He informed Sigel of Southern withdrawal and the arrival of the Ohio regiments, assuring him that with their arrival and "some effective cavalry I can protect the road and your supplies." To Halleck he reported that all seemed to be quiet, the trains running as scheduled. [55]

The raid netted the Confederates a number of successes. McNeill not only destroyed important rail and government properties at Piedmont but successfully jolted Federal and state authorities. Worse, stung by the surprise and the effective loss of five hundred troopers, coupled with the detachment of three hundred troopers under Boyd, Sigel had substantially weakened the cavalry component of his main column as he began moving up the Valley. Increasingly, he ran the risk of being destroyed in detail, whereas Imboden's hope of disrupting Federal plans came to nothing. [56] The diversion principally gave Breckinridge time to consolidate his army at Staunton in his move to confront Sigel.

On his return to the Valley on May 11, Imboden found the Federals probing his picket lines, even dashing briefly into Mount Jackson. In his absence, both Colonel George H. Smith and Captain Davis had kept Breckinridge well informed. Davis' scouts had watched the enemy movements closely and probed their lines to establish troop strength. On May 10 Davis sounded the alarm that the Federals were on the move. He estimated their strength at seven regiments and fifteen hundred to two thousand cavalry, discounting most citizen reports—figures of ten thousand infantry—as hyperbole. On the following day he informed Breckinridge that the enemy was camped at Cedar Creek. The Valley narrowed there,

55. *Ibid.*, 428, 430–31, 438–39; Kelley to Sigel, May 12, 1864, Sigel Papers.
56. *OR*, Vol. XXXVII, Pt. 1, p. 732.

and Davis' scouts found it difficult to secure accurate intelligence since the Federals were using larger patrols. Worse, the weather obscured enemy positions from observation points on Massanutten Mountain.[57]

Imboden, fearful that Sigel would get in his rear, withdrew to within three miles of New Market on May 12. Despite the cavalry dash into Mount Jackson, he remained uncertain over Federal intentions. He took note of Boyd's column, then proceeding down Page Valley toward New Market, but was unsure of their objective. However, as he wired Breckinridge, "If he [Sigel] comes on I will fight him here." Almost as a postscript, the operator reported sighting Boyd's men as they crossed the top of the mountain. Later that day, Imboden learned that Federals had briefly occupied Mount Jackson. In relaying that intelligence to Breckinridge, he informed him that his advanced unit was at Rude's Hill. Provided the Federals did not bring up infantry or artillery, he proposed to make a stand there. If they did, he intended to retreat to Lacey Spring, which, he believed, offered the next best position to challenge any advance. Anxious, Imboden queried, "By what hour can I expect support here?"[58]

Unexpected aid arrived in the person of Major Harry W. Gilmor. As a dashing, romantic, and controversial partisan cavalry officer, Gilmor had captured the popular imagination, but his exploits seldom matched his publicity. Approaching Captain Davis, he informed him that he was ready to resume command of his 2nd Battalion Maryland Cavalry, then on picket duty. Gilmor, accused of allowing his men to commit criminal acts during a raid on the Baltimore and Ohio Railroad in February, had just stood trial in Staunton. Even though he was acquitted by court-martial, it technically remained for Lee to review the decision before releasing him from arrest. However, Breckinridge, after reviewing the court's decision, restored him to command. He directed Gilmor to report to Imboden with the charge to get into "Sigel's rear, harass his supply trains and outposts." Breckinridge wanted time.[59]

---

57. *Ibid.*, 727–29.

58. *Ibid.*, 731, 733; Imboden, "Battle of New Market," 481.

59. OR, XXXIII, 1252, and XXXVII, 729; Harry Gilmor, *Four Years in the Saddle* (New York, 1866), 146–47; W. W. Goldsborough, *The Maryland Line in the Confederate Army* (1869; rpr. Gaithersburg, Md., 1987), 244; Special Orders No. 105, May 5, 1864, War Department and Special Orders No. 48 and Special Orders No. 1, Headquarters Valley District, May 10, 1864, Harry Gilmor Papers, MHS. For an evaluation of Gilmor and his book, see Kevin Conley Ruffner, "'More Trouble Than a Brigade': Harry Gilmor's 2nd Maryland

Gilmor's arrival posed a dilemma for Captain Davis. Though he had his doubts about Gilmor's leadership ability, Davis was reluctant to lose Gilmor's forty men, since that would leave him with twenty-six, and none for picket duty. But the sudden appearance of the Federal cavalry challenging Davis' pickets between Mount Jackson and Edinburg made the dispute academic. Galvanized, Gilmor immediately formed his men, then defiantly ordered them to charge while Davis formed a line. The shock of the charging troopers forced the Federals to retire. On reaching their front line, Gilmor wheeled and, under fire from carbines, hastily retreated at full gallop. Immediately the New Yorkers picked up the pursuit, but suddenly they found themselves strung out along the road. At Hawkinstown, Gilmor ordered, "By fours, right about wheel, march—charge!" The pursuers wheeled as well, and the Southerners chased them for half a mile until they reached a small bridge. There Major Charles G. Otis re-formed his 21st New York Regiment, and a volley halted the Southerners. Even though Gilmor successfully extricated his men, he sustained a wound in the back from a well-placed shot by Otis. Within half a mile of Mount Jackson, the Federals decided to give up the chase.[60]

On the following day, May 12, despite suffering considerable discomfort, Gilmor attempted a more daring mission. Heeding Breckinridge's instructions to strike at Sigel's rear, he and his men moved through a mountain pass into Powell's Fort Valley, parallel to the Shenandoah and Page Valleys, to Caroline Furnace. There they stalked a detachment of some fifty men of the 20th Pennsylvania Cavalry carrying dispatches to Boyd, but they succeeded in capturing only eleven troopers. When he learned of Imboden's success in routing Boyd's men, Gilmor regarded it as pointless to continue. Withdrawing to Caroline Furnace on May 15, he met a courier carrying orders from Breckinridge for him to destroy the bridge over the North Branch of the Shenandoah River. Unfortunately, with the battle already under way and the distance too great, the opportunity for him to help trap Sigel's army was lost.[61]

At Winchester, Sigel, fearing that the Confederates might send a force through one of the several gaps in the Blue Ridge to strike at his rear or

Cavalry in the Shenandoah Valley," *Maryland Historical Magazine*, LXXXIX (1994), 399–402, 410n, and James I. Robertson, Jr., "The War in Words," *CWT* (1977), 48.

60. *OR*, Vol. XXXVII, Pt. 1, p. 729, and Vol. LI, Pt. 2, p. 853; Gilmor, *Four Years in Saddle*, 148–51.

61. Gilmor, *Four Years in Saddle*, 151–56.

left flank, sent Colonel Boyd at the head of a cavalry detachment to operate on the east side of the mountains to watch for any such attempt. Ultimately the unit was to join the main army at New Market. Moving northward on the evening of May 8, the colonel escorted a wagon train as far as
Bunker Hill on the Martinsburg Pike. Turning eastward, he proceeded to
Summit Point and then on to Berryville. On the following day, discovering that Mosby's rangers had just ambushed a Federal squad on its way to
the town, he sought to capture them. After a brief and unsuccessful skirmish, he continued on through Millwood and White Post and then across
the Blue Ridge at Ashby's Gap. At Paris they again clashed with Mosby's
rangers. After pursuing them through Upperville and Rectorstown, Boyd
decided to move back into the Valley through the Manassas Gap. By May
13 he was advancing up the Page Valley to Luray. That afternoon, from
Massanutten Mountain, Boyd could see New Market in the distance and
troop encampments below the town, while further up the Valley he saw a
wagon train moving with a herd of cattle. Mistakenly, he assumed that
they were Sigel's men. Unfortunately for Boyd, the Confederates also
spotted him. [62]

Aware of Boyd's movement up Page Valley, the Confederates observed
the Federals from Shirley's Hill. Imboden reacted quickly. He ordered the
23rd Virginia and 18th Virginia Cavalry regiments to mount for action.
He intended to bag them. Boyd, despite protests, refused to accept the
possibility that the troops he saw in the Valley might be Confederate.
Captain James Stevenson, leading the advance down the mountain, observed with his field glasses a large body of men moving toward New Market. He believed they were Southern and immediately informed the colonel. Boyd differed and ordered him to continue the descent. Soon
Stevenson saw cavalry and a section of artillery advancing toward the
mountain. Again he sent word to Boyd. The colonel still refused to believe they were Confederates and again he ordered Stevenson to proceed.
On reaching the base of the mountain, the New Yorkers ran into Imboden's pickets, dressed in Union uniforms, at the bridge crossing Smith's
Creek. Boyd, bewildered by the news, assumed again that they were

62. James H. Stevenson, *"Boots and Saddles"*: *A History of the First Volunteer Cavalry of
the War* (Harrisburg, 1879), 260–64; Beach, *First New York (Lincoln) Cavalry*, 322–23; William P. Buck, ed., *Sad Earth, Sweet Heaven: The Diary of Rebecca Buck* (Birmingham, 1973),
253; Sigel, "Sigel in Shenandoah," 488; Imboden, "Battle of New Market," 481.

merely Sigel's men, uninformed of Boyd's possible appearance. Stevenson, however, sent a squad to force the pickets back. As the Southerners withdrew toward New Market without firing, the Federals conferred. Boyd decided to cross the bridge and then move downstream to get into the rear of the column observed from the mountain. If the body were Southerners, he reasoned, they could retreat down the Valley. But no sooner had Boyd's cavalry begun moving across the bridge than Imboden sprang his trap.[63]

The continuing advance of Boyd's men had surprised the Confederates. Colonel O'Ferrall of the 23rd Virginia, who watched as they persisted in approaching "the very jaws of our brigade," rightly suspected that they mistook them for Federals. Delighted, the Virginians "prepared to bag them."[64] With a two-to-one advantage, Imboden fully expected to crush them in the trap. As Boyd's men crossed the bridge and turned north along the creek, suddenly the 23rd Virginia appeared on a bluff overlooking the stream. Giving the "rebel yell," they fired a volley into them. The New Yorkers returned the fire, but as Stevenson noted, "the contest was unequal."[65] Soon they discovered the 18th Virginia moving to attack their flank. Boyd desperately attempted to open up a gap in a fence in his rear for an escape, but the shelling by the two guns of McClanahan's battery and the severity of the fire from the bluff broke the New Yorkers. Routed, they fled toward the mountainside. Adding to the chaos, a heavy downpour made climbing slippery slopes difficult at the very least. Others with better luck dashed down a road alongside the mountain. Boyd and Stevenson escaped, but Federal losses in terms of killed, wounded, and missing totaled over a hundred. Captain George Chrisman with his Rockingham Reserves rounded up some seventeen prisoners, and Lieutenant J. N. Potts gladly exchanged his "badly jaded" horse for a "splendid" new one.[66] Imboden wired Breckinridge that "we pitched into him, cut him off from the roads, and drove him into the Massanutten Mountain."[67] For Sigel the rout became the second disaster in less than a week. Boyd's deba-

63. OR, Vol. XXXVII, Pt. 1, p. 733; Stevenson, *"Boots and Saddles,"* 265; Beach, *First New York Cavalry*, 324, 331; Charles T. O'Ferrall, *Forty Years of Active Service* (New York, 1904), 94; Davis, *New Market*, 68–69; Delauter, *18th Virginia Cavalry*, 18.

64. O'Ferrall, *Forty Years of Service*, 94.

65. Stevenson, *"Boots and Saddles,"* 265–66.

66. J. N. Potts, "Who Fired the First Gun at New Market?" CV, XVII (1909), 453.

67. OR, Vol. XXXVII, Pt. 1, p. 73.

cle now added a loss of three hundred to Higgins' five hundred without succeeding in protecting Sigel's flanks. Imboden had reduced the Federal cavalry by a third with little loss to his own.[68]

In Staunton the news brought welcome relief from the disquieting dispatches coming from the southwest. No sooner had Breckinridge reached the town than he learned of Jenkins' defeat at Cloyds Mountain and the destruction of the New River bridge, accentuating his anxiety over his limited resources. Replying to McCausland's request for reinforcements, he tersely responded that he "can send no aid." McCausland's warning of his inability to thwart Crook brought additional pressure from Richmond. A worried War Department, notifying Stringfellow that neither instructions nor reinforcements could be sent, advised that McCausland "is best acquainted with the necessities of his case and must act according to his best judgment." Lee, learning the news on the following day, wired Breckinridge that "it may be necessary for you to return to protect Lynchburg, &c." Wisely, he left the decision up to the general: "You must judge."[69]

Meanwhile, pressure in the east intensified the need for additional forces there to fend off the Union offensive. Alarmed over the threat to Drewry's Bluff, Davis asked Lee if it would not be wise "to call Breckinridge and Imboden to you." For Davis it seemed that "affairs are critical."[70] Referring to Breckinridge's request for reinforcements, Lee reminded Davis that his withdrawal would leave "no opposition to Sigel" in western Virginia.[71] Lee wired Breckinridge, "If you can drive back the different expeditions threatening the Valley it would be very desirable for you to join me with your whole force."[72]

A warning from Robert Preston in Salem to an already apprehensive

68. Harrisonburg (Va.) *Rockingham Register*, May 20, 1864, in Lynchburg *Virginian*, May 23, 1864, and John W. Wayland, *A History of Shenandoah County, Virginia* (Strasburg, Va., 1969), 315–16; Stevenson, "*Boots and Saddles*," 265–70; Beach, *First New York Cavalry*, 324–27; Pratt to Colonna, Nov. 19, 1910, New Market Battle File; O'Ferrall, *Forty Years of Service*, 94–95; Lincoln, *Thirty-fourth Massachusetts*, 277–78; Eby, ed., *Virginia Yankee*, 224; T. H. Neilson, "The Sixty-Second Virginia—New Market," *CV*, XVI (1908), 60; Davis, *New Market*, 68–70.

69. *OR*, Vol. XXXVII, Pt. 1, pp. 727–28.

70. *Ibid.*, Vol. LI, Pt. 2, p. 929.

71. Dowdey and Manarin, eds., *Papers of Lee*, 730.

72. *OR*, Vol. XXXVII, Pt. 1, p. 735.

War Department heightened the alarm. Preston wired that "unless re-enforcements are sent Colonel McCausland at once, the Virginia and Tennessee road from Dublin to Lynchburg is at the mercy of the enemy."[73] Bragg immediately ordered General Samuel Cooper to direct Breckinridge, subject to contrary instructions from Lee, to send a brigade to Lynchburg to protect that point and to join McCausland in protecting the railroad. However, Breckinridge on the very same day wired Bragg that he intended to move down the Valley. On receiving Bragg's order, he strongly objected to it. He replied that Crook no longer threatened Lynchburg and that he expected "to meet enemy in this valley to-day or to-morrow." As to sending the brigade, he protested that "further division of my small force might endanger both Staunton and Lynchburg." Besides, he added, "My orders from General Lee give me discretion." However, he indicated that he would wait two or three hours to hear from Bragg before beginning his move. Without directly addressing the issue, Bragg capitulated and merely informed him that with Butler then attacking Drewry's Bluff, with Grant's cavalry operating on the north side of the James River, and with the railroads cut leading out of Richmond, sending any reinforcements for McCausland was impossible. Instead, he advised Breckinridge that "the forces in Western Virginia and East Tennessee must provide for any emergency there."[74] Interpreting the dispatch in accord with his own plans, Breckinridge responded, "I feel authorized to continue down the Valley," since "the distance from here to Southwest Virginia is too great to return now." He assured Bragg, "If I meet enemy, I will engage him—if he crosses Blue Ridge will try to thwart him."[75]

News coming from the lower Shenandoah was equally disquieting. On May 10, Davis had wired Breckinridge, "Sigel's whole force on the move up the Valley." Reports soon poured into Breckinridge's headquarters. Fortunately, the news coming from Stringfellow relieved Davis' concern over the crisis in the southwest. On May 11 he had cautioned Breckinridge that Federal cavalry occupied Christiansburg; if they advanced on Salem, he warned, they "intended to co-operate with Sigel and against you." Two days later, more optimistically, Stringfellow reported their movement

73. *Ibid.*, 731.
74. *Ibid.*, 732–35.
75. *Ibid.*, Vol. LI, Pt. 2, p. 932.

toward Newport but added that "their ultimate object [is], I think, unde-
veloped." But to Breckinridge, their route meant one thing, back into
West Virginia, and with that the end of the immediate threat there. He
quickly advised the War Department that the Federals were "not advancing toward Lynchburg." Further reports on the morning of May 15 confirmed his judgment.[76]

With his troops rapidly concentrating in Staunton, Breckinridge allowed them a day of rest while he waited for the arrival of the VMI cadets.
Wharton's men relaxed and prepared two days of cooked rations.[77] The
cadets, marching eighteen miles on a dusty road, made excellent time on
the first day. However, the mild weather suddenly changed that night.
Rain turned the roads into a sea of mud, and as Cadet Beverly Standard
complained to his parents, "We had to wade through like *hogs.*"[78] The cadets cockily marched into Staunton to the popular song "The Girl I Left
Behind Me." They became the toast of the town and the envy of veterans.
As Cadet John Wise remembered, the "whole population" turned out to
watch their dress parade. Citizens showered invitations on them to visit
families and attend parties in their honor. Their adoration by the town's
young ladies created considerable resentment among veteran officers, who
"could not and would not understand why girls preferred these little un-
titled whipper-snappers to officers of distinction." In retaliation, veterans
struck up "Rock-a-Bye Baby" as they marched by. Soldiers, cuddling their
guns in a rocking fashion, broke into "a perfect roar of amusement."[79]

Breckinridge's assembled army—a combination of veteran brigades, reserves, cadets with a section of artillery, a small company of engineers, and
two batteries—totaled almost 4,250. At New Market he would augment
his numbers with Imboden's force for a total army of 5,335 and eighteen
guns to challenge Sigel's considerably larger army.[80] Because they were
outnumbered, everyone assumed that Breckinridge would wait for the Federals to advance on Staunton. Entrenched behind breastworks, their defensive positions might well offset superior numbers. Instead, a determined

76. *Ibid.*, Vol. XXXVII, Pt. 1, pp. 731, 733–37, and Vol. LI, Pt. 2, p. 928.
77. Mastin Diary, May 12, 1864.
78. Barrett and Turner, eds., *Letters of a New Market Cadet*, 61.
79. Wise, *End of an Era*, 289–90; Wise, "West Point of the Confederacy," 465.
80. Davis, *New Market*, 53–54, 193–97.

Breckinridge preferred to confront rather than remain on the defensive. [81]
He ordered his men to cook two days' rations preparatory to taking up the
march at daybreak on the morning of May 13. Despite heavy rain, they
covered twenty miles on their first day. By the following day his troops
reached Lacey Spring, ten miles south of New Market. There a dispatch
from Imboden informed him of the Federal cavalry "hovering about me all
day yesterday." Prisoners, he reported, indicated that Sigel intended to resume the march from Woodstock on the morning of May 13. Poor weather
conditions obscured Federal activity from his signal corps on Massanutten
Mountain, and observers could not verify any of their movements. [82]

Initially, Imboden, believing that Sigel would not advance until the situation in Hampshire County clarified, concluded that the enemy "has
fallen back." [83] On learning that Breckinridge would reach Lacey Spring
on the afternoon of May 14, he hurriedly rode to see the general at his
headquarters. Aware of Sigel's cautious approach, Imboden believed that
he would not attempt to go beyond Meem's Bottom or Rude's Hill. But
the sudden and unexpected arrival of a courier shattered that assumption.
Interrupting their dinner, the messenger reported the presence of Major
Timothy Quinn with six hundred troopers at Rude's Hill. He further told
them that the Federals were vigorously pushing back his brother's 18th
Virginia, while Smith was attempting to form a line to cover their retreat.
Sounds of cannon fire in the distance underscored the urgency of the situation. With instructions to hold New Market at all costs until night and
then to fall back to Shirley's Hill, Imboden dashed off to his brigade. A
determined Breckinridge now prepared to confront his adversary the next
morning before Sigel could learn of his presence. [84]

On reaching New Market, Imboden found Smith well positioned and
his thinly spread line still holding the town. The line, stretching from a

81. Johnston, *Kentucky*, 186; Basil W. Duke, *Reminiscences of General Basil W. Duke,*
C.S.A. (New York, 1911), 183; Edward Raymond Turner, *The New Market Campaign, May*
1864 (Richmond, 1912), 20; Davis, *New Market*, 55.

82. General Orders No. 1, May 12, 1864, J. Stoddard Johnston Papers, MC; Circular,
May 12, 1864, Clarke Papers, MHS; OR, Vol. XXXVII, Pt. 1, p. 735; Mastin Diary, May
13–14, 1864.

83. OR, Vol. XXXVII, Pt. 1, pp. 732–33, 735.

84. Johnston, "Sketches of Breckinridge," 259; J. D. Imboden, "Battle of New Market,"
482; Davis, *New Market*, 73–74; Abbot, "General John D. Imboden," 112–13.

hillside on the west and extending across the turnpike toward Smith's Creek, created an appearance of greater numbers. The 18th and 23rd Virginia Regiments occupied the town and the area on the right, while the 62nd Virginia held the west. A forest concealed the extreme right, while McClanahan's battery anchored the left on a hill from which it could sweep the town and put the Federal artillery, occupying a lower elevation, at a disadvantage. As Quinn's New Yorkers reached the outskirts of New Market by 5 P.M., the batteries of Captains Chatham T. Ewing and Alonzo Snow also came up. A section of Ewing's guns, discovering a Southern attempt to screen a gun in an advanced position on the pike, moved to an elevated rise, fired on the piece, and forced the gunners back. Colonel John Wynkoop ordered his troopers to charge. They gained some ground, and skirmishing continued for more than two hours while frightened residents sought the safety of their basements. The arrival of Colonel Moor's infantry provided Wynkoop with additional support. Imboden, remembering his instructions, began pulling his men out of the town.[85]

Breckinridge hoped to goad the Federals into continuing to attack. He wanted to lure them south of New Market to a stronger position where he could then give battle. Imboden, satisfied in viewing the Federals from Shirley's Hill that the enemy had little chance of dislodging him that night, continued to harass Moor's men. At 8 P.M. he renewed the attack, only to retire. An hour later he sent a dispatch to Breckinridge that the Federals occupied New Market. Then at 10 P.M. he launched another probe, but the 1st West Virginia, with "every man clutching his rifle," was ready. As the Southerners approached, they rose to their knees and "poured a deadly volley" into the Confederates, who retired for the final time. The lack of a counterattack reassured Imboden of his security for the night. However, it also meant that Moor had refused to take the bait. Sporadic firing continued until 11 P.M., while Imboden, under the security of darkness and continuing rain, withdrew his troops south of Shirley's Hill.[86]

At Woodstock the news of the skirmishing greatly encouraged Sigel,

85. Lang, *Loyal West Virginia*, 112–13; Lincoln, *Thirty-fourth Massachusetts*, 278–79; J. D. Imboden, "Battle of New Market," 482; Davis, *New Market*, 75–76; Jasper W. Harris, "Sixty-Second Virginia at New Market," *CV*, XVI (1908), 461.

86. Wheeling *Daily Intelligencer*, May 23, 1864; Turner, *New Market*, 24–25; Davis, *New Market*, 77; J. D. Imboden, "Battle of New Market," 482; Wise, *Virginia Military Institute*, 299–300.

while at Lacey Spring, Breckinridge, unaware of the capture of his dispatches, believed that the element of surprise would be his the next morning. Determined, he ordered the army to move at 1 A.M. For Imboden it would be a short night. Awakened two hours before daybreak, he learned that Breckinridge's troops would arrive before sunrise. Using Imboden's men as a screen, Breckinridge prepared to confront Sigel.[87]

87. Beach, *First New York Cavalry*, 349; Davis, *New Market*, 78; Wise, *End of an Era*, 292–93; Edward Raymond Turner, "The Battle of New Market," CV, XX (1912), 72; Wise, "West Point of Confederacy," 466.

4

Valley of Humiliation

Enthusiasm ran high among Sigel's troops as they left Martinsburg on April 29 and marched up the dusty pike toward Winchester. Spring was much in evidence, and as the weather warmed, soldiers gladly discarded their overcoats and other items to lighten their load. Overall the troops exuded confidence in Sigel and his generals, yet reservations tempered the mood of a number of officers. "Fearing some disaster," Colonel Strother left his notebook with his wife and took only a small one with him.[1] Lieutenant Colonel William S. Lincoln of the 34th Massachusetts believed that "Sigel, with his present force, will be lucky indeed if he does not have to 'get out of this.'" He also doubted the army's fighting ability. Aside from the 54th Pennsylvania, which he regarded as fair, and the 12th West Virginia, which he considered "pretty good," Lincoln rated the troops as "barely passable."[2] Men of the 18th Connecticut predicted pessimistically, "We shan't get farther than Fisher's Hill, for a thousand men at that point will stop our whole force."[3]

Before leaving Martinsburg, Sigel received a dispatch from the general-in-chief. Grant, worried over rumors of an attempted Southern movement down the Valley, directed Sigel to collect intelligence on any such activ-

---

1. Hewitt, *Twelfth West Virginia,* 110; Eby, ed., *Virginia Yankee,* 221.

2. Lincoln, *Thirty-fourth Massachusetts,* 260–61.

3. William C. Walker, *History of the Eighteenth Regiment Connecticut Volunteers in the War for the Union* (Norwich, Conn., 1885), 210–11.

ity and keep him informed. Initial concern focused primarily on the location of Longstreet's corps, which Sigel feared might slip through Thornton Gap and enter Page Valley at Luray. From there they could strike at Front Royal or move into the Shenandoah Valley. Incoming reports generated additional anxiety. One refugee placed Longstreet at Sperryville or Luray, another at Wolftown. Some suggested that General Thomas Rosser was moving down the Valley. Exasperated, Sigel wrote Grant about the difficulty in securing accurate intelligence, complaining that the "cavalry here is in wretched condition, and can hardly protect my scouting parties." But with the discrediting of rumors, Sigel became more optimistic and wired Grant from Bunker Hill on April 30 that there were no Confederate forces of consequence north of Cedar Creek, nor any indications of a movement down the Valley. Longstreet was not at Luray. Sigel believed that no formidable force existed in the Valley. With a new sense of confidence, he informed Grant that "we will occupy Winchester to-day . . . and push our advance toward Cedar Creek." Yet he cautiously sent scouting parties in various directions to keep track of the enemy.[4]

Having rested overnight at Bunker Hill, Sigel continued the march toward Winchester. As the army approached the town, the countryside gave increasing evidence of the ravages of three years of warfare. Strother was struck by the number of "graves, bones, and dead animals."[5] Farmland lacked fences and livestock, and "it seemed as if the country was deserted by its inhabitants."[6] Entering the town, Sigel and his staff were impressed with the visible "destructiveness and paralyzing effects of the war." Dr. Neil observed that "one thinks of an eternal Sunday, as he wanders through her lonely streets and beholds ruined walls, tenantless houses, demolished churches." For him the scene provided a marked contrast with the town's reputation of "shaded avenues, princely mansions and handsome flower-gardens, the home of the aristocratic and wealthy."[7]

The Federal presence delighted Unionists, and the Union flag flew from a number of windows. Even a few waving handkerchiefs greeted the

---

4. OR, XXXIII, 997–98, 1006, 1014, 1022–23, 1025–26, and Vol. XXXVII, Pt. 1, pp. 363–64; John McEntie to Weber, April 26, 1864, B. G. to Melvin, April 27, 1864, Weber to Melvin, April 27, 1864, G. Putman to Weber, April 29, 1864, Weber to Sigel, April 28, 29, 1864, Sigel to Stahel, May 1, 1864, Sigel Papers.

5. Eby, ed., *Virginia Yankee*, 221.

6. Hewitt, *Twelfth West Virginia*, 104.

7. Eby, ed., *Virginia Yankee*, 221; Neil to Parents, May 5, 1864, Neil Letters.

troops. For Lieutenant Colonel Thomas F. Wildes of the 116th Ohio, the display demonstrated more patriotic feeling "than we had ever observed before." Strother agreed, noticing that "the feeling against Yankees is much modified in Winchester since Banks' first entry in 1862." Blacks were "greatly delighted to see the yankees once more."[8] Winchester resident Julia Chase was glad to be "once more under the protection of the Stars and Stripes."[9] As the 116th Ohio marched through town, Willie McFielly, the colonel's boy, led with a "marker." One excited lady called out, "That's right, little boy, raise it up high, clear up, and let everybody see it."[10]

Others noticed that "more often, scowling faces, *not always bearded,* could be seen looking from behind half closed doors."[11] To William Patterson they looked "bitter and black enough, rebel men bit their lips and hold their places."[12] Mrs. Hugh Lee, like other Southern ladies, stayed indoors, where she confided to her diary that "I did not see them, never going one inch out of my way to see an army of occupation, though I would walk miles to see them chased through the Valley, as they will be in a few weeks." She initially felt no fear about the Federals' presence, though she was anxious about their retreat. "Then may God protect us, for we will be at the mercy of a merciless foe." But her optimism radically changed the next morning, when she found that "the work of deviltry has already commenced."[13]

Winchester, a frequent battleground during the previous two years, served as the county seat of Frederick County. Prior to the war it thrived as a commercial center and transportation hub for the lower Valley. Shops, taverns, and the Taylor Hotel lined the main street. A striking Greek Revival courthouse with its columned portico dominated the center of town and symbolized its prosperity. Roads radiated out from its tree-

8. Elizabeth Davis Swiger, ed., *Civil War Letters and Diary of Joshua Winters* (Parsons, W. Va., 1991), 105–106; Eby, ed., *Virginia Yankee,* 223; Thomas F. Wildes, *Record of the One Hundred and Sixteenth Regiment Ohio Infantry Volunteers in the War of Rebellion* (Sandusky, Ohio, 1884), 83; Lincoln, *Thirty-fourth Massachusetts,* 260; C. J. Rawling, *History of the First Regiment, Virginia Infantry* (Philadelphia, 1887), 163; Walker, *Eighteenth Regiment Connecticut,* 215.

9. War Time Diary of Miss Julia Chase, 1861–1864, May 1, 1864, W-FCHS.

10. Wildes, *One Hundred and Sixteenth Ohio,* 83.

11. Frank S. Reader Diary, May 1, 1864, W&L.

12. Diary of William Patterson, May 1, 1864, SHC.

13. Mrs. Hugh Lee Diary, May 1, 1864, Mrs. Hugh Lee Collection, W-FCHS.

lined streets in all directions. The macadamized Valley Pike linked Winchester with the towns up the Shenandoah Valley, while the Winchester and Potomac Railroad, destroyed in the first year of the war, connected the town with the main line of the Baltimore and Ohio Railroad at Harpers Ferry. Because of its location, the town held considerable military importance. A Federal army occupying that point secured a number of advantages. Its presence not only safeguarded the railroad from attack but protected Washington's right flank as well. A Union army there also invariably posed a potential threat to Staunton and the important Virginia Central Railroad, some one hundred miles up the Valley. Conversely, a Confederate force controlling the town could raid the Baltimore and Ohio, advance into western Maryland and southern Pennsylvania, or even strike at Washington.

On the eve of the Civil War, Winchester, the largest urban center in the Valley, boasted a population of 3,004 whites, 680 free blacks, and 708 slaves, a total of 4,392 residents. Only Martinsburg, twenty miles to the north, with a population of 3,364, and Staunton, with 3,875, could challenge the town for size. During the secession crisis, Unionist sentiment dominated the area. Citizens adopted pro-Union resolutions and overwhelmingly elected like-minded delegates to attend the convention in Richmond. But in the aftermath of the firing upon Fort Sumter and the secession of Virginia, public sentiment radically changed. Loyalty to their state now dominated the region. Yet not all Unionist feeling vanished. Winchester's residents would pay a heavy price for their divided loyalties, and would suffer the ravages of warfare from the town's constant changing of hands between the two belligerents.[14]

Pronounced hostility marked the attitude of the town's Southern element toward "Yankees," who learned to repay it in kind. Prior to Sigel's arrival, two incidents in particular had intensified those antagonisms and set the tone for the May occupation. On April 24, a scouting party of the 21st New York Cavalry had passed through Winchester on their way to Middletown, and Captain Davis and his Maryland battalion waited to trap them. However, the New Yorkers discovered Davis' men and hastily retreated, the Marylanders chasing them back into Winchester. The Federal

14. Frederic Morton, *The Story of Winchester* (Strasburg, Va., 1925), 146–49; Garland R. Quarles, *Occupied Winchester, 1861–1865* (Winchester, Va., 1991), 2–4; Roger U. Delauter, Jr., *Winchester in the Civil War* (Lynchburg, 1992), 2; *Population of the United States in 1860: The Eighth Census* (Washington, D.C., 1864), 519–20.

troopers attempted to hide in Union homes, but their pursuers hounded them out. [15] Kate Sperry noted, "It was gay to see how we *secesh girls waved* and how the *Union girls raved* when our men went in their houses and hauled out several Yankees." [16] Julia Chase confided to her diary, "But, oh it was so humiliating and mortifying to see how badly our Troops manage things. . . . Shall the Unionists ever have good occasion to rejoice to see their army successful." [17]

Four days later, another incident further inflamed tensions. A Federal trooper's horse gave out as his unit moved up the Valley, so he asked permission to return to Martinsburg with a party taking some wounded there. But before he could leave Winchester, a boy surprised him on Loudoun Street and demanded his surrender. When the trooper refused, the boy shot him twice, took his horse and arms, and then fled. Major Quinn, assuming it was a case of "bushwhacking," ordered the arrest of the boy's father. With the father absent, he detained three citizens instead, but on discovering the full account of the shooting he paroled them as security. [18] An angry Julia Chase wanted more "vigorous measures" and lashed out at the decision, believing that "the boy's father should have been hunted up, if not found the house burned to the ground." [19] Some Union soldiers agreed. Several troopers set fire to the house. Only the pleas of the mother saved it from destruction. Disgusted with the "Secesh" element, Chase wrote that "some of the Secession girls and women were rejoicing over it, crying out—how brave. What a cool thing. May the Lord have mercy on these people." [20]

Such mutual antagonism became even more evident with the army's arrival. At his headquarters at Hollingsworth's Mill, Sigel attracted a curious crowd of country people wanting to see the new general. Annoyed, he asked them who they were. On hearing their reply, he threatened to arrest them "if they did not immediately disperse." [21] The following day, a fire

15. Thomas B. Gatch, "Recollections of New Market," CV, XXXIV (1926), 211; Mrs. Hugh Lee Diary, April 27, 1864; *American*, May 4, 1864; John C. Bonnell, Jr., *Sabres in the Shenandoah: The 21st New York Cavalry, 1863–1866* (Shippensburg, Pa., 1996), 33.

16. Kate S. Sperry, "'Surrender? Never Surrender!': The Diary of a Confederate Girl," transcribed by Lenoir Hunt, April 24, 1864, W-FCHS.

17. Chase Diary, 73.

18. Mrs. Hugh Lee Diary, April 30, 1864.

19. Chase Diary, 74–75.

20. *Ibid.*, 75.

21. Lang, *Loyal West Virginia*, 111; Eby, ed., *Virginia Yankee*, 221.

destroyed two large houses in the center of town. Even though soldiers co-operated with citizens in extinguishing it, many residents suspected that it had been set in retaliation for the shooting incident. "If they keep on," wrote Kate Sperry, "we wont even have a little piece of town left." [22] Sigel also imposed strict restraints on movements into or out of the town. Food-stuffs and wood, already in short supply, became even more scarce. Kate Sperry wrote, "Old Seigel [sic] is worse than Milroy, considering the short time he has been here—not a soul has been permitted to leave town or one citizen to come in." [23]

The Federals stayed in Winchester for over a week, their stay marked by drills, dress parades, and mock battles. Sigel delighted in watching the men parade to a cacophony of bands making a "terrible noise." A mock battle proved more chaotic than the grand parade at Martinsburg. With many of Sigel's staff unable to communicate well in English, and with few of his colonels knowing "anything at all about brigade drill," the various maneuvers became confused. Colonel Lincoln watched in horror, feeling fortunate that "this was playing war! and the guns unshotted! as otherwise our loss would have been fearful." [24] The poorly managed exercises dam-aged the prestige of Sigel and his staff among the troops. Colonel Wildes recalled, "There was never anything seen half so ridiculous, and it bred in everyone the most supreme contempt for General Sigel and his crowd of foreign adventurers." [25]

Never one to act recklessly, Sigel became increasingly cautious at Win-chester. At Bunker Hill he had assured Grant that he would push toward Cedar Creek—hardly a serious penetration up the Valley. But after reach-ing Winchester, and despite Grant's previous instructions for him to threaten Staunton, he asked the general to clarify his expectations. With

22. Sperry Diary, May 2, 1864; Patterson Diary, May 2, 1864; Eby, ed., *Virginia Yankee*, 223.

23. Sperry Diary, May 7, 1864; Patterson Diary, May 6, 1864; "Life in Winchester De-scribed by N.Y. Herald Correspondent," in *Valley News Echo: Monthly Civil War Newspapers* (Hagerstown, Md., 1965), V, no. 5, 2.

24. Lincoln, *Thirty-fourth Massachusetts*, 263; Circular, April 30, 1864, Sigel Papers; Diary of William M. Goudy, May 3–7, 1864, Civil War Diaries Collection, WVU; Reader Diary, May 5, 1864; Charles H. Lynch, *The Civil War Diary, 1862–1865, of Charles H. Lynch, 18th Conn. Vols.* (N.p., 1915), 57; Charles W. Bennett, Jr., ed., *"Four Years with the Fifty-Fourth": The Military History of Franklin Bennett, 54th Pennsylvania Volunteer Regiment, 1861–1865* (Richmond, 1985), 29.

25. Wildes, *One Hundred and Sixteenth Ohio*, 85.

his present troops, Sigel asserted, he could not advance beyond Strasburg without posting a sizable force at Front Royal to protect his left flank, rear, and lines of communication. If his army was "to make energetic and decisive movements," he would need an additional five thousand men. Yet, as he informed Grant, he was not asking for more troops but merely stating "how things are and appear to me."[26]

Grant replied that he did not want Sigel to go beyond Cedar Creek. He cautioned him to watch out for any attempted Southern movement down the Valley. Yet he reminded Sigel of his own modified plan, in which Crook contemplated advancing from West Virginia toward Lynchburg and then returning to Staunton. "Then you would want to meet them with train loaded with supplies." He reassured Sigel that additional reinforcements could be sent to him "should the enemy move down the Valley." Yet Grant wanted more. In a wire to Halleck on May 17, before he learned of the outcome at New Market, an exasperated Grant asked, "Cannot Gen'l Sigel go up Shenandoah Valley to Staunton?" Since the town was an important Southern depot, Sigel's destruction of the railroad there would be "of vast importance to us."[27] Sigel's May 2 dispatch to Weber at Harpers Ferry underscored his timidity. The army, he confided, would continue its advance up the Valley, or would remain at Winchester "if the force of the enemy are not far superior to mine." More telling, he outlined to Weber his arrangements for a possible retreat.[28]

Sigel did have cause for worry. Mrs. Lee of Winchester aptly summed up his conundrum: "I do not see how Siegel [*sic*] can carry his army up the Valley when he can scarcely protect his wagon trains, between Martinsburgh & Winchester."[29] Rumors of partisan activity circulated widely.[30] The vulnerability of Sigel's supply line troubled him. Mosby's, McNeill's, and Gilmor's rangers, as well as bushwhackers, continually preyed on the trains.

In late April, Stuart had directed Mosby to communicate with Imboden and possibly cooperate with him.[31] Lieutenant Colonel John S. Mosby, the most renowned and feared of the partisans, operated mainly in

---

26. OR, Vol. XXXIII, 901, and Vol. XXXVII, Pt. 1, pp. 363–64, 368–70;
27. *Ibid.*, Vol. XXXVII, Pt. 1, pp. 369, 475.
28. *Ibid.*, 369–70; Sigel to Weber, May 2, 1864, Sigel Papers.
29. Mrs. Hugh Lee Diary, May 7, 1864.
30. Chase Diary, May 11, 13, 1864.
31. "Field Letters from Stuart's Headquarters," *SHSP*, III (1877), 194.

the Piedmont region but occasionally ranged widely. He had organized his rangers—officially, the 43rd Battalion of Virginia Cavalry—in June 1863 under a law passed by the Confederate Congress in April 1862. Holding the unconventional belief that an enemy's most vulnerable point was its rear, Mosby theorized that "a small force moving with celerity and threatening many points on a line can neutralize a hundred times its own number."[32] Federal authorities decried such attacks as guerrilla warfare. Confederate authorities, despite uneasiness over the charges and the nature of Mosby's tactics, supported and continued to authorize the battalion. Technically, the 43rd Battalion, a part of the Army of Northern Virginia, operated under the command of Stuart and Lee primarily in a region of some 125 square miles centering on Loudoun and Fauquier Counties, east of the Blue Ridge Mountains. In the spring of 1864, with Grant's army operating against Lee's in eastern Virginia and Sigel's force moving up the Valley, the new configuration forced Mosby to spread his rangers thin to exploit points of vulnerability. As ranger James Williamson summed it up, this arrangement "gave us plenty of work."[33] Mosby divided his command into two components, with two companies operating in the Valley and the other two remaining east of the Blue Ridge. By attacking supply lines in the Valley, he wanted to force Sigel to detach men to protect his rear.[34]

Sigel learned the boldness of Mosby on the very day he entered Winchester. With ten men, the ranger captured eight wagons north of Darkesville, some fifteen miles north of Winchester. Stung by his audaciousness, Sigel directed Colonel Robert S. Rogers, commanding the post at Martinsburg, not to dispatch any trains without a proper escort. If Rogers was unable to provide adequate guards, then Sigel would. Rogers, painfully aware of his vulnerability, complained of his inadequate force. Two days later he reiterated his complaint. "At present," he warned, "it is not impossible for men to come into the post in small parties and in disguise." That very night, Mosby with twenty men stealthily proved his point, capturing and carrying off fifteen horses and several prisoners.[35]

32. John S. Mosby, "A Bit of Partisan Service," *B&L*, III, 148.

33. James J. Williamson, *Mosby's Rangers* (New York, 1909), 148.

34. *OR*, XXXIII, 1081, 1113, 1252, 1307; Williamson, *Mosby's Rangers*, 148–49, 165; Jeffry D. Wert, *Mosby's Rangers* (New York, 1990), 34–35, 160.

35. *OR*, Vol. XXXVII, Pt. 1, pp. 2–3, 371–72, 378, 386; Williamson, *Mosby's Rangers*, 413; John S. Mosby, *The Memoirs of Colonel John S. Mosby*, ed. Charles Wells Russell (1917; rpr. Bloomington, 1959), 272–73; Swiger, ed., *Letters and Diary of Winters*, 105; Mrs. Hugh Lee Diary, May 5, 1864.

Alarmed by the raid, Sigel took extra precautions at Winchester to prevent similar embarrassments there. He detailed five companies to guard various roads and strengthened his pickets, ordering them to fire on anyone approaching them at night. A third of the army remained on standby duty all night in case of an emergency. Sigel even attempted to spread rumors of troop movements to make potential attackers more wary. He sent a cavalry company to Bunker Hill to patrol and escort trains from that point on into Winchester. However, the security of Martinsburg and Winchester against an attack was not Sigel's chief concern. With the army on the move to Cedar Creek, Captains Adolphus E. "Dolly" Richards and William H. Chapman of Mosby's command were harassing his supply line. Near Newtown, Richards boldly attempted the capture of a well-guarded train on May 10, while Chapman's men attacked a scouting party of the 1st New York Cavalry.[36]

The rangers' boldness along the open stretches of road on the Valley Pike had a chilling effect on Sigel. On May 13, Chapman's men assailed a train at Fisher's Hill. The following morning the rangers struck another guarded train as it ascended Fisher's Hill. On the same day, bushwhackers struck another train moving from Martinsburg, first between Bunker Hill and Winchester and then again between Winchester and Middletown. The frequent attacks not only made Sigel more cautious but also accomplished Mosby's objective in forcing him to detach "a heavy force to guard their communications." By the time Sigel approached Woodstock on May 13, he had grown decidedly more defensive as a result of McNeill's raid on Piedmont, Chapman's operations, and harassment by bushwhackers.[37]

On May 8, Sigel had informed Grant of his intent to advance from Winchester. He expected to establish contact with Crook, who he believed would be in Lewisburg by May 14, and to form a junction with him. However, he said nothing to Grant about Staunton or the original plan for

36. OR, Vol. XXXVII, Pt. 1, p. 379; Hewitt, *Twelfth West Virginia*, 105; Neil to Parents, May 8, 1864, Neil Letters; Albert Artman Diary, May 5–10, 1864, USMHI; Diary of Jonas B. Kauffman, May 3–7, 1864, in Henry Wilson Storey, *History of Cambria County* (New York, 1907), II, 106; Williamson, *Mosby's Rangers*, 165–67; Wildes, *One Hundred and Sixteenth Ohio*, 86.

37. Williamson, *Mosby's Rangers*, 413–14; OR, Vol. XXXVII, Pt. 1, pp. 73, 446–47; John Scott, *Partisan Life with Col. John S. Mosby* (New York, 1867), 214–16; Samuel Clarke Farrar, *The Twenty-Second Pennsylvania and the Ringgold Battalion, 1861–1865* (Akron, 1911), 221; George Lyon to Sigel, May 14, 1864, Sigel Papers; Davis, *New Market*, 44.

movements in western Virginia.[38] Anticipating the move, Sigel five days earlier had sent the army's excess baggage back to Martinsburg. As Colonel Wildes noted, "We were down to our 'fighting weight.' " To conceal his movement, Sigel prohibited signaling for roll call. The impending move excited the troops. Private Frank Reader, having wanted "to get out of this place as soon as possible," breathed a sigh of relief. Many regarded the delay as a result of the general's procrastination.[39]

With "bands playing and colors flying," Sigel's army left their camps to move up the Valley. Members of the 22nd Pennsylvania Cavalry were "in high spirits," many believing "in their 'very bones' that this year would finish the job and down the rebellion."[40] The men of the 12th West Virginia began "whistling 'Yankee Doodle' keeping step to the music."[41] Scouting parties watched the various gaps of the Blue Ridge and the fords on the Shenandoah River. On the march, Sigel expected his men to become accustomed to breaking camp without the sound of a bugle and drum. Special orders permitted only regimental buglers to call reveille and tattoo. Josiah Staley rightly suspected that "they do not want the rebs to know the amount of our force."[42]

The day's march to Cedar Creek proved to be hot and dusty, and though the pace was leisurely, some men suffered from the heat. The route was littered with graves and decomposing horse carcasses. Men of the 18th Connecticut detected a decided change among civilians. Whereas in the preceding year local residents had taunted and jeered, now they seemed "very quiet and undemonstrative."[43] Few showed themselves to the passing regiments. That night, the rains returned.[44]

38. *OR*, Vol. XXXVII, Pt. 1, p. 407.

39. Wildes, *One Hundred and Sixteenth Ohio*, 83–84; Lincoln, *Thirty-fourth Massachusetts*, 271; Walker, *Eighteenth Regiment Connecticut*, 215–16; C. M. Keyes, ed., *The Military History of the 123d Regiment Ohio Volunteer Infantry* (Sandusky, 1874), 54; Jacob Campbell Diary, May 3, 1864, Jacob Campbell Papers, WVU; Reader Diary, May 8, 1864; Sigel to Stahel, May 8, 1864, Sigel Papers.

40. Farrar, *Twenty-Second Pennsylvania Cavalry*, 219.

41. Typescript Summary (4), n.a., n.d., n.p., Curtis Papers.

42. Josiah Staley to Wife, May 10, 1864, Staley Letters, Civil War Materials, MIC 17, Roll 19, OHS; Lincoln, *Thirty-fourth Massachusetts*, 273–74.

43. Walker, *Eighteenth Regiment Connecticut*, 216.

44. Reader Diary, May 10, 1864; Lynch, *Civil War Diary*, 57; Lincoln, *Thirty-Fourth Massachusetts*, 273; Keyes, *History of the 123d Ohio*, 54; Eby, ed., *Virginia Yankee*, 223–24; Swiger, ed., *Civil War Letters of Winters*, 106; Farrar, *Twenty-Second Pennsylvania*, 218–19;

Delaying only until the pioneers could build a bridge over the creek, they resumed the march on the following day, May 11. Through heavy rain, the army passed along the silent street in Strasburg and then up Fisher's Hill, a point dreaded by many veterans because of its "formidable natural defense." Many in the 18th Connecticut wondered why the Confederates did not contest their advance. At Fisher's Hill a shift in mood became noticeable.[45] Halting, officers ordered their troops to load their guns. First Lieutenant William Hewitt observed that "more than one brave man looked very serious as he tore the papers from his cartridge."[46] None too soon, for as they pushed on they encountered their first challenge from Imboden's cavalry. After a brief skirmish the Southerners rapidly withdrew toward Woodstock.[47]

There Sigel had a stroke of luck. Not only did he capture Woodstock easily, but he also found a number of important dispatches providing information on Breckinridge's movements. He learned the number of Southern troops en route to Staunton and had evidence of Confederate anxiety over the possibility of his moving across the Blue Ridge toward Charlottesville to join Grant. Sigel later wrote that this information "could not fail to prompt me to energetic action."[48] Yet he remained at Woodstock for two days. He became more defensive. In a wire to the War Department, he proclaimed that his objective was "to threaten Staunton, to divide the forces of Breckinridge, and to assist by these means General Crook." But then he asserted that with "the enemy . . . continuously on my flank and rear," he did not possess sufficient troops to fulfill his objective. Instead, he announced his intention of not advancing "farther than this place with my main force." He now planned to send out "strong parties in every direction" unless Breckinridge advanced against him, in which case "I will resist him at some convenient position." Despite his knowledge of Southern movements, he allowed the golden opportunity of stealing a march on his adversary to slip away.[49]

Neil to Friends, May 10, 1864, Neil Letters; Ephraim W. Frost to Mother, May 13, 1864, Ephraim W. Frost Letters, H. E. Matheny Collection, WVU.

45. Walker, *Eighteenth Regiment Connecticut*, 217; Swiger, ed., *Letters and Diary of Winters*, 106; Sperry Diary, May 14, 1864; Transcript Summary, [4], Curtis Papers.

46. Hewitt, *Twelfth West Virginia*, 105.

47. OR, Vol. XXXVII, Pt. 1, p. 427.

48. Sigel, "Sigel in the Valley," 488.

49. OR, Vol. XXXVII, Pt. 1, pp. 446–47; Captured Confederate Dispatches, Sigel Papers; Davis, *New Market*, 57–58, 61.

Meanwhile, incoming reports revealed that only Imboden opposed Sigel at New Market. Enticed by the idea of taking Mount Jackson and then seizing control of the important crossroads at New Market, Sigel made what William C. Davis has called "the biggest mistake of the campaign."[50] Summoning Colonel Moor to Stahel's headquarters, he directed him to take a "strong party" and gather intelligence on Imboden's position. The logical choice for the mission was Colonel Joseph Thoburn and his 2nd Brigade, but as Captain Henry A. Du Pont later charged, Sigel decided that "the reconnaissance should be commanded by a fellow-German."[51] Not only was Moor unfamiliar with the Valley, but Sigel never supplied him with scouts and a reliable map. But it was Sigel's choice, and Moor moved toward New Market with a combined force numbering some 2,350 men, a third of Sigel's army.[52]

At Mount Jackson, meanwhile, Major Quinn, expecting to contact Colonel Boyd and another unit, heard the gunfire of Boyd's skirmish but fell back to Edinburg. The following morning, May 14, an additional three hundred troopers arrived, along with orders for Quinn to proceed to Mount Jackson. Retracing his previous route, Quinn found the planks on the bridge over the North Fork of the Shenandoah River now torn up. In the distance he could see the Southerners on Rude's Hill. Quinn, after replacing the planking, masked his main body behind a hill and began probing the Confederate position. Repulsing a sudden Southern charge, they soon drove the pickets back to Imboden's main line. There the general's batteries opened up a barrage.[53]

Alerted to the sound of "occasional cannon shots," Moor sent Colonel Wynkoop to support Quinn. When Wynkoop arrived at the outskirts of New Market, he ordered Quinn to fall back on a rear line. With the infantry up, Moor unleashed his own artillery barrage. Imboden replied in kind, but after a brief duel he withdrew until around 8 P.M., when he attempted to probe Moor's right. Repulsed, Imboden waited until 10 P.M.; then he ordered another barrage and attack. Moor, pleased with the day's results,

50. Davis, *New Market*, 70.

51. Du Pont, *Campaign of 1864*, 10; OR, Vol. XXXVII, Pt. 1, p. 79; Lincoln, *Thirty-fourth Massachusetts*, 289.

52. Davis, *New Market*, 71.

53. OR, Vol. XXXVII, Pt. 1, pp. 73–75, 79; Farrar, *Twenty-Second Pennsylvania*, 222; Lang, *Loyal West Virginia*, 112.

wisely made no attempt to press the Southerners. His efforts seemed on
the verge of achieving Sigel's objective of controlling New Market.[54]

New Market, a town of 1,422 located at the crossroads of two major arteries, offered an important strategic prize. The Valley Pike, running the
length of the Shenandoah, crossed the east-west road from West Virginia
through the Alleghenies at Brock's Gap to New Market. Then it passed
east through New Market Gap across Massanutten Mountain into Page
Valley and across the Blue Ridge at Thornton's Gap into the Virginia
Piedmont. Sigel wanted to control those roads. Possession of New Market,
he reasoned, would sharpen Southern fears that he might move east to
join Grant. Yet in his desire to seize the point, he blundered in running
the risk of a battle without sufficient preparation. Strother, already a
strong dissenter over the detaching of Higgins' and Boyd's expeditions,
worried about pushing Moor some twenty miles ahead of the main column. He feared that the army could be "destroyed in detail."[55]

Meanwhile, Breckinridge's army formed at Lacey Spring, about eight
miles south of New Market. Around 1 A.M. on May 15, without the beat
of drums, his men started out. Wharton's and Echols' brigades led the way,
then the cadets and artillery. In the distance they could see Imboden's
pickets on the crest of a hill.[56] Originally, Breckinridge had hoped to provoke Sigel into taking the offensive. Briefed by Imboden, he carefully
chose a strong defensive position. Williamson's Hill, some two miles south
of New Market, offered an excellent anchor for his left flank. By daybreak
his troops—"weary, wet, and muddy"—began arriving. Yet despite consolidating his forces into an army of some 5,300 troops and eighteen guns,
Breckinridge remained dangerously outnumbered. Fortunately for him,
the factor of leadership weighed heavily on the Confederate side.[57] The

54. OR, Vol. XXXVII, Pt. 1, pp. 79–80; Rawling, *First Regiment Virginia*, 164–65.

55. *Population: 1860 Census*, 519; OR, Vol. XXXVII, Pt. 1, p. 447; Sigel, "Sigel in the
Valley," 488; Charles H. Porter, "The Operations of Generals Sigel and Hunter in the
Shenandoah Valley, May and June, 1864," PMHSM (Boston, 1907), VI, 66; Eby, ed., *Vir-
ginia Yankee*, 224.

56. OR, Vol. XXXVII, Pt. 1, p. 89; Johnston, "Sketches of Breckinridge," 260; Wise,
"West Point of the Confederacy," 466; John Clarke Howard, "Recollections of New Mar-
ket," CV, XXXIV (1926), 57; "Col. Francis Lee Smith," CV, XXVI (1918), 83–84; Davis,
New Market, 80–81.

57. Harrisonburg (Va.) *Rockingham Register*, May 20, 1864, in Wayland, *History of Shenandoah County*, 316; J. D. Imboden, "Battle of New Market," 482–83; Davis, *New
Market*, 53.

weather would complicate any battle that day. Rain had already soaked the area for three days, and it showed little sign of letting up. Soggy fields and roads made movements difficult, especially for the artillery. Local streams and the Shenandoah River ran high.

Again attempting to provoke Moor into attacking, Breckinridge sent a skirmish line forward. Shrewdly, Moor again refused to take the bait. Shifting tactics, Breckinridge now probed Federal lines more seriously. He sent Lieutenant Carter Berkeley's section and then First Lieutenant Randolph Blain Jackson's battery to Shirley's Hill. As Berkeley's guns moved down the hill toward the Federals, Snow's battery countered in a duel lasting more than two hours. Yet the ploy failed to provoke a counterattack.[58] Growing more determined, Breckinridge remarked to Imboden, "We can't wait any longer for them to attack us. We can attack and whip them here, and I'll do it."[59] Incoming intelligence buoyed his spirits. He knew the threat in the southwest was dissipating, while signals from Massanutten Mountain confirmed Moor's strength. Yet Breckinridge still assumed that Sigel remained unaware of his presence and that only a portion of his army faced him.[60]

Meanwhile, Moor, learning of the presence of Breckinridge, realized his danger and ordered his men back to their former position at Bushong's Hill. Then in the distance he began to see the emerging Confederate deployment. Moor decided to maintain a defensive position while Major Lang sent dispatches to Sigel for immediate aid.[61] On Stahel's arrival, he recognized Moor's untenable position and ordered him to pull back. Meanwhile, Breckinridge shrewdly maneuvered his men on Shirley's Hill to create an illusion of larger numbers prepared to advance.[62] On his right he sent Imboden with his troopers and two sections of McClanahan's artillery across Smith's Creek to strike at Sigel's rear and destroy the bridge over the Shenandoah River. A similar order went to Gilmor. The maneuver was daring, and if it failed Breckinridge would be deprived of the use of Imboden's 18th Virginia Cavalry in pursuing the Federal army. Finally,

58. OR, Vol. XXXVII, Pt. 1, p. 80; Potts, "Who Fired the First Gun at New Market?" 453; Charles Warner Buchanan, "Who Fired the First Gun at New Market?" CV, XVII (1909), 237; Davis, *New Market*, 82–83.

59. J. D. Imboden, "Battle of New Market," 483.

60. OR, Vol. XXXVII, Pt. 1, p. 736; Davis, *New Market*, 85.

61. Lang, *Loyal West Virginia*, 113–14; Davis, *New Market*, 86.

62. OR, Vol. XXXVII, Pt. 1, p. 80; Turner, *New Market*, 26–27.

Wharton's line began their descent. At the bottom Breckinridge allowed them to rest briefly; then they moved out.[63]

Breckinridge's aggressiveness forced Sigel into a confrontation he hardly expected or was prepared for. At Woodstock, incoming reports had heightened Sigel's anxiety. Michael Graham, a supporter of Sigel's, noticed that he "seemed to be restless as a chained Hyena. His eyes seemed to [be] piercing every object upon which he cast them, and especially as the dispatches from the front were received."[64] Considering his options, Sigel saw Mount Jackson "as a defensive point" providing a number of opportunities, and its proximity to New Market offered great appeal. Initially, he planned "to await Breckinridge's attack at that place."[65] Yet he remained uncertain whether he should attempt to advance beyond that town or merely confront the Confederates there.

Finally, at 5 A.M. on May 15, the Federal army moved toward Mount Jackson. At Edinburg, stragglers from Boyd's expedition greeted them as cannon fire in the distance became more distinct. Occasional rain continued to dampen the route. At Mount Jackson, Sigel learned of the presence of Breckinridge and the repulse of Southern attacks on the previous evening. Initially he ordered Moor to retire to Mount Jackson. But frustrated at the lack of a response, he decided "to move forward with my whole force."[66] Unfortunately, he failed to inform General Sullivan of the change.

As the cannonading became more "lively," Sigel crossed the Shenandoah River to reconnoiter the terrain as far as Rude's Hill.[67] Misleading reports strengthened his confidence. Calculating that his troops equaled approximately those of Breckinridge's and taking into consideration Moor's performance of the previous day, he concluded that "the advantage was on our side." He further believed that "a retreat would have a bad effect on our troops."[68] Conferring with his chief of staff, he asserted, "We may as well fight them to-day as any day. We will advance."[69] Before hur-

63. Davis, *New Market*, 90; J. D. Imboden, "Battle of New Market," 483; Edward Raymond Turner, "The Battle of New Market," CV, XX (1912), 73; George H. Smith, "More of the Battle of New Market," CV, XVI (1908), 570.

64. Michael Graham to Cole, May 17, 1864, Sigel Papers.

65. Sigel, "Sigel in Shenandoah," 488; Beach, *First New York Cavalry*, 349.

66. Hewitt, *Twelfth West Virginia*, 111; Eby, ed., *Virginia Yankee*, 224–25; Stevenson, *"Boots and Saddles,"* 275; Beach, *First New York Cavalry*, 349.

67. Eby, ed., *Virginia Yankee*, 225.

68. Sigel, "Sigel in Shenandoah," 488.

69. Quoted in Davis, *New Market*, 98.

rying off to confer with Moor and Stahel, he sent a dispatch back to the remainder of the army "to hasten their march toward New Market."[70] "With a great flourish" he arrived on the battlefield around noon. Suddenly Sigel comprehended the gravity of the situation.[71] Hoping to buy time by holding Breckinridge temporarily in check, he pulled Moor back to a new position and sent a dispatch to Sullivan "to bring forward all his troops without delay." Sullivan, meanwhile, had been advancing at a relaxed pace. Around noon, while resting his men only a few miles from the town, he received Sigel's order. He immediately sent Carlin's and Kleiser's batteries ahead, but not Du Pont's.[72]

Buoyed briefly by a report from Captain Richard G. Pendergast, Sigel believed that Sullivan's arrival was imminent and began developing a new line. However, what alarmed Major Lang was the leisurely pace at which his troops "began to come into line."[73] Breckinridge, after personally reconnoitering the Federal position, concluded that Sigel "had abandoned the offensive and assumed the defensive." Despite the enemy's "exceedingly strong defensive position," Breckinridge decided to attack. Needing to buy time to readjust his line, he ordered an artillery barrage. As his men moved into position, Breckinridge sent the artillery, with the exception of Blain's battery, to a position on the east side of the pike. There he personally posted them so that they could fire obliquely into the Federal line without risking his own men and so that they could serve as "a skirmish line of artillery" and relieve pressure on his troops.[74] Meanwhile, Imboden had discovered Stahel's cavalry massed in a woods. He suggested to Breckinridge that McClanahan's guns enfilade them from across Smith's Creek. The general agreed. As Breckinridge advanced, the Southern guns created considerable confusion among Stahel's troopers and forced them to withdraw to a more appropriate position. But in doing so, they uncovered Kleiser's battery.[75]

Despite heavy rain around 2 P.M., Breckinridge ordered the charge. As

70. Hewitt, *Twelfth West Virginia*, 112; Beach, *First New York Cavalry*, 349.

71. Lang, *Loyal West Virginia*, 114.

72. Du Pont, *Campaign of 1864*, 20; Sigel, "Sigel in Shenandoah," 488–89.

73. Hewitt, *Twelfth West Virginia*, 111–13; Lang, *Loyal West Virginia*, 114; Lincoln, *Thirty-fourth Massachusetts*, 289; Sigel, "Sigel in Shenandoah," 489.

74. Johnston, "Sketches of Breckinridge," 260–61; Wayland, *History of Shenandoah County*, 315–19; Davis, *New Market*, 102–103.

75. J. D. Imboden, "Battle of New Market," 483–84; Turner, *New Market*, 41–42; Davis, *New Market*, 109–10.

his men pushed forward, Sigel's gunners opened fire. Nothing seemed to be able to stop them as they struck Sigel's first line. The onslaught, which to one Ohioan seemed "like an avalanche upon our little band," threatened to overlap Moor's line. The 123rd Ohio, without orders, retreated toward the pike. The 18th Connecticut, recognizing that their "position was worse than useless," also hastily withdrew. [76]

Sigel's main line waited on Bushong's Hill. A number of his officers harbored reservations about the position. Strother concluded that it was "not so good a position as the first for defense." [77] Others believed that Rude's Hill would be better. However, Lieutenant Colonel John P. Wolfe of the 51st Virginia and Major Peter J. Otey of the 30th Virginia Battalion disagreed and believed that Bushong's Hill was a strong position. [78] Jennings S. Wise concluded that Sigel held "a position of great natural strength," [79] and Edward Raymond Turner considered the position "so well chosen and so well defended that for a while it seemed impossible to force it." [80] Yet Sigel's greatest mistake was giving battle there while his army remained spread along the pike. To William C. Davis it "was a blunder on a grand scale." [81]

Breckinridge fully realized the "ugly effort" that would come in dislodging the Federals from the hill. With Sigel presumably consolidating his entire army, an assault carried serious risk. Yet he accepted it. He gambled on using a single charge. Breckinridge supervised his men directly to animate them "to heroism by his immediate presence." [82] As his line briskly surged forward, he ordered Chapman's battery to advance. [83] On the hill, Sigel waited. Snow's, Carlin's, and Kleiser's batteries double-loaded their pieces. Sigel, riding the line, told Ewing's gunners, "I dinks we fight him a little." As Wharton's men appeared over the rise of the terrain, Ewing's men let go with a devastating fire, tearing holes in the right wing of the

76. Lincoln, *Thirty-fourth Massachusetts*, 284; Keyes, *History of the 123d Ohio*, 54–55; Walker, *Eighteenth Connecticut*, 220; Lynch, *Civil War Diary*, 60.

77. Eby, ed., *Virginia Yankee*, 226.

78. Wolfe to Colonna, June 23, 1911, and Peter J. Otey to Scott Shipp, April 14, 1875, New Market Battle File, VMI.

79. Wise, *History of Virginia Military Institute*, 309.

80. Turner, *New Market*, 78.

81. Davis, *New Market*, 111–13.

82. Johnston, "Sketches of Breckinridge," 261.

83. Davis, *New Market*, 114–16.

51st and 30th Virginia Regiments. Yet the Southerners pushed forward through the "loblolly" of mud. The writhing fire on the 51st Virginia's right flank slowed them; then suddenly the Virginians wavered and began pulling back. With that the whole line stalled. Worse for Breckinridge, a gaping hole opened between the 51st and 62nd Virginia and begged for a counterattack. Adding to the danger, Stahel's cavalry poised for an attack.

For Breckinridge the gap was critical, for a Federal thrust there would cut his line in two. Major Charles Semple asked Breckinridge to put the cadets there, and the general reluctantly ordered them forward. [84] Despite heavy fire, the corps closed the gap. Captain D. H. Bruce "saw them stand and fight like regulars. I never saw soldiers fight better than they did." [85] "Had the cadets given away at this point," Major Otey wrote, "it is very clear that the Yankees would have driven a wedge as it were into our attacking column." [86] Yet Wharton's line teetered on the verge of collapse. Casualties mounted. Rain caused problems with the wooden ramrods, while smoke hid Kleiser's battery so that only the legs of the gunners and the wheels of the guns remained visible. Worse, Sigel prepared to counterattack. The moment seemed ripe for disaster. [87]

Massed in squadrons, Stahel's cavalry readied. Aware of their presence, Breckinridge ordered his batteries to double-load with canister. As the troopers galloped down the road on the Southern right, Chapman's battery, Berkeley's section, Minge's VMI guns, and the men of the 22nd and 23rd Virginia Regiments waited. Soon they belched their discharges to fill the road with reeling and staggering cavalrymen. Stunned by the fire on their flanks and front, the charge broke in disarray. Some surrendered; others broke through the ranks of the 54th Pennsylvania, creating problems for them. The rout gave the Confederates a needed tonic at a critical moment. [88]

84. "John C. Breckinridge," *CV*, XIII (1905), 259; Davis, *New Market*, 121–22.

85. D. H. Bruce, "Battle of New Market, Va.," *CV*, XV (1907), 554, and *SHSP*, XXXV (1907), 155–56.

86. Otey to Ship, April 14, 1875, New Market Battle File.

87. Edgar to Smith, April 16, 1908, George S. Patton, Jr. Papers, LC; Lincoln, *Thirty-fourth Massachusetts*, 284; Wise, *History of Virginia Military Institute*, 17–18; Wayland, *History of Shenandoah County*, 321; "Battle of New Market," *RR*, XI, 517; Neilson, "Sixty-Second Virginia," 60; "Concerning V. M. I. Cadets at New Market," *CV*, XX (1912), 392; Smith, "More of the Battle of New Market," 569–70; Baltimore *Sun*, May 21, 1864; Davis, *New Market*, 117–24.

88. Memoranda, n.d., Frank Imboden Letters, UV; G. W. Gageby to Colonna, May 27,

Confusion developed along the Federal line. Highly excited, Sigel rode everywhere. He consulted with Moor and Stahel, "all jabbering in German," and as Strother noted, "the purely American portion of his staff were totally useless to him."[89] Stahel's repulse unsettled the general. For fear that the Confederates would regain their momentum, he now decided to attack and desperately ordered the charge against now superior numbers.[90] Federal gunners stepped up their barrage. The noise became deafening. But when the 1st West Virginians reached the crest of a rise, they "sustained a galling and destructive fire." They wavered. Before the 54th Pennsylvania hardily pushed forward, the Confederates came on "with redoubled fury." Suddenly the Federal line began collapsing, and for Sigel "the tide of battle now turned."[91] Though badly shaken, the Southern line now gained greater confidence. Colonel George Edgar, seeing the right wing of the 51st Virginia and the 30th Virginia Battalion crack, rushed his men up and began passing through them. Wharton on the left stabilized his line, and soon the mingling ranks formed a new one to retake their lost ground. Then, in the midst of a crashing thunderstorm, the line simultaneously surged forward. As one Federal remembered, they "came down on our second line like an avalanche."[92] Carlin's and Snow's batteries began withdrawing section by section. Snow's battery got away first, but Carlin's gunners soon lost three guns. The cadets, charging across a muddy depression later known as the "Field of Lost Shoes," headed for Kleiser's battery and snagged one piece as a trophy. On the right Patton's 22nd and Derrick's 23rd Virginia Regiments advanced, but more slowly than the cadets. As they picked up momentum, Federal resistance crumbled. Across Smith's Creek, McClanahan's gunners, hearing "the triumph yell of victory . . . fell to the ground, kicked up their heels and yelled with perfect delight."[93]

1911, and David R. Bryan to Colonna, March 8, 1911, New Market Battle File; Mastin Diary, May 15, 1864; Stevenson, *"Boots and Saddles,"* 275; Couper, *One Hundred Years,* II, 280–81; Turner, *New Market,* 63–64; Johnston, "Sketches of Breckinridge," 261; F. M. Imboden, "Gen. G. C. Wharton," *CV,* XIV (1906), 392; Neilson, "Sixty-Second Virginia," 61; Wise, "West Point of Confederacy," 468–69; Turner, "Battle of New Market," 75.

89. Eby, ed., *Virginia Yankee,* 226.
90. Davis, *New Market,* 129–31.
91. Turner, *New Market,* 59.
92. Cincinnati *Daily Gazette,* May 24, 1864.
93. *OR,* Vol. XXXVII, Pt. 1, pp. 84, 86; Du Pont, *Campaign of 1864,* 15; Couper, *One Hundred Years,* II, 281–82; Wheeling *Daily Intelligencer,* May 23, 24, 1864; Neil to Friends,

Soon Sigel's army was in full retreat. The demoralization could not be stopped. Even the sloping terrain gave Southerners the advantage in lobbing shells at them. Stahel attempted to cover the retreat, but his troopers created more confusion than support. Ewing's battery feebly tried, but failed. Du Pont's gunners arrived and effectively put a brake on the Confederates. Breckinridge now became cautious. Du Pont's actions, according to William C. Davis, "may have saved Sigel from annihilation."[94] Fearful that the Federals might re-form on Rude's Hill, Breckinridge briefly halted his men to allow them to rest and replenish their ammunition. Without cavalry to undertake a pursuit, he sent for Berkeley's section. He ordered the lieutenant, "Go at once; charge down the pike and drive them off the hill."[95] Joined by Lieutenant Collet's section, they excitedly headed toward Rude's Hill. As they approached, Berkeley saw Du Pont's artillery carefully limbering up to abandon the hill as the remainder of the army hurried across Meem's Bottom toward the bridge and safety.[96]

Sigel briefly attempted to form a line at Rude's Hill. He managed to gather some cavalry and the newly arrived but exhausted 28th and 116th Ohio Regiments to support his guns. However, in consultation with Stahel and Sullivan, he concluded that they should "not await another attack." Taking note of their severe losses, a diminishing supply of ammunition, and the commanding position of Southern guns, they feared that in case of defeat "we could not cross the swollen river, except by the bridge." By 6 P.M. Sigel's army, except for a company of cavalry and Du Pont's men, had succeeded in crossing. Once across, Du Pont's men tore up the bridge's planks to block the Southerners. One wit attributed the breaking off of the Confederate pursuit to "General Sigel's fame for conducting

---

May 19, 1864, Neil Letters; Lincoln, *Thirty-fourth Massachusetts*, 284–85; Rawling, *First Virginia Regiment*, 166–67; Storey, *History of Cambria County*, II, 137; Wise, *History of Virginia Military Institute*, 320–21; Howard, "Recollections of New Market," 58–59; Bruce, "Battle of New Market," 157; F. M. Imboden, "G. C. Wharton," 392; Davis, *New Market*, 131–44; quoted in Robert J. Driver, Jr., *The Staunton Artillery—McClanahan's Battery* (Lynchburg, 1988), 88.

94. *OR*, Vol. XXXVII, Pt. 1, p. 109; Du Pont, *Campaign of 1864*, 21–22, 27; H. A. Du Pont to B. A. Colonna, n.d., New Market Battle File; S. T. Shank, "A Gunner at New Market, Va.," *CV*, XXVI (1918), 191; Davis, *New Market*, 150.

95. Quoted in Driver, *Staunton Artillery—McClanahan's Battery*, 88.

96. Eby, ed., *Virginia Yankee*, 227; Turner, *New Market*, 94; Couper, *One Hundred Years*, 283; Driver, *Staunton Artillery—McClanahan's Battery*, 88–89.

'masterly retreats.' "[97] Withdrawing to the flooding Mill Creek, a mile north of the bridge, Sigel posted his army in battle formation. He believed that the army was "perfectly safe, as the creek was high and could not be forded."[98] With his cavalry out of position and the flooding of Mill Creek, Breckinridge's brilliantly conceived trap had failed.

More than a bridge lay in ruins. Sigel's army, badly bruised and shaken, survived to retire to Cedar Creek, but the general's reputation was not so fortunate. No one doubted his courage—Major Lang paid tribute to his "great personal bravery"—but his judgment was another matter.[99] As to his competency, Strother noted in his diary, "We can afford to lose such a battle as New Market to get rid of such a mistake as Major General Sigel." He summarized Sigel's ability with the notation, "The campaign was conducted miserably."[100] To the men of the 18th Connecticut, the defeat looked "like a case of mismanagement."[101]

The indictment contained substance. Since leaving Martinsburg, Sigel had allowed Southern forces to attack his army in detail. The disastrous Higgins and Boyd expeditions deprived him of a third of his cavalry at New Market. Underestimating Confederate strength, he sent Moor to probe far in advance of his main column without adequate support when he knew that Breckinridge was moving north. Worse, he allowed his army to stretch some twenty miles along the Valley Pike in the face of a potential attack. Sigel's willingness to give battle without concentrating his army proved disastrous. Du Pont, contrasting Sigel with Breckinridge, believed that the Confederate general acted on the Jomini principle of concentration, "while Sigel seems to have had no conception of its existence."[102] The lack of proper reconnoitering undoubtedly caused a number of mistakes, especially in the placement of artillery, which exposed a serious organizational deficiency. Without a chief of artillery, Sigel failed to benefit from an efficient and effective use of his guns. In ad-

97. Wildes, *One Hundred and Sixteenth Ohio*, 87.

98. Sigel, "Sigel in Shenandoah," 490; Frost to Mother, May 19, 1864, Frost Letters; Eby, ed., *Virginia Yankee*, 227–28; Du Pont, *Campaign of 1864*, 15–16; Charles H. Lynch to B. A. Colonna, Aug. 27, 1912, New Market Battle File; "Battle of New Market," *RR*, XI, 517.

99. Lang, *Loyal West Virginia*, 114.

100. Eby, ed., *Virginia Yankee*, 229–30.

101. Lynch, *Civil War Diary*, 61.

102. Du Pont, *Campaign of 1864*, 29.

dition, Sullivan's rigidity and lack of initiative deprived Sigel of reinforcements at the critical moment on Bushong's Hill. Compounding his flawed direction of his forces, the use of German by Sigel and his staff resulted in the failure to communicate his instructions adequately.[103]

Ironically, the New Market disaster allowed Grant to achieve his primary objective in western Virginia. By heightening Southern fears over the security of the Virginia Central Railroad, Sigel's advance up the Valley caused Richmond and Lee to focus on Staunton's safety. By concentrating a majority of the region's forces in the Shenandoah to meet that threat, Breckinridge by necessity left only a smaller and makeshift contingent to defend the southwest against Crook. With that region more vulnerable, the Army of the Kanawha destroyed not only large segments of the Virginia and Tennessee Railroad but the important New River bridge as well. In their choice of priorities, Confederate authorities unwittingly conformed to Grant's plans for western Virginia, although their choices were dictated by the need to sustain the Army of Northern Virginia. Despite Sigel's failure to "hold a leg," the Confederates allowed Crook to do the "skinning."

Exhausted, the Army of the Shenandoah poured into Mount Jackson. Residents watched the "gruesome and sickening sights" of wounded men struggling under the care of their "dispirited and despondent" comrades.[104] With the threat of an attack diminished, Sigel ordered the withdrawal to Cedar Creek. Around dark the army began treading its way north through the rain and mud. As their shoes wore out, many in the 116th Ohio merely threw them away and walked barefoot. The men of the 12th West Virginia changed their old chant to "We Fights no more mit Sigel."[105] Private Reader lamented, "How uncertain are my prophecies. Thought this morning that we could whip anything in the valley and would go right on to Staunton. But how different."[106] But the exhausted Southerners went into camp that night, as Colonel J. Stoddard remem-

103. "Battle of New Market," *RR*, XI (1868), 517; Turner, *New Market*, 101–102; Wildes, *One Hundred and Sixteenth Ohio*, 87–88; New York *Herald*, May 22, 1864.

104. Robert Hugh Martin, *A Boy of Old Shenandoah*, ed. Carolyn Martin Rutherford (Parsons, W. Va., 1977), 17–18; Neil to Friends, May 19, 1864, Neil Letters; Lincoln, *Thirty-fourth Massachusetts*, 290.

105. Sigel, "Sigel in Shenandoah," 490; Lynch, *Civil War Diary*, 61; Frost to Mother, May 19, 1864, Frost Letters; New York *Herald*, May 22, 1864.

106. Reader Diary, May 15, 1864.

bered, "with cheers of victory such as had not been heard in the Valley since Stonewall Jackson had led them."[107] An elated Breckinridge wired Lee the news of Sigel's defeat "with heavy loss." A delighted Staunton *Spectator* hailed it as "one of the most brilliant victories of the war."[108] To an admiring Colonel Frank Imboden, "Breckinridge on his splendid bay that day was indeed superb!"[109]

  107. Johnston, "Sketches of Breckinridge," 262.

  108. Breckinridge to Lee, May 15, 1864, Charles Venable Papers, SHC; OR, Vol. XXX-VII, Pt. 1, p. 87; Staunton (Va.) *Spectator*, May 24, 1864.

  109. F. M. Imboden, "G. C. Wharton," 392.

5

Hunter Takes Command

After retreating across the Shenandoah River, Sigel sent a terse message to the War Department: "A severe battle was fought to-day at New Market. . . . Our troops were overpowered by superior numbers." His reverse did not come as a total surprise. Although Grant had hoped Sigel could "hold one of the legs while others skinned," Halleck had anticipated nothing but disaster. "Instead of advancing on Staunton," Halleck telegraphed Grant on May 17, "he is already in full retreat on Strasburg. If you expect anything from him you will be mistaken. He will do nothing but run. He never did anything else."[1] The Cincinnati *Daily Commercial* agreed, informing its readers that "the retreat, it will be recollected, is General Sigel's favorite movement."[2] Colonel Strother quipped, "We are doing a good business in this department. Averell is tearing up the Virginia and Tennessee Railroad while Sigel is tearing down the Valley turnpike."[3] The defeat dashed Southern Unionist hopes. In Winchester, a despondent Julia Chase confided to her diary, "It seems that we are doomed to disaster in the Valley, not one victory has ever been gained over the Rebels since the Federals entered Virginia."[4]

1. OR, Vol. XXXVII, Pt. 1, pp. 76, 485, Vol. XXXVII, Pt. 2, p. 452, and Vol. XXXVI, Pt. 2, p. 840.

2. Cincinnati *Daily Commercial*, May 19, 1864.

3. Eby, ed., *Virginia Yankee*, 229; Miles O'Reilly, *Baked Meats of the Funeral* (New York, 1866), 300–301; Lang, *Loyal West Virginia*, 165.

4. Chase Diary, May 16, 1864.

With Sigel's removal now certain, Secretary of War Stanton proposed Major General David Hunter as his replacement. Halleck informed Grant of the possibility, noting that Lincoln would appoint him "if you desire it." The answer came immediately: "By all means I would say appoint Genl Hunter or any one else to the command of West Virginia."[5] On May 19 the War Department issued General Orders No. 200, and Hunter had finally secured the assignment for which he had long begged Lincoln.[6]

Born in 1802 in Princeton, New Jersey, David Hunter was the son of Andrew Hunter, a Presbyterian chaplain of the 3rd New Jersey Infantry Regiment during the American Revolution, and Mary Stockton, the sister of Richard Stockton, a signer of the Declaration of Independence. Born of a prominent Virginia family, Andrew Hunter possessed kinship ties in the Shenandoah Valley, counting among his relatives Robert T. M. Hunter, the secretary of state of the Confederacy. Little is known of David Hunter's early years, though his strict, Calvinist upbringing was evidenced later in his "deeply religious convictions." In 1818 he enrolled at West Point, and upon graduation in 1822 he was assigned to duty on the western frontier. For eleven years he served in the infantry, and in 1833 he was promoted to the rank of captain.[7]

In 1836, Hunter, now married and eager to promote his personal interests, resigned from the army and moved to Chicago to join his brother-in-law in real estate speculation. Five years later, disappointed by meager economic success, he decided to resume his military career. Successfully reinstated, Hunter became a major in the paymaster's office and served in a noncombatant role as chief paymaster under General Zachary Taylor during the Mexican War. In September 1850 he was promoted to the rank of lieutenant colonel.[8]

On the eve of the 1860 presidential election, Hunter was serving in the

5. OR, Vol. XXXVI, Pt. 2, pp. 840–41, and Vol. XXXVII, Pt. 1, pp. 485, 492.

6. OR, Vol. XXXVII, Pt. 1, p. 492.

7. Edward A. Miller, Jr., *Lincoln's Abolitionist General: The Biography of David Hunter* (Columbia, S.C., 1997), 1–3; William Hanchett, *Irish: Charles G. Halpine in Civil War America* (Syracuse, 1970), 36; Cornelia McDonald, *A Diary with Reminiscences of the War and Refugee Life in the Shenandoah Valley, 1860–1865* (Nashville, 1935), 316; John B. Hayes, ed., *Samuel Francis Du Pont: A Selection from His Civil War Letters* (Ithaca, 1969), II, 75, 80, 217; O'Reilly, *Baked Meats*, 330; Eby, ed., *Virginia Yankee*, 239.

8. Miller, *Lincoln's Abolitionist General*, Chap. 2; Robert W. Johannsen, ed., *The Letters of Stephen A. Douglas* (Urbana, 1961), 165; Lynda Lasswell Crist et al., eds., *The Papers of Jefferson Davis* (Baton Rouge, 1983, 1985), IV, 367, and V, 477.

Kansas Territory at Fort Leavenworth. There, revolted by the turmoil and atrocities on the frontier which resulted from slavery, he became an ardent abolitionist. His antislavery proclivities soon earned him the nickname of "Black David."[9] Politically minded, he supported Lincoln in the election and, violating an unwritten law that military officers refrain from such activities, became involved in partisan politics.[10] Privy to Southern gossip, he informed Lincoln of various plots designed to prevent his election.[11]

Hunter's political connections enabled him to rise rapidly from a colonel of the 6th United States Cavalry to command a division under General Irvin McDowell. Wounded in the Battle of First Manassas, he escaped the recriminations that followed the defeat. Once he had recovered sufficiently from his wound, the War Department assigned him to the Western Department on August 22, 1861, to assist General John C. Frémont.[12] Embroiled in the controversy over Frémont's emancipation proclamation, Hunter learned the importance of currying favor with the Radicals in Washington.[13] With the division of the department, the War Department placed him in command of the Department of Kansas. Impatient and mortified over the assignment, he agitated for a better command.[14]

In March 1862 the War Department appointed Hunter to command the Department of the South, which consisted of parts of South Carolina, Georgia, and Florida. Stanton, without Lincoln's knowledge and with his implied consent, agreed to allow Hunter to use his judgment on slavery.[15] Much to the joy of the Radicals, on May 9, 1862, Hunter issued an order freeing all slaves in the department. However, Lincoln, refusing to allow "such a thing, upon *my* responsibility, without consulting me," revoked the proclamation. Hunter's attempt to organize a black regiment that

9. O'Reilly, *Baked Meats*, 329; Robert C. Schenck, "Major-General David Hunter," *Magazine of American History*, XVII (1887), 140; Miller, *Lincoln's Abolitionist General*, 46.

10. Du Pont, *Campaign of 1864*, 38–39.

11. Hunter to Lincoln, Oct. 20, 1860, Nov. 1, 1860, Dec. 18, 1860, Abraham Lincoln Papers, LC; David Hunter, *Report of the Military Services of Gen. David Hunter, U.S.A.* (New York, 1873), 5–6.

12. *OR*, Vol. LI, Pt. 1, p. 353.

13. T. Harry Williams, *Lincoln and the Radicals* (Madison, 1941), 49, 54–55, 108, 136–37.

14. Hunter to Lincoln, Dec. 23, 1861, Lincoln Papers.

15. Benjamin P. Thomas and Harold M. Hyman, *Stanton: The Life and Times of Lincoln's Secretary of War* (New York, 1962), 234–35; Williams, *Lincoln and the Radicals*, 136–37.

summer also failed. Though abolitionists saw Hunter as a champion and many church pulpits rang with his praises, his actions triggered a storm of debate and criticism in Washington. In the House of Representatives he came under severe attack by conservatives and had to abandon the project of arming the former slaves.[16]

Given a leave of absence by the War Department, he left the Department of the South on September 3, 1862, for New York.[17] Smarting over his treatment by the administration in Washington, Hunter lobbied for a new command. He secured a number of short-term assignments, such as president of the court of inquiry investigating the surrender of Harpers Ferry to Stonewall Jackson by Colonel Dixon Stansbury Miles and then as president of the court-martial trial of Major General Fitz John Porter. Briefly he returned to South Carolina, but the failure of his attempt to take Charleston in cooperation with the navy accentuated his frustration there.[18] The War Department relieved him "temporarily" from command; he believed that this was "universally regarded as a censure on my conduct."[19] The department sent him to scrutinize Grant in November 1863 and then on another mission in April 1864 to investigate General Nathaniel Banks's command on the Red River. The War Department offered him the command of Union forces on the West Coast, but Hunter, preferring to serve under Grant, who was now rumored to become the new general-in-chief, shrewdly declined. He wanted—and received—a promise of a position in the East,[20] and with Sigel's disaster on May 19 he was assigned to be the new commander in the Department of West Virginia.[21]

There was little delay in Hunter's assuming command. At Martinsburg he received the proper military salute as he passed through town on May

16. Hunter, *Report*, 17–27; John Niven et al., eds., *The Salmon P. Chase Papers* (Kent, Ohio, 1993), I, 344; Basler, ed., *Works of Lincoln*, V, 219, 222–23; Williams, *Lincoln and the Radicals*, 137; Thomas and Hyman, *Stanton*, 234–37; Hanchett, *Irish: Charles Halpine*, 51; Walter M. Merrill, ed., *Let the Oppressed Go Free: The Letters of William Lloyd Garrison* (Cambridge, Mass., 1979), V, 93; Adam Gurowski, *Diary from March 4, 1861, to November 12, 1862* (Boston, 1862), I, 210.

17. Hunter, *Report*, 17.

18. Hunter to Lincoln, May 22, 1863, Lincoln Papers; Otto Eisenschiml, *The Celebrated Case of Fitz John Porter* (Indianapolis, 1950), 77–78, 170.

19. Hunter to Lincoln, June 25, 30, 1863, Lincoln Papers; Hunter, *Report*, 42–43.

20. Edward G. Longacre, "A Profile of Major General David Hunter," *CWT*, XVI (1978) 38; Dennett, ed., *Lincoln and Diaries of Hay*, 169.

21. *OR*, Vol. XXXVII, Pt. 1, p. 492.

21 on his way to Sigel's headquarters. A pleased Clifton M. Nichols, editor of the Springfield (Ohio) *Daily News* and then in Martinsburg, wrote to his paper, "Let us hope that the day of 'splendid retreats' is over."[22] Kate Sperry took note of his radical reputation as he rode through Winchester: "Exit Sigel and *Nigger* Gen. Hunter went through here to take his place."[23] Near sunset on that day he finally reached the Hite House, where the Opequon Creek crossed the Valley Pike below Newtown. Colonel Strother, standing on the front porch, watched as Hunter's entourage approached. As Hunter dismounted, Strother, a distant cousin, recognized him and walked down to greet him. Pulling the colonel aside, Hunter told him that he had come to relieve Sigel. Anxious officers and their men soon learned the reason for his presence and knew they had a new and more dynamic commander.[24]

Hunter's demeanor impressed Captain Du Pont, who considered the nearly sixty-two-year-old army officer "strong and robust physically."[25] General James A. Garfield took special note of Hunter's "keen grey eyes, a long nose, slightly aquiline, a large mouth with corners slightly depress and the whole shut with a sharp decisiveness."[26] Hunter stood approximately five feet, eight inches tall, paunchy with broad shoulders and a "swarthy and Indian look both in complexion and of feature."[27] Accenting his features, he wore a dark brown wig and a dyed drooping mustache. "The expression of his somewhat prominent features," Du Pont noted, "was stern and severe."[28] The severity Du Pont observed would not go unnoticed by Hunter's troops.

Despite the blow to its morale caused by the New Market defeat, the Army of the Shenandoah remained a dangerous adversary. Captain John Suter of the 54th Pennsylvania Regiment detected "a new spirit infused into all the men," for after "having already had a pretty sensible smell of

22. *Ibid.*, 505; Clifton M. Nichols, *A Summer Campaign in the Shenandoah Valley in 1864* (Springfield, Ohio, 1899), 42–43.

23. Sperry Diary, May 21, 1864.

24. Eby, ed., *Virginia Yankee*, 231–32.

25. Du Pont, *Campaign of 1864*, 37.

26. Theodore Clarke Smith, *The Life and Letters of James Abram Garfield* (New Haven, 1925), 260.

27. O'Reilly, *Baked Meats*, 330.

28. Longacre, "Profile of Hunter," 4; Farrar, *Twenty-Second Pennsylvania*, 227; Lynch, *Civil War Diary*, 62; Du Pont, *Campaign of 1864*, 37.

gunpowder, there are few who would take their furlough at present if offered." What now was needed was energetic leadership.[29] For his chief of
staff, Hunter appointed Strother. The colonel, never a member of Sigel's
inner circle, now became a chief adviser. In addition Hunter added two
new members, Lieutenant Colonel Charles G. Halpine as assistant adjutant general and his nephew Lieutenant Samuel W. Stockton of the 4th
United States Cavalry as aide-de-camp. He also consolidated the artillery
under Du Pont and made it an independent unit. Reluctantly, he retained
Sigel's staff.[30]

Displeased with the "disorganized and demoralized" condition of the
army, Hunter asked the War Department to send him some energetic and
efficient brigadiers. The cavalry, he felt, was "utterly demoralized from frequent defeats by inferior forces and retreats without fighting." He now
asked for a new general to command it, for "it would be impossible to exaggerate the inefficiency of General Stahel." The situation called for "a
commander of zeal, grit, activity and courage." In addition he asked for a
new brigadier general to replace Sullivan, whom he regarded as being "of
limited experience, energy, and reliability."[31] Although the War Department agreed with Hunter's assessment, Halleck reminded him that "energetic and efficient brigadiers are scarce." Pointing out that Hunter already
possessed three cavalry generals—Averell, Duffié, and Stahel—Halleck
wrote that "no one can be appointed till some one else is mustered out."[32]

Another problem, more politically sensitive, was Sigel. The administration feared the political impact of the general's removal. Lincoln fretted that "the Germans seem inclined to cut up rough about the removal
[of Sigel] from command in the Shenandoah." The president and the War
Department wanted to retain "the Dutch in some position if possible."[33]
Sigel, absent from headquarters on Hunter's arrival, found him sitting on
the front porch of the Hite House awaiting his return. They greeted each
other cordially, shook hands, and went into the house. The removal order

29. John Suter to D. J. Morrell, May 20, 1864, in Storey, *History of Cambria County*, II,
168–69.

30. OR, Vol. XXXVII, Pt. 1, pp. 508, 525, 531–32, and Pt. 2, pp. 366–67; Eby, ed., *Virginia Yankee*, 232–33, 237; Lang, *Loyal West Virginia*, 116; Du Pont, *Campaign of 1864*,
46–47.

31. OR, Vol. XXXVII, Pt. 1, pp. 508, 516–17.

32. *Ibid.*, 525.

33. Du Pont, *Campaign of 1864*, 34, 45.

stunned Sigel, who had been assured just a few days before by Major George Lyon, a personal friend, that Washington did not see the defeat as a disaster and that there still remained general confidence in him.[34] Strother, calling on Sigel the day after, found him with tears "in his eyes and his lips quivering." Sigel told him that he would rather "have died on that battlefield than to have suffered this disgrace."[35] "Actuated by an earnest patriotism," Sigel told Hunter that he "was anxious to take a division in this army or attend to any other duty." Hunter diplomatically assigned him to command the reserve division protecting the Baltimore and Ohio Railroad.[36]

Hunter's presence in the Valley shifted the focus in western Virginia fully to the Shenandoah and the capture of Staunton. Grant's basic objectives remained the same; only the thrust of Union forces in the region changed. Sigel's earlier dispatch to Crook to advance against Staunton and the Virginia Central Railroad between Staunton and the Jackson River Depot stood. Hunter reiterated the directive.[37] Initially, on May 18, Grant had suggested to Halleck that with Crook's expedition returning to Gauley Bridge, Halleck should send Sigel's surplus force to Harpers Ferry and then on to Grant or "up the Shenandoah as may then seem most advantageous." Two days later, after learning of Hunter's appointment, Grant repeated the same suggestion but took special note of Lee as "evidently relying for supplies greatly" on the Virginia Central. He also believed that Hunter could, by moving south, effectively guard the Baltimore and Ohio Railroad, thus providing more aid than if he were to "reenforce armies elsewhere." Instead, Grant, still determined to disrupt Lee's western supply lines, directed Halleck to inform Hunter of Sigel's instructions and to instruct Hunter to "reach Staunton and Gordonsville, or Charlottesville if he does not meet too much opposition." If that were not possible, then Hunter could still render an important service by holding at bay "a force equal to your own."[38]

Suddenly the situation in the Valley changed radically. On May 17, Breckinridge departed for Lee's army, leaving essentially a military vacuum. On the twenty-second, Grant reported to Halleck that "Breckin-

34. Lyon to Sigel, May 19, 1864, Sigel Papers.

35. Eby, ed., *Virginia Yankee*, 232; Baltimore *American*, May 24, 1864.

36. OR, Vol. XXXVII, Pt. 1, p. 524.

37. Ibid., 479, 482, 507.

38. Ibid., Vol. XXXVI, Pt. 3, pp. 3–4, and Vol. XXXVII, Pt. 1, pp. 485–86, 500, 507.

ridge is said to have arrived" to join Lee's army. On the next day the chief
of staff relayed the news to Hunter. On the twenty-fifth, Grant confirmed
the intelligence and wired that Breckinridge was "unquestionably here."
He now directed that "if Hunter can possibly get to Charlottesville and
Lynchburg, he should do so, living on the country." Grant wanted him to
break those supply lines "beyond possibility of repair for weeks." Once this
was accomplished, Hunter should either go back to his original base or
move toward Gordonsville to join the Army of the Potomac.[39] In conveying these instructions to Hunter, Halleck closed with the charge, "In your
movements live as much as possible on the country."[40]

Before setting his army in motion, Hunter reflected on past reasons for
Federal failures in the Valley. For him two factors contributed to Union
vulnerability there: the dependency on long supply lines operating
through a hostile countryside, and the constant opportunities for Confederate attacks to disrupt that support system. Couriers and small detachments made excellent targets, and guerrilla warfare and bushwhacking
posed an ongoing threat.[41] Mosby's rangers, in particular, were a menace.
Another threat came from McNeill's rangers, though they were more
troublesome to foraging soldiers who strayed too far from their command
than to Hunter's heavily guarded supply line in the upper Valley.[42]

Hunter, hoping to reduce guerrilla activity, decided to make such attacks on his men and supplies more difficult and to exact a price for them
from the civilian population. Mosby's support system became the focus of
his attention. Clifton Nichols in Martinsburg noted that "there are a
great many of these farmers by day and bushwhackers by night in this region."[43] To Hunter, "the laws of war of any civilized nation" did not permit the aiding and abetting of guerrillas and bushwhackers. He charged
Southern sympathizers with being "spies" and "abusing the clemency
which has protected your persons and property, while loyal citizens of the
United States residing within the rebel lines are invariably plundered of
all they may possess, imprisoned, and in some cases put to death." He

39. *OR*, Vol. XXXVI, Pt. 1, pp. 7–8, Pt. 3, pp. 171, 183, 208–209, and Vol. XXXVII,
Pt. 1, pp. 535–36; Eby, ed., *Virginia Yankee*, 235.

40. *OR*, Vol. XXXVII, Pt. 1, p. 543.

41. Wheeling *Daily Intelligencer*, June 15, 1864; Cecil D. Eby, Jr., "David Hunter: Villain of the Valley," *Iron Worker* (Spring, 1964), 2.

42. Williams, ed., *Rebel Brothers*, 194–95.

43. Nichols, *Summer Campaign*, 61–62, 68.

threatened that if such persons fired upon any Union train or soldier, "the houses and other property of every secession sympathizer residing within a circuit of five miles from the place of outrage, shall be destroyed by fire."[44]

For the destruction of Federal property, Hunter would assess civilians five times its value. To avoid such consequences, he advised them to tell guerrillas to withdraw from within his lines and to join "the regular secession army in my front or else where." In justifying his harsh attitude toward the civilians, he later wrote: "If there were any Union white men in the country, except a Quaker family in Winchester, I failed to find them."[45] A Federal officer expressed the sentiments of the army when he remarked to a citizen, "Why don't you people get up a petition to withdraw Mosby from the Valley and send it to Jeff Davis. Then you all would not be treated so badly by the Yanks." The reply: "We would rather suffer."[46] Hunter's troops agreed with the officer, a delighted Frank Reader hoping that Hunter "is going to put an end to this bushwhacking."[47]

On May 24, when a group of guerrillas fired from a house in Newtown on a cavalry detachment escorting a military train, Hunter immediately ordered Major Timothy Quinn to take his 1st New York troopers there to determine the building from which they fired the shots and then torch it and all of the outbuildings. The New Yorkers determined that the source of the attack was a Methodist parsonage and surrounded the building. As a soldier prepared to ignite it, a woman confronted Quinn, charging that "You go about this like you are accustomed to burning." "I am," Quinn replied sarcastically, "I have probably burned about 50." The pastor, returning home from riding circuit, arrived just in time to see his home in flames.[48]

Hunter also charged Quinn with informing the town's residents and those living along the Valley Pike that if guerrillas repeated the incident, "every rebel house within five miles" would meet a similar fate. A worried

44. "Secessions of West Virginia: Major-General Hunter's Order," Doc. 4, *RR*, X (1867), 172; Eby, ed., *Virginia Yankee*, 235.

45. David Hunter to Southern Claims Commission, June 30, 1874, Roll 5, RG 56, SCCP.

46. William D. Wintz, ed., *Civil War Memoirs of Two Rebel Sisters* (Charleston, W. Va., 1989), 36.

47. Reader Diary, May 26, 1864.

48. *OR*, Vol. XXXVII, Pt. 1, pp. 528, 557, 565; Wintz, ed., *Memoirs of Rebel Sisters*, 37; Eby, ed., *Virginia Yankee*, 235.

delegation requested an interview with Hunter, who sent Strother to meet with them. The colonel listened, then gave them a copy of Hunter's order and bluntly informed them that "vengeance would surely fall upon the country if these robberies and murders continued." The best way for them to protect themselves, he advised, would be to expose the guilty parties. The order and Strother's comments hit the mark, and the citizens told Strother that a Captain Glenn and a group of Marylanders, along with a Captain Sheerer of Winchester, operated in the area and that the home of a Mrs. Wilson served as their rendezvous point. Before returning to headquarters, Strother stopped at Middletown and delivered the same message; citizens there also agreed to provide information.[49] Hunter's order delighted many Valley Unionists. Julia Chase in Winchester thought that it was "exactly right," for "if persons will harbor these outlaws, they must expect the consequences."[50]

Acting upon Strother's intelligence, Hunter immediately directed the arrest of Mrs. Wilson for harboring guerrillas. When the arresting officer found that she rented her home, he ordered her to remove her possessions. Mrs. Wilson and her two daughters, thinking that only the house faced destruction, gladly complied. Much to her horror, while tied in a rocking chair, she watched soldiers pour oil on the pile and then ignite it. Adding to her humiliation, the officer tied her hands and then marched her off down the road in a downpour toward a guard tent. Finally, one soldier, taking pity on her, remarked, "Boys, I can't stand any more of this, what if it was your mother." He dismounted and let her ride his horse the rest of the way. On reaching the post, they required Mrs. Wilson to take an oath of allegiance to the government.[51]

On May 27, Captain George Ellicott went to burn a reputed bushwhacker's home near Woodstock. Finding on his arrival only a woman with three small children, he refused to torch the house. Upon Ellicott's return to headquarters, Hunter reprimanded him for his dereliction. When the captain replied that the house was not worth destroying, Hunter laughed and then dismissed him. On learning that some citizens at Woodstock had attempted to confuse his scouts, he sent Strother to investigate. The colonel, who frequently ameliorated the general's orders, felt

49. Eby, ed., *Virginia Yankee*, 235–36.
50. Chase Diary, May 24, 1864.
51. Eby, ed., *Virginia Yankee*, 236; Wintz, ed., *Memoirs of Rebel Sisters*, 38.

increasingly frustrated in dealing with the local populace. Himself a Virginian from the Valley region, Strother often felt moved to sympathy by the citizens' "outrage and distress." In order to be able to better fulfill his duties, he began distancing himself from social interaction with the population.[52]

Shortly after the Newtown incident, Gilmor's men fired on a supply train of sixteen wagons just outside the town, killing fourteen privates and two officers. Only the timely arrival of infantry saved the train from complete destruction. Furious at having his rear preyed upon as his army moved toward Staunton, Hunter on May 30 ordered a detachment of two hundred men from the 1st New York Cavalry under Major Joseph Stearns to Newtown and Middletown "for the purpose of burning every house, store, and out-building in that place," except for churches and the houses of known Unionists between the two towns. As the New Yorkers reached Newtown, they made their distaste for the assignment known by their "murmuring of disapproval."[53] The expressions "of mute helplessness" on the faces of old people and children strengthened their reluctance to burn the town. On interrogating citizens, they found that in the aftermath of the attack residents had cared for Federal soldiers wounded in the fray. Responsive to their troopers' objections, the officers agreed to disobey the order, instead merely administering an oath of allegiance to the citizens. Stearns, uncertain how Hunter would take the news, approached the general and gruffly told him. Hunter, surprised but "somewhat pleased" at his manner, dismissed him with a "good-natured grunt." Unknown to Stearns, Strother averted more serious consequences by pacifying Hunter as to the correctness of Stearns's decision.[54]

Determined to control civilian movements, Hunter prohibited them from passing through his lines. He recognized no passes, no matter their presumed authority, and required their bearers to report personally to his headquarters. Neither did dealings in contraband escape his attention. Hunter not only maintained a surveillance of sutlers and other tradesmen, but he showed a special interest in preventing the smuggling of proscribed items. He demanded the names and other intelligence about the traders,

52. Eby, ed., *Virginia Yankee*, 237–38.

53. *OR*, Vol. XXXVII, Pt. 1, p. 557; Asst. Adj. Gen. to Quinn, May 30, 1864, Letters Sent, #5680, II, Department of West Virginia, NA; Beach, *First New York Cavalry*, 355–56.

54. Beach, *First New York Cavalry*, 355–56; Stevenson, *"Boots and Saddles,"* 278–79; Eby, ed., *Virginia Yankee*, 241.

and directed provost marshals to scrutinize those dealing in goods. Finally, he ordered all sutlers, except those with express permission, back to Martinsburg.[55]

Meantime, Hunter readied the army to resume the campaign. Additional reinforcements arrived. Kelley, having received an order from Sigel for two regiments on May 17, immediately sent the 4th Virginia Regiment to Martinsburg. An Ohio militia unit and a detachment of the 34th Massachusetts left Martinsburg on the night of May 19 to join Sigel's army. Five days later, detachments of the 15th and 21st New York Cavalries were on their way from Cumberland. Yet Hunter's army remained badly short of stores and equipment, especially shoes. Even knapsacks to carry the required one hundred rounds of ammunition remained scarce, forcing unit quartermasters to order new ones from Martinsburg.[56]

Despite Hunter's efforts to minimize guerrilla activities, problems of supply remained serious. With supply lines becoming longer and more vulnerable to attack and harassment, he hoped to find the solution in Grant's suggestion that he should live off the country.[57] In General Orders No. 29 he prepared to do exactly that. Hunter was familiar with the constraints on living off the countryside contained in Grant's instructions for Sigel: *"Indiscriminate marauding should be avoided. Nothing should be taken not absolutely necessary for the troops, except when captured from an armed enemy."* Despite these lofty intentions, such a theoretical nicety would prove difficult to enforce in the face of necessity.[58]

Unknown to Hunter, forage and grain in Shenandoah and Rockingham Counties, just immediately to his southwest, remained scarce, and even Confederate forces in the area had trouble keeping troops supplied. In late February, Imboden had complained to Jubal Early, then temporarily in the Valley District, about the exhaustion of supplies and the difficulty of sustaining his cavalry there. In late March, Averell had noted in a report to Sigel that his train had left for Rockbridge County to secure supplies, since the country between that town and Timberville had "been exhausted."[59]

55. *OR*, Vol. XXXVII, Pt. 1, pp. 519, 525; Circular, May 27, 1864, Letters Sent, #5680, II, 254, and Special Orders No. 103, Special Orders, #5700, XX, 316, Department of West Virginia, NA.

56. *OR*, Vol. XXXVII, Pt. 1, pp. 478–79, 490, 505, 535; Wildes, *One Hundred and Sixteenth Ohio*, 89–90; Norton, *"Red Neck Ties,"* 36–37.

57. *OR*, Vol. XXXVI, Pt. 1, p. 8, Pt. 3, p. 183, and Vol. XXXVII, Pt. 1, p. 536.

58. *OR*, XXXIII, 765–66; Simon, ed., *Papers of Grant*, X, 236–37.

59. *OR*, XXXIII, 714, 1194–95.

As the army prepared to move on May 26, a correspondent of the Wheeling *Daily Intelligencer* noted that "before surprising the enemy Hunter took occasion to originate a more than little surprise 'at home.' "[60] He stripped his army down to bare essentials. Halpine, Hunter's assistant adjutant general, exhorted the troops: "We are contending against an enemy who is in earnest, and if we expect success, we too must be in earnest." So that "a glorious result may crown our effort," sacrifices and suffering would be required.[61] All excess baggage and equipment would be sent back to Martinsburg. Orders allowed each regiment only one wagon to "transport spare ammunition, camp kettle, tools and mess pans," and limited the amount of clothing to what a soldier could carry, plus an extra pair of shoes and socks. Knapsacks, he directed, would contain one hundred rounds of ammunition, four pounds of hard bread, and ten rations each of coffee, salt, and sugar. The men would have to make the provisions last for eight days.[62]

To Colonel Wildes, the "order looked like 'business.' "[63] Taken aback, Dr. Neil complained to his family that Hunter "issued some awful orders about one thing or another, one is we must fatten our mules and, if necessary, kill them for subsistence. He has cut our transportation down to almost nothing."[64] Colonel Lincoln noted that "the iron hand of the new Commander is already felt."[65] Private Reader, noting the four pounds of bread for what some expected to be a ten-day expedition, lamented, "We will have a hungry trip I fear."[66] The men of the 123rd Ohio grumbled that they were "being converted into a pack train." In response to an officer's query as to the name of his unit, one wit replied, "Troops! This is Hunter's ammunition train."[67]

As feeding the army became increasingly problematic for Hunter, the need arose for strict guidelines regarding the securing of provisions. He gave his officers the responsibility to obtain necessary foodstuffs from the

60. Wheeling *Daily Intelligencer*, June 15, 1864.

61. *OR*, Vol. XXXVII, Pt. 1, pp. 517–18.

62. Wildes, *One Hundred and Sixteenth Ohio*, 89–91; Goudy Diary, May 24, 1864; Patterson Diary, May 22, 1864; Lynch, *Civil War Diary*, 62; New York *Herald*, June 9, 1864.

63. Wildes, *One Hundred and Sixteenth Ohio*, 90.

64. Neil to Friends, May 23, 1864, Neil Letters.

65. Lincoln, *Thirty-fourth Massachusetts*, 292.

66. Reader Diary, May 23–24, 1864.

67. Keyes, *History of the 123d Ohio*, 59; Hewitt, *Twelfth West Virginia*, 145; Wildes, *One Hundred and Sixteenth Ohio*, 90–91.

countryside and to prevent waste, and directed Stahel to establish regulations supervising the acquisition of supplies under "reliable and just officers." For Unionist citizens he required the officers to issue certificates as payment for any stores taken. Hunter cautioned that officers were "to hold their men well in hand, and to allow no plundering or oppression of the inhabitants." Pillaging was forbidden. In compliance, officers, such as Colonel John E. Wynkoop, issued stringent directions that anyone leaving camp or the column on the march "would be punished severely."[68]

Sensitive to the need to maintain an adequate supply of horses for the cavalry, Hunter warned against any misuse of the animals, adding that "all who break down their horses from want of care or unnecessary hardship on the march will not be sent to the rear." Negligence would effectively mean joining the infantry.[69] For troopers, especially officers, the replacement of their horses with fresh ones became a necessity, and thus the breakdown of horses posed a serious problem for the local populace as well. Sergeant William McIlhenny's complaint that there was "no forage for our horses" was not an uncommon one.[70] As the cavalry moved up the Valley in Augusta County near Mount Sidney, two officers rode over to G. W. Hollar's farm and took his horse. In reply to his protest, as Hollar remembered, the officer "told me his own was near giving out and he must have another." The Alexander Clem family, despite their loyalty, quickly learned that troopers targeted stables. The Federals led their horse and one belonging to the widow of Clem's brother, killed by bushwhackers, back to their camp.[71] In a confrontation with Philip Engleman, a Rockbridge County farmer, soldiers told him that they had "orders to take all the horses they could get, their horses were broken down."[72] Officially, Hunter required all foraging squads to turn horses over to the acting provost marshal general for transfer to the chief quartermaster.[73]

68. OR, Vol. XXXVII, Pt. 1, pp. 546, 577; General Order No. 34, June 1, 1864, Robert Smith Rodgers Papers, DU; Porter, "Operations of Sigel and Hunter in the Shenandoah Valley, May and June, 1864," 71; Farrar, *Twenty-Second Pennsylvania*, 232–33.

69. Hunter to Stahel, May 23, 1864, Letters Sent, II, #5680, 55, Department of West Virginia.

70. William McIhenny Diary, May 28, 1864, USMHI.

71. G. W. Hollar file, #21827, and Alexander Clem file, #9309, RG 217, SCCP.

72. Philip Engleman file, #1104, microfile 966, RG 233, SCCP.

73. Circular, May 27, 1864, Letters Sent, #5680, II, 254, Department of West Virginia; Farrar, *Twenty-Second Pennsylvania*, 233–34.

At Woodstock, Hunter wrote to Halleck on May 28 that in advancing "I shall depend entirely on the country."[74] Later, at New Market on June 4, Hunter reiterated his orders that "No straggling or pillaging will be allowed." Acquisitions would be made properly and in an orderly fashion.[75] Only loyal persons would be given receipts for their property. In reality, officers and soldiers gave few receipts or vouchers to residents, whether loyal or not. Soldiers commonly told citizens that they would be paid for the items later. In time Hunter made the character of the expedition more explicit to the army. In General Orders No. 34 he explained the need for them to be cut loose from their base because of "the rapid manner in which it will be necessary to march for the successful accomplishment of our object." Those falling sick on the march would be left in the care of loyal residents, for it would be "inhuman to expose those who are seriously sick to the fatigues of rapid transportation."[76] As Hunter later stated, "In my march to Lynchburg, Virginia, I cut loose from my base of supplies, and lived entirely on the enemy. This I did on my own responsibility. We needed every thing we found in the way of supplies, and we took every thing."[77]

The matter of citizen loyalty became academic as the army moved up the Valley and the matter of simple survival grew more urgent. When pressed by a purported Unionist, officers or soldiers merely repeated the standard answer: payment would be made later. Mathew Tisdale, a Unionist farmer in Augusta County, protested the loss of his two horses. Since he "had obeyed Presdt Lincoln's proclamation," the Federals "should protect" his property. The officer had told him that "he was compelled to take them" and that Tisdale would be paid later.[78] Robert Gray of Rockingham County had actively campaigned against secession in 1861 and offered "Generals Fremont, Genl Hunter, & Genl Ricketts to make his house their headquarters," yet he sustained losses of 1,500 fence rails, 150 cords of wood, and 400 panels of plank fencing to Hunter's men for fuel.[79] George Kline, a Dunker known for his Unionist sentiments and activities, did not escape losing his horse to soldiers.[80]

74. OR, Vol. XXXVII, Pt. 1, p. 548.
75. Porter, "Operations of Sigel and Hunter," 71.
76. General Orders No. 34, June 1, 1864, Rodgers Papers.
77. Hunter to Southern Claims Commission, June 30, 2874, Roll 5, RG 56, SCCP.
78. Mathew Tisdale file, #7651, RG 217, SCCP.
79. Robert A. Gray file, #8935, RG 223, SCCP.
80. George Kline file, #15250, RG 223, SCCP.

Hunter fully expected that the upper Valley above the North River, un-spoiled by military operations, would provide the necessary subsistence. His intent to maintain discipline against plundering was admirable, but once the army actually began advancing, the number of serious incidents of pillaging and despoiling property grew. Scarcity of rations compounded the problem, for before the army had even passed Strasburg, shortages for some regiments were already becoming serious, particularly for the men of the 116th Ohio, who had suffered from "half rations of bread from the very start."[81] William Patterson complained that his command had "no bread at all for officers. . . . How the Gen. means to feed us don't know."[82]

Soldiers became experts at finding provender, and were often assisted in their efforts by slaves, who willingly pointed out the location of hidden provisions. Lieutenant William Beach observed that during a few minutes' rest in front of a farmhouse, "the men were busy as ants, bringing sacks full of shelled corn that had been stored in the attic."[83] The widow of Samuel Jones later charged that Captain Matthew Berry, who stayed with them, told his men "to take what they wanted."[84] Private Reader noted that "the boys are getting along finely in subsisting off this country and we will dev-astate it before we leave it."[85]

Hunter harbored no qualms in meting out punishments to those sol-diers who engaged in plundering. Sergeant George Case Setchell, a some-time scavenger himself, noted that the general "had as many as 100 men at a time marching up and down in front of his headquarters for being caught at it."[86] Ironically, instead of acting as a deterrent, his disciplinary actions created resentment, for as the men believed, "We can stand most anything but hunger. It did seem very strange to us that we could not for-age in the enemy's country." In another case, much to the indignation of his men, Sullivan disciplined a group by having them carry rails all after-noon and taking their money and other items from them.[87]

81. Wildes, *One Hundred and Sixteenth Ohio*, 91.

82. Patterson Diary, May 27–30, June 12, 1864.

83. Beach, *First New York Cavalry*, 359.

84. Samuel Jones file, #16654, microfiche 2201, RG 223, SCCP.

85. Reader Diary, May 30, 1864.

86. George Case Setchell, "A Sergeant's View of the Battle of Piedmont," *CWT*, II (1963), 43.

87. Lynch, *Civil War Diary*, 64–65.

On the morning of May 26, with the army reorganized and augmented and Breckinridge no longer a factor in the Valley, Federal units began to push southward from Cedar Creek. Hunter, along with some twelve thousand troops, made ready to strike for Staunton. As a precaution, he ordered the army to camp "in order of battle. The infantry in front, cavalry in rear, and artillery and trains in the center."[88] Reaching a point above Strasburg, the army stopped briefly to rest. The break allowed Hunter time to order the burning of several houses reputed to be rendezvous points for bushwhackers.[89]

The army's entry into Woodstock on May 27 sparked pandemonium. Colonel Strother observed that "the whole town was squalling with women, children, chickens and geese."[90] Soldiers busily gathered up produce and stock and threatened "to burn down every dwelling in the neighborhood."[91] James Rudy, a nearby farmer, lost five horses, eighteen sheep, a cow and heifer, and sixty chickens.[92] A few angry women derided the soldiers with the taunt, "We've seen 'em come back this way a might sight faster than they went up."[93] Hunter, however, was in high spirits. A band played "Just in Time for Lanigans Ball," and "the old fellow skipped around over the porch to it and it was real amusing."[94] He then ordered the local jail searched, "evidently seeking an apology [excuse] to burn something and proposed to set fire to the Hollingsworth Hotel." To dissuade him from doing so, the colonel told him that in the aftermath of a previous engagement the hotel housed wounded Union soldiers who received good care from local residents.[95]

Hunter halted in Woodstock until a supply train caught up with the army and delivered shoes for his men. Colonel Wildes estimated that as many as two thousand had lacked shoes when Hunter assumed command.

88. OR, Vol. XXXVII, Pt. 1, pp. 537–38.

89. Eby, ed., *Virginia Yankee*, 236; Wildes, *One Hundred and Sixteenth Ohio*, 91; Extracts of the Diaries of Levi Pitman of Mt. Olive, Shenandoah Co., Va., 1845–1892, May 26, 1864, p. 22, Shenandoah County Library, Edinburg, Va.

90. Eby, ed., *Virginia Yankee*, 237.

91. Pitman Diaries, May 28, 1864, 22.

92. James Rudy file #2568, microfiche 2221, RG 233, SCCP.

93. O'Reilly, *Baked Meats*, 299.

94. Reader Diary, May 27, 1862.

95. Eby, ed., *Virginia Yankee*, 238.

Many of them marched from Cedar Creek without them. Wildes found it "really a pitiful sight to see them marching along, leaving marks of blood on the ground."[96]

On May 29 the army began moving further south. Reaching the Mount Jackson area the same day, Federal units began experiencing a stiffening Confederate resistance. Yet with inferior numbers, Imboden could not seriously challenge Hunter. Pulling back, he informed Lee from New Market on May 27 that there was no point north of Mount Crawford "where I can successfully resist him, and there it is very doubtful, though I will do my best." He feared that Stahel's superior cavalry could easily outflank and envelop his men. Mount Crawford and the North River, he believed, offered a better defensive line. The most Imboden hoped for was that the skirmishing would delay the Union advance toward Staunton.[97]

After fording the North Fork of the Shenandoah River at Mount Jackson, Hunter halted at New Market on May 30. Remaining there until June 2, veterans took the opportunity to revisit the battlefield. Rain had washed away the soil in some places, uncovering graves and exposing corpses to the sun. Corporal Jonas B. Kauffman recoiled at "a sight beyond description."[98] Private Samuel Farrar saw a man who "was buried just where he died."[99] Colonel Lincoln found a mass grave of indiscriminately and poorly buried dead in which "feet, arms, and heads were protruding at all points of this festering mass."[100] Regimental burial details busily disinterred bodies and gave them proper graves with headboards.

In reflecting on the battle, many veterans reconsidered their opinion of Sigel. Many of the men of the 5th West Virginia Cavalry believed that the general "had no cause whatever, for getting whipped. All that hurt him was, that he couldn't handle his troops." Hunter's reputation grew in comparison, and the West Virginians believed that "the whole command is eager to try the Rebels under Gen. Hunter."[101] He also won high praise from Theodore Wilson, a correspondent for the New York *Herald*, for inspiring his troops "by his persevering activity, his presence and his counsel."[102]

96. Wildes, *One Hundred and Sixteenth Ohio*, 89, 91–92.

97. OR, Vol. XXXVII, Pt. 1, p. 749.

98. J. B. Kauffman to B. A. Colonna, n.d., New Market Battle File.

99. Farrar, *Twenty-Second Pennsylvania*, 233.

100. Lincoln, *Thirty-fourth Massachusetts*, 295.

101. Reader Diary, May 30, 1864.

102. New York *Herald*, June 9, 1864.

Before moving further south, Hunter waited to establish contact with Crook. The delay gave his army a respite to rest and forage, much to the despair the local population. Soldiers scouring the countryside took "everything eatable, and many other things." According to a sergeant in the 22nd Pennsylvania Cavalry, "The ladies took it all coolly; rich, modest and refined, I pitied them."[103] Men of the 123rd Ohio, out of hardtack, got their first flour since enlisting and made "slap-jacks." As Private Reader observed, the West Virginians welcomed the opportunity to live "off the *fat of the land.*"[104]

By June 2, Hunter was ready to move again. The 34th Massachusetts Regiment, breaking camp at 5 A.M., briskly marched out of New Market with their band playing as wounded Federals cheered from the windows of makeshift hospitals. Residents, however, remained quiet. As the 18th Connecticut passed through town, "those who did show themselves looked angry and threatening."[105] Shortly beyond the town, cavalry units began clashing with Southern pickets, and then they encountered a small force near Lacey Spring.[106]

News of the renewed movement spread up the Valley. Residents in Harrisonburg anticipated the Federals' arrival with apprehension. A cavalryman brought the news of their approach, and immediately a squad of scouts rode down the pike to verify the report's accuracy. Within half a mile of town they watched as "the head of the enemy's column rose black over Gambill's hill. . . . They continued to pour over the hill in solid Columns . . . and came on quietly, their horses at a walk." The squad spread the alarm and sent a warning to Staunton, then waited at the courthouse for the Federals to appear. Seeing the Southerners, the approaching troopers fired at them and then charged, pursuing "at break-neck speed" until they reached Imboden's troops on the edge of Harrisonburg. Reining in their horses, the Federals pulled back until reinforcements could arrive. Soon the Southerners, consisting of regulars and some Rockingham reserves, began retreating toward Mount Crawford.[107]

Federal troops overran Harrisonburg. The band of the 34th Massachu-

103. Farrar, *Twenty-Second Pennsylvania*, 232.
104. Keyes, *History of the 123d Ohio*, 60.
105. Lincoln, *Thirty-fourth Massachusetts*, 296; Walker, *Eighteenth Connecticut*, 228.
106. Patterson Diary, June 2, 1864.
107. "Hunter's Raid, 1864," SHSP, XXXVI (1908), 96–98; *Harrisonburg, Virginia: Diary of a Citizen* (Berryville, Va.), June 1–2, 1864.

setts paraded through town playing patriotic music, while many of their hospitalized comrades cheered from windows and doors.[108] The residents of Harrisonburg, a small town of just over a thousand, felt the sting of another occupation.[109] As the 123rd Ohio camped, a detachment of 150 men was sent into town for picket duty. Yet soldiers had already began searching houses for foodstuffs such as meat and flour. Foraging parties also discovered other commodities, such as muslin, valued at $2,000, and a bale of batting. The following day the Ohioans broke up into small parties to scour the countryside, and soon they deposited seventy-five barrels of flour and large quantities of tobacco, plus caches of meat, sugar, and corn, on the courthouse lawn.[110] Peter Blosser looked on as foragers looted his garret and took from his farm a carriage, a mare, two cattle, fourteen hogs, twelve sheep, and 280 pounds of bacon.[111]

Meanwhile, soldiers searched the old brick courthouse. When they discovered that city authorities were preparing the county records for shipment to safety, they removed the records and burned them. Soldiers also gutted the offices of the local paper, the *Rockingham Register* and destroyed its press and type, fouling Strother's and Halpine's plan to publish an edition of the paper to amuse the troops.[112]

Plundering became severe. "This is not necessary and should not be permitted," Strother noted, "especially as there are some wounded Union soldiers here who have been well treated by the citizens."[113] William McIlhenny agreed, noting in his diary that "we had some pretty bad boys among us." One enterprising soldier persuaded the proprietor of a saloon to let him "take charge of the place." Finding a barrel of whiskey, he was soon doing business "over the counter at a lively rate." Hunter, seeing some of his men returning to camp drunk, investigated, stopped the sale, and arrested the men.[114]

The Federals were surprised by how little serious opposition they had encountered in their advance to Harrisonburg, but with Imboden posi-

108. Lincoln, *Thirty-fourth Massachusetts*, 297.

109. *Population: Eighth Census*, 519.

110. Keyes, *History of the 123d Ohio*, 60–61; Wildes, *One Hundred and Sixteenth Ohio*, 92.

111. Peter Blosser file, #16500, microfiche 1438, RG 233, SCCP.

112. Hanchett, *Irish: Charles Halpine*, 114; Eby, ed., *Virginia Yankee*, 241.

113. Eby, ed., *Virginia Yankee*, 241.

114. William McIhenny Diary, June 3, 1864.

tioned at Mount Crawford, Hunter knew the situation would shortly change. He spent most of the remainder of the day attempting to ascertain Southern strength. Intelligence reported strong entrenchments, with the North River in Imboden's front. Felled trees blocked all the fords, and a 24-pound howitzer and a 20-pound Parrott on the heights commanded the fords and the bridge. With reports estimating Imboden's augmented force at twenty-five hundred, an assault might be costly, and Strother advised strongly against attacking his position on the North River. Instead, Strother suggested flanking the Confederate position by moving to Port Republic. There, he reasoned, Hunter would easily be in a position to send cavalry units south to Waynesboro, where his troopers could cut the Virginia Central Railroad and thereby isolate Staunton from the east. Such a strategy, he argued, would demoralize Imboden's army. Hunter agreed.[115] That evening, a courier brought news that Crook was near Buffalo Gap. Hoping to signal him, Hunter sent a number of rockets aloft to apprise him of their position, but he received no response.[116]

Early the following morning, June 3, the army, expecting to engage the Confederates at Mount Crawford, took up its march at 5 A.M. As a feint to conceal their movements, and also "to amuse" himself, Hunter, at the urging of Strother and Lieutenant John Meigs, sent Meigs with a cavalry detachment toward Mount Crawford.[117] McNeill's rangers observed the Federals closely as they left Harrisonburg and were surprised that they turned left onto the Port Republic Road rather than continue up the Valley Pike toward Staunton. McNeill exclaimed, "Where do they go to?" Another ranger suggested that he should turn his binoculars to the other road. Quickly seeing the Federals, he exclaimed, "Ah! there go the rascals—horse, foot and dragoon." Immediately he dispatched a courier to Mount Crawford to inform Imboden.[118] The rangers were not alone in their surprise. Hunter's troops, anticipating a much different route, found that "the move rather astonishes all of us."[119]

115. Eby, ed., *Virginia Yankee*, 241.

116. OR, Vol. XXXVII, Pt. 1, p. 94; Lang, *Loyal West Virginia*, 117; Humphreys, *Lynchburg Campaign*, 30; Eby, *"Porte Crayon,"* 114; Lincoln, *Thirty-fourth Massachusetts*, 297; Patterson Diary, June 3, 1864.

117. OR, Vol. XXXVII, Pt. 1, p. 94; Eby, ed., *Virginia Yankee*, 242; Wheeling *Daily Intelligencer*, June 21, 1864; Baltimore *American*, June 14, 1864.

118. "Hunter's Raid, 1864," 98–100; Williams, ed., *Rebel Brothers*, 195.

119. Reader Diary, June 4, 1864.

Marching through heavy rain, the army easily made its way to Port Republic without fear of harassment as Meigs's troopers drove Imboden's skirmishers back toward Mount Crawford. At the South Branch of the Shenandoah River, the high and swift-running water forced them to halt while they constructed a pontoon bridge. Despite the high water, Stahel risked sending the 20th Pennsylvania Cavalry across to secure the other side. The train carrying canvas pontoons finally arrived, but constructing the bridge became a torturous affair and it was 6 P.M. before troops could move across it. An anxious Hunter shouted orders, "Men, break step," to divide the weight on the "frail bridge." The crossing progressed slowly, and finally, at dusk, the rear guard reached the other side and went into camp. The delay, Strother feared, had sacrificed "all the benefits of our early march."[120]

Meanwhile, Stahel's cavalry had driven out the few Confederates in Port Republic and snared thirteen wagons of a large supply train. Captain Ellicott complained that "they should have captured a hundred, but the cavalry was cowardly." Scouring the countryside for additional prizes, a squad of troopers overtook Elijah Sibert driving his horses and carriage. They arrested him, took him back to Port Republic, and put his carriage to good use the next day as an ambulance.[121] That evening, Hunter's men destroyed a local woolen mill and its machinery. Corporal Lynch observed that "a number of women were crying as the mill burned."[122] Strother also lamented, but not for the burnt factory. In the delay they had "lost the opportunity of making a dash to Waynesboro." For the army, sleeping on their arms, the night of June 4 was "fearful, dark, rainy." Early the next morning, Hunter woke his chief of staff. Hearing the sounds of skirmishing, they both realized that the day would undoubtedly bring a battle.[123]

---

120. Eby, ed., *Virginia Yankee*, 242; Lynch, *Civil War Diary*, 66–67; Walker, *Eighteenth Connecticut*, 228; Keyes, *History of the 123d Ohio*, 62; Setchell, "Sergeant's View of Battle of Piedmont," 43.

121. Elijah Sibert file #17089, microfiche 2223, RG 233, SCCP.

122. Lynch, *Civil War Diary*, 68.

123. Eby, ed., *Virginia Yankee*, 242; David Powell, Memoirs of a Union Officer During the Civil War, 69, USMHI.

Brigadier General William Woods Averell (seated)
Courtesy of U.S. Army Military History Institute

Major General John C. Breckinridge
Courtesy of Library of Congress

Major General George Crook
Courtesy of Library of Congress

Benjamin West's depiction of the charge of the
VMI Corps of Cadets at the Battle of New Market.
Courtesy of Virginia Military Institute Archives

Lieutenant Colonel John S. Mosby (standing, center) and some of his vaunted raiders, ca. 1862

Courtesy of the author

Ruins of the Virginia Military Institute
Courtesy of Virginia Military Institute Archives

Lieutenant General Jubal A. Early shortly after the war
Courtesy of Library of Congress

Major General David Hunter
Courtesy of U.S. Army Military History Institute

Brigadier General John D. Imboden
Courtesy of Library of Congress

Brigadier General John McCausland
Courtesy of West Virginia State Archives, Charleston

Major General Franz Sigel
Courtesy of Library of Congress

Colonel David H. Strother
Courtesy of Library of Congress

6

Piedmont

News of the New Market victory, coming at the beginning of a new campaign season, had greatly boosted Southern morale. On May 16, a joyful Lee immediately wired Breckinridge "to offer you the thanks of the army for your victory over General Sigel." Four days later, after learning "the completeness of your success," he praised him "for the ability and zeal you have displayed in the management of the affairs of your department and of the Valley District." Lee was especially thankful for "the relief it has afforded me."[1] Soon after his arrival at Hanover Junction on May 20, Breckinridge's reputation with the War Department soared even higher when he repulsed General Philip Sheridan's attempt to destroy the bridge over the South Anna River in Lee's rear. Veterans of the Army of Northern Virginia cheered him as he appeared in their camps.[2] Major Josiah Gorgas, chief of the Ordnance Bureau, noted on June 1 that "General Breckinridge appears to be rising in favor as a dashing commander."[3]

For the public, Breckinridge's victory evoked memories of Stonewall Jackson's Valley campaign of 1862. Exulting over the achievement, the Richmond *Daily Dispatch* wrote that "Gen. Breckinridge, in celerity of

1. OR, Vol. XXXVII, Pt. 1, pp. 737, 744–45.

2. Johnston, "Sketches of Breckinridge," 317.

3. Frank E. Vandiver, ed., *The Civil War Diary of General Josiah Gorgas* (University, Ala., 1947), 110–11; Davis, *Breckinridge*, 431.

movement, has proven himself a worthy successor of Jackson."[4] The Richmond *Whig*, comparing him to Jackson and Turner Ashby, boasted that the gallant Kentuckian had added to the fame of Southern arms "by renewing the performances of the first and second years of the war."[5] The Harrisonburg *Rockingham Register* referred to him as "that accomplished and fearless leader," noting that "the enemy has fallen back down the Valley much faster than he came up, and has been severely punished for his temerity."[6]

Sigel's defeat partially frustrated Grant's design in western Virginia. Staunton remained momentarily safe, and the important Virginia Central Railroad continued to link that section with the east. Sigel's debacle also renewed the possibility of a Confederate initiative in the Valley. As early as April, such a prospect had suggested itself as the means of relieving Federal pressure on the region. The virtues of such a move were not lost on Lee. Along with his congratulations, on May 16 he urged Breckinridge to "press them down the Valley, and, if practicable, follow him to Maryland." Later that day, however, Lee's enthusiasm became more tempered. Pressed by Grant, he wired that if "your command is not otherwise needed in the Valley or in your department, I desire you to prepare to join me."[7]

Lee's need for reinforcements became increasingly acute as the savage battles from the Wilderness to Spotsylvania Court House severely taxed the Army of Northern Virginia.[8] He desperately needed to reinforce his army to combat Grant's aggressive tactics and his two-to-one advantage in men. Buoyed by a May 17 newspaper report of Beauregard's success at Bermuda Hundred, he wired Davis that if the changed situation around Richmond permitted, "I recommend that such troops as can be spared be sent to me at once." If he did not receive reinforcements, he warned, the question would be "whether we shall fight the battle here or around Richmond."[9]

4. Richmond *Daily Dispatch*, May 19, 1864.

5. Richmond *Whig*, May 17, 1864.

6. Extract of Harrisonburg (Va.) *Rockingham Register* in Lynchburg *Virginian*, May 23, 1864.

7. Lee to Breckinridge, May 16, 1864, Telegram Book, Lee's Headquarters Papers; *OR*, Vol. XXXVII, Pt. 1, pp. 737–38.

8. E. B. Long, *The Civil War Day by Day: An Almanac, 1861–1865* (Garden City, N.Y., 1971), 494, 505.

9. Dowdey and Manarin, eds., *Papers of Lee*, 733; Douglas Southall Freeman, ed., *Lee's Dispatches* (Baton Rouge, 1994), 186–87.

Meanwhile, intelligence reports from West Virginia indicated a diminished threat from that region. The news of Crook and Averell's uniting at Union but moving toward Lewisburg lessened fears, [10] while Sigel's retreat to Cedar Creek reassured Southern authorities. The Federals were "much disorganized and demoralized," Imboden wired Breckinridge. "They seem to have no idea of moving from Cedar Creek, and have circulated a report that they are awaiting re-enforcements." Such news provided a new sense of security for the Valley. [11] Optimistic newspaper reports assumed the disappearance of the threat and Sigel's return to Martinsburg. The *Rockingham Register* chortled that "the Dutch Yankee General Sigel . . . has concluded that it is best for him to keep as low down the Valley as possible." [12]

Lee, noting the diminished threat from Averell and Crook, suggested to Breckinridge on May 17 that before leaving the Valley he should organize a Valley guard and then proceed to Hanover Junction with his infantry and any cavalry that could be spared. On the following day, acting on reports that reinforcements going to Grant were from Sigel's army, Lee wired that "if this be true, you can with safety join me." In reply, Breckinridge assured him of his intention to "move as rapidly as possible." [13] When Breckinridge joined the Army of Northern Virginia on May 20, Lee positioned him at Hanover Junction, not merely to guard the main route to Richmond with its important railroad bridges across the North and South Anna Rivers but also to allow him the flexibility to "speedily return to [the] Valley if necessary." [14]

At the time, Lee believed that sufficient forces remained in western Virginia to resist a renewed threat by Sigel. "Grumble" Jones in the southwest had informed Lee that he possessed "4000 infantry & dismounted cavalry, 1000 mounted men & plenty of artillery," while Imboden reported a strength of 3,000 men. [15] In reality, however, the numbers were inflated. As Hunter began his movement south from Cedar Creek on May 26, Imboden's strength was closer to 1,200 men. Imboden's command consisted of two regiments, the 18th Virginia, 23rd Virginia Cavalry, and

10. *OR*, Vol. XXXVII, Pt. 1, p. 738.

11. *Ibid.*, 739, 743.

12. Harrisonburg (Va.) *Rockingham Register*, quoted in Richmond *Whig*, May 31, 1864.

13. *OR*, Vol. XXXVII, Pt. 1, pp. 738, 742–44, and Vol. LI, Pt. 2, p. 943.

14. Freeman, ed., *Lee's Dispatches*, 189, 194; Johnston, "Sketches of Breckinridge," 317; Davis, *Breckinridge*, 433–34.

15. Dowdey and Manarin, eds. *Papers of Lee*, 767.

McClanahan's battery of six guns, plus Gilmor's Maryland Battalion, Davis's Maryland Battalion, and McNeill's rangers. The 62nd Virginia Mounted Infantry, his largest regiment, despite his pleas, had gone with Breckinridge to join Lee. Local reserves, armed with hunting rifles, shotguns, and various other firearms, provided another 1,100. An additional 700 boys and old men, mainly mounted on workhorses, afforded another source of manpower. Yet the necessity of watching Federal activity in West Virginia and the lower Valley stretched his forces thin, and in an emergency it would take time to concentrate them. [16]

Imboden's scouts closely watched for any surreptitious probings or canards. Captain Davis refused to honor a flag of truce for the purpose of recovering the body of a captain for fear that it was merely a ruse. At Fisher's Hill on May 18, his men stopped a wagon carrying medical supplies, escorted by a squad of cavalry destined for Union wounded. They allowed the wagon to continue but demanded that the troopers wait for its return. [17] Imboden engaged in a number of ruses himself in an attempt to conceal Breckinridge's departure, hoping to create the impression "that you were still in command." [18] However, reported Federal probings increasingly concerned him and, fearing that "I shall soon have urgent need for all my men," he began pressing Breckinridge for the return of the 62nd Virginia, which "is small now, and will be of little value to you." [19] Federal activity soon justified his fears. Southern vigilance quickly spotted Hunter's movement, and even before the Federals camped at the end of their first day he knew of their advance. [20]

Breckinridge's departure raised the question of command in western Virginia. In the void, "Grumble" Jones wired the War Department on May 20, "Must I assume command of Western Virginia?" Three days later, from Abingdon, having not yet received an order merging his department with western Virginia, he again asked for instructions. Since Jones held the senior commission, Seddon assigned him to the Department of South-

16. J. D. Imboden, "The Battle of Piedmont," *CV*, XXXI (1923), 459; J. D. Imboden, "Fire, Sword, and the Halter," 171–72; Marshall Moore Brice, *Conquest of a Valley* (Verona, Va., 1965), 25–26.

17. *OR*, Vol. XXXVII, Pt. 1, pp. 742, 745; *The Medical and Surgical History of the War of the Rebellion* (Washington, D.C., 1875), I, pt. 1, Appendix, 227.

18. *OR*, Vol. XXXVII, Pt. 1, p. 745.

19. *Ibid.*, 744.

20. *Ibid.*, 748.

western Virginia.[21] Military units in the Valley District, however, remained under Imboden, although Lee retained supervisory authority. Meanwhile, Lee, recognizing the need to appoint a competent replacement for Breckinridge, urged the War Department on May 25 to send "a good commander . . . at once" and informed Seddon that he would return Breckinridge as soon as he could.[22]

That same day Imboden wired Lee that scouts reported a "massing at Beverly for a raid on Staunton."[23] Lee told him to ready the reserves, assuring him that he would "return General Breckinridge as soon as I can."[24] The next day Imboden wired more accurate news, reporting that Hunter's army was advancing from Strasburg to Maurertown with eight days' rations and a train carrying canvas pontoons. Two days later his anxiety became even more pronounced when Federal units reached Mount Jackson. "His cavalry outnumbers ours two to one," he informed Lee, "his infantry four to one; his artillery four to one." Compelled to fall back, he despaired of the lack of any defensive position north of Mount Crawford where he might "successfully resist him, and even there," he feared, "it is very doubtful, though I will do my best."[25]

Driven back through New Market, Imboden, rather than risking a direct confrontation, relied on the tactics of delay. Hoping to increase Federal caution, he spread rumors that in falling back he expected to receive reinforcements. He realized that in the open Valley he could not offer any serious opposition for fear that Stahel's more sizable cavalry could easily flank and envelop his men. At Lacey Spring he received a report of a Federal column headed toward McDowell and of the Federals' continuing movement from the west. With Hunter's army moving southward from Mount Jackson, an alarmed Imboden wired Jones for aid. To him the Federal objective was clear: Staunton.[26]

On June 1, Imboden detailed his strategy to Jones. He wanted to induce

21. *Ibid.*, Vol. XXXIX, Pt. 2, pp. 616–17, and Vol. XXXVII, Pt. 1, pp. 745–47.

22. *Ibid.*, Vol. XXXVII, Pt. 1, pp. 747–49, and Vol. LI, Pt. 2, pp. 981–82.

23. *Ibid.*, Vol. XXXVII, Pt. 1, p. 748.

24. Lee to Imboden, May 25, 1864, 230. Telegram Book, Lee's Headquarters Papers.

25. OR, Vol. XXXVI, Pt. 3, p. 836, and Vol. XXXVII, Pt. 1, p. 749.

26. *Ibid.*, Vol. XXXVII, Pt. 1, p. 749; J. D. Imboden, "Fire, Sword, and the Halter," 172; Battle of Piedmont, Virginia. Fought on Sunday, June 5th, 1864, Account Taken Directly from Original Letter of General J. D. Imboden to Col. I. Marshall McCue, October 1st, 1883, p. 2, MC.

Hunter "to follow me up as far as Mount Crawford," but he feared that since Hunter was "playing a devilish cautious" game, he "may not take the bait." If he did, he assured Jones, "we can get him on 'a run,' we can ruin him." With Crook moving from Greenbrier toward Staunton, Imboden would hold the North River line while Jones "thrash[ed] Crook and Averell, and then we can pay our respects jointly to Mr. Hunter."[27] Federal delays at New Market and Harrisonburg provided Imboden with valuable time, though not to effect his impractical plan. Lee, already concerned, ordered Jones with all available forces to go to Imboden's aid.[28] Unable to spare even a regiment, much less the small 62nd Virginia Regiment, he ordered Jones to call out the reserves. In addition, "Mudwall" Jackson at Jackson River, with Jones's approval, marched to join Imboden.[29] At Bang's depot, Colonel B. H. Jones, with the 60th Virginia and Bryan's battery, boarded a train and headed for Staunton by way of Lynchburg and Charlottesville.[30] Meanwhile, "Grumble" Jones wired Richmond on May 31 that he was on his way to join Imboden.[31] Pleased, Lee telegraphed him to "proceed with all dispatch with your troops."[32] On the night of June 2, Jones wired Imboden that he would arrive shortly with three thousand troops.[33]

Meanwhile, Imboden summoned all available men in Augusta County to form companies. He even called on minor government officials, normally exempted, to go to Mount Crawford. In a broadside he shamed any who might shirk the call: "I see no reason why Magistrates & Constables should not *fight for their homes* in a pinch like this."[34] Captain James F. Jones of the Nitre and Mining Corps ordered his men to report to him at Staunton, and on June 3 some 130 of them assembled.[35] Meanwhile, after being easily driven from Harrisonburg on June 3, Imboden's troopers skirmished with the Federals at Lacey Spring and then continued to retire. At

27. David Strother, "Operations in West Virginia," *RR*, XI, 486; J. D. Imboden, "Fire, Sword, and the Halter," 172–73.

28. *OR*, Vol. XXXVII, Pt. 1, p. 750.

29. *Ibid.*, 750–51.

30. Humphreys Autobiography, II, 318; Humphreys, *Lynchburg Campaign*, 30; Jenning Diary, June 1–3, 1864.

31. *OR*, Vol. XXXVII, Pt. 1, p. 751.

32. Lee to Jones, June 1, 1864, Telegraph Book, 233, Lee's Headquarters Papers.

33. J. D. Imboden, "Battle of Piedmont" (1923), 459.

34. Quoted in Brice, *Conquest of Valley*, 30.

35. *OR*, Vol. LI, Pt. 1, p. 1225.

Mount Crawford they crossed over to the south side of North River to wait for Hunter's approach.[36]

On June 2, Imboden had informed Lee of his retreat, noting that his force contained only "about 3,000 men and ten guns. . . . My artillery ammunition is exhausted and none at Staunton." He feared that Hunter might attempt a flanking movement with his cavalry through Brown's Gap to strike at Charlottesville and then Staunton. Could Lee "give additional aid to the Valley"?[37] Busily his men fortified various fords. A 20-pound Parrott gun guarded the bridge, while a 24-pound howitzer secured other points. Meanwhile, Jones's troops slowly traveled by rail to Lynchburg and then on to Staunton. Yet much to Imboden's dismay, the number of arrivals fell well below the expected three thousand. None of the approaching units was sizable. "Mostly they were in companies, and parts of companies."[38] By June 2 a number of small detachments had arrived, as well as the reserves of Augusta and Rockingham Counties. Bryan's battery, reaching Staunton before their horses could catch up with them, temporarily impressed local mounts, refitted them with wagon harnesses and single-trees, and then pressed on to the front.[39] In North Carolina near Newton, General John C. Vaughn's brigade rapidly left for Bristol, where they boarded freight cars for Lynchburg. Changing trains at Lynchburg, they hurried on toward Staunton and then immediately headed for Mount Crawford. Vaughn's Tennessee cavalry added approximately eight hundred men to the army. Meanwhile, with the aid of Captain Frank B. Berkeley, Imboden spent the night of June 3 dividing up his men into two small brigades and deploying them. Before sunrise, just prior to Vaughn's arrival, Jones reached North River and assumed control of the army.[40]

Brigadier General William E. "Grumble" Jones was one of the most controversial officers in the Confederate service.[41] Born in Washington

36. Humphreys, *Lynchburg Campaign*, 30; J. D. Imboden, "Battle of Piedmont" (1923), 459.

37. *OR*, Vol. LI, Pt. 2, p. 981.

38. J. D. Imboden, "Battle of Piedmont" (1923), 459.

39. Humphreys Autobiography, II, 318; Jenning Diary, June 3, 1864.

40. Imboden to McCue, Oct. 1, 1883, pp. 3–4, MC; John Berrien Lindsley, ed., *The Military Annals of Tennessee* (Nashville, 1886), 141; J. L. Henry, "First Tennessee Cavalry at Piedmont," *CV*, XXII (1914), 397.

41. Richmond *Daily Dispatch*, June 7, 1864; Richmond *Whig*, June 7, 1864; Lynchburg *Virginian*, June 8, 1864; Richmond *Sentinel*, June 24, 1864; Richmond *Examiner* in Baltimore *American*, June 13, 1864.

County, Virginia, in 1824, Jones graduated from West Point in 1848. While serving in the Oregon territory he earned a reputation as a disciplinarian. Noted for his eccentricities, this "small, thin blackeyed and whiskered man" dressed plainly, if not at times shabbily, and often without any insignia on his uniform, with the result that he was frequently mistaken for a private by his own men.[42] In 1852 his new bride died in a storm in the Gulf of Mexico. Never fully recovering from the loss, Jones became a withdrawn and cantankerous widower. Aptly nicknamed from "his grumbling disposition and manner," he could be curt, quarrelsome, and suspicious. His profanity became legendary, and though some regarded him as a misanthrope, he commanded great respect among his men for his courage and bravery and for his willingness to share their hardships in the field.[43]

Jones served in the United States Army until 1856, when he resigned and returned to Virginia to farm. With secession he organized the Washington Mounted Rifles and served under Jeb Stuart. A clash of personalities estranged them, and in 1863 Stuart had Jones arrested for disrespect. Lee attempted to ameliorate their animosity but failed, and when a court-martial found Jones guilty the War Department reassigned him to the Department of Western Virginia.[44] There, under General Samuel Jones, "Grumble" took charge of the cavalry. With Breckinridge at Hanover Junction with Lee, Jones had temporary command of the Department of Southwestern Virginia.

When Jones arrived at Mount Crawford, Imboden explained the deployment of his men. Jones approved. He found a makeshift army that included convalescents, dismounted cavalrymen on furlough, reserves, and other nondescripts. As Sergeant Humphreys of Bryan's battery noted, the

42. Richmond *Sentinel*, June 24, 1864.

43. Thomas W. Colley, "Brig. Gen. William E. Jones," *CV*, XI (1903), 266–67; " 'Grumble' Jones: A Personality Profile," *CWT*, VII (1968), 35–36; Edward A. Pollard, *The Last Year of the War* (New York, 1866), 33n; Mosby, *Memoirs of Colonel John S. Mosby*, ed. Russell, 23; William N. McDonald, *A History of the Laurel Brigade*, ed. Bushrod C. Washington (1907), 109; Henry Kyd Douglas, *I Rode with Stonewall* (Chapel Hill, 1940), 157; Vandiver, ed., *Diary of Gorgas*, 113; Edward G. Longacre, *Mounted Raids of the Civil War* (London, 1975), 28, 127. See also Dobbie Edward Lambert, *Grumble: The W. E. Jones Brigade of 1863–1864* (Wahiawa, Hawaii, 1992).

44. W. W. Blackford, *War Years with Jeb Stuart* (Baton Rouge, 1993), 16, 51–52, 62–63; McDonald, *Laurel Brigade*, 168–70; "Jones: A Personality Profile," 40; Adele H. Mitchell, ed., *The Letters of Major General James E. B. Stuart* (1990), 271–72, 291.

force "consisted of troops from every quarter, hastily thrown together, and altogether undisciplined."[45] No unit was larger than a battalion; many were parts of companies or fragments put together between southwestern Virginia and the North River. Imboden estimated the army at slightly over four thousand.[46] "Perhaps at no time during the war," he later wrote, "were such heterogenous materials brought together so suddenly and compacted into harmonious and obedient bodies of troops."[47]

With his army well positioned, Jones, expecting an attack on the morning of June 4, waited confidently for Hunter's appearance. Much to his surprise, the Federals, instead of attacking at Mount Crawford, marched toward Port Republic. Jones and Imboden initially discounted the reports from Captain McNeill's courier. When the captain reached Mount Jackson, he shouted to Imboden, "General you are flanked; you are almost surrounded by Hunter's whole army." Now galvanized, Imboden hurried his men back along the Valley Pike toward Staunton and then veered off eastward toward New Hope.[48]

Improvisation became a strategic necessity. Jones, unfamiliar with the countryside except for the Valley Pike, relied on Imboden's advice. Well acquainted with the topography of the region, Imboden explained to Jones what he believed would be Hunter's probable route and made a rough map for him. He strongly urged a concentration at Mowry's Hill, three miles below and west of New Hope and overlooking Long Meadow Run. That position, he asserted, would be advantageous and could offset Hunter's numerical superiority. Jones, according to Imboden, agreed "without hesitation." Then Imboden furnished Jones with two guides and suggested that he would use his own brigade, without risking a serious engagement, as a screen. Vaughn, entitled by the date of his commission to assume command of the cavalry, offered instead to remain with Jones. Screening the main column, Imboden moved to Mount Meridian and sent pickets to watch the various fords of North River. He hoped to provide Jones with sufficient time to concentrate at Mowry's Hill.[49]

45. Humphreys Diary, June 4, 1864.
46. J. D. Imboden, "Battle of New Market," 485; Humphreys, *Lynchburg Campaign*, 30.
47. J. D. Imboden, "Battle of Piedmont" (1923), 460.
48. "Hunter's Raid, 1864," 98–100; J. D. Imboden, "Fire, Sword, and the Halter," 173; Richmond *Sentinel*, June 24, 1864; Richmond *Whig*, June 25, 1864.
49. J. D. Imboden, "Battle of Piedmont" (1923), 460; J. D. Imboden, "Fire, Sword, and the Halter," 173–74; Imboden to McCue, Oct. 1, 1883, MC; Humphreys, *Lynchburg Campaign*, 31.

Bivouacking at Mount Meridian for the night, Lieutenant Colonel George William Imboden, the general's brother, closely scrutinized Federal activity. Learning that they occupied Port Republic, he sent some twenty pickets to the east at the fork of the Weyer's Cave road, while the remainder bivouacked at Crawford's farm. Early the next morning, June 5, the sounds of fighting between his scouts and the 1st New York Cavalry alerted him and his brother. Rushing to the aid of their fleeing men, the 18th Virginia Cavalry formed in a field and then, "yelling like fiends," charged and pushed the New Yorkers back to where their remaining men waited.[50] Repulsing a Federal countercharge, Southern troopers, buoyed by their success, pushed dangerously beyond their support. The sudden arrival of the 21st New York Cavalry with the remainder of the 1st New York quickly changed the equation, and in the ensuing melee the New Yorkers surrounded and captured Captain Frank M. Imboden and some eighty of his men. General Imboden, realizing that he was more seriously engaged than his security or instructions warranted, escaped only by "the speed and great power of my horse" to rejoin his remaining men at Bonnie Doon. The New Yorkers now easily drove the Southerners through Mount Meridian for approximately a mile.[51]

Only the timely arrival of reinforcements saved the Virginians from complete capture. General Imboden was able to extricate his men from a narrow sunken road, lined with fences on either side. Spotting a flanking movement on their right, they rapidly pulled back to a rocky bluff.[52] The skirmish threatened to expand into a major engagement, contrary to Imboden's objective, which had been merely to force Hunter into deploying his army. If he was successful, though, the process of resuming the advance would cost the Federals at least two hours. Time, he believed, was what Jones needed. To accomplish his ruse, he knew, he would have to make an effective demonstration of resistance. Sending off a courier to Jones, he asked for a section of McClanahan's battery and five hundred men. Much to his surprise, even before the dispatcher left his sight, Jones appeared.

50. Stevenson, "*Boots and Saddles,*" 279.

51. George W. Imboden to Mollie, June 10, 1864, Book 28, #15–30, Lewis Leigh Collection, USMHI; McIhenny Diary, June 5, 1864; Imboden to McCue, Oct. 1, 1883, MC; Powell, Memoirs, 69–70; J. D. Imboden, "Battle of Piedmont" (1923), 460.

52. Imboden to McCue, Oct. 1, 1883, MC; J. D. Imboden, "Battle of Piedmont" (1923), 460; O'Ferrall, *Forty Years of Service,* 98; John N. Opie, *A Rebel Cavalryman* (Chicago, 1899), 219–20,

Queried about the dispatch, Jones acknowledged its receipt and said that the guns and men would arrive within five minutes. It quickly became clear to Imboden that the entire army was only "a few hundred yards" away, and the sudden appearance of Federal units quickly settled any question as to the site of the engagement.[53]

Fearing that Hunter's greater strength would result in "a fearful loss of life on our side," Imboden strongly protested the decision to engage at Piedmont instead of Mowry's Hill. Jones was unmoved and indicated that if Hunter did not attack, "I will go over there and attack him where he is."[54] In fairness to Jones, as Milton Humphreys points out, Imboden's plan to concentrate at Mowry's Hill would have uncovered Staunton. Hunter could have easily returned to the Valley Pike, avoided a battle, and moved directly on the town and waited for the Army of the Kanawha to join him.[55] As for Jones's decision, Strother noted that the "position was strong and well chosen."[56] The site undoubtedly helped to offset Hunter's superior numbers.[57]

The arrival of Berkeley's section of guns and the massing of Federal cavalry in their front made a continued argument academic. A well-placed shot crippled one of Ewing's guns, and another shell exploded in the rear of the New Yorkers, forcing them to retire in some confusion.[58] Hunter, when told of the forming Confederate battle line, remarked that he would "just as soon fight him now as at any other time." Du Pont promptly

53. J. D. Imboden, "Battle of Piedmont" (1923), 460–61, and XXXII (1924), 18; Imboden to McCue, Oct. 1, 1883, 6–7, MC; J. D. Imboden, "Fire, Sword, and the Halter," 174; Opie, *Rebel Cavalryman*, 219–20; O'Ferrall, *Forty Years of Service*, 98. For full details of the battle see Scott C. Patchan, *The Forgotten Fury: The Battle of Piedmont, Va.* (Fredericksburg, Va., 1996).

54. Imboden to McCue, Oct. 1, 1883, 7, MC; Milton Humphreys doubted the nature of the altercation as presented by Imboden. Otherwise, as he notes, Jones would have placed him under arrest. Humphreys, *Lynchburg Campaign*, 51.

55. Humphreys, *Lynchburg Campaign*, 51.

56. Eby, ed., *Virginia Yankee*, 243; OR, Vol. XXXVII, Pt. 1, p. 94; Hunter to Adjutant General, June 8, 1864, Edwin McMasters Stanton Papers, LC; Lang, *Loyal West Virginia*, 117.

57. Estimates of Jones's strength vary from Imboden's 4,200 to Vaughn's 5,600. Humphreys believed the number was close to the lower figure, but Patchan accepts Vaughn's figures. Humphreys, *Lynchburg Campaign*, 34–35; Brice, *Conquest of Valley*, 63; Patchan, *Forgotten Fury*, 227.

58. Carter Berkeley, "Augusta's Battle," Staunton (Va.) *Spectator and Vindicator*, July 29, 1904; Imboden to McCue, Oct. 1, 1883, 7, MC; Stevenson, *"Boots and Saddles,"* 280.

brought up his own battery and Snow's and effectively countered Southern fire.[59] Meanwhile, Jones began deploying his men, confidently allowing the terrain to determine the shape of his line. In directing Colonel
Beuhring H. Jones to form his 1st Brigade on the left, he remarked that
"the country would suggest the position that I should take."[60] Unfortunately, in massing his infantry on the left and the cavalry and four of Bryan's long-range guns on the right, the general left a gap of some six hundred yards between the two wings. "The line," as Milton Humphreys
observed, "was a very irregular one. We had no centre."[61] When Imboden
asked for instructions, Jones, pointing to Round Hill opposite his position,
told him to send out flankers to its foot in order to protect his right flank,
since he expected Hunter to attempt to turn his "position *there.*" Imboden remembered his remark that "if you can prevent *that*, it is all I shall
ask of you."[62] Later, Imboden maintained that Jones added, "I'll attend to
the rest of the field."[63] Sadly, both Imboden and Vaughn believed that
their orders were peremptory to hold their positions *"till further orders,"*
without any discretionary authority.[64]

As the 21st New York and 14th Pennsylvania Cavalries cautiously
pressed toward Piedmont, they drove the Southern skirmishers back.
Twice the Confederates repulsed them, but with increasing Federal
strength and aggressiveness they retreated back to their main line of rail-
pens. Now behind pens, some ten to twelve feet deep and slanting toward
an open field, they blazed away. Sergeant George Case Setchell recalled
that "we could fire only at their blooming rails."[65] Their obvious strength
caused Colonel William Ely to be cautious. Recalling his men, he re-
formed his 18th Connecticut Regiment along the edge of the opposite
woods.[66]

---

59. Du Pont, *Campaign of 1864*, 55–56; Powell Memoirs, 70–71; Humphreys, *Lynchburg Campaign*, 36.

60. Report of Colonel B. H. Jones, n.d., 1, Thornton Tayloe Perry Collection, VHS; J. D. Imboden, "Fire, Sword, and the Halter," 174.

61. Humphreys Diary, June 5, 1864.

62. J. D. Imboden, "Battle of Piedmont" (1924), 18.

63. Imboden to McCue, Oct. 1, 1883, 8, MC.

64. J. D. Imboden, "Battle of Piedmont" (1924), 19; Humphreys, *Lynchburg Campaign*, 35.

65. George Case Setchell, "A Sergeant's View of the Battle of Piedmont," *CWT*, II (1963), 45.

66. OR, Vol. XXXVII, Pt. 1, p. 117; Lynch, *Civil War Diary*, 68–69; Walker, *Eighteenth Connecticut*, 231–32; Wildes, *One Hundred and Sixteenth Ohio*, 93.

Taunting them, Southerners suddenly cried out, "New Market! New Market!" and surged forward, threatening to overlap Colonel Moor's right flank. However, with Du Pont concentrating his artillery and enfilading the charging Confederates, the 116th Ohio drove them back to their fortifications.[67] Du Pont's masterful use of his guns became one of the battle's critical components. His tactic of using concentrated mass fire, especially his "most effective work" on the Southern line, earned him Hunter's commendation for "the fine practice of our artillery" in silencing "the enemy's batteries."[68] In contrast, Milton Humphreys maintained that Jones's handling of his artillery was so inept that it was unworthy of study.[69]

Confederate rail-pens proved almost impregnable. Yet Moor's brigade again attacked, while Wynkoop's 2nd Brigade probed the left. Repulsed and in a developing pattern of response, the Southerners counterattacked, with the same results. Even the Federals' addition of two howitzers from Kleiser's battery failed to break the deadlock. Another Confederate assault almost encircled the two pieces but failed after severe fighting. The attack jolted Hunter. Fearing a mass attack, he ordered his wagon trains to prepare for a retreat.[70]

Jones felt increasingly optimistic. He assured his staff that victory was near and that Hunter "was desperately beaten."[71] Yet initially, Jones seemed unconcerned over the gap in his line. Worse, despite warnings of Federal activity on his right flank, he ignored its danger until it was too late to execute a realignment. Instead, he seemed to be shifting from a defensive mode to an offensive one by massing men on the left. Hunter took advantage of the gap and counterattacked.[72]

---

67. Wildes, *One Hundred and Sixteenth Ohio*, 93–94; Humphreys, *Lynchburg Campaign*, 38; Brice, *Conquest of Valley*, 69–70.

68. OR, Vol. XXXVII, Pt. 1, p. 95; Du Pont, *Campaign of 1864*, 58–59; Humphreys, *Lynchburg Campaign*, 40.

69. Patchan, *Forgotten Fury*, 119.

70. OR, Vol. XXXVII, Pt. 1, p. 117; Du Pont, *Campaign of 1864*, 60; Wildes, *One Hundred and Sixteenth Ohio*, 93–94; Lynch, *Civil War Diary*, 69; Walker, *Eighteenth Connecticut*, 232–33; Rawling, *First Regiment Virginia*, 172–73; Setchell, "A Sergeant's View," 45–46; William J. Kimball, "The 'Outrageous Bungling at Piedmont,'" *CWT*, V (1967), 45.

71. T. J. Doyle to J. Lewis Peyton, May 18, 1882, in J. Lewis Peyton, *History of Augusta County, Virginia* (Staunton, Va., 1882), 237.

72. Humphreys Autobiography, III, 321; Humphreys, *Lynchburg Campaign*, 42; Berkeley, "Augusta's Battle"; Willene B. Clark, ed., *Valleys of the Shadow: The Memoir of Confederate Captain Reuben G. Clark, Company I, 59th Tennessee Mounted Infantry* (Knoxville, 1994), 30–31; Patchan, *Forgotten Fury*, 119–20, 134–35.

After hesitating for fear of a massive Southern assault, Hunter ordered Colonel Thoburn, not yet fully engaged, to shift the 34th Massachusetts and 54th Pennsylvania Regiments, reinforced by a unit of the 1st New York Cavalry, up a hollow to the left to attack the right flank of the Southern infantry and exploit the gap.[73] Fortunately for the Federals, the Confederates' intense assault on Moor's brigade diverted their attention. Then Hunter ordered a general assault. Following a preliminary artillery barrage on Southern fortifications, Thoburn's brigade suddenly charged at around 3 P.M. The men of the 60th Virginia were caught by surprise, and the 34th Massachusetts rapidly began to overlap Southern entrenchments. Jones, now fully realizing the danger of the breach, tried to stem a collapse by leading Harper's and Harman's reserves and Berkeley's section to the aid of the Virginians. In vain he attempted to stop the stampede by adjusting the regiment's line. By now the entire Federal line was surging forward and clambering over Southern fortifications. For the Confederates the fighting became desperate and hopeless, and many "threw up their hands . . . and begged for mercy" once the Federals made it over the rail-pens.[74]

Jones's courageous attempt to rally his men proved not only futile, but fatal. A volley cut him down, and suddenly the army became leaderless. His adjutant general, Captain Walter K. Martin, sounded the alarm and the benediction for the battle: "General Jones is killed! We have no leader now!" Already hard pressed, the Southerners broke.[75] Many escaped in the chaos that followed, but the number captured was sizable. Hunter estimated that over 1,000, including 60 officers, surrendered, and that Confederate killed and wounded numbered 600. But the victors also paid a price, with roughly 800 killed and wounded.[76]

The most perplexing aspect of the engagement was the role of the Con-

73. Lang, *Loyal West Virginia*, 117–18; Powell Memoirs, 72; Lincoln, *Thirty-fourth Massachusetts*, 299–300; Wheeling *Daily Intelligencer*, June 21, 1864; Patchan, *Forgotten Fury*, 134 n. 357.

74. Berkeley, "Augusta's Battle"; Lincoln, *Thirty-fourth Massachusetts*, 300; Humphreys, *Lynchburg Campaign*, 44; Wheeling *Daily Intelligencer*, June 21, 1864; Neil to Friends, June 8, 1864, Neil Letters; Brice, *Conquest of Valley*, 73–75; Patchan, *Forgotten Fury*, 147–59.

75. Humphreys, *Lynchburg Campaign*, 44; Opie, *Rebel Cavalryman*, 221; Berkeley, "Augusta's Battle."

76. Brice calculates Confederate losses at "1,500 dead, wounded and captured," while Patchan sets the figure at 1,488. Patchan cites Federal losses at 165 dead, 620 wounded, and 39 prisoners, plus 7 officers, for a total of 831 men. *OR*, Vol. XXXVII, Pt. 1, p. 95; Brice, *Conquest of Valley*, 78–79; Patchan, *Forgotten Fury*, 223.

federate cavalry. Vaughn's and Imboden's brigades, estimated by Imboden at between 1,600 and 1,800, outnumbered the two Federal regiments by two to one, yet during the battle they only watched as Thoburn's brigade overran the infantry.[77] Imboden later maintained that the woods "enabled Hunter, unseen by us, to throw a brigade" into that position,[78] but Colonel O'Ferrall of the 23rd Virginia Cavalry disagreed, noting that the two regiments were "seen moving double-quick up a depression in a field, which concealed them from our infantry, but not from our cavalry." For O'Ferrall there was no misunderstanding of Federal intent.[79] Imboden admitted that just prior to the attack "we saw this flanking brigade emerge from the woods and move at quick time up a gentle slope directly on Jones' flank." Actually, the movement created tremendous excitement, and Imboden seemed eager to attack. However, as he pointed out, the advance occurred "immediately in front of Vaughn's Brigade, distant perhaps 600 yards." He also noted that "a rapid charge on the left flank of this flanking brigade of the enemy would have at least checked it and given Jones time to change front to the right and repel it." The ultimate rationale for the failure to do exactly that rested on the fact that Jones had left no discretion with his "peremptory" order.[80] In an 1883 letter, Imboden underscored this point, writing, "One word 'Charge!' given to Vaughan['s] brigade & mine, or to either, at the right moment, would almost certainly have prevented the flank attack at the road."[81]

A more serious question pertains to the lack or breakdown of communications between the two cavalry leaders and Jones. They both denied ever having received an order directing them to attack the Federal left. However, Captain Berkeley understood from Captain Martin that Jones sent couriers to both with such instructions. And one of the couriers, Reuben T. Tanner, maintained that he did deliver "an order to operate against the two regiments in front of him, and that Imboden said to tell General Jones he would do it immediately."[82]

Further complicating this question is Vaughn's dispatch of two Tennes-

77. Humphreys, *Lynchburg Campaign*, 44–45; Opie, *Rebel Cavalryman*, 221.

78. J. D. Imboden, "Battle of Piedmont" (1924), 19.

79. O'Ferrall, *Forty Years of Service*, 99–100.

80. J. D. Imboden, "Battle of Piedmont" (1924), 19; Humphreys, *Lynchburg Campaign*, 44–45.

81. Imboden to McCue, Oct. 1, 1883, 14, MC.

82. Humphreys, *Lynchburg Campaign*, 52; Brice, *Conquest of Valley*, 81.

see regiments on Jones's order to the left.[83] Obviously Vaughn received an order, but a question remains regarding its contents, as well as whether another one, undelivered, was sent by Jones to Imboden. Later, in a report that drew on the accounts of a number of officers for particulars, Colonel B. H. Jones wrote that "the conclusion is almost irresistible, that there was a misapprehension of orders on the part of some one, a misapprehension, disastrous indeed in its consequences."[84] And why was Vaughn inflexible? Obviously, Jones in making shifts in his line, which included the Tennessean's own men, was changing his battle strategy.[85]

With Jones's death, Vaughn assumed command of the army. Born in 1824 in Roane County, Tennessee, John Crawford Vaughn grew up in the eastern section of the state. He entered local politics on reaching his majority, and during the Mexican War he served as a captain of a company in the 5th Tennessee Volunteers. On returning home he became a merchant in the village of Sweetwater. A secessionist, in 1861 he organized a company in Monroe County and then assisted in raising a regiment in Knoxville in May. He became colonel of the 3rd Tennessee Regiment and left for Lynchburg with his men to serve the South even before his state seceded. There on June 4, 1861, they entered Confederate service. After initially serving in western Virginia and participating in the First Battle of Bull Run, Vaughn returned to east Tennessee. In September 1862 the War Department promoted him to brigadier general. Transferred to Vicksburg, he commanded a brigade at Chickshaw Bayou and surrendered to Grant. After being exchanged, he returned to the Department of East Tennessee and Western Virginia, where he again led a mounted brigade. With Hunter's threat, his cavalry had rushed to Imboden's aid at Mount Crawford.[86]

On learning of Jones's death, Vaughn conferred with Imboden. Already sensing defeat, Imboden undertook preparations to protect the retreat of the infantry. Since Vaughn did not know the country and Imboden did, Vaughn told him that "I will adopt your suggestions." Imboden then explained the necessity of gaining the road to New Hope and, if necessary,

83. Clarke, ed., *Valleys of the Shadow,* 30–31.

84. B. H. Jones Report, Perry Collection.

85. Humphreys Autobiography, III, 326.

86. James D. Porter, *Tennessee,* Vol. VIII of *Confederate Military History,* ed. Clement A. Evans (Atlanta, 1899), 339–40; Lindsley, ed., *Military Annals of Tennessee,* 137–41; Warner, *Generals in Gray,* 316–17; Steward Sifakis, *Who Was Who in the Civil War* (New York, 1988), 674–75.

fighting their way back to Mowry's Hill. Initially he proposed using that place as a defensive position. To Vaughn the plan appeared unrealistic, and instead they decided that the army should move toward New Hope. If necessary, they would resist Hunter along a wooded area above the Beard farm, between Piedmont and New Hope, but they hoped to reunite the army at another point. After providing Vaughn with guides, Imboden shifted his brigade to the Crumpecker farm, where he planned to take a defensive position. [87] Hoping to regroup their fleeing men, he stationed Captains Sturgis Davis and John Opie in New Hope on the road to Waynesboro. [88] Vaughn also directed O'Ferrall to remain there with two squadrons until nightfall. Then he was to retire to Fisherville. [89]

Rapidly, the two generals salvaged as much of the army as they could. Vaughn with his cavalry moved to Beard's farm, while Imboden with two sections of Bryan's battery attempted to cover part of the army's retreat. At Beard's farm, Captain Berkeley found Lieutenants Paul Collet's and H. H. Fultz's sections. Rapidly they positioned their guns facing the East Road as it emerged from the woods, while eighty Tennessee riflemen arrived and arranged themselves behind a strong rail fence. They waited for any pursuing Federals. Then, as Colonel Andrew T. McReynolds with two hundred men approached them at a gallop, their guns "poured a *salvo*" of canister and grape into the cavalrymen. [90] The fire devastated McReynolds' men. After another salvo, they retreated to re-form. Imboden, despite the arrival of his brigade, rejected a suggestion to charge. Instead, he formed a line and waited. Again the Federals charged, and again they were repulsed. Badly bloodied, the Federals fell back toward Piedmont. Imboden, fearing that pursuit would be hazardous, made none. [91]

Over Strother's protests, Hunter halted any further efforts. "The worthlessness of our cavalry," Strother believed, caused the general "to content himself with the affair as it stood." [92] Later, Imboden confirmed

87. J. D. Imboden, "Battle of Piedmont" (1924), 19; Imboden to McCue, Oct. 1, 1883, p. 12, MC; Brice, *Conquest of Valley*, 82.

88. Opie, *Rebel Cavalryman*, 222.

89. O'Ferrall, *Forty Years in Service*, 100–101.

90. Imboden to McCue, Oct. 1, 1883, p. 11, MC.

91. J. D. Imboden, "Battle of Piedmont" (1924), 19–20; Berkeley, "Augusta's Battle"; Opie, *Rebel Cavalryman*, 221–22; Peyton, *History of Augusta County*, 235; Driver, *Staunton Artillery—McClanahan's Battery*, 95–96.

92. Eby, ed., *Virginia Yankee*, 246.

Strother's instinct, noting that "if the pursuit had been more vigorous it would have been far worse for us."[93] Confederate disarray became dangerous. Neither Davis nor Opie could stop the skedaddling by either cajoling or threatening physical force, "so great was their terror."[94]

Imboden's brigade now withdrew in a more orderly form. At New Hope the two generals again met and decided that Vaughn should push ahead to Fisherville and establish telegraphic communication with Lee and the War Department. They were eager to learn the contents of the department's dispatches to Jones for fear of their impact on Hunter's movements, since they knew of Crook's movement toward Staunton. They also fully recognized the shattered condition of their army, which now numbered only 2,000 to 2,500 men. Vaughn departed for Fisherville, where he wired Lee the bad news. "I will try to protect Staunton," he said, but added that reinforcements would be needed. He also wired Seddon, repeating the plea for additional men and the warning for Staunton's safety. At 10 P.M., Vaughn reassured the War Department that his artillery and wagons were safe, but, he added, with the Federals pursuing he feared that he would be forced to retreat from the Valley. He further advised the secretary that Crook was now reported to be within twenty miles of Staunton and that the town "cannot be held."[95]

When Imboden reached Fisherville that evening around 11 P.M., the two generals discussed Lee's reply and the hopelessness of receiving aid from him. Unable to prevent a move on Staunton, they withdrew to Waynesboro and Rockfish Gap. Fearing a Federal pursuit the following morning, Vaughn undertook a ruse to gain time to concentrate his army in safety at Waynesboro. He gave Colonel O'Ferrall a note asking for the return of the bodies of General Jones, Captain Robert Doyle, and Colonel W. H. Browne (the latter was presumed dead), and sent him out to intercept any advancing Federal unit. On encountering the 21st New York Cavalry, O'Ferrall asked Major Charles G. Otis for permission to present the dispatch personally to Hunter. Hunter refused to grant him either an audience or the return of the bodies, despite O'Ferrall's protests.[96] The

93. Imboden, "Fire, Sword, and Halter," 175.

94. Opie, *Rebel Cavalryman*, 222.

95. *OR*, Vol. XXXVII, Pt. 1, pp. 150–51, and Vol. LI, Pt. 2, pp. 989–90; Imboden to McCue, Oct. 1, 1883, 12–13, MC; J. D. Imboden, "Battle of Piedmont," 20; J. B. Jones, *A Rebel War Clerk's Diary* (Philadelphia, 1866), II, 227.

96. O'Ferrall, *Forty Years of Service*, 101–104.

stratagem may have gained the Confederates some time, but it was Hunter's decision to turn west at the junction of the Waynesboro and Staunton
Roads that actually provided Vaughn's army with its needed security.

The following day, Vaughn wired Bragg that he possessed "not over
3,000 effective men, including Imboden's cavalry, 800." Staunton, he
wrote, had fallen that morning, and he expected Crook to unite with
Hunter there that evening or the next morning.[97]

97. OR, Vol. XXXVII, Pt. 1, p. 151; Imboden to McCue, Oct. 1, 1883, 12–13, MC; J. D.
Imboden, "Battle of Piedmont" (1924), 20.

7

Staunton, At Last!

Washington was jubilant. Staunton at long last lay uncovered and within the grasp of the Union army. On June 14, Secretary of War Stanton wired Hunter the administration's and country's thanks for "the recent brilliant victory" which had "wipe[d] out the antecedent disasters to our arms in former campaigns in the Shenandoah Valley."[1] Grant's chief of staff, General Rawlins, noted enthusiastically that "Hunter is doing what we expected Sigel to do some time since."[2] The victory at Piedmont was, indeed, no small achievement. Colonel Strother later summed up its significance to Grant's campaign as "the virtual annihilation of the enemy's military power in West Virginia and the valley of the Shenandoah. All the country west of the Blue Ridge was at our mercy. As this country was the source from which the enemy drew its principal supplies of meat, grain, forage, salt, lead, and iron, we were well aware that its possession was essential to the maintenance of his army."[3]

The Army of the Shenandoah exuded a new confidence. Hunter's popularity soared, and the troops cheered when they saw him.[4] Hunter waited until the privacy of a farmhouse before he gave vent to the exhilaration of success. There he embraced both Halpine and Stockton, kissed them on

1. OR, Vol. XXXVII, Pt. 1, p. 103; Porter, "Operations of Generals Sigel and Hunter," 74.
2. James Harrison Wilson, *The Life of John A. Rawlins* (New York, 1916), 227.
3. Strother, "Operations in West Virginia," 485.
4. Hewitt, *Twelfth West Virginia*, 141.

their cheeks, and slapped them on their backs. That night the staff enjoyed "a triumphant evening." Strother watched and listened as "the bands played and the men sang and shouted. The army was intoxicated with joy."[5] The victory, as Chauncey S. Norton of the 15th New York Cavalry noted, wiped out "the disgrace of New Market."[6] Corporal Jonas Kauffman recorded in his diary that "we slept on the Johnnies' blankets and ate their corn cakes."[7]

Hunter's victory, though, exacted a price: nearly 840 Federals wounded, dead, or missing.[8] With casualties still littering the battlefield, local houses and barns were converted into temporary hospitals. Details busily worked the entire night to bury the dead, the sounds of suffering continuing well into the morning as exhausted surgeons and medical orderlies worked to save lives and comfort the wounded.[9] Dr. Neil caught the poignancy of that night for his family: "How heart rending to hear the groans & shrieks of dying men as we went over the battlefield that night with torches, hunting up the wounded. Rebs and Union lay side by side, praying loud & fervently to God to have mercy on them." Neil admitted that "the Surgeon cannot do very much on the field, except to administer a little cordial occasionally or ligate a bleeding artery & see that they are carefully handled by the stretcher bearers."[10] To Private James W. Mulligan of the 15th New York Cavalry "it seems a sin to see the men laying ded . . . in pils be hind their brest work."[11] Corporal Lynch, carrying some blankets to the field hospital, recoiled at the "sickening sight."[12] As the army moved toward Staunton the next morning, many of the wounded went along. From Staunton, Hunter would send the 14th Pennsylvania Cavalry with ambulances back for the remaining wounded.[13]

The celebration supplied a needed tonic for the army, but the following morning, June 6, the reality of campaigning quickly returned. "Cheering

5. Eby, ed., *Virginia Yankee*, 246; Hanchett, *Irish: Charles Halpine*, 116.

6. Norton, *"Red Neck Ties,"* 38.

7. Kauffman Diary in Storey, *History of Cambria County*, I, 108.

8. OR, Vol. XXXVII, Pt. 1, p. 95; Brice, *Conquest of Valley*, 78–79; Patchan, *Forgotten Fury*, 222–25.

9. Farrar, *Twenty-Second Pennsylvania*, 236–37.

10. Neil to Friends, June 8, 1864, Neil Letters.

11. Mulligan to Wife, Aug. [?] 15, 1864, Mulligan Letters.

12. Lynch, *Civil War Diary*, 70.

13. Artman Diary, June 7, 1864.

and singing," the troops reached the juncture of the Staunton and Waynesboro Roads, where the army briefly halted before turning westward toward Staunton. Strother objected, wanting to take "the Waynesboro Road to finish Imboden," but "the General kept on the [road to] Staunton." In doing so, Hunter undoubtedly missed an opportunity to destroy Vaughn's shattered army, but with Crook's army approaching Staunton from the west, he wanted to effect a junction with him and take the prize which had eluded Federal armies for so long. [14]

Staunton was indeed a trophy. At the beginning of the Civil War, the town, with its population of nearly four thousand, was the leading commercial hub in the upper Valley, and with the secession of Virginia it became an important military depot and popular refugee center as well. The town served as the county seat of agriculturally rich Augusta County. Only three other counties in the state outranked it in wheat production, while in rye and corn it ranked second. By 1860 its land ranked as the most valuable in Virginia, with the average per-acre price of farmland more than three times the state average. With the region's prosperity rooted in that agricultural richness, a radiating system of transportation routes made Staunton the region's most important commercial center. [15]

The macadamized Valley Pike, running northeastward, connected the town with Winchester and Martinsburg in the lower Valley, while roads leading south linked it with Lexington and Buchanan. Other roads, stretching to the west, tapped the Allegheny hinterland over to Parkersburg, while to the east they connected to Waynesboro and at Rockfish Gap crossed the Blue Ridge Mountains into the Virginia Piedmont and reached Charlottesville. In 1854 the Virginia Central Railroad—stretching from Jackson's Depot in the west to Charlottesville, Gordonsville, and Richmond by 1860—had begun to tap Staunton's commerce. The completion of the Blue Ridge Tunnel in 1858 reduced cost and travel time to the Virginia capital by an hour. By 1860 the railroad constituted a vital artery of trade for the upper Shenandoah Valley, and with the beginning of the war it became a major supply line for the Army of Northern Virginia.

Commercial activity during the 1850s had spurred Staunton's popula-

14. Eby, ed., *Virginia Yankee*, 246; Walker, *Eighteenth Connecticut*, 244.

15. *Population: Eighth Census*, 509, 519; Richard K. MacMaster, *Augusta County History, 1865–1950* (Staunton, Va., 1987), 7, 20–22; Mary Elizabeth Massey, *Refugee Life in the Confederacy* (Baton Rouge, 1964), 77.

tion growth by as much as 65 percent and spawned a wide variety of industries and businesses in the surrounding area. Sixty-two grist mills, twenty-two sawmills, and eighteen distilleries dotted the countryside. Ten coopers produced flour barrels, while seventeen blacksmiths plied their trade. In addition a variety of other small industries enhanced the area's vitality, including three manufacturers of agricultural implements, five carriage makers, three wagon makers, a large woolen mill, a foundry, and a shoe factory, along with cobblers and saddlers. Staunton boasted three banks, hotels, and eighty houses of business. In 1860 its businesses had gross sales of nearly one million dollars.[16]

As the town prospered, Staunton's social, cultural, and civic life expanded. Its location made it a logical choice for a number of governmental institutions, such as the Western Lunatic Asylum and the Deaf, Dumb, and Blind Institute. The Virginia Supreme Court held sessions in Staunton to serve the western section of the state. The town boasted two daily newspapers, the *Vindicator* and the *Spectator*, as well as numerous common schools, plus a male academy and three institutes for women. An advertisement for the Virginia Female Seminary vaunted the school as "strictly first class and with a very large first class patronage from all the Southern States."[17]

With its strategic location in the upper Valley, Staunton was transformed by the war into a bustling city and an important supply depot for the Confederacy. The presence of soldiers and a growing military complex changed its character and quickened its life with all the vices and problems of a boomtown. With the influx of clerks, workers, soldiers, and refugees, the city's population more than doubled. The government constructed and converted stables, arsenals, and shops for military use, while commissary and quartermaster warehouses soon lined the tracks of the Virginia Central Railroad. The Ordnance Department and the Nitre and Mining Corps set up offices in Staunton. Government spending spurred the local economy and gave rise to new enterprises. Confederate authorities established a number of military hospitals, including one at the Deaf,

16. MacMaster, *Augusta County*, 21; Brice, *Conquest of Valley*, 4; Marshall Moore Brice, "Augusta County During the Civil War," *Augusta Historical Bulletin* (Staunton), I, 5–6.

17. MacMaster, *Augusta County*, 21–22; Brice, *Conquest of a Valley*, 4–5; Brice, "Augusta County During the Civil War," 7; Mary Custis Lee DeButts, ed., *Growing Up in the 1850s: The Journal of Agnes Lee* (Chapel Hill, 1984), 75.

Dumb, and Blind Institute, and a stockade for military prisoners. Staunton soon became one of the largest military depots in Virginia.

On the eve of secession, residents of Augusta County had clearly supported the Union. As the presidential candidate for the Southern Democratic Party, Breckinridge fared poorly in the 1860 election. He received only 218 votes in the county, while the two Union candidates, John Bell of the Constitutional Union Party and Stephen A. Douglas of the national Democratic Party, received 2,553 and 1,094 votes, respectively. During the secession crisis, citizens held public meetings at which they adopted Unionist resolutions and elected three delegates to the state convention. At the convention, the delegates opposed secession until the final ballot, when finally two of them changed their votes to favor it. With the firing upon Fort Sumter and Lincoln's call for troops, sentiment in Augusta County changed radically, and with the passage of the referendum on secession, Southern support exploded. On April 17, 1861, local citizens excitedly poured into town. The West Augusta Guard and the Staunton Artillery, led by then-captain John D. Imboden, left by train for Harpers Ferry to defend Virginia.[18]

Prior to 1864, Federal armies had seriously threatened Staunton with capture only once. Union efforts to trap Stonewall Jackson in the spring of 1862 had brought Federal forces as far south as the North River, but Jackson's dazzling movements in striking first at General John C. Frémont at Cross Keys on June 8 and then at General James Shields's column at Port Republic the following day had blunted Union moves toward the town. Until Grant's concerted strategy made Staunton and its supply line to Richmond a prime target, the town remained relatively secure. Sigel's movement had offered a potential threat, but Breckinridge's victory at New Market provided a respite. However, with Lee's stripping the Valley of forces to aid him in the east, the remaining troops lacked sufficient power to combat the renewed threat from Hunter.

For more than a week before Hunter's move from Cedar Creek, reports and rumors had circulated in Staunton that the Federal army was again on the move. The *Spectator*, attempting to reassure its readers, bragged on May 31 that "they will be met, and will probably be again thunder-struck as they were at New Market." Breckinridge would "swoop upon them, like

---

18. Jos. A. Waddell, *Annals of Augusta County, Virginia* (Harrisonburg, 1979), 454–57; Abbot, "General John D. Imboden," 90; Peyton, *History of Augusta County,* 226–30.

an eagle upon its prey."[19] Confederate authorities were less confident. They became increasingly apprehensive on June 4, when Colonel Edwin G. Lee, who had just that day assumed command of the town, learned of Hunter's flanking Jones at Mount Crawford and movement toward Port Republic. Fearing a cavalry dash, Lee worked feverishly to prepare military stores and official papers for shipment to safety.[20]

The crisis came the next day. On Sunday afternoon around 5 P.M., Colonel Lee received a note revealing that the army was "broken and routed." Immediately he wired General Lee, "We have been pretty badly whipped. . . . I fear Staunton will go." Official notification from Vaughn would not come until 11 P.M.[21] Relying on his own judgment, Colonel Lee began supervising the evacuation. In a flurry of activity he "strained every nerve to get all stores and supplies away," but "time was so limited." Having been in command only one day, he did not know "what was here, and had no time for inquiries." Worse, Jones's troops, on their way to Mount Crawford, had sequestered most of the quartermaster's wagons there, and Lee found it impossible to transport all of the stores.[22]

Yet as a result of his preparations the previous day, Lee managed to safeguard a considerable amount: 900 sacks of salt, a large quantity of leather, most of the ammunition and bacon, and much of the quartermaster's supplies. Fearing that the Federals would destroy the rest and burn the warehouses, he kept the buildings open all night while a town official distributed the remaining stores to citizens. What could be saved he shipped by railroad to Fisherville and Lynchburg. Additional wagon trains, accompanied by convalescents and blacks, left to escape across the Blue Ridge Mountains at the Tye River Gap. Haste forced Lee to abandon stores belonging to the Ordnance Department and valued at $400,000. As Hunter's men entered the town on June 6, Lee fled on horseback.[23]

Earlier that Sunday morning, Joseph Addison Waddell, returning home after securing his papers at the quartermaster's office, had climbed a hill behind his house to join others in watching the columns of smoke rising

19. Staunton (Va.) *Spectator*, May 31, 1864.

20. *OR*, Vol. XXXVII, Pt. 1, pp. 153–54.

21. *Ibid.*, 151.

22. *Ibid.*, 152–54; Joseph Addison Waddell Diary, June 5, 1864, UV.

23. *OR*, Vol. XXXVII, Pt. 1, p. 153; Randolph H. McKim, *A Soldier's Recollections* (Washington, D.C., 1983), 217; Alexandra Lee Levin, " 'Why Have You Burned My House?': Henrietta Lee and the Burning of Bedford," *Virginia Cavalcade*, XXVIII (1978), 86.

from the direction of Piedmont. Initially, since they heard no musketry or cannon fire, they assumed that it was merely from burning mills. However, they soon learned that the smoke came from the raging battle. By midday, as the haze receded, many began to believe the Confederates had won, but news from the battlefield shattered that hope. The succinct report that "Gen Jones is killed and our army routed" rapidly cast a pall over the city. "I cannot depict the horror of our feelings," Waddell confided to his diary.[24]

Soon fleeing fugitives, carrying "furniture, stock of all kinds, contrabands, &c." with their horses and cattle, crowded the Greenville road leading to Lexington. Already alarmed by Federal movements, Mrs. Baldwin and her two sisters decided to "refugee." Large numbers of government officials and employees joined the exodus. Waddell, as he rode out of town, "was inescapably sad and anxious." Many turned off the Greenville road with the government trains and headed for the Blue Ridge Mountains. Their route would prove to be a dangerous one.[25] As refugees reached Lexington the day after Staunton fell, Margaret Junkin Preston noted that "all has been wild excitement this afternoon. Stages and wagons loaded with negroes poured in from Staunton."[26]

A defenseless city waited, but not for long. On Monday morning, June 6, Major Lang asked Hunter to allow him and his men the honor of leading a charge into Staunton to fulfill a long-standing dream of the West Virginians to capture the town. His troopers briefly encountered resistance from a squad of cavalry on the main road under a bridge, but after a brisk exchange of fire the Southerners, leaving some eighteen of their men as prisoners, scurried away. As news of Lang's entry reached the main army, cheers spread along the marching line from regiment to regiment.[27]

24. Waddell Diary, June 5, 1864; Waddell, *Annals of Augusta County*, 488–89.

25. Waddell Diary, June 5, 1864; John Milton Hoge, *A Journal by John Milton Hoge, 1862–5: Containing Some of the Most Particular Incidents That Occurred During His Enlistment as a Soldier in the Confederate Army, Written by Himself, at Guest Station, Wise Co., Va., August, 1865*, ed. Mary Hoge Bruce (Cincinnati, 1961), June 6, 1864, 15, UV; J. Kelly Bennette Diaries, June 6, 1864, J. Kelly Bennette Papers, SHC; Luther Emerson to Wife, June 21, 1864, Emerson Family Papers, UV; Randolph Barton, *Recollections, 1861–1865* (Baltimore, 1913), 56–57; Bruce S. Greenwalth, ed., "Life Behind Confederate Lines in Virginia: The Correspondence of James D. Davidson," *CWH*, XVI (1970), 224.

26. Allan, ed., *Life and Letters of Preston*, 184.

27. Lang, *Loyal West Virginia*, 119; George W. Imboden to Mollie, June 10, 1864, Book 28, Leigh Collection.

As the Federals arrived, white flags hung from several houses, leading one Federal to wonder whether this was "indicative of submission or with a view to securing protection."[28] Most residents merely observed as the army passed, more often than not showing Hunter's army a coolness with no display of patriotism.[29] Yet Strother observed that along the way to Staunton some citizens seemed "very glad to see us. They greeted us pleasantly, waved their handkerchiefs, such as had them, and brought buckets of water or milk to quench our thirsts." Near the town "a dozen or more girls" presented the soldiers with flower bouquets, but the colonel could not tell "whether this compliment was sincere and loyal or meant as a propitiation of the demons."[30] William Patterson was surprised to find that "some women were glad Jones was killed for he had [im]pressed their sons & husbands."[31]

Strother ordered two bands with a large American flag to accompany Hunter's staff as it marched into town. Bands paraded along the town's streets playing "Yankee Doodle" and "Hail Columbia."[32] Proceeding in triumph through the city, Hunter and his staff established their headquarters at the American Hotel, across from the railroad depot, and "Had a good dinner."[33] For the Federals the day provided an exhilarating experience: first the victory at Piedmont, and now the occupation of Staunton. As Private Frank Reader noted, "We are the first yankees ever here and it is almost worth a fellows life to gain such a victory and follow it up as we have." Not surprisingly, "Gen. Hunter is adored by his troops now."[34]

The mayor, town council members, and a number of other prominent citizens went to see Hunter at the hotel, and the general sent for Strother to meet with them. Alexander Stuart—a former U.S. congressman, secretary of the interior under Millard Fillmore, a Unionist delegate to the Virginia convention, and an opponent of secession—served as spokesman for the group. After listening to their concerns, the colonel informed them that the army was "warring according to the rules of civilized nations."

28. Hewitt, *Twelfth West Virginia*, 142.

29. Beach, *First New York Cavalry*, 367; Walker, *Eighteenth Connecticut*, 245.

30. Eby, ed., *Virginia Yankee*, 246; Benjamin F. Zeller, Reminiscences, June 7, 1864, 9, Benjamin F. Zeller Collection, USMHI.

31. Patterson Diary, June 6, 1864.

32. Eby, ed., *Virginia Yankee*, 247; Farrar, *Twenty-Second Pennsylvania*, 238.

33. Eby, ed., *Virginia Yankee*, 247.

34. Reader Diary, June 6, 1864.

His men would destroy all military stores and buildings, but private property, schools, and charitable institutions would remain safe and protected. He warned the delegation to expect possible disorderly acts by "an ill-disciplined soldiery" but reassured them that the army intended to maintain peace and order. For the town fathers, Strother noted, the discussion seemed "to give satisfaction and allayed the evident 'tremor' which our coming had produced."[35]

The hopes of Staunton's citizens for an orderly occupation would prove to be unrealistic. Hunter's army managed to maintain order the first night. Although some thievery occurred—Lucas P. Thompson returned home to find that soldiers had stolen "more than three-fourths of my bacon, half of my flour, and a sword and pistol"—most citizens got through "without much alarm and without being much annoyed by so many Yankees coming to the hydrant for water and to the kitchen for food."[36] But then, on "Tuesday morning early" as one Staunton lady wrote, "the burning commenced."[37] Strother rode into town to find "everything in shocking confusion." Flames engulfed railroad property, government buildings, and public stores. Mobs consisting of soldiers, blacks, "Secessionists," camp followers, and general riffraff engaged in plundering what they could.[38] Soldiers searched houses for provisions, forced open shops, and dispersed their goods. As Charley Cochran, proprietor of a tobacco shop, sat talking to the editor of the *Spectator*, soldiers entered his store, took what they wanted, and left. Unable to express his outrage, Cochran just sat there "like the boy the calf ran over."[39] Soldiers forced owners of dry goods stores to open them or risk having them broken into and robbed. At the Virginia Hotel, provost guards broke open barrels of apple brandy and let their contents spurt into the street and stream down its gutters. Strother watched the brandy flow "with floating chips, paper, horse dung, and dead rats" as an array of soldiers and "vagabonds" got down on their hands and knees to drink it. The more fastidious used their canteens to collect the precious liquid.[40]

35. Eby, ed., *Virginia Yankee*, 247; Waddell Diary, June 7, 1864.

36. Greenwalth, ed., "Life Behind Confederate Lines: Correspondence of Davidson," 225.

37. Waddell Diary, June 6, 1864; Waddell, *Annals of Augusta County*, 490.

38. Eby, ed., *Virginia Yankee*, 248.

39. Richard Mauzy, "Vandalism by General Hunter, 1864," *Augusta Historical Bulletin*, XIV (1978), 53.

40. Eby, ed., *Virginia Yankee*, 248; Waddell, *Annals of Augusta County*, 490; Richmond *Sentinel*, June 21, 1864; Richmond *Daily Dispatch*, June 24, 1864.

Fearful that the unchecked fire of warehouses and stores would spread to private property, a group of citizens pleaded with Hunter not to burn the workshops. He agreed, but only on the condition that they tear down the buildings themselves. As soldiers prepared to set fire to a shoe and boot factory, a lady approached Hunter and pleaded that the flames would spread to the houses of "innocent people" and would render "a great many families . . . homeless." He relented and ordered only the machinery destroyed. Informed of the decision, a group of women eagerly scurried to round up relatives and friends to assist in carrying out the task.[41]

Despite such efforts, soldiers torched a number of buildings without notice. The conflagration, coupled with troopers' galloping through the streets, terrified residents, many of whom feared that the Federals intended to burn all of Staunton. Strother managed to intervene on several occasions to contain the destruction. In one such case, Alexander Stuart persuaded him to allow citizens to tear down a carriage factory. The colonel agreed, and Lieutenant Meigs supervised its demolition. Wisely, Strother also prevented the burning of a warehouse next to a hotel for fear of the fire spreading to it.[42]

The town's two newspapers became special targets of Federal wrath. Ironically, in 1860 both papers had opposed secession and attacked the "fire-eaters." Their former Unionist position would offer them no shield against retaliation in 1864. Federal officers gained access to the *Spectator*'s office through a ruse. Two members of Hunter's staff, under the pretext of wanting some printing done, approached Richard Mauzy, the paper's editor, who was sitting on the steps of the building. They asked Mauzy to do some work for them, and he replied that his printers had left to join the army at Piedmont. The officers then told him that they possessed their own printers. Once in the plant, they saw that his equipment was still there. One of the officers then asked, "You were not expecting us?" Mauzy replied that he expected Crook to occupy Staunton and that the general would not permit the shop's destruction. The officers denied any such intent on their part. On leaving, they assured him of the building's safety and issued a note of protection. They also prepared a duplicate note for the provost marshal, who arrived just as they left. With the stationing of a guard by the provost, Mauzy felt secure.[43]

41. Waddell Diary, June 7, 1864; Waddell, *Annals of Augusta County*, 490.

42. Eby, ed., *Virginia Yankee*, 248–49; Margaret Briscoe Stuart Robertson, *My Childhood Recollections of the War* (n.p., n.d.), 9; Point Pleasant (W. Va.) *Weekly Register*, June 30, 1864.

43. Mauzy, "Vandalism by General Hunter," 50–53.

Much to the editor's horror, the following morning he found the soldier preparing to leave. Left to protect his own property, he waited uneasily. Shortly a squad of soldiers, ignoring the note and claiming to have different orders, entered the shop. Using bludgeons, they demolished the press, threw its fragments and type into the street, and gutted the building. The *Vindicator* would have likely met a similar fate, but the editor had sent his type off to safety and succeeded in hiding some of his tools. Nevertheless, soldiers ransacked the office and threw his Washington press into the street.[44]

Staunton's area tobacco warehouses became a special target for soldiers, who plundered and then burned the buildings, throwing into the street the tobacco they did not take. Soldiers so stuffed their knapsacks with "the weed," as William Hewitt called it, that "the army might have been tracked by the tobacco plugs strewn along the road."[45] The patients of the Confederate hospital received quantities of it from the men of the 18th Connecticut.[46] In the plundering, Colonel Lincoln observed that "the men have had no hesitation in appropriating to their own use, whatever would contribute to their personal comfort."[47]

Hunter spared from destruction the two large public institutions, the Deaf, Dumb, and Blind Institute and the Western Lunatic Asylum, which had been functioning as military hospitals. The surprise of the Union victory had left hospital authorities no time to evacuate patients. When Federals approached the asylum, they informed black servants congregating outside the building of their "liberty to either go or stay, just as they pleased." The servants responded jubilantly, having believed that "when de Yankees com'd dey all be free." They then proceeded to tell the Federals where hospital officials had concealed valuables. Conducting a search of the buildings, a provost marshal found an estimated $300,000 worth of property.[48]

Fully recognizing the purpose of the complex, the Federals respected the hospitals and molested none of the patients. Hunter paroled some five hundred convalescing Southerners, as well as physicians.[49] Dr. Neil found

44. *Ibid.*, 53–54; Brice, *Conquest of Valley*, 100–101.
45. Hewitt, *Twelfth West Virginia*, 143; Wildes, *One Hundred and Sixteenth Ohio*, 101.
46. Lynch, *Civil War Diary*, 73.
47. Lincoln, *Thirty-fourth Massachusetts*, 305.
48. Point Pleasant (W. Va.) *Weekly Register*, June 30, 1864.
49. *OR*, Vol. XXXVII, Pt. 1, p. 95.

the surgeons "very gentlemanly fellows, but put on a good deal of style."[50] Impressed with the facilities, Colonel Hayes wrote to his wife that the "Secesh were friendly and polite; not the slightest bitterness or unkindness between the two sorts. . . . If I am to be left in hospital this is the spot."[51] The numbers at the hospitals swelled with the arrival of Federal wounded from Piedmont.

With the arrival of Crook's army on June 8, Federal officers grew more concerned about pillaging and destruction of property. Hunter ordered Averell to provide guards to protect private property in the vicinity of his camps and directed that "no soldiers will be allowed to enter the town without a pass from division headquarters." Crook deplored the "many acts committed by our troops that are disgraceful to the command" and the men's "utter disregard of General Orders, No. 11." He instructed his officers to enforce the order and authorize foraging parties only for the purpose of gathering supplies. He demanded the arrest of all marauders.[52] Yet despite the order, Captain John Young doubted whether "there will be anything left for the Rebels to live on after we leave this valley. . . . Just think of twenty or thirty thousand men and horses eating off a country like this," he wrote his wife, particularly "after the Rebels have gleaned the country before us."[53]

Little remained safe from a needy army. Soldiers broke into Jacob Humbert's house at night and stole his bacon and the blankets off his bed, then reappeared the next morning and took his flour. In justification an officer told Humbert that "they are compelled to do so as they were cut off from their supplies."[54] An officer explained to Martin Garber that "the army was making a raid and that they had orders to take horses and cattle and flour and bacon and everything else necessary for the use of the army," particularly because they had "lost a good many horses the day before."[55] Alexander Anderson was luckier. Despite confiscating some 390 pounds of bacon and other commodities, an officer refused to allow his men to take all of Anderson's horses.[56]

50. Neil to Friends, June 8, 1864, Neil Letters.

51. Williams, ed., *Diary and Letters of Hayes*, II, 473.

52. OR, Vol. XXXVII, Pt. 1, p. 607.

53. Young to Emma, June 9, 1864, Young Papers.

54. Jacob Humbert file #2524, microfiche 471, RG 233, SCCP.

55. Martin Garber file #2537, RG 217, SCCP; John Bates file #16245, microfiche 4041, RG 233, SCCP.

56. Alexander Anderson file #2133, RG 217, SCCP.

Horses were a highly sought commodity. John Brown, a Unionist blacksmith near Churchville, lost two horses, but he remarked to a neighbor that "he would rather they had been taken by that army than that the rebel devils should have them."[57] Lewis Defenbaugh protested as his two horses were taken away, but "it did no good they said they wanted to mount cavalry."[58] Amelia McGray begged soldiers not to take her three horses, "as they were all she had or at least to leave her a horse in place of hers."[59] Unionist Elizabeth Garber, despite her pleas that "she needed them more than the army did," lost her two horses.[60] Henry Eakle went to Staunton to see Hunter about recovering his horse, but the general merely told him that "they had lost some horses in the battle . . . and that they were compelled to take some." Hunter mentioned nothing about reimbursement.[61]

When Hunter's army left Staunton, the town bore witness to the ravages of the occupation. The railroad depot and its buildings lay in ruins. All the public workshops and factories in the vicinity exhibited similar destruction. For six miles the telegraph line ceased to exist. The rail line toward Waynesboro looked like a twisted road of iron. The men of the 12th West Virginia, on Hunter's orders, had efficiently wrecked long sections of it. Piling up ties and rails into heaps, they ignited them and watched as the rails bent into unserviceable forms.[62] For the better part of six miles, the Virginia Central showed their handiwork.[63]

Having successfully occupied Staunton, Hunter turned his attention back to Jones's shattered army in the Waynesboro area. He wanted to attack there and then move on Charlottesville. Such a maneuver would conform to his instructions from Halleck on May 21 and was in accordance with his directive to Crook and Averell. In his reply to Halleck's instructions, Hunter had expressed his intention, once the two armies joined at Staunton, to "move directly east, via Charlottesville and Gordonsville." Five days later, Halleck had reiterated the order for Hunter "to

57. John Brown file #22264, RG 217, SCCP.

58. Lewis Defenbaugh file #11252, microfiche 1453, RG 233, SCCP.

59. Amelia McCray file #6898, microfiche 63, RG 233, SCCP.

60. Elizabeth Garber file #2545 and Lydia Fishburn file #19558, RG 217, SCCP.

61. Henry Eakle file 16218, microfiche 3979, RG 233, SCCP.

62. Wildes, *One Hundred and Sixteenth Ohio*, 101; Hewitt, *Twelfth West Virginia*, 143; Lynch, *Civil War Diary*, 72.

63. *OR*, Vol. XXXVII, Pt. 1, pp. 95, 153; Richmond *Sentinel*, June 21, 1864.

push on if possible to Charlottesville and Lynchburg" and destroy the railroad, a movement both Washington and Grant wanted. [64]

Grant, who had been unable to deal Lee's army a telling blow, now believed, as C. A. Dana told Stanton, that "the effective destruction of the Virginia Central Railroad" was "an indispensable element" of his "plan of campaign." [65] On June 6 he sent more explicit instructions to Hunter, informing him of Major General Philip Sheridan's expedition to strike at Charlottesville to destroy the Virginia Central. He wanted Hunter to proceed to Lynchburg, warning that because "that point is of so much importance to the enemy," the Confederates would put up a stiff resistance. Noting past instructions, he specified that Hunter's route "should be from Staunton via Charlottesville." Once Hunter and Sheridan accomplished their mission, they were "to join the Army of the Potomac." [66]

However, Grant's June 6 dispatch failed to reach Hunter. Nevertheless, by June 9 Hunter and his staff assumed the existence of a raid directed at Charlottesville and factored Sheridan's role into the planning of the army's route. Earlier, at Rude's Hill, a May 27 issue of the *Rockingham Register* had fallen into Hunter's hands. The paper mentioned the loss of communications between Staunton and Richmond for five days. Hunter, concluding that the break resulted from Federal cavalry operations and that Sheridan "has doubtless got possession of the Virginia Central Railroad." [67] Actually, Sheridan, then just returning from defeating Jeb Stuart at Yellow Tavern, anchored Meade's left flank, where Grant initially intended using him as a shield and decoy for a flanking movement against Lee. Not until the afternoon of June 5 did Sheridan receive orders to undertake the Trevillian Station–Charlottesville raid to cooperate with Hunter. [68] Nevertheless, on June 9, Strother, confident as a result of the news in the Harrisonburg paper, told Crook that if Lee detached "a division or two" to defend Lynchburg, they "would be cut off by Sheridan who

64. *OR*, Vol. XXXVII, Pt. 1, pp. 507, 543.

65. *Ibid.*, Vol. XXXVI, Pt. 1, p. 89, and Pt. 3, p. 599.

66. *Ibid.*, Vol. XXXVII, Pt. 1, p. 598.

67. Eby, ed., *Virginia Yankee*, 236; Du Pont, *Campaign of 1864*, 70; George E. Pond, *The Shenandoah Valley in 1864* in *Campaigns of the Civil War* (New York, 1963), VI, 42–43; [Judith White McGuire], *Diary of a Southern Refugee, During the War* (New York, 1867), 276; William B. Feis, "A Union Military Intelligence Failure: Jubal Early's Raid, June 12–July 14, 1864," *CWH*, XXXVI (1990), 218.

68. *OR*, Vol. XXXVI, Pt. 3, pp. 628–29, and XXXVII, Pt. 1, p. 593.

was moving with his cavalry toward Charlottesville and would cooperate with us."[69]

A Federal move on Charlottesville posed serious consequences for Lee and for the security of Lynchburg. If successful, it would block a major rail line and make reinforcing the city difficult. Fortunately for the Confederates, the original order allowed differing interpretations.[70] Initially, on June 7, Hunter intended to take the route Grant suggested, but his staff as well as other officers resisted and approached Strother to use his influence against it. The colonel, sympathetic to Hunter's proposal, believed that such a move was a good one but now counseled him to delay making a final decision until he talked it over with Crook. Hunter agreed.[71]

At Meadow Bluff, on receiving Sigel's and then Hunter's orders, Crook had begun readying his troops on May 30. His position at Meadow Bluff was a good one, since he could, if necessary, join Sigel in accordance with the original plan. There he learned of the defeat at New Market and received the order "to make a demonstration on Staunton as soon as possible." In a second dispatch he learned that Hunter now commanded the department. The message also reiterated the directive to advance on the town in order to unite with Hunter's army in carrying out the strike on Lynchburg.[72]

The Army of the Kanawha, however, was in no condition to undertake a new campaign immediately. The torturous march to Meadow Bluff from the New River bridge had exhausted the army. As Captain Hastings observed, "From Newburn Bridge to this place we should have marched in four days, but the constant rain storms, causing muddy roads and swollen creeks and rivers, so delayed us that nine days were occupied."[73] Many wagons had to be abandoned, and rations became scarce. When the 15th West Virginia reached Meadow Bluff, they "were in a pitiful plight and in a state of semi-starvation." One West Virginian wrote to his family that "three days last week all I had to eat was a little corn meal baked on a stone and one cup of coffee. I have not changed my clothes since I started

69. Eby, ed., *Virginia Yankee*, 250.

70. *OR*, Vol. XXXVII, Pt. 1, p. 536; Simon, ed., *Papers of Grant*, X, 487–88.

71. Eby, ed., *Virginia Yankee*, 248.

72. *OR*, Vol. XXXVII, Pt. 1, pp. 120, 478, 507; Schmitt, ed., *George Crook*, 115–16.

73. *OR*, Vol. XXXVII, Pt. 1, p. 120; Hastings Autobiography, May 20, 1864, XI, 17; J. E. D. Ward, *Twelfth Ohio Volunteer Infantry* (Ripley, Ohio, 1864), 76.

and have none to put on. . . . My coat is in ribbons, and my pants hardly hold together. . . . I am about as hard a looking fellow as ever you saw."[74] Many were also without shoes. Captain John Young complained that his men "think that I am the cause. Think I don't do my duty. Annoys me very much."[75] Sickness had also taken its toll. A diet of green beef without bread, coffee, or salt on the march had a deleterious effect on the men, and diarrhea plagued the camps. Young noted that on several mornings twenty in his company reported sick. With no hospitals, "no care [was] taken of the sick."[76]

The respite at Meadow Bluff not only proved beneficial for the health of the army but also allowed Crook time to reprovision his men with supplies from Gauley Bridge. He realized the necessity of obtaining sufficient subsistence, since provisions would be scarce along his projected route to Staunton. On May 20 supplies began to arrive at Meadow Bluff, and for the first time in ten days the men received full rations. As Colonel Hayes observed, the "rations . . . filled our camp with joy last night."[77] The delay, Crook complained, resulted from the "miserable transportation" furnished by the quartermaster's department.[78] A correspondent for the Cincinnati *Daily Gazette* agreed, charging that the department used "worn out wagons, decayed horses and mules, and, worse than all, two year old unbroken mules" which were "perfectly unfit for such service . . . in this rocky, mountainous country."[79]

The men of the 2nd West Virginia Cavalry had "no idea what wee will do next or where wee will go," but Private Tall well knew that "it is not likely that wee will lay idle while the grand struggle is going on."[80] Despite the failure to fully refit his troops, Crook, "with many of my men barefoot and scantily supplied with rations," and with each regiment limited to one supply wagon, began the march toward Staunton on May 31. The Army of the Kanawha was "now well fed and rested, with new clothing, except shoes," but as Captain Hastings observed, it was also "much reduced by

74. Wheeling *Daily Intelligencer*, May 26, 1864.

75. Young Diary, May 20, 1864.

76. *Ibid.*, May 22–24, 26, 28, 1864, pp. 6–7; Young to Emma, May 24, 1864, Young Papers; Abraham to Sister, May 27, 1864 in Benson, comp., *With the Army*, 96.

77. Extracts from Hayes Diary, May 21, 1864.

78. *OR*, Vol. XXXVII, Pt. 1, pp. 120, 561.

79. Cincinnati *Daily Gazette*, June 3, 1864.

80. Tall to Mother and Sisters, May 21–22, 1864, Tall Letters.

battles, sickness and the expiration of the three year's terms of service."[81] Some were not able to resume the march.[82] Crook would need to "drain the country of all supplies as I pass through."[83] Despite shortages, morale remained high. Colonel Hayes wrote to his wife, "We feel well about the future. General Crook is more hopeful than ever before." To his uncle, Hayes confided, "We all believe in General Crook. . . . He is the best general I have ever been with, no exceptions."[84] Many of the men "were passably happy as each man knew we were going over the Allegheny Mountains into the Shenandoah Valley."[85]

Averell's troopers were in no better shape than the infantry. Duffié's brigade was "almost entirely broken down from lack of rations" and "very much disorganized and demoralized."[86] Many suffered from sickness. Averell considered "our late trip one of the very hardest campaigns of the war." The arrival of the 8th Ohio Cavalry, with fresh horses and new clothes, made their condition more poignant. Private J. J. Sutton and his fellow West Virginians, "with open mouths, as we stood in our half naked condition, saw them file by and go into camp."[87] Encamped at Bunger's Mills in Greenbrier County, some ten and a half miles from Meadow Bluff, Averell too was forced to wait for supplies, especially horses, horseshoes and nails, shoes, and clothing. The failure of the "miserable, inadequate, and insufficient transportation furnished from the Kanawha" forced his troopers to subsist on half rations. When he resumed the march, Averell estimated that out of his 3,200 mounted and 1,200 dismounted men, 600 were without shoes and other articles of clothing. As a result his men "suffered terribly," but as he proudly noted, "without complaint." On June 3, three days after the departure of Crook's infantry, the cavalry moved out, with Lieutenant Blazer and his scouts taking the advance—"almost as destitute as when we came," complained Private Sutton.[88]

81. Hastings Autobiography, May 31, 1864, XII, 2.

82. Davis Diary, May 31, 1864.

83. OR, Vol. XXXVII, Pt. 1, p. 561.

84. Williams, ed., Letters and Diary of Hayes, II, 466–67.

85. Abraham to Sister, May 27, 1864, in Benson, comp., With the Army, 9.

86. OR, Vol. XXXVII, Pt. 1, pp. 500–501.

87. Sutton, Second Regiment: West Virginia, 125.

88. OR, Vol. XXXVII, Pt. 1, pp. 145, 500–501, 584; Cincinnati Daily Commercial, July 12, 1864; James A. Thomson, "The Lynchburg Campaign, June, 1864," G.A.R. War Papers, I, 123; Benson, comp., With the Army, 97; Lang, Loyal West Virginia, 376; Sutton, Second Regiment: West Virginia, 125.

With reduced forces in the region, the Confederates could do no more than harass Crook's movement. As John McNulty Clugston of the 36th Ohio observed, "There seems to be no rebel force in this part of the country except bushwhackers and about one thousand men under Jackson."[89] Initially, on May 20, "Mudwall" believed that Crook's army would move toward the Kanawha Valley, but as the troops remained near Lewisburg, Southerners became increasingly apprehensive.[90] Reports of a Federal buildup at Beverly created additional concern. Positioning two companies in Pocahontas County to watch Federal activity there, Jackson moved his troopers to Gallaghan's. From there on May 29 he reported to Stringfellow at Dublin that there was no movement yet, although he thought "they are preparing and watching closely."[91] When reports of Federal presence at Beverly proved to be false, Jackson, at Imboden's request, moved his men to the Jackson River Depot and then to Millborough, while "Grumble" Jones directed McCausland to occupy the former place.[92] By the end of May, Southerners steeled themselves for Crook to strike at Staunton or Salem.

McCausland, a newly promoted brigadier general and in command of Jenkins' brigade, ordered his command to rendezvous near Gap Mills for inspection. With the mortal wounding of Jenkins at Cloyds Mountain, leadership had fallen to McCausland as second in command. The War Department, recognizing his performance there and at New River, promoted him on May 24. By 1864, McCausland had acquired a reputation as a "gallant and accomplished officer," and Richmond regarded him well.[93] After Jenkins' death, questions had been raised over who should command in southwestern Virginia. Bragg suggested transferring Echols to the department. Lee demurred, although he recognized the urgency for a new overall commander and one for Jenkins' brigade. He asked Seddon to return Breckinridge to the region as soon as possible. However, the day before receiving Lee's reply, Richmond assigned McCausland to head the brigade.[94]

89. Clugston Diary, June 3, 1864.

90. *OR*, Vol. XXXVII, Pt. 1, p. 746.

91. *Ibid.*, 748–50.

92. *Ibid.*, 750–51.

93. Shirley Donnelly, "General 'Tiger John' McCausland: The Man Who Burned Chambersburg," *WVH*, XXIII (1962), 141–43; Vandiver, ed., *Diary of Gorgas*, 100.

94. *OR*, Vol. XXXVII, Pt. 1, pp. 747, 752; Freeman, ed., *Lee's Dispatches*, 216–18.

John McCausland possessed a considerable military background. He stood first in his 1857 graduating class at the Virginia Military Institute. After attending the University of Virginia for a year, he returned to VMI as an assistant professor of mathematics and as an assistant instructor in artillery tactics under the supervision of then-professor Thomas Jackson. With the outbreak of the war he organized a battery of artillery in Rockbridge County. Governor John Letcher offered him its command, but he declined both the appointment and election as its captain. Instead, Lee sent him to the Kanawha Valley to raise troops.[95] There he organized the 36th Virginia Regiment and received the rank of lieutenant colonel. He soon developed a reputation as a tenacious fighter and earned the nickname "Tiger John." Once asked about his short temper, McCausland replied that "a lively colt makes a high stepping carriage horse."[96] McCausland possessed one marked advantage over his sparring partners. He knew West Virginia well, and especially the Shenandoah Valley. "My kith and kin lived along the route taken by Hunter," he later remarked, "and everything that would stimulate a man to almost superhuman efforts were here found to help and force me to do my utmost."[97]

Those in Jenkins' old command, possessing a reputation of being "badly disciplined mountaineers," became apprehensive over the appointment. As General Bradley T. Johnson later found out, they "would fight like veterans when they pleased, but had no idea of permitting their own sweet wills to be controlled by any orders, no matter from whom emanating."[98] They respected McCausland as "a gallant and accomplished officer" yet feared that he would be a "strict disciplinarian." James McChesney of the 14th Virginia Cavalry wrote that "he is said to be very profane and hard

95. Garnett L. Eskew, "Last Surviving Confederate General, McCausland, One of the Saviors of Lynchburg," clipping in John McCausland Biographical File, V.M.I; Garnett Laidlaw Eskew, "They Called Him 'Town Burner' " *WVR*, XVI (1938), 42.

96. Donnelly, "General 'Tiger John' McCausland," 141. See Michael J. Pauley, *Unreconstructed Rebel: The Life of General John McCausland C.S.A.* (Charleston, 1993), David L. Phillips and Rebecca L. Hill, *Tiger John: The Rebel Who Burned Chambersburg* (Leesburg, Va., 1993), James Earl Brown, "Life of Brigadier General John McCausland," *WVH*, IV (1943), 239–93.

97. Quoted in Brown, "Life of McCausland," 269.

98. Quoted in Robert K. Krick, " 'The Cause of All My Disasters': Jubal A. Early and the Undisciplined Valley Cavalry," in Gary W. Gallagher, ed., *Struggle for the Shenandoah: Essays on the 1864 Valley Campaign* (Kent, Ohio), 80–82, and Jeffrey C. Weaver, *22nd Virginia Cavalry* (Lynchburg, 1991), 25.

on his men."[99] Captain Thomas Feamaster believed that he was "disliked generally by all & never can fill the vacancy caused by the death of Gen. Jenkins."[100] Characterizing his brigade, McCausland later recalled that "I call it cavalry, it really wasn't anything but mounted infantry—mostly western Virginia boys who had formed their local militia companies and joined up with us." He added, "none better. But they were undisciplined."[101]

On June 1 the new general moved his brigade toward Sweet Springs. There he occupied a position on the route Crook undoubtedly would take if he advanced toward Staunton. Jones wanted him to watch Crook and, if possible, prevent him from joining Hunter. At Covington, McCausland "got ahead" of the Federals and readied his men to challenge their advance. He adopted a strategy of delaying Crook "without fighting a pitched battle," hoping to provide "Grumble" time to fight Hunter. With only about eighteen hundred men, McCausland knew that any attempt at serious resistance "would have utterly destroyed my smaller force."[102] Another factor was the condition of his brigade. "The horses were mere skeletons—most all Confederate horses were skeletons in '64. We carried little or no rations and had to live off the country we happened to be marching through."[103]

Yet the Federals, in passing through narrow valleys, were well aware that "a small force can easily hold a large one."[104] Southern scouts and guerrillas continually harassed them, while blockaded roads impeded their advance. Once past White Sulphur Springs, Blazer's men became increasingly involved in a series of skirmishes with McCausland's. At Covington on the Jackson River on June 2, Blazer's scouts spotted the Confederates. Dismounting, they waded the river, then charged double-quick into the town. Initially successful, they drove the Southerners for a mile until the

99. James McChesney to Lucy, March [May] 31, 1864, H. E. Matheny Collection, WVU.

100. Thomas Feamaster Diary, June 9, 1864, Feamaster Family Papers, LC.

101. Quoted in Jack L. Dickinson, *16th Virginia Cavalry* (Lynchburg, 1989), 43, and Eskew, "They Called Him 'Town Burner,' " *WVR*, XVI (1938), 42.

102. McCausland to Chas. M. Blackford, Jan. 30, 1901, McCausland Letter, W&L and John W. Daniel Collection, UV.

103. Quoted in Catherine Henderson, "The Man Who Never Knew Defeat," *CWT*, XXIII (1984), 38–39.

104. Williams, ed., *Diary and Letters of Hayes*, II, 470.

Confederates formed a battle line. After skirmishing for about two hours, Blazer's men broke off the engagement and retreated back through town to the main body.[105]

On June 5 at Cow Pasture River, the 91st Ohio found the Southerners entrenched. With the aid of the 13th West Virginia the Ohioans charged with bayonet. Driven out of their position, the Confederates fell back. The Federals attempted to call up the cavalry, but Blazer, annoyed at their slow response, shouted to his scouts, "Come on, boys!" and dashed into the retreating Rebels at full tilt, killing and capturing several.[106] After pausing to destroy the bridge, Blazer's men began systematically destroying small bridges and culverts along their route. Of the Confederates, Corporal Ellis boasted in his diary that "we drove them like sheep" toward Panthers Gap.[107]

The narrow mountain gap, with its lofty and precipitous bluffs on each side, offered McCausland's smaller force a stronger position from which to challenge Crook. Fortifying the Gap, his men piled up rocks for cover at various intervals and cleverly stretched a telegraph wire to prevent cavalry charges. Chaplain A. H. Windsor of the 91st Ohio Regiment, observing the Southern position, believed that it would be "madness . . . to attempt to drive the enemy away by charging though the gap."[108] Crook shrewdly sent a detachment across the mountain on an old road to make a flank attack on their rear. Suddenly realizing their danger, the Southerners fled and barely escaped.

Without further opposition, Crook's men easily reached Goshen on June 5. The next morning they began systematically tearing up the Virginia Central Railroad. As Hayes observed, the rail line could "be destroyed by troops marching parallel to it, very fast," but the work considerably slowed the pace of the army.[109] "Today we became experts at

105. Journal of the 23rd Regiment, 18; Clugston Diary, June 3–4, 1864; Montgomery, *Blazer*, 16; Cincinnati *Daily Gazette*, June 20, 1864; Edwin B. Meade, ed., *Memoirs: Early Life and Civil War Days of Captain Edwin E. Bouldin* (Danville, Va., 1968), 14–15.

106. Montgomery, *Blazer*, 16; Thomson, "Lynchburg Campaign," 124–25.

107. Ellis Diary, June 5, 1864.

108. Windsor, *Ninety-First Regiment O.V.I.*, 47.

109. Feamaster Diary, June 5, 1864; Cracraft Journal, June 5, 1864; Achilles James Tynes to Wife, June 13, 1864 [copy from Achilles James Tynes Papers, SCH], Hunter's Raid File, W&L; Windsor, "Letter from the 91st Ohio," Athens (Ohio) *Messenger*, July 21, 1864; James Z. McChesney, "The Hunter Raid into West Virginia, May 1864" 1–2, H. E.

destroying railways," observed Captain Hastings, "the Brigade destroying eight miles in such a way that the rails would have to be sent to a rolling mill to be straightened."[110] As usual, the method was to stack rails and cross-ties and then fire the wooden ties. Weights attached to the ends of the rails helped to bend them. Captain James A. Thomson of the 34th Ohio recalled the procedure: "The entire command stack arms, form in single rank along the track, take hold of the rails, lift the entire mass on one side, and turn it completely over."[111] Occasionally they made a point of bending some rails into the form of the letters *US* as evidence of their visit.[112]

As Crook approached Buffalo Gap on June 6, he learned of the concentration of McCausland's and "Mudwall" Jackson's units there. Using his cavalry as a screen, he avoided them by crossing over North Mountain at Pond Gap and then marching into the Valley on an abandoned road. As the army descended the mountain, a courier reached Crook from Hunter. He informed him of the victory at Piedmont and the capture of Staunton. Captain Hastings, reflecting the army's relief over the news, confided to his diary, "We were glad enough to learn that Hunter had been successful, otherwise we should have had to skedaddle back to the Kanawha Valley as best we could."[113] Now more confident, the Army of the Kanawha brushed aside a small Southern force and marched into the Valley at Middlebrook, some eleven miles southwest of Staunton.

Middlebrook's stunned residents got their first sight of Union soldiers in their neighborhood. Not all, however, felt cowed. A number of local women refused to disguise their sentiments and openly "predicted our annihilation."[114] Others, like the Dunkards, received them cordially. One Dunkard lady gladly gave them pies and cakes to feast on.[115] Andrew Stiarwalt of the 23rd Ohio observed that the Unionists "are very glad to See

---

Matheny Collection; James M'Chesney [McChesney], "Scouting on Hunter's Raid to Lynchburg, Va.," CV, XXVIII (1920), 173; Extracts from Hayes Diary, June 6, 1864.

110. Hastings Autobiography, June 6, 1864, XII, 3.

111. Thomson, "Lynchburg Campaign," 125.

112. Cracraft Journal, June 6, 1864; Ward, *Twelfth Ohio*, 77.

113. Cincinnati *Daily Gazette*, June 20, 1864; Hastings Autobiography, June 8, 1864, XII, 4.

114. Thomson, "Lynchburg Campaign," 127.

115. Cincinnati *Daily Gazette*, June 25, 1864.

us Coming."[116] But they also suffered from being overrun by hungry soldiers.

Low on food and supplies, soldiers foraged in the area. Peter Roebush
lost 150 pounds of bacon, half a bushel of flour, and a cow, as well as two
horses for the Federal artillery.[117] After suffering the loss of two horses,
two head of cattle, and 300 pounds of bacon, Unionist Mary Blackburn
told an officer that "I thought he might leave me a little flour."[118] The Emerson family, fearing intrusions during the night, established a rotating
watch. Yet the army's restraint in the Middlebrook area surprised many
residents.[119] One woman was relieved that the soldiers did not do "as
much damage as we expected," while Lewis Bumgardner was greatly
pleased when a "very gentlemanly" officer provided protection for his
family.[120]

Early the next morning, June 8, Crook's army continued its march
toward Staunton to form the long-awaited juncture with Hunter. As they
approached, the men of the 8th Ohio Cavalry noticed that "Union feeling began to manifest itself to a greater extent." Ladies stood beside the
road with "buckets of water and tin-cups in their hands, from which they
gave to many a fatigued, thirsty and dirt coverd soldier a drink of cool
water." Others waved "handkerchiefs, dishcloths, and other articles of like
character." But like Hunter's men before them, Crook's soldiers questioned the sincerity of these expressions, for "we were unable to tell
whether they proceeded from a genuine feeling of patriotism or a hypo-
critical desire to save their *onions*."[121] On reaching Staunton, the Army of
the Kanawha proudly entered the town "in grand style, with bands playing
and flags flying." Their only regret was that they could not "claim a share
of the glory of its capture."[122] There was great cheering for the event, in
part because long-awaited necessities and shoes were there.[123] With some
disappointment, the men of the 23rd Ohio also discovered that "all the

116. Stiarwalt Diary, 19.

117. Peter Roebush file #1388, microfiche 1001, RG 233, SCCP.

118. Mary Blackburn file #41694, RG 217, SCCP.

119. Diary of Nancy Emerson, July 8, 1864, Emerson Family Papers, UV.

120. Bettie W. Memphy [?] to Brother, June 10, 1864, and Lewis Bumgardner to James
Bumgardner, June 10, 1864, Hunter's Raid File.

121. Reminiscences, June 7, 1864, Zeller Collection.

122. Point Pleasant (W. Va.) *Weekly Register*, June 23, 1864.

123. *OR*, Vol. XXXVII, Pt. 1, p. 145.

business houses have been sacked by our forces."[124] Yet they could now wash, repair clothing, and enjoy their new provisions.[125]

For those veterans of the 23rd and 28th Ohio whose enlistments had expired, their journey ended in Staunton. Strother and Hunter hit on a practical plan for sending them home: the men would form a guard of 800, under the command of Colonel Moor, to escort a train with some 1,040 prisoners to Beverly and then on to the north. Both Stahel and Major Lang would accompany them. The remaining members of the depleted 12th Ohio and the 23rd Ohio now merged into the 23rd Ohio.[126]

The junction of the two armies made Grant's staff optimistic about military operations in western Virginia. An excited Halpine confided in his diary, "We can laugh at anything less than one of Lee's Army Corps to reenforce the valley troops."[127] General Rawlins, writing to his wife on June 7, predicted that "their combined forces will be sufficiently strong to enable them to strike a staggering blow against the Confederacy."[128] Hunter now possessed not only the necessary manpower to destroy Lee's supply lines but, more important, the possibility of fulfilling Grant's design of a turning movement. Lee could not ignore the threat the Army of West Virginia posed to the Army of Northern Virginia's left flank and rear.

Hunter's four-day respite in Staunton provided not only time to rest and equip his men but also a chance to reorganize his cavalry. Since Stahel had been wounded at Piedmont, he relieved him of command and divided the cavalry into two divisions. The first one he assigned to Duffié, the second to Averell. He temporarily reassigned Stahel to duty in the lower Valley and gave him the task of organizing a force for the defense of the Baltimore and Ohio Railroad and a guard for a supply train to follow after the army. Presumably Stahel would then "with all discreet speed rejoin this command." Hunter tactfully emphasized Stahel's temporary assignment and expressed appreciation for his "faithful, zealous, and gallant

124. Cracraft Journal, June 8, 1864.

125. Hastings Autobiography, June 9, 1864, XII, 4; Patterson Diary, June 9, 1864; Thomson, "Lynchburg Campaign," 127, 129; Windsor, "Letter from 91st Ohio," Athens (Ohio) *Messenger*, July 21, 1864.

126. OR, Vol. XXXVII, Pt. 1, p. 606; Eby, ed., *Virginia Yankee*, 250; Hastings Autobiography, June 9, 1864, XII, 4; Journal of 23rd Regiment, 19; Cracraft Journal, June 9, 10, 1864; Lang, *Loyal West Virginia*, 376.

127. Quoted in Hanchett, *Irish: Charles Halpine*, 116.

128. Wilson, *Life of Rawlins*, 227.

services." To Halleck, Hunter commended Stahel's performance at Piedmont and voiced regret in parting with him.[129]

Yet Stahel's departure in fact pleased Hunter. At Cedar Creek he had
complained to Halleck about the state of the cavalry and asked "most urgently" for "a commander of grit, zeal, activity, and courage." He had
claimed that "it would be impossible to exaggerate the inefficiency of
General Stahel" and confided to Strother that he was "determined to be
rid of him." The cavalry's performance at Piedmont infuriated Strother,
who believed that the "worthlessness of our cavalry" and its failure to follow up the victory had induced Hunter "to content himself with the affair
as it stood."[130]

With Crook now at Staunton, the delayed decision over the army's
projected route in striking at Lynchburg came into sharp focus. The day
before his arrival, Hunter had consulted with Strother as to his views. The
colonel proposed moving through Lexington to Buchanan, then crossing
the Blue Ridge by the Peaks of Otter Road and marching through Liberty
to Lynchburg.[131] Two dispatches found on the body of General Jones
helped to reshape Strother's and Hunter's thinking. One contained an
item from the commandant at Lynchburg to Richmond asking for more
troops to defend the city against "a sudden raid." The second came from
Jefferson Davis, who urged Jones to guard "against raids into the western
portion of North Carolina." The wire implied that such a penetration
would create serious political and military problems. Presumed Southern
weakness there, coupled with reports of Grant's progress, encouraged
Hunter and Strother to expand their strategy to embrace a plan for an
"extensive and damaging campaign." The prospect of being able to conduct military operations from Lynchburg against both the South Side
Railroad and the Richmond and Danville Railroad, as well as being able
to liberate prisoners at Danville, enticed them. If Lee did detach a force to
defend Lynchburg, they reasoned, they would accomplish an important
function by weakening Lee and thereby relieving pressure on Grant. In
case of adversity, Strother believed, "We had always safe lines of retreat
open to the westward, through the passes of the mountains."[132]

To carry out the plan, Hunter fully accepted the necessity of cutting his

129. OR, Vol. XXXVII, Pt. 1, pp. 612–14.
130. Ibid., 516–17; Eby, ed., Virginia Yankee, 232, 246.
131. Eby, ed., Virginia Yankee, 249.
132. Strother, "Operations in West Virginia," 486.

army off from its supply base at Martinsburg. His supply line, already tenuous at best, would be even more difficult to maintain beyond Lexington and into the Virginia Piedmont. The potential for dangerous shortages of ammunition and provisions was great. Grant's charge to live off the countryside now took on a larger significance than it had in merely striking at Charlottesville. At New Market, Hunter had explicitly informed the army of his intention of cutting "loose from its base," yet the real test of the practicality of this strategy—both for the army and for the civilian population that would be required to support it—lay south of Staunton in the route crossing the Blue Ridge into the Virginia Piedmont to attack Lynchburg.

Further refinement of the strategy came on June 8, when Averell, then in high favor, met with Hunter and proposed a highly ambitious plan. Averell suggested that the main column should continue up the Valley to Buchanan, but he further recommended detaching Duffié's cavalry to move eastward to threaten the Confederate position at Rockfish Gap as a feint, then to continue moving along the western slope of the Blue Ridge to demonstrate against any Southern forces stationed at the various gaps in the mountains. In addition, he suggested that Duffié should send scouting parties across the mountains to strike at the Orange and Alexandria Railroad, which linked Charlottesville and Lynchburg. Once he reached White's Gap, Duffié could advance with his entire cavalry on Amherst Court House, where his troopers could destroy the railroad and he could send a detachment toward Lynchburg. Duffié's main body could then move below the city, cross the James River, and operate against the South Side Railroad until he formed a junction with Hunter in that area. Averell estimated that it would take five days to complete the movement.[133]

Hunter was impressed and approved the plan. He gave Duffié verbal instructions as to his route and a written memorandum for his use.[134] But not everyone was optimistic about the strategy. Crook harbored serious reservations and questioned the operation's objective. Strother replied that the move was designed to force Lee out of Richmond by cutting his transportation lines to the west and south. When Crook questioned whether the Army of West Virginia possessed sufficient strength to carry out the plan, Strother assured him that it did, arguing that the army could

133. Eby, ed., *Virginia Yankee*, 249–50.
134. OR, Vol. XXXVII, Pt. 1, p. 146; Lang, *Loyal West Virginia*, 376.

defeat any Confederate force then in West Virginia or western Virginia. With Grant closely pressing Lee, he believed, the Army of Northern Virginia could not spare troops for the defense of the Valley. If Lee attempted such a move, he assured Crook, Sheridan's cavalry, then moving toward Gordonsville, would cut them off.[135]

Crook, still skeptical, warned that they might take Lynchburg but that Lee, "for want of supplies," would not allow them to hold it. He also cautioned that "if we expected to take Lynchburg at all we must move upon it immediately and rapidly." Strother agreed but pointed out the army's "lack of ammunition." Hunter's troops had paid a high price for the victory at Piedmont in their expenditure of ammunition, and a move on Lynchburg without supply lines would be hazardous. Brushing that objection aside, Crook asserted that his command possessed plenty and offered to move on Lynchburg alone with his own division. For him, "celerity was more important than numbers or ammunition." Reporting back to Hunter, Strother stressed Crook's fear of delaying too long. Understanding his reservations, Hunter replied that "a good deal of delay was unavoidable."[136]

Finally, on the morning of June 10, and despite Crook's reservations, all was in readiness. After a restless night spent fearing a guerrilla attack, Hunter set off toward Lexington "in high good humor" with a combined army of some twenty thousand men and thirty-six pieces of artillery on four parallel roads. Crook's division took the main road toward Brownsburg, with Averell's cavalry on one to its west. Sullivan's infantry marched on the Greenville Road, while Duffié's cavalry rode eastward toward the Blue Ridge Mountains. The troops maintained a state of readiness to concentrate if one group suddenly became engaged. Crook's troops had hardly left Staunton before they began skirmishing with McCausland's men.[137]

Earlier at Buffalo Gap, on June 6, McCausland, learning of Jones's defeat at Piedmont, had feared that Crook's flanking movement would trap him between the two armies. To prevent that, he made a "dead race to get to Middlebrook" before Crook's men entered the Valley.[138] Already on

135. Eby, ed., *Virginia Yankee*, 250.

136. *Ibid.*, 251.

137. OR, Vol. XXXVII, Pt. 1, pp. 618–19; Campbell Diary, June 10, 1864; Cecil D. Eby, Jr., "David Hunter: Villain of the Valley," *Proceedings of the Rockbridge Historical Society*, VI (1966), 87.

138. Tynes to Wife, June 13, 1864, Hunter's Raid File.

the evening of June 9 his men had tangled with Federal pickets and then retreated. "Tiger John" fully intended to delay any further Union advance up the Valley, but this time he faced a combined Federal army. Despite overwhelming odds, his brigade continued to torment Hunter's men up to the very gates of Lynchburg itself.

For Hunter, who estimated McCausland's brigade at some fifteen hundred, "Tiger John" became a source of annoyance as well as a retarding force. Crook placed Hayes's 23rd Ohio Regiment at the head of the advance. "Don't let those fellows delay us," Hayes ordered.[139] They easily forced McCausland's rear guard to keep retiring,[140] but near Brownsburg the Southerners had prepared a surprise. Two Southern scouts halted behind a barricade of fence rails and began firing at the oncoming Federals. Then they quickly fell back. In their rear, on a hill commanding a bend in the road, McCausland's main column lay waiting, concealed on the hill's crest along a wooded area. At a distance they saw the Union cavalry closing up in fours for their charge on their rear guard. As the Federals reached them, suddenly they opened fire with a roar that Private J. Scott Moore believed "would have waked the snakes in February." The Federals "reeled, and shook, and fled." Without orders, Captain Edwin E. Bouldin with Company B of the 14th Virginia countercharged. In less than half an hour, as Major Achilles James Tynes lamented, McCausland's men, despite their courage "against such odds," were again retreating toward Brownsburg, pressed closely by Crook's men.[141]

Meanwhile, at Newport, Averell, hoping to use a circuitous route to get into the enemy's rear, turned to the west toward Walker's Creek Valley.[142] As Major Tynes observed, "We were in what may be a called *a very tight place*. If we turned our backs 'twas a ruinous rout; if we moved back fighting, *slowly*, the flanking columns, one, two thousand, & there other fifteen hundred strong (cavalry) would pass & engulf us."[143] A small Confederate contingent in Brownsburg bravely overran a squad of six Federals leading the advance, but a second unit, less than a hundred yards behind, checked them. Captain Hastings noted that "this taught them a lesson as no fur-

139. Hastings Autobiography, June 10, 1864, XII, 6.
140. Journal of 23rd Regiment, 19.
141. J. Scott Moore, "General Hunter's Raid," *SHSP*, XXVII (1899), 181–83; Meade, *Memoirs: Bouldin*, 15; Tynes to Wife, June 13, 1864, Hunter's Raid File.
142. OR, Vol. XXXVII, Pt. 1, p. 120; Eby, ed., *Virginia Yankee*, 252.
143. Tynes to Wife, June 13, 1864, Hunter's Raid File.

ther attack of this nature was made."[144] Capturing a wounded Confederate, they asked him when McCausland intended to stop and fight. The
soldier reputedly replied that "if you can tell me when Crook will stop
pursuing I can tell you when I will stop running."[145]

Weary of Confederate tactics, Federal soldiers had no intention of tol-
erating hostile acts by local civilians. As Colonel J. N. Waddell and his
12th West Virginia Regiment with Hunter's column marched by a burning home, he saw a lady bitterly weeping as she sat on a trunk in her front
yard. Her husband had vowed to shoot the first Federal he saw, and when
a sergeant leading an advanced guard stopped at the house to ask for a
drink of water, he fulfilled his promise. Immediately the sergeant's men
"peppered [him] full of holes." They gave the man's wife five minutes to
get her things out of the house, then set fire to it. "In one short hour,"
Waddell noted, "that beautiful home and all it contained went up in flame
and smoke."[146]

Crook's men camped near Brownsburg that night. The soldiers were
soon foraging about the countryside, and a group of ten or fifteen visited
James Potter's farm. They quickly deprived him of twenty sheep, a heifer,
a hog, fifty pounds of bacon, and two bushels each of wheat and corn. The
men killed all the sheep and the heifer in their camp, some four hundred
yards from Potter's house.[147] The next morning, June 10, Crook's column
pushed toward Lexington, and McCausland's forces continued to retreat.
The constant skirmishing and pulling back took a heavy toll on the Confederates. Captain Bouldin complained "on several occasions . . . that it
was too hard to keep the officers & men . . . on duty all day & night for
days & nights." He once asked McCausland if they could be relieved, but
the general refused, explaining that they would have to wait until "the
danger was over."[148]

That night, the "foot sore, hungry & exhausted" brigade camped a mile
in front of Lexington across the North River. Lexington's residents nervously listened to their preparations as they watched the Confederate
campfires light up the hillsides.[149] McCausland went into Lexington to

144. Hastings Autobiography, June 10, 1864, XII, 6.
145. Wheeling *Daily Intelligencer*, July 15, 1864.
146. Clipping, "Hunter's Lynchburg Raid," J. N. Waddell Collection, WVA&HL.
147. James Potter file #5652, microfiche 1826, RG 233, SCCP.
148. Meade, *Memoirs: Bouldin*, 16.
149. Charles W. Turner, ed., "General David Hunter's Sack of Lexington, Virginia,
June 10–14, 1864: An Account by Rose Page Pendleton," *VMH&B*, LXXXIII (1975), 175.

discuss plans to delay Hunter's army with General Smith at the Virginia Military Institute. Early the following morning "the thunder of Crooks guns" roused the Southerners.[150] Positioned behind rail breastworks, they offered some resistance, but Hayes's men easily dislodged them. "Hotly pressed by the enemy," they hurriedly retreated toward the covered bridge spanning the North River. Already loaded with bales of hay and soaked with turpentine, the bridge contained only a single aisle for their passage. As the last trooper scurried across, the sappers torched the structure.[151]

Buying time, McCausland deployed his men the best he could along the North River's southern bluffs. The river provided a formidable barrier. The depth of the river before the town, coupled with high banks on either side, made fording extremely difficult. To cross the river, the Federals would have to go five miles downstream or two miles to the west. The south bank and the heights immediately behind it rose perpendicularly, forming a ridge along the river, to the height of fifty or sixty feet in many places. Thickets of cedars on the heights made concealment easy. To the right of the bridge, behind the cedars and slightly to the west, rested the buildings of the Virginia Military Institute, where McCausland positioned sharpshooters along the cliff and in some of the stores near the bridge. He placed a battery on the northwest corner of the institute's parade ground on North Hill overlooking the opposite bank. In addition, he sent small units of cavalry up and down the river to picket the fords and sound an alarm if an attempt was made to flank the town.[152]

Excited by the flight of the Southern rear guard toward the bridge, Crook's skirmishers dashed down the surrounding hills after them. As they approached the river, they abruptly came under heavy musket and artillery fire from the southern bluff of the river. After a shell killed one and wounded six, they quickly drew back. Advanced units rapidly moved up for support, while Du Pont's battery moved to a hill overlooking the town on the left of the pike and began firing at the institute. Crook noted the formidable Southern position. With field glasses he could easily discern the location of the sharpshooters on the high bluffs. Meanwhile, Hunter's

150. Tynes to Wife, June 13, 1864, Hunter's Raid File.

151. *Ibid.*; Feamaster Diary, June 11, 1864; Diary fragment, 5th Cavalry Brigade, June 12, 1864, Tavenner, Cabell, and Alexander Scott Withers Tavenner Papers, DU; Wise, *End of an Era*, 310–11.

152. OR, Vol. XXXVII, Pt. 1, p. 96; "General Hunter's Expedition," 527; Eby, ed., *Virginia Yankee*, 252–53; Lexington (Va.) *Gazette*, July 19, 1864.

and Sullivan's infantry hurried toward the fighting. Crook, holding the Confederates in his front with the 36th Ohio, sent his 2nd Brigade under Colonel White in a flanking movement up the northern side of the river to find a suitable ford. Captain McMullin brought up a section of artillery and opened fire on the Southern guns. His Ohio and Kentucky batteries positioned themselves on the right of the pike, with the 1st Kentucky placed to cover White's brigade as it moved up the river. In addition, Hunter sent Averell's cavalry, which had been unsuccessful in cutting off McCausland's retreat from Brownsburg, on a flanking movement across the North River some eight miles above Lexington to "fall upon the enemy's flank and rear."[153]

McCausland's challenge infuriated Hunter, who felt that the Southerner's attempt "to defend an indefensible position against an overwhelming force by screening himself behind the private dwellings of women and children, might have brought justifiable destruction upon the whole town." He also had no desire to reduce his ammunition supply any more than was necessary. Preferring "to spare private property and an unarmed population," Hunter decided against making extensive use of his artillery.[154] Instead, he limited the barrage and relied on Averell's flanking movement to accomplish the capture of Lexington and, he hoped, McCausland. Provoked by Confederate fire seemingly coming from the institute, Du Pont fired on the barracks, but after a single round he ordered his guns to stop.[155] His decision saved the cadet corps from serious injury. Had the guns been aimed at the center of the building, shells would have caught them in formation and exploded in their midst. Instead, his fire merely struck the institute's cupola.[156]

Confederate resistance ended with Crook's infantry encirclement from the west and south. White's 2nd Brigade, fording two miles up the river, sent McCausland's pickets scurrying back toward Lexington. Meanwhile, with the arrival of the remainder of his division, Crook prepared for an assault across the river into the center of town. Braving fire from sharpshooters, his engineers, using lumber from several nearby buildings, sufficiently

153. OR, Vol. XXXVII, Pt. 1, p. 97; "General Hunter's Expedition," 527.

154. OR, Vol. XXXVII, Pt. 1, pp. 96–97.

155. Du Pont, *Campaign of 1864*, 68; "General Hunter's Expedition," 527; Thomson, "Lynchburg Campaign," 129.

156. Couper, *One Hundred Years*, III, 24–25.

repaired the bridge allow Crook's men to cross.[157] To the east of town, others busily constructed a pontoon bridge over the backwater of Jordan's Mill Dam. More important, they destroyed the locks of the dam, thereby lowering the water and allowing troops easily to ford the river.[158] Soon Hayes's 1st Brigade, singing "John Brown's Body," boldly marched up Main Street into the center of Lexington.[159] Symbolic of the town's plight, as resident Rose Page Pendleton observed, "three houses hoisted white flags in token of surrender."[160] Elated, the men of the 2nd Division believed that "Genl Crook can *proudly* say that his Command did the work without any assistance."[161] Hayes saw the battle as merely "an artillery and sharpshooter's duel." For the colonel, whose men suffered the few casualties inflicted, the skirmish could be summed up as a "very noisy affair, but not dangerous."[162]

McCausland's decision to defend the town, despite Hunter's overwhelming numbers and the protests of General Smith, had its rationale. In the aftermath of Cloyds Mountain, he had gained possession of Grant's instructions for Crook to join Hunter in a move on Lynchburg. He fully realized that he could not stop the Federals, yet his orders, which he showed to Smith, called for him to retard their movement. The superintendent disapproved of the decision, for if it would only retard the Federals for "a few hours," Smith "was not willing to make such a sacrifice or run such a risk." However, he held the cadets "on the parade grounds ready to give support." Despite his reservations, time, as "Tiger John" knew, was and would be the principal enemy for Hunter. Any delay reduced his chances for a successful drive to capture Lynchburg.[163]

157. Lynch, *Civil War Diary*, 74.

158. John Beard Gibson and David Robert Revelet to Thomas Harding Ellis, Aug. 24, 1864, John Alexander Gibson Papers.

159. Hastings Autobiography, XII, 9.

160. Turner, ed., "Hunter's Sack of Lexington," 176; "The Shelling of Lexington, Va." CV XXXII (1924), 378.

161. James Thomson to Fannie Nelson, June 12, 1864, Thomson Papers.

162. *OR*, Vol. XXXVII, Pt. 1, pp. 96, 120, 757; Williams, ed., *Diary and Letters of Hayes*, II, 474.

163. McCausland to Chas. M. Blackford, Jan. 30, 1901, Daniel Collection; Francis Smith to W. H. Richardson, June 17, 1864, Superintendent Letter Book: Outgoing Correspondence; O'Reilly, *Baked Meats*, 311–12.

8

On to Lynchburg

Southerners had expected that Staunton, a military target, would experience the brunt of Hunter's fury. Lexington, in contrast, was not a military depot with warehouses brimming with uniforms and shoes or guns and ammunition, nor was it a transportation hub serving a network of roads crisscrossing its streets, or a railroad center. Only a branch of the James River and Kanawha Canal linking the town with Lynchburg held any real military importance, and then only a minor one. A much smaller town than Staunton, Lexington was the commercial center of agriculturally rich Rockbridge County. With a population of 17,248, of which 422 were free blacks and 3,985 slaves, the city was the site of Washington College and the Virginia Military Institute, and the home of former governor John Letcher.[1] Visiting Lexington in the 1850s, Strother had found it "beautifully situated on an eminence in the midst of the great valley . . . its horizon is bounded on all sides by blue mountains, whose outlines are uncommonly diversified and pleasing."[2] Colonel Lincoln believed that the region's surrounding fields of wheat and other crops "would seem to be enough to supply the wants of Lee's entire army."[3]

1. Edwin L. Dooley, Jr., "Lexington in the 1860 Census," *Proceedings of the Rockbridge Historical Society*, IX, 189–96; *Population: 1860 Census*, 517, 519.

2. [David Hunter Strother], "Virginia Illustrated," *Harper's New Monthly Magazine*, XI (1855), 302.

3. Lincoln, *Thirty-fourth Massachusetts*, 307.

For the past three years Lexington had remained secure. Even in early May 1864, the Lexington *Gazette* had exuded confidence and discounted the possibility of a raid from the northwest into the Valley. As late as May 25, the paper, in reporting the calling up of the county reserves, continued to show little alarm but merely cautioned military authorities against creating a shortage of farm labor in the region. "We believe that Gen. Kemper and Gen. Imboden will both take a common-sense view of this most important interest," the editor wrote, "and that they will be in favor of leaving at home, as large a proportion as possible as our agricultural population."[4]

Local residents were not so optimistic. News on June 3 that Crook was some forty miles from Lexington "this side of Covington" created considerable alarm. Although a short respite of hope came the following day with reports of McCausland's presence between Lexington and the Federals and of Jones's movement from Salem, news of the Piedmont disaster destroyed any confidence. "No sooner is one alarm over than another comes," lamented Margaret Junkin Preston. With the influx of refugees bearing stories of the burning of Staunton, "wild excitement" swept the town.[5]

On June 7, reports of Averell's cavalry moving toward Lexington further heightened the tension. "People are more certain to-day of 'the Yankees coming' than they have been at all yet," Mrs. Preston observed, "because there is not a soldier between them and us."[6] Preparations commenced immediately. School officials began securing the institute's library, moving books and other items to adjacent Washington College, a private school. Since VMI was government property, the Federals might burn it. Assuming that "soldiers would take everything they could lay hands on of any value," citizens began securing their property. Later that day, with the receipt of more news on retreating Confederate forces and accounts of the destruction in Staunton, the commotion intensified. Returning from her daily prayer meeting, Mrs. Preston saw "people moving flour, goods, &c.; driving out their cows; ladies flying about in a high state of excitement."[7]

4. Lexington (Va.) *Gazette*, May 4, 25, 1864.

5. Allan, ed., *Life and Letters of Preston*, 182–83.

6. *Ibid.*, 184.

7. *Ibid.*, 185; Henry Boley, *Lexington in Old Virginia* (Richmond, 1936), 113; Rawling, *First Regiment Virginia*, 180.

On the evening of June 10, warnings of Hunter's approach ended any uncertainty. The noise of troop movements and the light of campfires springing up on the northern side of the river confirmed the presence of McCausland's retreating men and the imminent arrival of the Union army. Realizing the impossibility of defending the town, citizens undertook their final efforts in securing their valuables.[8] Brigadier General William Nelson Pendleton's family hid cadet uniforms and cloth from the institute in the upstairs dormitory of their grammar school.[9] Many men, fearing the consequences of capture, hurriedly left town. Former governor Letcher was unable to evacuate his entire family and departed alone that evening for Richmond.[10] Cornelia Peake McDonald, after listening to her husband's final instructions as he prepared to leave town, wrote in her diary, "I scarcely heard what he said, for I felt that the future was nothing if only terrible present was not here, portentous and dreadful."[11] Refugees driving wagons containing their possessions and herding their slaves and cattle crowded the roads toward the mountains and up the Valley. As the Federals pushed toward Lexington, Captain Feamaster watched "the people . . . all refugeeing at a terrible rate, a general stampede."[12] Lexington's remaining citizens slept little that night. For Cornelia McDonald, "the vigil of that June night, near the shortest of the year, seemed more like an Arctic night, so lonely and so creepy."[13]

The next morning, the smoke rising from the burning bridge gave residents full warning of what was to come. The skirmishing and ensuing artillery fire sent many into their cellars for protection as Union batteries sent "shells screaming, shrieking, bursting & whizzing all over the crest of the hills."[14] "Shells fell everywhere in the town," Mrs. Pendleton wrote to her husband,[15] and dozens of buildings soon bore the scars of the bombardment. A number of residents agreed with Hunter's outrage at Mc-

---

8. "Shelling of Lexington," 378; Edward A. Moore, *The Story of a Cannoneer Under Stonewall Jackson* (Freeport, N.Y., 1971), 236.

9. Turner, ed., "Hunter's Sack of Lexington," 175–76.

10. F. N. Boney, *John Letcher of Virginia* (University, Ala., 1966), 206.

11. McDonald, *Diary with Reminiscences*, 203.

12. Feamaster Diary, June 8, 1864.

13. McDonald, *Diary with Reminiscences*, 204n.

14. Tynes to Wife, Jan. 13, 1864, Hunter's Raid File.

15. Quoted in Robert J. Driver, Jr., *Lexington and Rockbridge County in the Civil War* (Lynchburg, 1989), 63.

Causland's "unsoldierly and inhuman attempt . . . to defend an indefensible position," although for an entirely different reason. Mrs. Pendleton felt that "surely a more dastardly thing has not been done by them during the war than the shelling of this defenseless town."[16] Despite its price to Lexington, however, the skirmishing succeeded in delaying the Union army and afforded McCausland's men, the cadets, and others precious time to exit the town safely.

Avoiding the debris and splinters from an exploding shell hitting the institute, the cadets were the first to leave Lexington. "Bidding adieu to such of its residents as we had known in happier days," they marched off toward Balcony Falls, a water gap through the Blue Ridge Mountains, with only an hour's edge on Averell's cavalry.[17] A Mrs. Barton aided their escape by giving their pursuers false information as to their route. When asked by an officer which direction they took, she pointed and said, "Right straight out the road in the direction you are now going."[18] The cadets stopped to rest after five miles on a height with a view of Lexington. Taking a final look at the town, they watched the rising smoke and presumed that the institute was ablaze. That evening they camped on the Blue Ridge some two miles from Balcony Falls, and General Smith posted pickets and deployed the cadets on the mountainside to ward off possible pursuers.[19]

In Lexington, the cadets' departure had merely begun the process of retreat. A flanking movement by Crook's infantry and Averell's cavalry in fording the North River at Leyburn's Mill and moving toward the town from the west and south made any continuing delay dangerous for the Confederates. A squadron of the 14th Virginia Cavalry, sent up the river to watch for crossing Federals, fell back from the ford after skirmishing and sustaining one casualty. On vidette duty, Sergeant James Z. McChesney, from a position in the rear of Washington College, soon observed Averell's cavalry "descending a distant hill."[20] The maneuver threatened to block

16. McDonald, *Diary with Reminiscences,* 203; Allan, ed., *Life and Letters of Preston,* 188; Turner, ed., "Hunter's Sack of Lexington," 176; Moore, "General Hunter's Raid," 185; Eby, "Hunter: Villain of the Valley," 88.

17. Wise, *End of an Era,* 312.

18. Quoted in William Couper, *History of the Shenandoah Valley* (New York, 1952), 935.

19. Couper, *One Hundred Years,* III, 25–26.

20. James Z. McChesney, "A Reminiscence of the Hunter Raid to Lynchburg," 7, H. E. Matheny Collection; M'Chesney [McChesney], "Scouting on Hunter's Raid," 174; Feamaster Diary, June 11, 1864.

the Confederates' retreat to Buchanan, and McChesney immediately reported the sighting to McCausland. Spurred by the news and the successful departure of the cadets, the general now ordered his cavalry to begin moving up Main Street for their own exit. Federal shelling, however, forced them to detour along a parallel street.[21] As Crook's men approached by Mulberry Hill, pandemonium overtook the town.[22]

Around 4 P.M., Hunter's troops proudly marched up Main Street, and soon half-starved soldiers swarmed over the town in search of food as residents—mainly women, children, and the elderly—watched "behind closed blinds."[23] For two hours, Mrs. Preston observed a "continuous stream of cavalry, riding at a fast trot, and several abreast" passing through the center of town. Mrs. Pendleton recoiled as they "came shouting in, as though they had captured some very valuable post."[24]

After three years of safety, the lawlessness of war became a reality for Lexington's remaining citizens. Hungry soldiers, as "insolent as possible," "cursed and swore" as they foraged for food and, at times, any other item that took their fancy. They invaded gardens and rooted out turnips and other vegetables. Residents attempted to pacify them by giving them food, but many possessed limited quantities of provisions themselves. Mrs. Preston appealed to the soldiers that she was a "lone woman, with no protection," but to little avail. A soldier demanded that she open her cellar or they would burn her house. "I told him to burn it," and with that they broke into the basement and looted it.[25] John, the servant of Rev. William S. White, told the Presbyterian minister, "Master, these Yankees are the best of all the rogues I ever saw, black or white."[26] But in defense of his regiment, C. J. Rawling of the 1st Virginia noted that foraging was something the men "only resorted to in order to prevent starvation."[27]

Sunday brought the full impact of the terrors of occupation. Not only did the looting and searches for contraband intensify, but warehouses, mills, and other buildings on the river were put to the torch.[28] Hunter or-

21. Turner, ed., "Hunter's Sack of Lexington," 176; "Shelling of Lexington," 378.

22. Susan P. Lee, ed., *Memoirs of William Nelson Pendleton, D.D.* (Philadelphia, 1893), 344.

23. Hastings Autobiography, June 11, 1864, XII, 9.

24. Allan, ed., *Life and Letters of Preston*, 189; Turner, ed., "Hunter's Sack of Lexington," 176; "Shelling of Lexington," 378; Zeller Reminiscences, June 11, 1864, 12.

25. Allan, ed., *Life and Letters of Preston*, 189–90; Memoirs of Sallie White Bruce, W&L.

26. Quoted in Driver, *Lexington and Rockbridge County*, 73.

27. Rawling, *First Regiment Virginia*, 178.

28. Lincoln, *Thirty-fourth Massachusetts*, 306.

dered the destruction of a number of homes. Earlier, upon entering Lexington on Saturday and stopping at the residence of Major William Gilham, a professor at the institute, Hunter informed Gilham's wife that
since the house belonged to the state, she should remove her furniture, for
he intended to burn it the next morning. Stoically accepting his decision,
she hospitably offered them "good applejack" as refreshments, "apologiz-
ing [that] she had nothing better."[29] Since her brother was a Union army
officer, a number of officers, including Captains Du Pont and William B.
McKinley, gladly assisted in removing her personal belongings and furniture.[30]

    That Sunday morning, Hunter consulted with Strother on whether to
burn the institute. Southerners regarded VMI as the West Point of the
South, and the institute drew its student body from prominent families of
that region. The faculty had contributed a number of generals to the Confederate army, and seven of its graduates, including Wharton and Echols,
had led troops at New Market. Jefferson Davis saw the institute as cultivat-
ing the South's future leaders, "the seed corn of the Confederacy."[31]
Strother regarded the school as a "dangerous establishment where treason
was systematically taught," pointing out to Hunter the institute's emphasis "that the Cadet in receiving this education from the sovereign state
owed allegiance and military service to the state alone." Further, its pro-
fessors and cadets had, "as an organized corps," taken up arms against the
Union, the cadets even using the school "as a fortress" while participating
in the defense of Lexington.[32]

    Hunter had expected Averell's advanced 1st Brigade under Colonel
Schoonmaker to burn the institute on their entry into town the previous
day. Instead, the colonel, finding that McCausland had merely stationed
guards there and at the adjacent Washington College, did not harm the
school. Angered, Hunter temporarily relieved Schoonmaker from command, informing him that in the future "he would put an officer in charge
of his advance who would know what to do under like circumstances."[33]
With the decision made, Strother watched plunderers stream out of the

    29. Eby, ed., Virginia Yankee, 253.
    30. Du Pont, Campaign of 1864, 68–69; Eby, "David Hunter: Villain of Valley," 88.
    31. Wise, "West Point of Confederacy," 461; Couper, One Hundred Years, II, 294.
    32. Eby, ed., Virginia Yankee, 254–55.
    33. McDonald, Diary with Reminiscences, 327–28; Couper, One Hundred Years, III,
30–31; Wise, Military History of V.M.I., 368; Eby, "Hunter: Villain of the Valley," 88.

building as his men began applying the torch. A number of officers joined in the looting. Lieutenant Meigs carried out a number of fine instruments, while Dr. Patton, Hunter's medical director, secured "a beautiful skeleton." Others robbed the library of its remaining "beautifully illustrated volumes." As Strother watched, the burning building "made a grand picture, a vast volume of black smoke rolled above the flames and covered half the horizon." The school's towers soon fell, and then the arsenal exploded, giving a Wagnerian flourish to the occasion. Hunter "seemed to enjoy this scene."[34] The general rubbed his hands together and chuckled, "Doesn't that burn beautifully?"[35]

Some officers, however, were uncomfortable with the burning of the institute. Halpine disliked destroying a "seat of learning," but he could "do nothing" to dissuade Hunter. Though "fully satisfied of the justice of the act," he watched "with feelings of inexpressible regret."[36] Captain Du Pont saw the burning as "entirely unnecessary, besides being contrary to the conventions of civilized warfare."[37] General Crook also objected, recording later in his autobiography that "I did all in my power to dissuade him, but all to no purpose."[38] Hunter "would have burned the Natural Bridge could he have compassed it," Crook was later reputed to have said.[39] Colonel Hayes concurred, confiding to his diary that "this does not suit many of us. Gen Crook, I know, disapproves. It is surely bad."[40]

Hunter spared the home of VMI's superintendent. Informed by Mrs. Smith that her daughter was upstairs with a two-day-old child, the general replied, "Very well we will make your house my headquarters."[41] The home of the former governor did not fare so well. On entering Lexington, West Virginia troops, deeply resenting "Honest John," shouted threats as they marched by his home. Apparently Hunter did not initially intend to

34. Eby, ed., *Virginia Yankee*, 256.

35. Beach, *First New York Cavalry*, 371.

36. O'Reilly, *Baked Meats*, 312; Hanchett, *Irish: Charles Halpine*, 118.

37. Du Pont, *Campaign of 1864*, 69.

38. Schmitt, ed., *George Crook*, 117.

39. G. Moxley Sorrel, *Recollections of a Confederate Staff Officer*, ed. Bell Irvin Wiley (Wilmington, N.C., 1987), 275.

40. Williams, ed., *Diary and Letters of Hayes*, II, 473, 479; Hastings Autobiography, June 12, 1864, XII, 10.

41. Eby, ed., *Virginia Yankee*, 254, 257; Eby, "David Hunter," 6.

burn it, for he detailed a guard to protect the house, and Dr. Patton demanded lodgings and spent the night there. An officer on Hunter's staff,
believing assurances of the house's security, attempted to allay Mrs. Letcher's fears. However, before leaving the next morning, Patton half-jokingly
told the governor's daughter that she had eaten her last meal there.[42]

Hunter's attitude changed radically when soldiers looting the institute
discovered a proclamation issued by Letcher when he was governor in
which he called upon citizens to resist, as Hunter noted, by "inciting the
population of the country to rise and wage a guerrilla warfare" against the
"vandal hordes of Yankee invaders." When Hunter read the proclamation
he became enraged. Believing that it violated his May 24 order prescribing
penalties "against persons practicing or abetting such unlawful and un-
civilized warfare," he ordered the house burned and allowed the governor's
family only ten minutes to vacate the premises.[43] Shocked, Mrs. Letcher
asked to see the order. Captain Berry told her that it was verbal. She then
asked for a delay in order to see Hunter. Berry refused. He gave her five
minutes to leave the house and denied her request to remove any clothing.
"Tearless and calm," Mrs. Letcher with five of her children sat on a stone
in the street and watched as her home became engulfed in flames. Next
door, the home of the governor's mother barely escaped a similar fate.
When hot embers ignited its roof, Berry's men refused to allow her black
servant to put the fire out, but one of Hunter's staff officers arrived and ordered the flames extinguished.[44]

For Corporal Lynch, "It was a grand and awful sight to see so many
buildings burning at the same time."[45] Dr. Neil, reflecting on the destruction that day, concluded that "Hunter is desperate" and predicted that the
general "will soon stand as high in the rebel estimation as 'Beast Butler.'"[46] The sight of so many buildings in flames accentuated the panic

42. Richmond *Sentinel*, July 20, 1864; O'Reilly, *Baked Meats*, 309–10; Boney, *John
Letcher*, 207; Hanchett, *Irish: Charles Halpine*, 118.

43. *OR*, Vol. XXXVII, Pt. 1, p. 97; Eby, ed., *Virginia Yankee*, 256.

44. Richmond *Sentinel*, June 24, 1864; Margaret Letcher Showell, "Ex-Governor Letch-
er's Home," *SHSP*, XVIII (1890), 394; McDonald, *Diary with Reminiscences*, 207–208; J. D.
Imboden, "Fire, Sword, and Halter," 178; Douglas, *I Rode with Stonewall*, 288; Boney, *John
Letcher*, 207–208.

45. Lynch, *Civil War Diary*, 75.

46. Neil to Friends, June 12, 1864, Neil Letters.

among the townspeople. To Cornelia McDonald "it seemed as if the Evil One was let loose to work his will that day."[47] Many residents feared that Hunter intended to destroy Lexington entirely.

Washington College, closed since 1861, barely escaped the fiery fate of its neighbor. Soldiers broke open the school's doors, smashed windows and sashes, and destroyed much of its scientific equipment. They stole half of the library's books, while the remaining ones suffered defacement. Ironically, much of the institute's equipment and books stored there met the same fate.[48] Private J. O. Humphreys of the 1st Independent Ohio Artillery noted with amusement that "it is doubtful if ever an army was so devoted to literature as was our Corps."[49] But others failed to find the humor. "It's all wrong," thought Sergeant John Booth of the 36th Ohio.[50] When the army left Lexington, soldiers threw away some books, burned others, or sent them along with assorted souvenirs to their families. The scientific equipment of both schools, not purloined, lay in shambles. Mistaking the statue of Washington on top of the main building for Jefferson Davis, soldiers initially pelted it with stones. Later the college's faculty summarized the havoc in a letter to the board of visitors as "a scene of desolation and destruction which could hardly be surpassed."[51]

Preparatory to burning the school, soldiers packed wood shavings in the building. David E. Moore, a school trustee, went to Strother to plead for the school's safety and asked for a guard to prevent further sacking. Moore explained that the college, endowed by Washington himself, honored the first president. The colonel quickly dispatched a guard, then attempted to explain why they were burning the institute but sparing the college. The undiplomatic trustee cavalierly replied, "I do not wish to discuss the matter, Sir." Angered, Strother, pointing to the institute, retorted, "You perceive that we do not intend to discuss it either."[52] Colonel Schoonmaker and two others urged Strother to persuade Hunter not to

---

47. Eby, "Hunter: Villain of Valley," 91; McDonald, *Diary with Reminiscences*, 207.

48. Board of Trustee Meeting of August 4, 1864, Washington College: Records of Board of Trustees, Feb. 21, 1845–Sept. 1873, W&L; Reader Diary, June 12, 1864; Lexington (Va.) *Gazette*, July 6, 1864; Moore, "General Hunter's Raid," 186.

49. Quoted in Couper, *One Hundred Years*, III, 35.

50. Booth Diary, June 12–13, 1864.

51. Washington College: Board of Trustees, Aug. 4, 1864, W&L.

52. Eby, ed., *Virginia Yankee*, 256.

commit such an act, arguing that "it was certain to lose to him the moral support of his army."[53]

As in Harrisonburg and Staunton, the local newspaper became a target. The editor of Lexington's *Gazette*, fearful of the paper's destruction, attempted to bury his printing press in the woods. When the press was discovered, Hunter ordered it broken into pieces and its fixtures at the paper's office burned. The editor also found himself under arrest. Claiming his loyalty, he produced an 1861 Unionist issue of his paper, but to no avail. After the Federals departed he managed to secure a smaller press and resumed publishing the *Gazette* on half sheets.[54]

At least one segment of the population greeted the Union army enthusiastically. Colonel Lincoln found blacks "wild with joy, . . . throng[ing] our camps, giving information and proffering assistance."[55] They provided the army with a variety of reliable intelligence as to where their masters had hidden goods, cattle, and horses, frequently leading foragers to the hiding places. Yet the Federals treated this source of information warily. Their caution stemmed from the slaves' obsequiousness, which, Strother believed, made them want "to tell us what they think will be agreeable to us rather than what they know." "Still," the colonel added, "there is no doubt of their good will to us." In one instance, their information led Blazer's scouts to capture and destroy seven boats hidden some nine miles down the canal. Two of the boats, loaded with six cannons and nine thousand rounds of artillery ammunition plus other powder and stores, created such a cannonade when ignited as to remind Strother "of a well-contested battle." Despite such betrayals, Strother noted, the slaves' masters "firmly believe that their Negroes are so much attached to them that they will not leave them on any terms."[56] Their delusion was destroyed when three hundred to five hundred blacks departed with Federal troops as they left Lexington.[57]

The behavior of blacks and their treatment by the army created consid-

53. McDonald, *Diary with Reminiscences*, 328.

54. Eby, ed., *Virginia Yankee*, 257–58; Lincoln, *Thirty-fourth Massachusetts*, 307; Lexington (Va.) *Gazette*, July 6, 1864.

55. Lincoln, *Thirty-fourth Massachusetts*, 307.

56. OR, Vol. XXXVII, Pt. 1, p. 97; Eby, ed., *Virginia Yankee*, 254, 258; Montgomery, *Blazer*, 17; Wellsburg (W. Va.) *Herald*, July 8, 1864; Wheeling *Daily Intelligencer*, July 2, 15, 1864.

57. Lexington (Va.) *Gazette*, July 15, 1864.

erable anger among Lexington's white residents. "The lamentation on the part of the white population," Colonel Lincoln found, "is both loud and deep."[58] Cornelia McDonald was upset by the presence of two black women riding beside an officer as his column moved up the street on the army's entry into town. Whites especially resented the "exultant" blacks who joined with soldiers in pillaging and who "were seen scudding away in all directions bearing away the spoils of the burning barracks." In the looting of Washington College, soldiers distributed much of the school's furniture to them. Their reputed entertainment at Crook's headquarters galled Mrs. McDonald. With the house well lit and a band playing, she assumed that "all held high carnival."[59] William Wilson, a provost guard, after searching Mrs. Pendleton's home, turned to her and remarked, "You treat those niggers good, they is free as you." She quickly retorted, "Do you suppose they have to wait for you to come here and tell them that?" After the Federal departure, she expressed the consensus of many southern whites: "My horror of the American Yankees is great, but of the *African Yankees!* it is impossible to express it."[60]

By June 12, Hunter badly needed to press on to Lynchburg before Lee had time to reinforce it. Two factors had contributed to his delay. The first was the late arrival of a supply train from Martinsburg. A convoy of some two hundred wagons had reached Staunton on June 10, shortly after the army's departure. The general then sent the 116th Ohio back to escort the train to Lexington. When it finally arrived on the eleventh, he welcomed the ammunition it delivered, though he did not appreciate "the thirty loads of forage which we did not want" or the "superfluous clothing." The general told Halpine to prepare a dispatch for Sigel, directing that in the future he not send "one pound of any kind of stores, except ammunition," and only "a scant supply of subsistence for the escort."[61] The supply train was "most welcomed" by Hunter's army for relieving some of their more immediate needs, but foraging remained the primary source of the Federals' provisions.[62]

58. Lincoln, *Thirty-fourth Massachusetts*, 307.

59. McDonald, *Diary with Reminiscences*, 205, 207; Washington College: Board of Trustees, Aug. 4, 1864.

60. Turner, ed., "Hunter's Sack of Lexington," 180; Lee, ed., *Memoirs of Pendleton*, 349.

61. OR, Vol. XXXVII, Pt. 1, pp. 97, 628, 630–31; Wildes, *One Hundred and Sixteenth Ohio*, 102–103; Thomson, "Lynchburg Campaign," 131.

62. Rawling, *First Regiment Virginia*, 177; Lynch, *Civil War Diary*, 74–75; James Dixon

While waiting at Lexington, the cavalry faced the task of rounding up horses to replace their own worn-out and broken-down ones. Rumor quickly spread through the countryside that the Federals "took the horses of 'friend & foe.'" William Ott protested the confiscation of his six horses, plus harnesses, two saddles, and bridles, but the officers told him that "orders were given to take all the horses."[63] A group of some twenty soldiers took the horse of William McKenny, telling him, "Old man I expect you think hard of me but we are in the inimy's country and when our horses break down we must take others whenever we can get them." McKenny was told that he would have been "paid for my beast" if he were a Union man.[64]

Hunter's second, more immediate cause for delay was his uncertainty regarding the whereabouts of Duffié's brigade. Duffié's expedition had lost contact with the army after detaching from the main column at Staunton on June 10, and by the following day Hunter was growing increasingly apprehensive.

Brigadier General Alfred Napoleon Alexander Duffié, commanding the 1st Cavalry Division, was born in Paris in 1835 and graduated from the military college of Saint-Cyr. While in the French army he served in Algiers and Senegal and won four medals in the Crimean War. In 1859 he moved to the United States and married into a prominent New York family. At the outbreak of the Civil War he resigned from the French army and accepted a commission as a captain in the 2nd New York Cavalry. Serving in the eastern theater, he was promoted to brigadier general in June 1863. That year, the War Department transferred him to the Department of West Virginia to serve under General Kelley.[65]

There, in command of the cavalry, Duffié whipped his men into shape and earned a reputation as "one of the best drill masters we had during the war."[66] At the outset of the 1864 spring campaign, the War Department temporarily attached him to Averell's cavalry division. Personal differences led to animosities between the two, and Duffié asked to be "relieved

file #15179, microfiche 1455, RG 233, SCCP; John Lamm file #18551, microfiche 3197, RG 233, SCCP.

63. William Ott file #17163, microfiche 966, and Andrew Shaver file #17162, microfiche 1004, RG 233, SCCP.

64. William McKenny file #1103, microfiche 992, RG 233, SCCP.

65. Warner, *Generals in Blue*, 131–32; Sifakis, *Who Was Who*, 193.

66. Quoted in Johnson, *United States Army Invades New River Valley*, 11.

from duty" on May 20 to return to Charleston to reorganize his command.[67] Instead, with Hunter's restructuring of the cavalry at Staunton,
he now commanded the 1st Cavalry Division. Yet discord continued with
Averell, "who nagged him and minimized every thing he did."[68]

After receiving "complete and comprehensive verbal instructions"
from Averell regarding his movement on Hunter's left flank, Duffié had
left Staunton before dawn on the morning of June 10. Initially he made a
feint toward Waynesboro by using two squadrons of the 15th New York
Cavalry under Lieutenant Colonel A. R. Root to probe Confederate positions there, while the main column moved on the road toward the Tye
River Gap. Encountering Southern pickets within six miles of Waynesboro, his troopers drove them in. The New Yorkers were surprised to find
Vaughn's army there in force. Root threw out a skirmish line and began
challenging the Confederates. Fortunately, the Southerners made no effort to charge him, and as Root began to think his situation was becoming
critical, suddenly the Southern command, fearing that Duffié's main force
might be preparing to attack its rear, withdrew toward Rockfish Gap. Root
took the opportunity to catch up with the main column on the eastern
side of the Blue Ridge.[69]

Meanwhile, Duffié, intending to avoid a general engagement, had
wisely continued to move southward on a road through the rough and
mountainous terrain south of Waynesboro leading toward the Tye River
Gap. After briefly skirmishing with "Mudwall" Jackson's rear guard on its
way to join Vaughn at Waynesboro, the Federals finally camped that night
close to the source of the Tye River. Unexpectedly, they also discovered
Mount Torry Furnace, the largest ironworks west of the Blue Ridge and
just refitted to produce pig iron for the Confederate government. Duffié
quickly ordered its destruction.[70]

The next morning he sent two parties across the mountains to strike at
the Orange and Alexandria Railroad while he attempted to contact

67. OR, Vol. XXXVII, Pt. 1, pp. 500–501.
68. Wilson, "Lynchburg Campaign," 139; Starr, *Union Cavalry in the Civil War*, II,
219–20.
69. OR, Vol. XXXVII, Pt. 1, pp. 139, 146; Norton, *"Red Neck Ties,"* 38–40; Stevenson,
"Boots and Saddles," 283; Hoge, *Journal*, June 8–10, 1864.
70. OR, Vol. XXXVII, Pt. 1, pp. 139–40, 155, 625; Farrar, *Twenty-Second Pennsylvania*,
239–40; Beach, *First New York Cavalry*, 369; George Hawke, "History of Once-Important
Mount Torry Furnace Traced," *Augusta Historical Bulletin*, XIV (1978), 35–36.

Hunter's headquarters, thought to be at Midway. Unable to communicate with Hunter, he left one regiment to secure the Gap and advanced into the Tye Valley. Again he attempted to contact Hunter, but again with no success.[71] Continuing to advance into the Piedmont, his troopers intercepted a dispatch from Staunton for Lynchburg which revealed that a wagon train carrying supplies and other materials was traveling only twelve miles ahead of him. Immediately he sent off a squadron of Marylanders to overtake it. They succeeded in capturing a number of prisoners and horses and returned with half a dozen wagons loaded with foodstuffs. They burned much of the remainder, which contained not only stores but Confederate bonds and currency, commissary records, and other documents. Some of the troopers filled their pockets with Confederate money, which they used during the remainder of the raid.[72]

The second party, consisting of ten men and a sergeant of the pioneers, struck toward Arrington Depot on the Orange and Alexandria Railroad. Their objective was to cut the rail line between Lynchburg and Charlottesville. Despite destroying large quantities of military stores and damaging the railroad, they failed to fully accomplish their mission.[73] They disrupted rail traffic between the two cities, but in less than two days the line was again in use. By retaining a regiment at the Gap and selecting only a small squad of troopers to strike at Arrington, Duffié lost the opportunity to burn the important wooden bridge, just south of the depot, which crossed the Tye River and was then quite vulnerable.[74]

Fortunately for the security of Lynchburg, the Botetourt Artillery, then on its way to Staunton via Charlottesville, had arrived in Lynchburg on June 10. The following day, unaware of the Federals in the Arrington area, the gunners boarded a mail train, used the attached flatcars to carry their guns, and headed for Charlottesville to join Breckinridge. On reaching Amherst Station, the conductor informed Captain Henry Clay Douthat that Federals were ahead wrecking the line. Concerned for the safety of the Tye bridge, the captain persuaded him to take them as far as they could go. At the next depot, some six miles from Arrington Depot, they

71. *OR*, Vol. XXXVII, Pt. 1, pp. 624–25.

72. *Ibid.*, 140; McIhenny Diary, June 11, 1864; Stevenson, *"Boots and Saddles,"* 283; Beach, *First New York Cavalry*, 369; C. Armour Newcomer, *Cole's Cavalry; or, Three Years in the Saddle* (Baltimore, 1895), 126.

73. *OR*, Vol. XXXVII, Pt. 1, p. 140.

74. Humphreys, *Lynchburg Campaign*, 54–55.

could see the smoke rising from the burning station. As Adam Plecker, a member of the battery, remembered, "Now we knew if the enemy got to that bridge the loss would be great."[75] Though they lacked horses to unload their artillery, someone remembered that one of the cars contained small arms and ammunition. Armed with forty rounds of ammunition, Douthat's men headed at double-quick for the bridge, some three miles ahead. Reaching it by nightfall, Douthat positioned two pickets on a hill some five hundred yards beyond the bridge with orders to fire on any advancing cavalry and then to retreat rapidly to the bridge. Hearing an approaching group of horsemen at midnight, the pickets called on them to halt for identification. Not receiving an acknowledgment, they opened fire. The Federals turned and retreated "at a rapid rate." With the threat gone and the battery's guns already on their way back to Lynchburg, the artillerists marched back toward the city.[76]

Meanwhile, Duffié, failing to establish contact with Hunter on the night of June 10 and not knowing the general's position, followed his original instructions. Hoping to inflict additional damage on the railroad, he pushed his cavalry toward Amherst Court House. There he expected to attack the rail line and then detach a smaller force to strike at a railroad bridge over the James River, some eight miles east of Lynchburg. However, within five miles of the town he received a dispatch from an increasingly worried Hunter, who ordered him to return to the army "by the most practical route and with as little delay as possible."[77]

Obeying, Duffié retired toward White's Gap to reenter the Valley. Moving northward on June 12, he encountered some three hundred Confederate troopers on the Piney River attempting to obstruct his route, but two squadrons of the 20th Pennsylvania Cavalry easily drove them back. From captured prisoners he now learned that Imboden was near and on his way to Lynchburg. Just before reaching the Gap, his troopers overtook another wagon train, this time with refugees. Easily capturing it, they destroyed everything not of use and stopped to spend the night at the Gap. The next morning they discovered and burned some two thousand cords of wood to have been used in charcoal production for a nearby iron fur-

75. A. H. Plecker, "Who Saved Lynchburg from Hunter's Raid?" *CV*, XXX (1922), 373.

76. Charles M. Blackford, "The Campaign and Battle of Lynchburg," *SHSP*, XXX (1902), 284–85; Plecker, "Who Saved Lynchburg," 372–73; Lynchburg *Virginian*, June 13, 1864; Markham, *Botetourt Artillery*, 59–60,

77. *OR*, Vol. XXXVII, Pt. 1, pp. 140, 624–25.

nace. Finally, on the afternoon of June 13, with bands playing patriotic music, Duffié's men marched through the streets of Lexington.[78]

Unfortunately, Duffié's absence and lack of contact with headquarters had seriously damaged his standing with Hunter. The general's staff discounted the value of Duffié's raid. Halpine sneered that the expedition had lost its way in the mountains, "as was usual with its leader," and Averell, still somewhat in Hunter's confidence, also enjoyed deprecating Duffié's ability. Both Strother and Crook developed jaded opinions on listening to Duffié's verbal report of his exploits, Strother finding it "exaggerated."[79] Crook was impatient over the lost time, and he also doubted Duffié's honesty. He suspected that Duffié "had been mostly engaged in pilfering."[80]

More important, however, was the fact that Duffié brought back intelligence on Federal and Confederate movements in eastern and central Virginia, as well as some eighty prisoners. Strother closely interrogated several of them and managed to extract considerable information. The prisoners recounted a severe rebuff to Grant and the turning back of Sheridan's attempt to establish contact with Hunter. They also claimed that Breckinridge had reinforced Vaughn at Rockfish Gap with four or five thousand men and that Ewell's corps was "advancing with a powerful column." But Strother was skeptical, "setting it down to ballying [bragging]."[81]

The following day, June 14, a courier from Averell brought what Strother considered more reliable information. Newspapers from Richmond and Lynchburg confirmed Sheridan's advance toward Charlottesville and the beginning of the siege of Richmond. "This is the information" Strother and Hunter had "wanted for some days." Other intelligence, regarded as reliable, reported that Lynchburg remained undefended and in a state of panic, its inhabitants fleeing at the prospect of Sheridan's approach. The news confirmed their decision to strike at Lynchburg. Even though the two realized that they lacked totally reliable intelligence, they decided to make a "bold and decisive advance on the

78. Ibid., 140–41; Farrar, Twenty-Second Pennsylvania, 242.

79. O'Reilly, Baked Meats, 319; Eby, ed., Virginia Yankee, 258.

80. Schmitt, ed., George Crook, 117.

81. Ibid., Vol. XXXVII, Pt. 1, p. 98; Eby, ed., Virginia Yankee, 258; Strother, "Operations in West Virginia," 486.

city."[82] Their plan called for the army to continue up the Valley to Buchanan, the western terminus of the James River and Kanawha Canal, and
then to cross the Blue Ridge at the Peaks of Otter and move directly on
the city. Unfortunately for Hunter, the circuitous route, combined with
the delay at Lexington, failed to heed Crook's earlier call for celerity of
movement.

Actually, Hunter had tentatively developed the strategy even before
Duffié's arrival in Lexington on June 13. Earlier the previous day, Strother
had prepared the order for Averell to move on Buchanan to secure the
bridge over the James River before McCausland could destroy it. Hunter
also sent a detachment of two hundred troopers to probe, gather intelligence, and cut Lynchburg's communications by riding around that city.
On the morning of June 13, Colonel Powell's brigade led Averell's main
column up the Valley toward Buchanan. Hunter charged Averell with
sending back information on "the roads and fords of the river," as well as
all newspapers dated after June 9 which might reveal Confederate movements.[83]

After reorganizing his train, Hunter's main column left Lexington on
June 14.[84] "The troops," Private Reader noted, "are in excellent condition
and anxious to finish the grand work they have commenced." The day
would be so hot and dusty that, as Major James M. Comly complained,
they "could scarcely see the wagons sometimes." As the army moved out
of Lexington, the town's residents "were in high spirits . . . there never was
so much rejoicing in town." For Mrs. Pendleton it was "inexpressible relief." Henry Boswell Jones, a local farmer, was glad to see them go. "They
have done us much injury," he recorded in his diary. "Oh! Lord have
mercy upon us and them."[85]

Shortly after leaving Lexington, Averell's cavalry encountered Mc-
Causland's men. Determined to delay them, the Southerners destroyed
bridges and culverts, cut trees to block the road, and with Enfield rifles
fired at them from behind rocks and trees as they advanced. Confederate
resistance occasionally forced Averell to bring up infantry support. Once

82. Eby, ed., *Virginia Yankee*, 258; Strother, "Operations in West Virginia," 486.

83. OR, Vol. XXXVII, Pt. 1, pp. 97, 627, 633; Eby, ed., *Virginia Yankee*, 257.

84. OR, Vol. XXXVII, Pt. 1, pp. 631–32.

85. Reader Diary, June 13, 1864; Extracts from Comly Diary, June 14, 1864; "Shelling
of Lexington," 378; Lee, ed., *Memoirs of Pendleton*, 348; Charles W. Turner, ed., *The Diary
of Henry Boswell Jones of Brownsburg (1842–1871)* (Verona, Va., 1979), 87.

the Federals formed in battle line, the Southerners suddenly retreated, only to repeat the tactic at another point.[86] Major Tynes felt that he had "never been so *chased, pursued, dogged*" before. Writing from the vicinity of Natural Bridge on June 13, he told his wife that Crook's men had sworn "that they would drive McCausland to Hell" and that from "the way he has put us through there [Buffalo Gap] to this place [it] seems like he would be able to keep his word."[87] With little relief, the Federals continued to drive them toward Buchanan. Within eight miles of the town the pace of Averell's troopers increased to "a gallop . . . endeavoring to save the bridge at that place."[88]

However, McCausland, attempting to buy time, had prepared an ambush. As the general and Captain Bouldin approached Buchanan, McCausland told him about a skirt of woods a little over a mile before the bridge where the road entered an open area. He instructed the captain to take a squadron of his Charlotte Cavalry and wait for the Federals there. Bouldin agreed on condition that McCausland leave a single fieldpiece "with the best horses he had to pull it." The general agreed, and Captain Feamaster proceeded to position his gun in an open area near the woods facing the sharp turn in the road. As McCausland's column passed, Bouldin's squadron waited, then charged up the road to engage the approaching Federals. After tangling with them in a "hand to hand engagement" and forcing them back, the Confederates quickly withdrew. While retreating, Bouldin's men suddenly turned off the road, and the Federals unknowingly continued their charge into range of the artillery piece. Suddenly, Feamaster's gun rapidly belched its deadly grape shot and "piled their men & horses up in the road & made them think they had run up on an infantry line in these woods." With several shots halting the Federals, the captain's men hurriedly made for the old covered wooden bridge, now loaded with bales of hay saturated with coal oil.[89]

Positioned across the river, McCausland's remaining artillery provided cover for the hotly pursued Southerners. As Bouldin's men hurried across

86. Artman Diary, June 13, 1864; John Harper Dawson, *Wildcat Cavalry: A Synoptic History of the Seventeenth Virginia Cavalry Regiment* (Dayton, 1982), 42.

87. Tynes to Wife, June 13, 1864, Hunter's Raid File.

88. Sutton, *Second Regiment: West Virginia*, 126–27.

89. Meade, *Memoirs: Bouldin*, 16–17; Harry Fulwiler, Jr., *Buchanan, Virginia: Gateway to the Southwest* (Radford, Va., 1980), 213; Feamaster Diary, June 13, 1864; Driver, *14th Virginia Cavalry*, 36–37.

the structure, the artillery opened fire on the Federals. Then McCausland
and Captain St. Clair ignited the bridge. Still on the north side of the
James, the general escaped by crossing on a small boat under the burning
bridge.[90] As flames from the burning bridge spread to houses and buildings
in the vicinity and threatened to engulf the entire town, a brief skirmish
ensued. The Federals brought up artillery and positioned their guns on a
hill behind the local cemetery, then fired into the town for some forty
minutes while units moved a mile up the river to ford it. Then the troopers
entered Buchanan "in full tilt."[91] Meanwhile, pioneers constructed a foot-
bridge over the smoldering wreckage.[92] A group of residents on the ve-
randa of a house across the river watched and cheered them on with their
work. After crossing, the soldiers responded in kind as they marched by
the house. Members of the 18th Connecticut noted that this was the first
time they had experienced such a greeting since leaving Winchester.[93]
With flowers pinned on their coats and bayonets sporting bouquets of
mountain ivy, Hunter's troops triumphantly marched down the main
street as the band struck up "Hail Columbia."[94]

Such Unionist sentiment was not shared by most of the residents in the
vicinity. Frightened by reports and rumors of Hunter's approach, large
numbers of citizens had fled with their wagons loaded with valuables. Others hid their possessions in presumably safe places, even in caves. Young
men, fearing arrest and rough treatment, hurriedly left to escape capture.
Only women, children, and old men remained. Residents had earlier protested to McCausland that the bridge's destruction was militarily unnecessary. Much to their surprise, Averell's men learned of the protest and
helped to extinguish the burning town.[95] Nevertheless, Buchanan sustained considerable damage. A few months later, Anne Taylor wrote to
her sister that the town appeared as "a desolate looking place," no more

90. McCausland to Charles Blackford, n.d., 6–7, Daniel Collection; Fulwiler, *Buchanan, Virginia*, 213; Blackford, "Campaign and Battle of Lynchburg," 298–99; E. E. Bouldin, "Charlotte Cavalry," *SHSP*, XXXVIII (1900), 73–74.

91. *OR*, Vol. XXXVII, Pt. 1, pp. 147; Fulwiler, *Buchanan, Virginia*, 214–15, 221–22.

92. Campbell Diary, June 14, 1864; Hewitt, *Twelfth West Virginia*, 144.

93. Walker, *Eighteenth Connecticut*, 250; Beach, *First New York Cavalry*, 373.

94. *OR*, Vol. XXXVII, Pt. 1, pp. 98, 147; R. H. Early, *Campbell Chronicles and Family
Sketches* (Lynchburg, 1927), 250–51; "The Capture of Buchanan," reprint clipping from
Buchanan News, April 30, 1936, in Beaumont W. Whitaker Collection, JML.

95. *OR*, Vol. XXXVII, Pt. 1, p. 98; Allen Diary, June 13, 1864; Eby, ed., *Virginia Yankee*,
259; Sutton, *Second Regiment: West Virginia*, 127; Fulwiler, *Buchanan, Virginia*, 222–23.

than "a mass of ruins. All the lower part of Buchanan looks like it is only fit for the habitation of owls and bats."[96]

As the Federals secured the town, McCausland's men fled eastward on the Peaks of Otter Road. Averell sent two brigades in pursuit, but local residents, aiding the retreating Southerners, had cleverly devised a variety of obstructions for them. In one case, they had succeeded in destroying the road as it rounded "a most precipitous point" on the side of a mountain. Averell's troopers eventually terminated the chase and returned to Buchanan. Any further intention to renew it ended with a dispatch from Hunter ordering the general to remain there until his arrival.[97]

The wait allowed Averell's troopers time to begin the destruction of property that afforded military use. Soon soldiers wrought havoc on canal locks and inflicted considerable damage on the embankments of the James River and Kanawha Canal. Squads swarmed over the countryside pursuing refugees, provisions, and other prizes.[98] One officer told an outraged Joseph Graybill, smarting over the loss of a horse, that if he went back to camp with him and recognized it, he could retrieve it. However, with the presence of so many soldiers Graybill feared leaving his home unprotected.[99] When a group of soldiers appeared at Susan Dawson's farm, they told her that "they were nearly starved and broken down and had been on a 'forced march' for some time." As she remembered, "they came into the house and begged for everything and anything to eat," then left with 450 pounds of bacon.[100] For fear of the marauders, Lucy Breckinridge at nearby Grove Hill plantation used her dress to hide family valuables. She admitted that she was "so burdened with letters, journal, silver, etc., that I don't think I could have walked far."[101] A more serious loss came in the form of labor. Corporal Albert Artman of the 14th Pennsylvania Cavalry observed "hundreds of negroes coming to our lines every day."[102]

Hunter's arrival quickly sharpened the tension between residents and the army. His attitude soon earned him a reputation for being "very rude

96. Letter to Sister Elly, July 6, 1864, quoted in Fulwiler, Buchanan, Virginia, 222–23.

97. OR, Vol. XXXVII, Pt. 1, pp. 147, 633.

98. Allen Diary, June 15, 1864; Hastings Autobiography, June 14, 1864, XII, 10.

99. Joseph Graybill file #19333, microfiche 3184, RG 233, SCCP.

100. Susan Dawson file #8092, microfiche 3169, RG 233, SCCP.

101. Mary D. Robertson, ed., Lucy Breckinridge of Grove Hill: The Journal of a Virginia Girl, 1862–1864 (Kent, Ohio, 1979), 184.

102. Artman Diary, June 14, 1864.

and gruff to the people." Residents became apprehensive about approaching him for protection against looting. His demeanor emphasized that sternness. To underscore his admonition against bushwhacking, he had one marauder shot. Denying requests for the man's burial, Hunter ordered the body left alongside the road as a warning.[103]

For the first time in its move up the Valley to Buchanan, the army penetrated the heartland of Virginia's iron region in Augusta, Rockbridge, and Botetourt Counties. In his instructions on March 29, Grant had especially targeted the ironworks at Fincastle for destruction, regarding its forges as "of much importance."[104] Intent on carrying out those directions, Averell sent a detachment there. A number of foundries would suffer devastation during the brief occupation, including the Cloverdale furnace (a major supplier of gun metal), the Grace furnace (important for its cannon iron), both of the Tredegar Iron Works of Richmond, and the J. W. Jones foundry.[105]

The Anderson family, which owned the Tredegar Iron Works, became a special target for Hunter's wrath. Near Buchanan stood Mount Joy, the home of Colonel John Thomas Anderson, a member of the Confederate Congress and elder brother of General Joseph Reid Anderson, who managed the ironworks in Richmond. Initially, Hunter sent an officer to burn the property, but he set fire to only the barn and outbuildings. When the general learned that the mansion had been spared, he sent a company of cavalry back to carry out the order fully. Anderson's niece requested permission to save her uncle's papers in his library, but the officer refused. He gave her an hour to get her own things out of the house before applying the torch.[106]

The flaws in Hunter's plan to "live off the country" grew more apparent as the army continued south. Maintaining a supply line secure from bushwhackers and guerrillas was becoming increasingly difficult as the army got closer to Lynchburg. Yet the army's needs were not being met through

103. Allen Diary, June 18, 1864.

104. OR, XXXIII, 758.

105. *Ibid.*, Vol. XXXVII, Pt. 1, p. 147; Charles B. Dew, *Ironmaker to the Confederacy* (New Haven, 1966), 164–65; Eby, ed., *Virginia Yankee*, 259; O'Reilly, *Baked Meats*, 322.

106. Fulwiler, *Buchanan, Virginia*, 215, 217, 219; J. D. Imboden, "Fire, Sword, and the Halter," 179; John T. Anderson, "General Hunter in the Valley: John T. Anderson to J. D. Imboden, April 2, 1877," *Tyler's Quarterly Historical and Genealogical Magazine* XII (1931), 197–98.

foraging, and serious shortages began to surface periodically despite the efforts of Blazer's scouts and others in rounding up hidden cattle and other commodities.[107] As the 34th Massachusetts had continued up the Valley, Colonel Lincoln observed that "the land, although generally in pretty good state of cultivation, is apparently less productive than in the lower part of the Valley." By the time his regiment reached Buchanan they lacked hardtack and their flour was in short supply, although as Lincoln admitted, "we still have beef and mutton in plenty."[108]

Early on the morning of June 15, Crook's division took the lead toward the Peaks of Otter. The journey over the Blue Ridge Mountains, with the Peaks of Otter dominating the terrain, prompted Colonel Lincoln to observe that "the scenery along our route is magnificent; mountain is piled high upon mountain."[109] Captain Hastings remarked on the "gorgeous display of rhododendrons . . . all being in full bloom! . . . I felt it was a sight never to be equaled."[110] A less romantic William Patterson, no doubt with the full agreement of many others, evaluated the terrain differently: "Rockiest road down the mountain ever saw."[111] Several of Hunter's staff took advantage of the occasion to scale the Peaks for the extraordinary view, but as Strother commented, they "got no sight of the enemy."[112]

The narrow, serpentine road over the mountainous terrain, with precipices of up to fifteen hundred feet, offered serious difficulties and hardships.[113] Surprisingly, except for some harassment by small groups of bushwhackers, they encountered little resistance. Colonel Lincoln wondered why, aware that "a small and resolute band would have found it easy work to have held at bay . . . our whole column."[114] Instead, Federal scouts merely killed a number of bushwhackers and as warnings left their bodies along the road. As the men of the 18th Connecticut passed them, Corporal Lynch observed that the corpses "looked frightful, with their long black beards and white faces in death."[115]

107. Montgomery, *Blazer*, 17.
108. Lincoln, *Thirty-fourth Massachusetts*, 308.
109. *Ibid.*; Powell Memoirs, 74–75.
110. Hastings Autobiography, June 15, 1864, XII, 11.
111. Patterson Diary, June 16, 1864.
112. Eby, ed., *Virginia Yankee*, 261.
113. O'Reilly, *Baked Meats*, 323.
114. Lincoln, *Thirty-fourth Massachusetts*, 308–309.
115. Lynch, *Civil War Diary*, 77; Walker, *Eighteenth Connecticut*, 251; Keyes, *History of the 123d Ohio*, 66.

Too far outnumbered to put up any serious opposition, McCausland's men littered the road with obstacles in an attempt to cause delays. Hunter's pioneer corps, however, quickly and efficiently cleared the debris to provide passage for the wagons. Colonel J. W. Watts, in charge of obstructing the road, later complained that "they cleared the road in less time than it took him to blockade it."[116] At various bends where the road narrowed, his men endeavored to cut it away and even blow it up with gunpowder. Where streams could be used, they diverted their flow onto the road. The treacherous route demanded great skill and patience by teamsters in handling their horses and mules. Despite their caution, a number of teams and wagons tumbled down the steep cliffs.[117] The men of the 23rd Ohio and the 5th West Virginia Cavalry, despite being used to rough, mountainous campaigning, greeted the more rolling countryside of Piedmont Virginia with pleasure. For the West Virginians it "was one of the most magnificent views . . . [they] ever saw. As far as the eye can reach a fine undulating country is seen." At the foot of the Blue Ridge the Ohio band enthusiastically played "Out of the Wilderness."[118]

That evening, Crook halted his advanced units at Fancy Farm at the foot of the mountains, some seven miles from Liberty, and waited for the remainder of the army to come up. With his advanced position and reports of Breckinridge's presence at Balcony Falls, he feared an attack on his unprotected rear and left flank. As a precaution he ordered Averell's cavalry, then following in the rear, to halt temporarily. Determined to ascertain the validity of the reports, Hunter sent squadrons of Duffié's men to reconnoiter the region and "find out where Breckinridge is." Meanwhile, Averell sent Colonel Powell's men ahead to scout the area toward Liberty, some twenty-four miles from Lynchburg. McCausland, surprised at Hunter's timidity, wondered why "Averell did not press on with his cavalry. He certainly outnumbered my cavalry three to one."[119] Hunter, however, exhibiting new vigor, informed Sullivan and Averell that "it becomes vitally important that we concentrate and move with all available speed upon Lynchburg tomorrow."[120]

116. Blackford, "Campaign and Battle of Lynchburg," 301; Powell Memoirs, 74; Wildes, *One Hundred and Sixteenth Ohio*, 105; OR, Vol. XXXVII, Pt. 1, p. 98.

117. O'Reilly, *Baked Meats*, 324–25.

118. Reader Diary, June 15, 1864; Journal of 23rd Ohio, June 15, 1864.

119. OR, Vol. XXXVII, Pt. 1, pp. 120, 147, 642; Eby, ed., *Virginia Yankee*, 261; "General Hunter's Expedition," 528; Wheeling *Daily Intelligencer*, July 15, 1864.

120. OR, Vol. XXXVII, Pt. 1, pp. 640–41.

Crook's infantry, picking up the march early the next morning, June 16, easily entered Liberty by 8 A.M. The town, as the county seat of Bedford County and an important railroad depot, was a commercial hub for the region. In the mid-1850s Strother had found it to be "a pleasant, and to all appearance, a thriving little town."[121] On the eve of the Civil War it had become an increasingly important economic center for an agriculturally varied farming community. Crops of tobacco and corn dominated the economy, with eleven tobacco manufacturers and a number of flour and meal mills. Local prosperity spawned a variety of businesses in the town involving wool, lumber, leather, and hides. Liberty boasted having two newspapers as well.[122] Captain Feamaster saw it as "a beautiful town, buildings fine, yards nicely fenced," with evergreens and shrubbery.[123]

The war had brought a number of changes to Liberty. Its residents, remote from the military campaigning in northern Virginia, initially came to know the horrors of war only vicariously with the arrival of casualties from distant battlefields. The Liberty General Hospital—consisting of two cabinet factories, four tobacco factories, the former Piedmont Institute, and two new buildings, with a total capacity of some eight hundred patients—became the largest hospital complex on the Virginia and Tennessee Railroad, while smaller hospitals dotted the countryside.[124] Their number surprised the Federals, and to some the area appeared as "almost nothing but a rebel hospital." Colonel Wildes of 116th Ohio observed that "every village we entered east of the Blue Ridge . . . was filled to repletion with wounded men."[125]

On entering Liberty, Hunter ordered his bands to play "Hail Columbia" and "Yankee Doodle" to announce the Federal presence.[126] To residents the men appeared as a descending swarm of locusts as hungry and weary soldiers began pillaging widely. The men of the 1st West Virginia Regiment had been "subsisting on a pint of flour, three-quarters of a

121. Cecil D. Eby, Jr., ed., *The Old South Illustrated by Porte Crayon: David Hunter Strother* (Chapel Hill, 1959), 97.

122. W. Harrison Daniel, *Bedford County, Virginia, 1840–1860: The History of an Upper Piedmont County in the Late Antebellum Era* (Bedford, Va., 1985), Chap. 7.

123. Feamaster Diary, June 16, 1864.

124. Horace H. Cunningham, *Doctors in Gray* (Baton Rouge, 1993), 53–54; Powell Memoirs, 76.

125. Wildes, *One Hundred and Sixteenth Ohio*, 106.

126. "General Hunter's Expedition," 527.

pound of beef, and half-ration of coffee and sugar per day."[127] Strother deduced that "our troops I fear are plundering and misbehaving terribly," since "women and children are besieging the General's door for protection."[128] Sam Taylor of Company A of the 18th Connecticut took one family's last three pints of meal, rationalizing that they were "the cause of the war and the ones who ought to suffer for it."[129] The presence of officers hardly curbed the looting. On one occasion it took a squad with bayonets to stop the indiscriminate looting of one large house.[130]

Hunter refused to tolerate bushwhacking or sniping at his troops as they moved toward Lynchburg. On learning that such fire came from one fine house, he immediately ordered it burned.[131] Corporal Lynch noticed that "many fine appearing ladies weep while their homes are burning. All they can do is to look on. One cannot help but feel sorry for them."[132] Many soldiers believed that local citizens treated them decently, although according to Colonel Wildes, "Some of the more ignorant people, who had never seen a 'Yank' before, were surprised to see us without horns and all the other traditional appendages of 'Old Nick.'"[133]

Depredations and retaliatory actions for hostile acts by the local populace were incidental to the Federals' principal targets of public property and the railroad. After setting fire to the depot at Liberty, Crook's men began systemically to burn ties and bend rails.[134] The superintendent of the line reported on August 10 that Federal troops totally destroyed the railroad between Liberty and the Big Otter bridge, some six miles. The company lost eight thousand railroad ties and sixty kegs of spikes.[135] One group of soldiers, discovering a hidden outbuilding containing hams, quickly looted it and hoisted their prizes on their bayonets as they marched away. Captain Young of the 11th West Virginia noted in his diary, "Camped on a rich farmer. Gave him his rights."[136]

127. Rawling, *First Regiment Virginia*, 182; Patterson Diary, June 16, 1864.

128. Eby, ed., *Virginia Yankee*, 262.

129. Walker, *Eighteenth Connecticut*, 253.

130. Keyes, *History of the 123d Ohio*, 66–67.

131. Hewitt, *Twelfth West Virginia*, 146.

132. Lynch, *Civil War Diary*, 78.

133. Wildes, *One Hundred and Sixteenth Ohio*, 106.

134. Wheeling *Daily Intelligencer*, July 15, 1864; "General Hunter's Expedition," 528.

135. Board of Director's Minutes of the Virginia and Tennessee Railroad, August 10, 1864.

136. Young Diary, June 16, 1864.

Inflicting such damage on the railroad consumed time that Hunter could hardly spare. Captain Hastings observed that Crook's men "went into camp disgusted and cross. How Genl. Crook fretted over the delay!" Hunter "kept us at destroying the railway, instead of dashing on and into Lynchburg," Crook later wrote.[137] The Federals would need to make a quick advance on the city to reach it before it could be reinforced.

The brief stay at Liberty did net Hunter some very valuable intelligence. Averell came into contact with a Confederate soldier's wife who had just arrived from Lynchburg and knew the situation there. In an interrogation she told Strother that "the place is not strongly fortified" and that "in this direction the only works were shallow rifle pits." Excited, Hunter ordered the army to advance. Yet as the army went into camp that night, Strother felt "a vague uneasiness. . . . Lee will certainly relieve Lynchburg if he can. . . . If he does succeed in detaching a force, our situation is most hazardous."[138]

Meanwhile, Averell's detachment, sent out at Lexington to reconnoiter the region around Lynchburg, rejoined Hunter at Liberty on June 15. They had managed to inflict some damage on the Orange and Alexandria Railroad at Amherst Court House before crossing the James River below the city. Once across the river, they turned back toward Liberty, then successfully attacked Concordia Station on the South Side Railroad line, with its important connections to Petersburg and Richmond. After destroying two trains and other property and damaging some fifty yards of track, the troopers hurried to rejoin the main army. Unfortunately for Hunter, though, they did not bring back "any clear or reliable information" on the military situation in the Lynchburg vicinity.[139]

In advance, Averell's main column reached the Little Otter River, where they found the bridge burned. Halting temporarily to repair it, they then rode on to the Big Otter River, forded that stream, and headed toward New London. As they approached the town near sunset, Southern units began challenging their advance. McCausland, just reinforced by Imboden, began engaging them in brief skirmishes. Imboden was frustrated with the tactic of skirmishing until the Federals deployed their infantry. That evening, as the Federals renewed their attack, McCausland

137. Hastings Autobiography, June 16, 1864, 1864, XII, 12; Hastings Memoirs, 8.
138. Eby, ed., *Virginia Yankee*, 262–63.
139. *OR*, Vol. XXXVII, Pt. 1, pp. 98, 156–57; Richmond *Daily Dispatch*, June 15–16, 18, 1864; Thomson, "Lynchburg Campaign," 132; Du Pont, *Campaign of 1864*, 71.

observed a massing in his front preparatory to a charge, while Imboden noticed that a double line of infantry was beginning to overlap his right flank. Fearing their increasingly untenable position, the Confederates withdrew toward Lynchburg. In a dispatch to Breckinridge, Imboden warned that he expected a renewal of the engagement early the following morning and alerted him to "expect the whole Yankee army up tomorrow." However, he expressed his hope that he could "probably delay its march so far as to prevent an attack on you till next day."[140]

Averell sent news of the clash to Hunter, who immediately roused his staff at 2 A.M. He sent Strother to Sullivan to apprise him of the situation and direct him to move his infantry toward New London to aid Averell. Another order went to Crook, camping near the Big Otter River on the Forest Road, to flank and trap the Confederates.[141] Crook moved rapidly along an obscure road north of the railroad. However, Strother experienced a series of frustrating delays while trying to reach Sullivan's headquarters. He spent two hours attempting to obtain an orderly to accompany him; then he found that most sentries did not even know the location of their regimental headquarters. "I never saw such damnable ignorance and carelessness," Strother fumed. "This want of system in this respect is common to our army and is the cause of great delay."[142]

After reaching Hunter, Sullivan's men moved out, only to halt at the Big Otter River, where the bridge had been destroyed. More precious time was wasted when a controversy erupted over how to repair it. Finally, Captain John F. Welch of the pioneer corps made the repairs, but the delay cost Sullivan some four hours. Once the artillery and trains crossed, the men moved more rapidly despite dense underbrush and heavily timbered terrain. Meanwhile, Crook's troops, reaching the main pike at 10 A.M., halted to await Sullivan's arrival. Sullivan caught up at 4 P.M., and Crook resumed the march. When they finally reached Averell at a crossroads, Crook's men found the cavalry already engaged beyond that point.[143]

In advancing toward Lynchburg, Averell's troopers had met with increasing Southern resistance as they approached the city. When they reached the vicinity of a Quaker meeting house, some four miles from

140. OR, Vol. XXXVII, Pt. 1, pp. 147, 157–60.

141. Ibid., 645.

142. Eby, ed., *Virginia Yankee*, 263; OR, Vol. XXXVII, Pt. 1, p. 99, 121.

143. Wildes, *One Hundred and Sixteenth Ohio*, 106–107; Lincoln, *Thirty-fourth Massachusetts*, 310; Keyes, *History of the 123d Ohio*, 67; Brown, "Life of McCausland," 267.

Lynchburg, Averell realized that Imboden with his three brigades in-tended to give battle there. The Southerners had chosen their position well. The peculiarities of the terrain put cavalry at a disadvantage. As one of Blazer's scouts noted, "The rebels had a clear field to take aim, while they were behind cover."[144] After briefly reconnoitering, Averell prepared to attack. Schoonmaker's 1st Brigade moved forward as a strong skirmish line. At intervals, columns of fours supported the brigade. The troopers re-mained mounted but prepared to charge mounted or dismounted across the open field. Oley's brigade, in column, shifted to the right, while Powell's men positioned themselves on the left. As Averell's men ad-vanced, Imboden's troops offered little resistance; instead they retired. As Schoonmaker's men approached the crest of the hill where the Quaker meeting house rested, Imboden's men unmasked their position and opened fire with artillery. Dismounting, Schoonmaker's and Oley's men pushed ahead. A section of artillery, supported by Powell, galloped for-ward and commenced firing. Suddenly the Federals discovered that the Southerners were there in strength. Initially the Confederates succeeded in repulsing them, but the timely arrival of Crook's division altered the situation. Responding to Averell's call for support, White's and Hayes's brigades "double-quicked all the way" to the skirmish line, while Crook sent Campbell's brigade to the left to clear the woods in that area.[145]

White's men easily stopped the Southern advance. Then they began to drive them back over a mile to their fieldworks. The 91st and 12th Ohio, despite intense artillery fire, charged across the open field toward the rail pens "filled with angry rebels" while the Confederate artillery "frowned death" on the advancing Ohioans.[146] Overrunning the fortifications, they drove the Confederates back into the inner defenses of Lynchburg. On the left, Campbell's men charged, overran the barricades, and "using their clubbed muskets and bayonets," engaged in hand-to-hand combat. The intense fire soon set the woods ablaze "with a mighty crackling and roar, only pierced by the terror stricken screams of the mangled men."[147] They drove Imboden's men for nearly a mile. Initially they captured four pieces of artillery, but they succeeded in actually carrying off only one. The 1st

144. Montgomery, Blazer, 19.

145. OR, Vol. XXXVII, Pt. 1, pp. 121, 147; Journal of 23rd Ohio, June 17, 1864; Sutton, Second Regiment: West Virginia, 129; Bennett, "Four Years with the Fifty-Fourth," 45.

146. Windsor, Ninety-First Ohio, 48–49.

147. O'Reilly, Baked Meats, 343–44,

Brigade, elated and confident, waited in line until 8 P.M. to undertake a night attack. But as night fell, the Federals grew more cautious.[148]

Hunter and his staff were satisfied with their first probe of the outlying defenses of Lynchburg, believing it was a "handsome little affair."[149] Despite the growing darkness, Crook and Averell prodded Hunter to continue the attack that evening. Powell wanted to make a dash and begged permission for his 3rd Brigade to make the attempt.[150] Private I. G. Bradwell of the 31st Georgia thought Hunter "could have marched into Lynchburg with little opposition" if he had "been more energetic."[151] However, caution ruled, and Strother noted that the generals ultimately "thought it more prudent to wait for the morning light." They retired for the night to the nearby residence of Major George C. Hutter, an old acquaintance of Hunter's. Boasting that they intended to take Lynchburg the following day, Hunter and his staff, in "high spirits," had "a good supper and slept profoundly."[152]

Those in the ranks, however, would not sleep so well, as exchanges of gunfire continued throughout the night. The proximity of the Confederate line prohibited the use of fires in making coffee or for cooking, so the men washed down their "hard tack and raw bacon" with "water from a canteen." The men of the 18th Connecticut remained in line, and after "getting a little feed, we dropped down on the ground to try and get a little sleep and rest."[153] The 23rd Ohio "could hear trains arriving, bands playing and thought by the sound troops were marching from the depot to the works in front of us." To Captain Hastings it meant one thing: "By the tardiness of our Commander our chance of success for the next day seem very slim."[154]

148. OR, Vol. XXXVII, Pt. 1, pp. 125–28; "General Hunter's Expedition," 528; Powell Memoirs, 76; Eby, ed., *Virginia Yankee*, 264.

149. Eby, ed., *Virginia Yankee*, 264.

150. Lang, *Loyal West Virginia*, 190; Wilson, "Lynchburg Campaign," 42.

151. I. G. Bradwell, "First of Valley Campaign by General Early," CV, XIX (1911), 230.

152. Eby, ed., *Virginia Yankee*, 264; E. Alvin Gerhardt, Jr., "The Battle of Lynchburg, June 17–18, 1864," *Lynchburg Historical Society and Museum Papers*, VIII, No. 3, p. 6.

153. Lynch, *Civil War Diary*, 79.

154. Hastings Autobiography, June 17, 1864, XII, 13.

9

The Threat, Lee, Lynchburg

Word of the defeat at Piedmont had come as "painful news" for Richmond. "The battle at New Hope [Piedmont] was a severe disaster to us," lamented Colonel Gorgas of the Ordnance Bureau.[1] In a letter to his wife, Colonel Walter Herron Taylor, Lee's adjutant, reflected the concern of many on the general's staff: "Plague take that force at Staunton say I. I fear it will be increased & prove troublesome to us."[2] The Federal victory not only opened up western Virginia to the ravages of Hunter's army but posed a menace to all of central Virginia as well. Such a threat uncovered and exposed Lee's extended left flank and jeopardized his ability to continue to defend Richmond. Conditions in the western region and the danger to Lynchburg, despite the risks, demanded a forceful response from Lee.

Jones's badly mauled army, now under the temporary command of Vaughn, rested at Waynesboro on June 6 and 7. Vaughn's telegrams of Jones's death and defeat jolted the Confederate capital. Secretary of War Seddon sent the dispatches of the battle to Jefferson Davis, informing the president that he intended to ask for the counsel of both Bragg and Lee "for the retrieval of this disaster, which endangers, if it has not lost, the

---

1. Vandiver, ed., *Diary of Gorgas*, 114–15.
2. R. Lockwood Tower, ed., *Lee's Adjutant: The Wartime Letters of Walter Herron Taylor, 1862–1865* (Columbia, S.C., 1995), 166.

Valley." Lee was already aware of the extent of the calamity. Immediately following the battle, Colonel E. G. Lee in Staunton had wired him the news. The colonel advised him that Vaughn had fallen back toward Fisherville and needed reinforcements. He further warned, "I fear Staunton will go."[3]

Others in Richmond agreed with the assessment of the defeat. Robert Garlick Hill Kean, head of the Bureau of War in the War Department, feared that "Staunton is at his [Hunter's] mercy."[4] The Richmond *Whig*, "not a little vexed at this temporary reverse," expressed alarm that Southern losses might be "some 13 or 1400, a serious disaster."[5] Richmond's *Examiner* asserted that "the withdrawal of Breckinridge was a sad mistake, and the Yankees took advantage of the weakness of the force under Jones to overpower them."[6] But "Who ordered Gen. Breckinridge to leave the Valley after the defeat of Sigel?" The *Whig* suspected the culprit was Bragg.[7] "If Breckinridge had been retained in the Valley after the defeat of Sigel, as he should have been," the Lynchburg *Virginian* asserted, "the prestige of his success and the spirit of his troops would have prevented our late disaster."[8]

Bragg, however, did not intend to take the blame for the decision to withdraw Breckinridge. "All was left to his [Lee's] better judgment," Bragg wrote to Seddon, "especially as he has directed all the movements of Breckinridge, Jones, and Imboden, down to this time." Bragg only "offered him my services to facilitate the movements he might desire."[9] John B. Jones, a War Department clerk, confided to his diary that Bragg "says Gen. R. E. Lee has command there as well as here, and was never interfered with."[10] Lee, though sensitive to the magnitude of the reverse, accepted the defeat with equanimity, counseling his wife, "It is useless for us to

3. OR, Vol. XXXVII, Pt. 1, pp. 150–51, and Vol. LI, Pt. 2. pp. 989–90.

4. Edward Younger, ed., *Inside the Confederate Government: The Diary of Robert Garlick Hill Kean* (New York, 1957), 154.

5. Richmond *Whig*, June 12, 1864.

6. Richmond *Examiner* in Baltimore *Sun*, June 11, 1864, and New York *Herald*, June 11, 1864.

7. Richmond *Whig*, June 13, 1864.

8. Lynchburg *Virginian*, June 13, 1864.

9. OR, Vol. XXXVII, Pt. 1, p. 150; Younger, ed., *Inside Confederate Government*, 154.

10. Jones, *Rebel War Clerk's Diary*, II, 227.

grieve for the calamity at Staunton or elsewhere. We will bear everything with patience that is inflicted on us."[11]

Lee read the recent dispatches from the Valley with a heightened concern for the vulnerability of his exposed western rail connections. The news that Vaughn, not Imboden, was in command immediately sharpened the question of leadership in western Virginia.[12] Lee, admitting that he did not know Vaughn, suggested to Davis on June 6 that "some good officer should be sent into the Valley at once to take command there." In considering various possibilities he discounted Echols as incapacitated, and Breckinridge, as he pointed out, was temporarily in Richmond recuperating from an injury sustained at Cold Harbor in repulsing a Federal attack.[13] Badly bruised when his horse "Old Sorrel" pinned down his leg, Breckinridge would require several weeks before he could ride again. Nevertheless, he remained Lee's obvious choice, especially after reporting that he would be "well in a day or two." Lee recommended sending Breckinridge "to take command & do what is practicable in rousing the inhabitants & defending the country."[14]

Lee intended to send Echols' and Wharton's brigades, constituting some 2,100 muskets, then in reserve, along with Breckinridge. With the order to prepare two days' rations, he had begun making preparations for their departure. He made inquiries in Richmond as to how quickly they could be sent to Staunton. In a cautionary note, Lee told Davis that "it is apparent that if Grant cannot be successfully resisted here, we cannot hold the Valley. If he is defeated, it can be recovered. But unless a sufficient force can be had in that country to restrain the movements of the enemy, he will do us great evil & in that event I think it would be better to restore to Genl Breckinridge the troops drawn from him." Later that day, Lee continued to press his recommendation: "G Breckenridge I think ought to go at all events if able—he can do a great deal personally in rallying the troops & People." Agreeing with Davis that "we require here every man we can get," Lee nevertheless hoped that Wharton's brigade would

11. Dowdey and Manarin, eds., *Papers of Lee*, 769.

12. *OR*, Vol. LI, Pt. 2, p. 990; Freeman, ed., *Lee's Dispatches*, 215.

13. Freeman, ed., *Lee's Dispatches*, 216–18; *OR*, Vol. LI, Pt. 2, pp. 983–84; Richmond *Whig*, June 6, 1864; Davis, *Breckinridge*, 437–38.

14. Freeman, ed., *Lee's Dispatches*, 217–19; Dowdey and Manarin, eds., *Papers of Lee*, 767; Johnston, "Sketches of Breckinridge," 317.

"assist in beating Hunter & then return to us."[15] Sending for Wharton, he told the general that he was dispatching him to drive Hunter from the Valley. To underscore the assignment's importance, Lee repeated three times, "General Wharton, *you must whip Hunter.*" "Then I will whip him," the general replied.[16]

The following day, June 7, Breckinridge's division set out for Rockfish Gap, charged with regaining the Shenandoah and protecting Charlottesville and the Piedmont. Echols' and Wharton's brigades boarded cars at Richmond. On reaching the South Anna bridge, they disembarked and then marched to the Beaver Dam Station.[17] At Bumpass Station they again boarded cars. Bypassing Charlottesville, they reached the Blue Ridge Tunnel on the evening of June 8. Passing through the tunnel, Wharton's troops camped for the night on the western slope of the Blue Ridge on the outskirts of Waynesboro. Hearing cannon fire in the distance, Wharton sent a company of skirmishers toward Fisherville, and the following day he ordered the regiment to form a battle line west of Waynesboro.[18]

With the army lacking confidence in Vaughn, Wharton strongly urged Breckinridge to join his men as soon as possible, sure that the general's presence would raise their morale. Breckinridge reached Lynchburg on the afternoon of June 8. Still unable to ride, he nevertheless began to consolidate and coordinate his military units. Finding a battery of four guns belonging to Vaughn's command there, he immediately sent them off to Charlottesville. He wired Vaughn that reinforcements were on the way and for him "to hold fast in the best positions, if the enemy advances." Warning him to expect an attempt by cavalry units to pass through the mountain gaps south of him in an effort to penetrate the Piedmont, Breckinridge suggested that Vaughn should "spare a good mounted force under enterprising leaders to operate on their flanks and rear." Yet, fearing the likely disorganization of Vaughn's cavalry, he telegraphed Bragg to suggest "that Morgan be ordered to the Valley." He then wired Colonel G. B. Crittenden, then in temporary command of his department at Gade Spring, to report to him. If, however, Morgan was operating near the

15. Freeman, *Lee's Dispatches*, 219; Dowdey and Manarin, eds., *Papers of Lee*, 767–68.

16. J. U. H. Wharton, "Gen. G. C. Wharton," CV, XIV (1906), 318.

17. Manarin, ed., "Diary of Woolwine," 437.

18. *Ibid.*; Johnston, "Sketches of Breckinridge," 318; Mastin Diary, June 7–9, 1864; Lowry, *26th Battalion Virginia Infantry*, 50–51.

mouth of the Sandy River, Breckinridge suggested that "he might sweep up Kanawha Valley and attack enemy now at Staunton in flank and rear."[19] As he moved to join Vaughn, Breckinridge was looking to the offensive in driving Hunter out of the Valley.[20]

An alarmed Vaughn wired Breckinridge on June 8 that the Federals were within a mile of Waynesboro and that he possessed only sixteen pieces of artillery and not "over 2500 muskets." Even though he had "a tolerable supply" of ammunition, he worried about his limited ordnance and urged the sending of ammunition and commissary supplies. In reporting the uniting of Crook and Averell with Hunter at Staunton, he assured Breckinridge that he would hold his position as long as possible. But he urged him to hurry: "I wish you would come immediately, if you have to come on an engine." In reply, Breckinridge exhorted Vaughn to "inspire the troops. We will soon drive the enemy out or destroy them."[21]

On arriving in Charlottesville on the morning of June 9, Breckinridge wired Lee the news of the uniting of Union forces at Staunton. He also noted that the Federals were "said to be strong with great deal of artillery." He asked for Colonel Floyd King's battalion, or "if you can't spare all . . . send him, with one good battery." He proposed to put King in charge of his artillery. Wiring Bragg, he asked him to order all local reserves to report to him.[22] When he reached the Blue Ridge Tunnel, Breckinridge organized the infantry of some five thousand men into two divisions under Wharton and Vaughn. He telegraphed Bragg that when McCausland arrived he would have nearly four thousand cavalry. Initially, he advised the War Department that Duffié and his men were advancing on Waynesboro, but he soon noted their shift southward toward either Lexington or the mountain gaps. He sent word to Imboden "to watch him."[23] Breckinridge realized that he could not defeat Hunter's larger army, yet he hoped that with his smaller force he could at least provide protection for Rockfish Gap and Charlottesville.

Also on June 9, Breckinridge received the first reports of Hunter's move toward Lexington. To bolster the morale of his troops, he spoke to them

19. OR, Vol. XXXVII, Pt. 1, pp. 753–56.

20. Humphreys Autobiography, III, 324; Humphreys, *Lynchburg Campaign*, 53; Johnston, "Sketches of Breckinridge," 318.

21. OR, Vol. XXXVII, Pt. 1, p. 755.

22. *Ibid.*, Vol. LI, Pt. 2, p. 1000.

23. *Ibid.*, 1002.

"with a powerful oration" which revived much of their confidence.[24]
Seeing no immediate threat from Hunter, he decided to take the initiative
in probing the Valley. He wanted to strike at Hunter's rear by way of
Greenville, expecting that Imboden's and McCausland's troopers would
be sufficient to block the gaps in the Blue Ridge and "whip his cavalry." If,
however, Imboden was unable to stop Hunter and divert a threat to
Lynchburg, Breckinridge hoped that "some troops can be thrown there to
detain him twenty-four hours."[25] After marching some twelve miles, he
learned of Lexington's fall. To Breckinridge the news meant one thing:
Hunter intended to strike at Lynchburg. Instead of pursuing him, he decided "to get ahead of him" and immediately directed his men back across
the Blue Ridge. Commandeering a supply train, he filled it with soldiers
for transport to Charlottesville. At Meechum's River Depot, Breckinridge
received confirmation of his suspicions from a telegraph operator, who
told him of Hunter's movement toward Buchanan. The news gave urgency
to his immediate "return to Charlottesville, so as to hasten to Lynchburg
to intercept Hunter."[26]

From Charlottesville he hurried ahead of his men to Lynchburg. His
troops required two days of marching and a day of rest before they would
reach a point within twenty miles of the city. Still suffering from his injury, Breckinridge reached Lynchburg on June 15. The physical strain of
the trip forced him to rest in bed on his arrival. Exhausted, he relied heavily on surrogates.

Securing accurate intelligence was his first priority. Prior to his arrival,
reports on Federal activity had begun to arrive at the headquarters of Brigadier General Francis T. Nicholls, commander of the post at Lynchburg.[27]
Imboden had alerted Nicholls on June 13 to cavalry penetration through
White's Gap toward Amherst Court House, adding: "You are in no danger
of attack, except by cavalry, for a day or two." On the fifteenth, Vaughn
relayed intelligence from the Lexington region that the Federals had

24. Humphreys, *Lynchburg Campaign*, 53–54.

25. *OR*, Vol. LI, Pt. 2, p. 1007.

26. Humphreys Autobiography, June 12, 1864, III, 325; Humphreys Diary, 13–14,
1864; Humphreys, *Lynchburg Campaign*, 56; Johnston, "Sketches of Breckinridge," 318;
Manarin, ed., "Diary of Woolwine," 437; "Hunter's Raid, 1864," 102; Davis, *Breckinridge*,
439–40.

27. *OR*, Vol. XXXVII, Pt. 1, p. 760; William Gilmore Beymer, *On Hazardous Service*
(New York, 1912), 7–10.

"spoke[n] boldly of their intentions, that they intended going to Bonsack's, thence up to Lynchburg."[28] The scout estimated their numbers at eighteen thousand. Though the reports confirmed Breckinridge's suspicions, he still had his doubts. To obtain more reliable information, as soon as he arrived in Lynchburg he sent out three of his own men to determine Federal strength and objectives.[29]

While waiting for confirmation, he readied his forces to defend the city. The operations of the cavalry, he concluded, were inefficient under Imboden, and new leadership was desperately needed. Though there was little doubt about Imboden's energy or commitment—his performance in the Valley up to the battle of New Market had been excellent[30]—there remained questions about his ability to control his men, whose lack of discipline had earned them a bad reputation.[31] Frustrated by the general's more recent performance, Breckinridge believed that his troopers had accomplished "less than nothing"[32] and complained to Bragg that "if a good general officer cannot be sent for them at once they will go to ruin."[33] Members of Imboden's own command agreed with this assessment. Trooper J. Kelly Bennette was perplexed by the general's constant maneuvering and feared that "our commander Gen. Imboden is not the man for cavalry."[34]

Richmond also agreed with Breckinridge's assessment and called for a new commander. Confidence in Imboden was not high in the department, with Robert Kean calling his performance "worse than ridiculous."[35] Earlier, on June 12, Jefferson Davis had alerted Major General Robert Ransom, Jr., that he was Davis' choice to command the cavalry in western Virginia. Relieving Ransom from command of the Department of Richmond on the fourteenth, the department ordered him "with the least practicable delay" to take command of the cavalry in western Virginia.[36] On the fifteenth, Breckinridge was growing anxious for Ransom's arrival

28. OR, Vol. XXXVII, Pt. 1, pp. 760–62.
29. *Ibid.*, 759–62; Davis, *Breckinridge*, 440.
30. Turner, "Battle of New Market," 73.
31. Lynchburg *Virginian*, June 27, 1864.
32. Breckinridge to Lee, June 15, 1864, Venable Papers.
33. OR, Vol. XL, Pt. 2, p. 658.
34. J. Kelly Bennette Diaries, June 11–12, 14, 1864, Bennette Papers, SHC.
35. Younger, ed., *Inside Confederate Government*, 156.
36. OR, Vol. LI, Pt. 2, p. 1006, and Vol. XXXVII, Pt. 1, pp. 760–61.

and wired Bragg to hurry him along. Even Early, who never fully appreciated the role of cavalry, waited nervously. Ransom would not arrive until the afternoon of June 18, during the battle for Lynchburg.[37]

Reports coming into the War Department had increasingly alarmed Bragg. Colonel Gorgas, reflecting on the news from all quarters, confided to his diary on June 9 that "affairs look to me more and more critical. I cannot see where farther [sic] reinforcements are to come from."[38] Robert Kean worried that the sequence of events in western Virginia and the cutting of the Orange and Alexandria Railroad at Arrington Depot "indicate a progress there which will soon grow into a vast disaster."[39] Bragg on the twelfth again called Davis' attention to conditions in western Virginia and the inadequacy of Confederate forces there to deal with Hunter. Incorrectly estimating Union forces at a minimum of 14,000, with an expected addition of 4,000 under Pope, compared with some 9,000 under Breckinridge, of which he judged only a little more than 5,000 were reliable, Bragg believed that "pressing necessity" demanded the sending of "at least 6,000 good troops to re-enforce Breckinridge." Seddon, despite concurring "if they can be possibly spared," thought the estimates of Union forces exaggerated and Confederate forces depreciated.[40]

Back on June 3, Grant, concerned about Hunter's expedition, had informed Meade that he wanted to maintain the pressure on Lee to prevent him from detaching any forces to meet that threat until Hunter "gets well on his way to Lynchburg."[41] On the sixth, deciding temporarily "to hold substantially the ground now occupied," Grant decided to apply pressure on Lee by using a cavalry raid to strike at the Virginia Central Railroad. Accordingly, Meade directed "Little Phil" to advance as far as Charlottesville, wrecking rail connections between Richmond and the Valley and Lynchburg, making "every rail on the road . . . so bent or twisted as to make it impossible to repair the road without supplying new rails."[42] Later that evening, Grant orally conferred with Sheridan to amplify his instruc-

37. *Ibid.*, XXXVII, Pt. 1, p. 762, and XL, Pt. 2, p. 658; Jubal Early, *A Memoir of the Last Year of War for Independence* (Lynchburg, 1867), 42.

38. Vandiver, ed., *Diary of Gorgas*, 114.

39. Younger, ed., *Inside Confederate Government*, 155.

40. OR, Vol. XXXVI, Pt. 3, p. 897, and Vol. XXXVII, Pt. 1, p. 758.

41. *Ibid.*, XXXVI, Pt. 3, p. 526; Simon, ed., *Papers of Grant*, XI, 13.

42. Simon, ed., *Papers of Grant*, XI, 19–21; OR, Vol. XXXVI, Pt. 1, p. 795, and Pt. 3, pp. 598–99; Philip H. Sheridan, *Personal Memoirs of P. H. Sheridan* (New York, 1888), I, 414.

tions and give him an order to deliver to Hunter, then at Staunton. He expected Hunter to move on Charlottesville, and he wanted Sheridan to join him there. Once united, they were to destroy the Virginia Central Railroad and the James River and Kanawha Canal. Once reaching a point between Charlottesville and Lynchburg, he suggested, they should send a cavalry unit ahead to destroy the canal. Underscoring that objective, Grant closed his order with the charge, "Lose no opportunity to destroy the canal." After accomplishing their mission, they were then to join the Army of the Potomac.[43]

Meade concurred, for without the destruction of the railroad "we can not compel the evacuation of Richmond, even if we succeed in seizing or breaking the Southside and Danville Roads."[44] General Rawlins, Grant's chief of staff, saw the juncture of Sheridan's cavalry and Hunter's army as creating a "force of great strength, able to take care of itself in an open country, and which will, I have no doubt, inflict great injury upon the enemy."[45] On the morning of June 7, Sheridan with two-thirds of the cavalry of the Army of the Potomac left its camp at New Castle. Shortly after their departure, Lee received intelligence of the expedition.[46]

Lee sent Major General Wade Hampton's and Major General Fitzhugh Lee's cavalries to intercept Sheridan. On the morning of June 11, Hampton's men clashed with Wesley Merritt's brigade. From prisoners Sheridan learned that Hunter was not moving toward Charlottesville but continuing up the Valley. They also informed him that Breckinridge's infantry was on its way toward Gordonsville and was either there or at Charlottesville. Ewell's corps, they said, was headed toward Lynchburg along the south side of the James River. Fearing that another full engagement would seriously diminish "the supply of ammunition to a very small compass," and with Hunter's changed position, Sheridan decided to abort the raid. Six days later, he finally reached White House to rejoin Grant.[47]

---

43. Simon, ed., *Papers of Grant*, XI, 24–25.

44. George G. Meade and George G. Meade Jr., *The Life and Letters of George Gordon Meade, Major General United States Army*, ed. George G. Meade III (New York, 1913), II, 236; Freeman, *R. E. Lee*, III, 361; Charles W. Turner, "The Virginia Central Railroad at War, 1861–1865," *JSH*, XII (1946), 531.

45. Wilson, *Life of Rawlins*, 230.

46. OR, Vol. XXXVI, Pt. 3, p. 888; Freeman, *Lee's Lieutenants*, III, 516.

47. OR, Vol. XXXVI, Pt. 1, pp. 26, 795–97, 806–809; Sheridan, *Memoirs*, 418–25; Freeman, *Lee's Lieutenants*, III, 516–22.

With the detachment of Hampton's and Fitzhugh Lee's men, coupled with Grant's superior army in his front, Lee possessed little manpower to spare for any attempt to retake the Valley. Yet dispatches coming into Richmond underscored the seriousness of conditions there and reported Hunter's move on Lexington. Lee realized that Breckinridge's small force was hardly sufficient to combat the threat, but the increasing menace from western Virginia demanded a decision.[48]

Lee mistakenly believed that the bloody fighting in the Wilderness and at Spotsylvania had "very much shaken" and dampened the resolve of the Army of the Potomac. Bragg, in a June 7 dispatch to General Johnston, then in Georgia, concurred that Grant had been "much crippled by his constant repulses."[49] Four days later, writing to Davis, Lee saw "no indications of his attacking me in his present position."[50] Finally, Lee decided on a bold move. On the evening of the twelfth, while the II Corps rested in reserve behind the III Corps near Gaines's Mill, he conferred with General Early. He instructed Early to hold his corps and two battalions of artillery under General A. L. Long in readiness to march to the Shenandoah Valley. He directed him to strike at Hunter's rear while Breckinridge engaged his front. The corps' detachment would reduce Lee's infantry by approximately 25 percent and leave him only some forty-one thousand troops to combat Grant.[51]

Following the interview, Early met with his division chiefs, and after nightfall written instructions followed. The directions transcended the mere destruction of Hunter's army and envisioned the possibility of a subsequent joint move by Early and Breckinridge down the Valley into western Maryland to threaten Washington. Such a move, Lee hoped, would force Grant to send troops to the capital's defense and thereby relieve pressure on him. The following day, June 13, Early's army was in motion. At 3 A.M. they marched through Mechanicsville and around Richmond, then headed northwest for Louisa Court House and westward to Charlottesville.[52]

48. Dowdey and Manarin, eds., *Papers of Lee*, 767; Walter H. Taylor, *Four Years with General Lee*, ed. James I. Robertson Jr. (Bloomington, 1962), 136; George Edgar Turner, *Victory Rode the Rails* (Indianapolis, 1953), 346.

49. *OR*, Vol. XXXVIII, Pt. 4, p. 762.

50. Dowdey and Manarin, eds., *Papers of Lee*, 774–75.

51. Freeman, *R. E. Lee*, III, 401; Blackford, "Campaign and Battle of Lynchburg," 286.

52. Early, *Last Year of the War*, 40; Jubal A. Early, *Jubal Early's Memoirs: Autobiographical Sketch and Narrative of the War Between the States* (Baltimore, 1989), 371; Dowdey and Ma-

Fortunately for Lee, Grant, in deciding "to make no further assaults" on the north side of the James River, had begun his move toward Petersburg on the evening of June 12. In contrast to Lee's belief that Grant's army was "very much shaken," the Union commander reassured Congressman E. B. Washburn that "All the fight, except defensive and behind breast works, is taken out of Lee's army." Grant had expected the enemy to remain in their entrenchments.[53] His judgment was a blunder. Surprisingly, considering his initial concern for Hunter's army,[54] he released pressure on Lee and undercut his own strategy embracing the capture of Lynchburg, the destruction of western rail lines and the canal, and the potential for a turning movement on the Army of Northern Virginia's left flank or rear from the west. Worse, his action potentially endangered Hunter's army, then departing from Lexington to strike into central Virginia, by leaving it without any supporting pressure to prevent a major Confederate countermove.

On the morning of June 13, Confederate skirmishers were surprised to find the Army of the Potomac gone and the trenches at Cold Harbor empty. Equally astonished, Grant's cavalry, now out of position, had failed to detect Early's departure. It would be nearly a month before Grant learned the whereabouts of the II Corps.[55] Lee, perplexed at losing contact with his adversary, was fortunate that the Federals were no longer there to probe his weakened lines either.[56] For Hunter, the withdrawal of pressure on Lee could be fateful. Strother, confiding in his diary three days later, reflected that "Lee will certainly relieve Lynchburg if he can. If he cannot, the Confederacy is gone up. If he does succeed in detaching a force, our situation is most hazardous."[57] Even Rawlins harbored reservations about their ability to capture the town, for he believed that it "would be a terrible blow to the rebels."[58]

---

narin, eds., *Papers of Lee*, 782–83; Jennings Cropper Wise, *The Long Arm of Lee* (Lincoln, Nebr., 1991), II, 827; Archie P. McDonald, ed., *Make Me a Map of the Valley* (Dallas, 1973), 211.

53. Simon, ed., *Papers of Grant*, XI, 32.

54. Ibid., 13.

55. Feis, "A Union Military Intelligence Failure," 211–12, 214–16.

56. Freeman, *R. E. Lee*, III, 402–403.

57. Eby, ed., *Virginia Yankee*, 263.

58. Wilson, *Life of Rawlins*, 230; Brian Holden Reid, "Another Look at Grant's Crossing of the James, 1864," *CWH*, XXXIX (1993), 302.

Lynchburg, situated on a series of hills overlooking the steep banks of the James River, was the largest city in central Virginia. Its 1860 population of 6,853, including 357 freedmen and 2,694 slaves, was surpassed only by Richmond, Petersburg, Norfolk, and Portsmouth in the east and Wheeling on the Ohio River.[59] A network of six turnpikes, the James River and Kanawha Canal, and three railroads aided Lynchburg's increasing commercial prosperity and made it an important transportation hub for the region. The canal allowed merchants to tap the western region all the way to Buchanan and Lexington, and also connected Lynchburg with Richmond, the canal's eastern terminus, some 110 miles down the James River. Some five hundred bateaux, employing an estimated fifteen hundred men, used it to transport goods. The Virginia and Tennessee Railroad linked the city with southwestern Virginia and eastern Tennessee, while the Orange and Alexandria Railroad provided a rail connection to Charlottesville, where the Virginia Central Railroad linked Lynchburg with Staunton as well as with Richmond. Running south of the James River, the South Side Railroad crossed the Richmond and Danville Railroad at Burkeville and ended at Petersburg.

The importance of the canal and the rail system transcended their purely economic value. As a transportation hub the city became an important supply depot for the Confederate capital and Lee's Army of Northern Virginia, sustaining military operations in Virginia and eastern Tennessee. Troops and supplies could readily be moved to threatened points by using interior lines. As a result, Lynchburg's capture would seriously threaten the defense of Richmond itself.[60] As Colonel Benjamin W. Crowninshield wrote, "Lynchburg on the north was to . . . rebel armies what Atlanta was to the south."[61] Grant knew that its capture was of great strategic importance, telling Meade in his June 6 dispatch that "it would be of great value to us to get possession of Lynchburg for a single day."[62]

59. J. Alexander Patten, "Scenes from Lynchburg," in Eugene L. Schwaab, ed., *Travels in the Old South* (Lexington, Ky., 1973), II, 537; *Population: 1860 Census*, 519.

60. Philip Lightfoot Scruggs, *The History of Lynchburg, Virginia, 1786–1946* (Lynchburg, n.d.), 104; Blackford, "Campaign and Battle of Lynchburg," 279–80; E. Alvin Gerhardt, Jr., "Battle of Lynchburg, June 17–18," *Lynchburg Historical Society and Museum Papers*, VIII, no. 3, 1.

61. Benjamin W. Crowninshield, "Cedar Creek," PMHSM, VI (1907), 156.

62. OR, Vol. XXXVII, Pt. 1, p. 598.

Nine days later, Rawlins wrote to his wife that "nothing could tell more terribly against Richmond unless it were the defeat of Lee's army."[63]

Lynchburg supported a number of profitable industries. The city was a major center for tobacco, boasting numerous warehouses and some eighteen factories that employed more than five hundred workers. Tapping Virginia's rich iron deposits, four foundries operated in the area. The Piedmont Works, the largest and owned by Francis B. Deane, not only produced wrought iron but also manufactured railroad cars, both passenger and freight, for the Virginia and Tennessee Railroad. The Deane foundry, making a transition to war production, became a major supplier of ordnance for the Southern army, and as early as May 1861 the foundry had begun shipping columbiad shells to Richmond. By the end of that summer, Deane had secured a government contract to supply the Confederate government with forty 12-pound howitzers. With the war the Lynchburg Machine Works had converted to manufacturing powder and balls, while a textile mill began making uniforms. With the Federal occupation of Alexandria, the Orange and Alexandria Railroad constructed new repair shops in Lynchburg to handle their rolling stock. In addition, eleven gristmills operated in the region. The city also was the home of a variety of other businesses which produced commodities such as clothing, furniture, and fertilizers, plus four banks and savings institutions, to make it a dynamic financial center. Centrally located in the rich Virginia Piedmont, the city's thriving agricultural and commercial trade and its relative security offered the Army of Northern Virginia and Richmond an important supply point for commissary and quartermaster stores.[64]

Lynchburg's location made it a popular haven for refugees, soldiers, and the sick and wounded. Some seventeen hospitals served the army there, making the city a major medical supply center. Medical demands converted warehouses, hotels, a college, and a number of other buildings into

63. Wilson, *Life of Rawlins*, 232.

64. Patten, "Scenes from Lynchburg," II, 535, 539, 539 n. 6; George S. Morris and Susan L. Foutz, *Lynchburg in the Civil War* (Lynchburg, 1984), 1–3, 12, 15; Scruggs, *Lynchburg Virginia*, 99, 102; Angus James Johnston II, *Virginia Railroads in the Civil War* (Chapel Hill, 1961), 13; George Graham Morris, "Confederate Lynchburg, 1861–1865" (M.A. thesis, Virginia Polytechnic Institute and State University, 1977), 4–6; Edley Craighill, "Lynchburg, Virginia, in the War Between the States," *Iron Worker*, XXIV (Spring, 1960), 3.

places of care for the wounded. The largest facility was Chimborazo Hospital. Except for Richmond, no other city in Virginia cared for more casualties than Lynchburg. As Peter W. Houck notes, the city filled the criteria of the "three R's—room, railroad, and remoteness."[65] By 1864 the number of convalescents had increased tenfold since 1861. Their presence, along with the local militia, provided a reservoir of manpower to build fortifications in defense of the city, but only against a minor assault.[66]

For Jubal Early, a native of the region, going to Lynchburg's defense was not just another military assignment. Born to a prominent family in Franklin County, southeast of Lynchburg, in 1816, Early had attended West Point, graduating eighteenth in the class of 1837. He freely admitted that "I was never a very good student,"[67] ranking near the top of his class only in the number of demerits received for disciplinary violations. After a short stint in the army he returned to Virginia, became a lawyer, and entered local politics as a Whig. Except for brief military service in the Mexican War, he served as a commonwealth attorney until 1852. As a delegate to the Virginia Convention of 1861 he adamantly opposed secession, and only after adoption of the ordinance did he reluctantly sign it. He tendered his services to Governor Letcher, who appointed him as a colonel in the Virginia militia. His first assignment was in Lynchburg in assembling and organizing volunteers into three regiments.[68]

Aged forty-seven in 1864, Early stood some five feet, ten inches tall, though he stooped and suffered from rheumatism which he had developed during the Mexican War. His men dubbed him "Old Jube," but this was not necessarily a term of endearment. With his dark flashing eyes and a satirical smile, and with gray hair and a full beard which "looked like a very

65. Peter W. Houck, *A Prototype of a Confederate Hospital Center in Lynchburg, Virginia* (Lynchburg, 1986), 6.

66. *Ibid.*, 8, and Chaps. 2 and 3; Gerhardt, "Battle of Lynchburg," 1; Peter W. Houck, ed., *Confederate Surgeon: The Personal Recollections of E. A. Craighill* (Lynchburg, 1989), 80; Mary Jane Bouldin, "Lynchburg, Virginia: A City in War, 1861–1865" (M.A. thesis, East Carolina University, 1976), 1.

67. Early, *Memoirs*, xxxix.

68. See Charles C. Osborne, *Jubal: The Life and Times of General Jubal A. Early, C.S.A.* (Chapel Hill, 1992), Chaps. 1–4; Millard K. Bushong, *Old Jube: A Biography of General Jubal A. Early* (Boyce, Va., 1961), Chaps. 1–4; J. C. Featherson, "Gen. Jubal Anderson Early," CV, XXVI (1918), 430.

malignant and very hairy spider,"[69] Early was a "crusty old bachelor" with a sharp wit and a rasping tongue more suitable at times for a prosecuting attorney. His profanity became legendary. Colonel Taylor, Lee's adjutant, confided to his wife, "I have feared our friend Early wd not accomplish much because he is such a *Godless* man. He is a man who utterly sets at defiance all moral laws & such a one Heaven will not favour."[70]

Early was also fond of tobacco, especially when agitated,[71] and liquor. Rumor held that "the inevitable canteen" at his side carried brandy or his favorite drink, Kentucky "Old Crow." On one occasion Lee, chiding him for his bad habits, called him "my bad old man." Early disliked "display," and his slovenly dress contrasted sharply with that of his fellow officers. One observer later described him as "always very shabbily dressed in a dingy old gray suit, with the stars on the collar so tarnished as to be barely visible. On his head he wore the queerest imaginable old gray felt hat, almost like one of the hats the clown wears in a circus, with a single feather, like the tail-feather, stuck in it."[72]

A strict disciplinarian, Early could be intolerant of mistakes and sharp with subordinates. George H. T. Greer, a teen-aged courier and clerk on Early's staff in 1862, noted that he was "very rigid in enforcing army regulations and military orders—which makes him disliked by shirking and sinecure officers."[73] Major Henry Kyd Douglas saw him as "arbitrary, cynical, with strong prejudices,"[74] yet the general took "great pleasure in rewarding merit." No one doubted his bravery. Captain John Goode, a volunteer aide-de-camp who observed him under fire on several occasions, had "never known a man who seemed to be so utterly destitute of fear and so entirely insensible to danger."[75] General John B. Gordon, despite difficulties stemming from Early's ignoring an important intelligence report

69. "Recollections of Jubal Early," *Century Magazine*, LXX (1905), 311; John Esten Cooke, *Wearing of the Gray* (New York, 1867), 110–11; Jeffrey D. Wert, "Jubal A. Early and Confederate Leadership," in Gallagher, ed., *Struggle for the Shenandoah*, 22–23; George H. T. Greer, "Riding with Early: An Aide's Diary," *CWT*, XVII (1978), 30.

70. Tower, ed., *Lee's Adjutant*, 177; Freeman, *Lee's Lieutenants*, I, 86, and II, xxviii.

71. Freeman, *Lee's Lieutenants*, I, xix.

72. "Recollections of Early," 311; Osborne, *Jubal*, 4.

73. Greer, "Riding with Early," 30.

74. Douglas, *I Rode with Stonewall*, 33.

75. John Goode, *Recollections of a Lifetime* (New York, 1906), 63.

from him at the Battle of the Wilderness, attested to the fact that he was "one of the coolest and most imperturbable of men under fire and in extremity." [76] Most regarded him as a man of great integrity and honor, although his negative peculiarities sometimes caused resentment and overshadowed his other qualities.

Early first distinguished himself at First Manassas, and by early 1863 he had received a promotion to major general for his performance from Cedar Mountain to Salem Church. Despite his controversial role during the Gettysburg campaign and flawed performance in the Wilderness, Lee assigned him to temporary command of A. P. Hill's III Corps on May 8. Then, as Grant began a new movement, and with General Richard Stoddert Ewell suffering from poor health, Early assumed command of the II Corps on June 4, with a promotion to lieutenant general as of May 31. [77]

Under cover of night and with written orders in hand, Early had his troops marching before dawn on June 13 toward Louisa Court House. On the following day Lee told Davis that "if the movement of Early meets with your approval, I am sure it is the best that can be made, though I know how difficult it is with my limited knowledge to perceive what is best." If Davis believed that it was unwise and should be recalled, he wrote, "please send a trusty messenger to overtake him to-night." But as he noted, Early's "troops would make us more secure here, but success in the Valley would relieve our difficulties that at present press heavily upon us." [78] As Lee undoubtedly expected, Davis made no recall.

For Lee, the secrecy of Early's departure was essential. He feared the possibility of any reports reaching Grant. On learning that a correspondent from the Richmond *Enquirer* knew about it, he immediately wrote to Davis to underscore the need for secrecy as an "important element of Gen. Early's expedition." He urged the president to send a notice to the newspapers "not to allude even by implication [to] any movement, by insinuation or otherwise." He assured Davis that the reporter agreed and asked his paper not to publish the information. [79] Fortunately for Lee, with the

76. John B. Gordon, *Reminiscences of the Civil War* (New York, 1903), 317; William C. Davis, " 'Jubilee': General Jubal A. Early," *CWT*, IX (1970), 44.

77. OR, Vol. XXXVI, Pt. 2, p. 974, and Pt. 3, p. 873.

78. Freeman, ed., *Lee's Dispatches*, 240–41; Dowdey and Manarin, eds., *Papers of Lee*, 777.

79. Freeman, ed., *Lee's Dispatches*, 240–41.

Federal move already under way, Grant's cavalry was not in a position to discover Early's departure.

Early's meeting with his generals and division chiefs the previous evening had alerted them that "an important movement was on hand," and they anticipated "some distant expedition." More telling evidence came with the order "to cook rations and be ready to move early the next morning."[80] Some believed that the movement was intended to shift them to the right of Lee's army, while others maintained that the design was to send them toward the south side of the James River. More perceptive observers like Captain John Paris believed that Charlottesville was the objective, "as we all believed without knowing anything."[81] The men of the 21st Virginia Infantry "gave up guessing, except that possibly Jackson's old corps was going back to the valley."[82] Even Brigadier General Bryan Grimes of Major General Robert Rodes's division remained unsure. He believed that they were either going "after Hunter or going into Maryland." If it was Maryland, he prayed "God that it will end more successfully than the other invasion."[83] Despite all speculations, as Captain Blackford remembered, only "Early knew where they were going."[84]

Rodes's division led Early's troops of some eight thousand muskets with twenty-four guns through Mechanicsville, then to Goodall's Tavern by way of the Brooke Turnpike and the Plank Road. At the tavern they turned along the Old Mountain Road to camp on the banks of the South Anna River near Auburn Mills. With the June weather heating up, the roads became quite dusty.[85] As Private George Peyton recorded, straggling

---

80. G. W. Nichols, *A Soldier's Story of His Regiment* (Kennesaw, Ga., 1961), 165; William H. Runge, ed., *Four Years in the Confederate Artillery: The Diary of Private Henry Robinson Berkeley* (Chapel Hill, 1961), 82.

81. Leonidas Polk to wife, June 16, 1864, Leonidas Lafayette Polk Papers, SHC; Diary, June 13, 16, 1864, II, John Paris Papers, SHC; Nichols, *A Soldier's Story of His Regiment*, 165.

82. John H. Worsham, *One of Jackson's Foot Cavalry* (New York, 1912), 227.

83. Pulaski Cowper, *Extracts of Letters of Major-General Bryan Grimes to His Wife*, ed. Gary W. Gallagher (Wilmington, N.C., 1986), 56.

84. Blackford, "Campaign and Battle of Lynchburg," 287.

85. McDonald, ed., *Make Me a Map*, 211; Frank E. Vandiver, *Jubal's Raid* (New York, 1960), 26; Robert Daniel Funkhouser Journal, June 13–14, 1864, in Laura Virginia Hale and Stanley S. Phillips, *History of the Forty-Ninth Virginia Infantry C.S.A.: "Extra Billy Smith's Boys"* (Lynchburg, 1981), 145–46; A. L. Long, "General Early's Valley Campaign," *SHSP*, XVIII (1890), 81.

became "awful," and by the third day of the heat men were throwing "away everything that we could spare."[86] To give relief from the dust, Early moved his wagon trains on a parallel road to the southwest of the one for the infantry. On the first day's march it soon became obvious to Captain Cary Whitaker that their "destination was the Valley to attend to Hunter Crook and their crowd."[87] Four miles west of Louisa Court House, Peyton's regiment heard "men yelling and could not imagine what was up. When we passed over a small hill we could plainly see the Blue Ridge and the sight was so welcome they greeted it with cheers."[88] As Rodes's division camped near Gordonsville on June 15, General Grimes now fully believed that "we will move up the Valley."[89]

At 4:30 A.M. on June 14, from the South Anna River, Early wired Lee, who had assumed that he had taken a more direct route to Charlottesville, to explain why he was taking such a roundabout one. He had heard reports of the clash between Fitzhugh Lee's and Hampton's cavalry with Sheridan's troopers. If true, the reports justified his going "by Louisa Court-House" to "try and smash up Sheridan and then turn off to Charlottesville." He also feared that "my trains will not be safe" if the Federals remained in the area.[90] Briefly halting at Trevillian Station, his men saw the remains of the intense engagement. Railroad crews were already busily working to repair the road, although by June 1864, even without the destruction by Sheridan, the Virginia Central Railroad in its dilapidated condition could hardly transport all the supplies needed by Lee's army.[91]

The march resumed at sunrise on June 16. "The troops [are] in fine spirits," Captain Paris noted, "thinking [they] are on the way to Pennsylvania." Reaching the vicinity of Charlottesville that day, they learned that their destination was Lynchburg.[92] "We are all doing well," Lieutenant Leonidas Lafayette Polk wrote to his wife, "considering we have marched

86. Diary of George Quintus Peyton, June 15, 1864, UV.

87. Cary Whitaker Diaries, June 13, 1864, SHC; Funkhouser Journal, June 14, 1864, in Hale and Phillips, *History of the Forty-Ninth Virginia*, 146.

88. Peyton Diary, June 14, 1864.

89. Cowper, *Letters of Grimes*, 56.

90. OR, Vol. LI, Pt. 2, p. 1012–13; Freeman, ed., *Lee's Dispatches*, 240.

91. J. G. Bradwell, Recollections of the Civil War: draft for Chap. 3, n.p. [typecopy, 1], J. G. Bradwell Papers, MHS; Turner, *Victory Rode the Rails*, 344.

92. Paris Diary, II, June 16, 1864; Abram Miller to Julia, June 22, 1864, pp. 23–24, Abram Schultz Miller Letters, James Miller Collection, W-FCHS.

80 miles in less than 4 days. Through the most intolerable dust & heat."[93] Some found "ramshackle trains on a piece of patched-up track" which they used to transport themselves for a short distance.[94] When they reached Charlottesville, the town exploded with enthusiasm. Joyous citizens treated them royally. Treated to ice cream and cherries, ice water, and tobacco "by the fairest of damsels," the men thoroughly enjoyed themselves.[95] Exuberant members of the 31st Georgia, passing some old men digging entrenchments on the edge of town, called to them to "quit throwing up them breastworks here in the town, and go with us and help drive them Yankees away."[96]

Ignorant of Hunter's movements in the Valley and the exact whereabouts of Breckinridge, Early had wired Lee from Louisa Court House that he would be near Charlottesville on the following evening and asked him to send him any information on the "state of things in the Valley."[97] When Early, riding ahead of his troops, reached the town, he found a telegram waiting for him. Breckinridge informed him that the Federals were then in Bedford County, about twenty miles west of Lynchburg. Early now knew Hunter's position and his intention. Galvanized into action, he telegraphed Lee that he intended to deviate from the original plan and, unless countermanded, go to the assistance of Lynchburg.[98] He reassured Breckinridge of that intention and emphasized that his "first object is to destroy Hunter, and the next it is not prudent to trust to telegraph."[99]

Realizing the need to reach Lynchburg promptly, he saw the Alexandria and Orange Railroad as the most expeditious means of transport. Fortunately, the rail line between Charlottesville and Lynchburg had escaped any severe damage from Duffié's men, and through strenuous efforts the line had been repaired sufficiently by the morning of June 17 to resume its use. However, only one train belonging to the Virginia Central, then

93. Polk to Wife, June 16, 1864, and Diary, June 15, 1864, Polk Papers; Robert Grier Stephens Jr., ed., *Intrepid Warrior: Clement Anselm Evans* (Dayton, Ohio, 1992), 419.

94. I. G. Bradwell, "Cold Harbor, Lynchburg, Valley Campaign, etc., 1864," VC, XXVIII (1920), 139.

95. Polk Diary, June 17, 1864; Joseph Lambeth Diary, June 17, 1864, VHS; Diary, William Beavans Books, II, June 15, 17, 1864, SHC; Allie S. Clark to Carrie Clark, June 22, 1864, Carrie H. Clark Papers, SHC.

96. Bradwell, "First of Valley Campaign," 230.

97. OR, Vol. XXXVII, Pt. 1, p. 761.

98. Early to Lee, June 16, 1864, no. 10, Venable Papers.

99. OR, Vol. XXXVII, Pt. 1, p. 763.

about to depart for Waynesboro, was available. Early immediately commandeered it. [100]

Suspicious from past experience about the reliability of railroad superintendent H. W. Vandergrift, Early wired Breckinridge to send all of the Alexandria and Orange's rolling stock to him at once. "Hold on and you will be amply supported," he reassured him. Less than an hour later he wired asking "what the railroad agents can and will do." In no mood for delay, Early underscored the necessity for prompt action and assured Breckinridge of his authority, warning that "if they fail take the most summary measures and impress everything that is necessary in the way of men or means to insure the object . . . I will hold all railroad agents and employees responsible with their lives for hearty cooperation with us." Two hours later, again stressing the need for urgency, he wired, "I shall come as soon as trains from Lynchburg arrive. I cannot start sooner for fear of interruption on the road if trains start in both ways." His troops had already "marched twenty miles today," he added. [101]

Not until sunrise the next morning, June 18, did Early secure trains and begin transporting his troops. General Rodes, a native of Lynchburg, requested for his division the honor of being the first to reach the city, but after a heated exchange, Early refused. With just six trains, only Major General Stephen D. Ramseur's division and a brigade of Gordon's were loaded on the cars. By necessity, the remaining infantry—Rodes's division and the remainder of Gordon's men—marched along the track until the returning trains picked them up. [102] The wagon trains and artillery left at daylight and moved by road. Not until late afternoon did all of Early's infantry manage to arrive in Lynchburg. Private Henry Robinson Berkeley's battery reached the city the following morning, with its horses and carriages following that evening. [103]

On reaching Lynchburg, Early found an excited and highly apprehensive citizenry. Rumors had run wild on the receipt of news of the Piedmont

100. *Ibid.*; Early, *Last Year of the War*, 42.

101. *OR*, Vol. XXXVII, Pt. 1, pp. 762–63.

102. Beavans Books, II, June 17, 1864, 71; Whitaker Diaries, June 18, 1864; Blackford, "Campaign and Battle of Lynchburg," 287–88; Vandiver, *Jubal's Raid*, 36.

103. Nichols, *Soldier's Story*, 166; Gordon, *Reminiscences*, 300; Robert C. Black III, *The Railroads of the Confederacy* (Chapel Hill, 1952), 246–47; Bradwell, "First of Valley Campaign," 230: Blackford, "Campaign and Battle of Lynchburg," 287; Runge, ed., *Four Years in Confederate Artillery*, 83.

disaster. Many residents fully expected an attack from Hunter at any moment, and some assumed that the situation "was almost hopeless and desperate."[104] Reports of the depredations committed by Hunter's army in the Valley had intensified that anxiety. On June 11, accounts of Duffié's cavalry near Arrington Depot—just twenty-eight miles from Lynchburg—had briefly thrown the city "into considerable excitement."[105] A short respite came with the news of Sheridan's reverse at Trevillian Station. But Breckinridge's wire to General Nicholls warning that Hunter was at Greenville and might turn eastward in a move on the city renewed fears.[106] Rumors soon circulated that Hunter was before Lexington.[107]

The confirmation of Lexington's fall and reports of Hunter's move eastward had caused further alarm. Rumors that the Federals were marching toward the city on two different routes spurred intense activity in preparing government stores, machinery, and other valuables for shipment to safety. The announcement on June 16 that Hunter occupied Liberty caused businesses to suspend their operations. Soon able-bodied men of all ages gathered to dig trenches on the city's outskirts. Yet local optimism held that something would prevent Lynchburg's capture, that Lee would somehow intervene.[108]

Confederate authorities, presuming the city would remain secure in central Virginia, had ignored its defenses and stationed no regular troops there. Upon his arrival in March, General Nicholls, though incapacitated from losing his left arm at the Battle of First Winchester and his left foot at Chancellorsville, had immediately marshaled what men he could, forming the more able convalescents and orderlies of the various hospitals into companies.[109] As a precautionary measure he also included those too old or young for army service as well as the guards and inmates of the local

104. Houck, *Confederate Surgeon*, 73; W. Asbury Christian, *Lynchburg and Its People* (Lynchburg, 1900), 217.

105. Lynchburg *Virginian*, June 13, 1864; Janet Cleland Diary, June 12, 1864, JML.

106. *OR*, Vol. LI, Pt. 2, p. 1005.

107. Lynchburg *Virginian*, June 13, 1864.

108. Susan Leigh Blackford, comp., *Letters from Lee's Army* (New York, 1962), 262; Cleland Diary, June 12, 18, July 4, 1864; Henry C. Sommerville Diary, n.p., Beaumont W. Whitaker Collection, JML; W. Craighill to Daniel, Nov. 30, 1905, Daniel Collection; Bradwell's Recollections, n.p. [typecopy, 1]; Houck, *Confederate Surgeon*, 75; Lynchburg *Virginian*, June 21, 1864; Christian, *Lynchburg and Its People*, 217.

109. Houck, *Confederate Hospital Center*, 123–24.

military prison.[110] He closely monitored incoming reports of Hunter's movements and maintained contact with the War Department. When on June 10 he learned of the pending fall of Lexington, he immediately wired Bragg the news. On the following day he reported the attack on the railroad near Arrington Depot. When he learned that Federal cavalry was approaching White's Gap and would cross there, Nicholls telegraphed Richmond for reinforcements.[111]

Suspicious of unverified reports, Nicholls complained to the War Department that "I have to depend upon scouts, not known to me."[112] In an attempt to rectify this deficiency, he sent Major Robert Chancellor Saunders out to reconnoiter the western area on the morning of June 14. As he moved toward the Big Island Road, Saunders ran into a Federal vidette. Escaping detection, he made his way back to the Forest Road Depot, where he woke the agent and told him that "the enemy would be on him early next day." Saunders, roused by their approach after a few hours' sleep, galloped off to report to Nicholls. He reported seeing "the dust clouds rising from the enemy's infantry, guns and wagons" extending "from the Peaks Gap to one or two miles this side of Liberty."[113] A wire from McCausland confirmed the report.[114] Then a courier from McCausland warned Nicholls that his exhausted troopers could delay Hunter's arrival at Lynchburg for no more than two days.[115]

Initially, Nicholls feared an attack from the north. Preparatory to such an assault, on June 11 he assembled the militia, some five to six hundred men, and led them to Amherst Heights on the north side of the river. Dr. E. A. Craighill, skeptical of the fighting ability of the militia, "never doubted but that a single company of seasoned soldiers could have routed our whole army."[116] Still worried, Nicholls sent a scout northward on the fourteenth to gather more accurate intelligence. Returning two days later,

110. Lynchburg *Virginian,* March 7, 1864; Houck, *Confederate Hospital Center,* 125–26.

111. OR, Vol. XXXVII, Pt. 1, pp. 756–58, 760, and Vol. LI, Pt. 2, pp. 1007–1008.

112. *Ibid.,* Vol. XXXVII, Pt. 1, p. 758.

113. R. G. Saunders to Blackford, Feb. 5, 1901, Daniel Collection; B. W. Whitaker, ed., "Hunter's Coming: A Rebel's Experiences in Hunter's Raid on Lynchburg," *Virginia Country's Civil War Quarterly,* VI (1986), 30–32; Blackford, "Campaign and Battle of Lynchburg," 301.

114. OR, Vol. XXXVII, Pt. 1, p. 155.

115. Dr. J. J. Terrell letter (typescript), n.d., Beaumont W. Whitaker Collection, JML.

116. Craighill to Daniel, Nov. 30, 1905, Daniel Collection; Lynchburg *Virginian,* June 13, 1864.

the scout reported that Federal activity there was merely a cavalry demon-stration "to mask Hunter's advance on the city." He now marched his men back through the city to meet the expected challenge coming from the west.[117]

To supplement his force, Nicholls ordered hospitals to "transfer every man from your ward that can walk to Camp Nicholls," outside the city. Both the militia and citizens hurriedly began constructing a line of breast-works from the city's cemetery to Daniel's Hill and onto the river, while Breckinridge's men guarded the city's approaches on the Salem Pike and Forest Road. To Private Bradwell "it looked . . . like a hopeless effort on their part, but they were game and meant business."[118] The Lynchburg *Virginian* expressed pleasure at "the alacrity with which they responded to the call" and noted that two colonels had led their commands while on crutches.[119] Despite assurances that they could combat Hunter success-fully, residents felt an uneasiness over their real effectiveness.[120]

The first signs of aid had come with the arrival of Breckinridge and some troops on Wednesday evening, June 15. For the people it was "a most reassuring sight."[121] Local women, "waving their handkerchiefs and cheer-ing them," greeted the "bronzed and dirty looking veterans, many of them barefooted." Sergeant John H. Worsham noted that "we were cheered to the echo, and the ladies waved their hands and gave up lunches and cool water as we marched through the city."[122] Women provided them with blankets, food, hot drinks, and clothing.[123] The news that Early was on his way to reinforce Breckinridge served as an additional tonic to morale. Sensing the altered mood, Sergeant Worsham noted, "Our presence brought an immediate change."[124] The following day more of Breckin-ridge's troops, along with the corps of cadets, arrived.[125]

117. Fred Menagh, "Civil War Surgeon's Account of the Battle of Lynchburg," clipping from Lynchburg *News*, June 14, 1959, McCausland Biographical File, VMI; Lynchburg *Virginian*, June 13, 21, 1864; Houck, *Confederate Surgeon*, 72; Markham, *Botetourt Artillery*, 60–61.

118. Bradwell's Recollections, n.p. [typecopy, 1], Bradwell Papers.

119. Lynchburg *Virginian*, June 22, 1864.

120. Craighill to Daniel, June 30, 1905, Daniel Collection.

121. Blackford, "Campaign and Battle of Lynchburg," 309.

122. Worsham, *One of Jackson's Foot Cavalry*, 229.

123. Craighill to Daniel, June 30, 1905, Daniel Collection.

124. Worsham, *One of Jackson's Foot Cavalry*, 229.

125. Couper, *One Hundred Years*, III, 45–46.

Suddenly, on June 17, the tension broke. From Lynchburg could be heard in the distance "the scream of a locomotive . . . and soon a dense cloud of pine smoke was seen." The anticipation of Early's arrival sent an "electric shock" of jubilation surging through the city. As the packed train crossed the bridge, "a joyous shout went up." [126] General Nicholls rode out to the lines and told the men that reinforcements were on the way. [127] Even more important, a fighting general had arrived. His appearance now galvanized residents, who felt that "Lynchburg was safe once more." [128]

Breckinridge, still suffering from his injury, lay exhausted from his hurried trip to Lynchburg and was not even able to inspect the city's defenses. His condition surprised Dr. E. A. Craighill, an attending physician. Craighill, who had met the general in 1859, found that Breckinridge "looked twenty years older, his hair and moustache having turned iron gray, almost white, and he looked sick and worn." Complicating his injuries, the general suffered from a number of maladies, including chronic diarrhea. Craighill considered him "entirely unfit for active service." [129] Fortunately, Lieutenant General Daniel H. Hill, an old friend of the general's, was then in Lynchburg. Breckinridge asked him to supervise the deployment of artillery and troops at his chosen defensive positions on the hills around the city. [130]

On June 17 Early wired Bragg, "Arrived here with sufficient troops to make all safe." [131] He then went to see Breckinridge. Finding him bedridden, Early gave him his confidential instructions from Lee. Breckinridge readily agreed to serve under him. He asked Early to place Hill, despite his informal position, temporarily in charge of his troops. Breckinridge also asked for the replacement of Vaughn, just rebuked for failing to comply with instructions. Early accepted both recommendations and wired the War Department to ask for Hill's appointment and for "another commander" to replace "the senior brigadier." [132] Richmond rejected the re-

126. Craighill to Daniel, June 30, 1905, Daniel Collection.

127. Blackford, "Jubal Early," 296.

128. Craighill to Daniel, June 30, 1905, Daniel Collection; Christian, *Lynchburg and Its People*, 219.

129. Craighill to Daniel, Nov. 30, 1905, Daniel Collection; Houck, *Confederate Surgeon*, 72–73.

130. Davis, *Breckinridge*, 441–42.

131. *OR*, Vol. LI, Pt. 2, p. 1020.

132. *Ibid.*

quest for Hill and instead ordered General Arnold Elzey to report immediately to Lynchburg from Richmond.[133]

With the necessary protocols completed and, more important, the establishment of his authority and lines of command, Early, accompanied by Hill, went out to reconnoiter and inspect the works hastily thrown up on College Hill to cover Salem Pike and Forest Road. Designed so that a small force could readily challenge a superior one, his defenses consisted of a broken line along the city limits, with its strongest point on College Hill. Breckinridge's men manned the hill, while invalids, reserves, and the cadets held other positions. Even though Early, considering the circumstances, understood the necessity of the fortifications, he harbored reservations, feeling that "they might just as well have been on Main St. as College Hill." Early possessed one fear: If Lynchburg was attacked, the positions allowed the city to be exposed to artillery fire.[134]

Mounting a defense of the city was not Early's primary strategy. Instead, he was "determined to meet the enemy with my troops in front" to offset the possibility of a bombardment.[135] Searching for Imboden, Early found him near the Quaker meetinghouse skirmishing with Averell's troops. Despite their precarious position and fear of a flanking movement, Imboden's troopers were managing to hold Averell's force in check at least until the arrival of Crook's troops. Then the situation changed. The possibility of a renewed attack put Imboden's men in jeopardy and threatened to shatter and panic the Southern line. Recognizing the danger, Early immediately sent a messenger back into Lynchburg to bring up Ramseur's division, whose forward companies had just reached College Hill. He ordered them to move rapidly to a redoubt approximately two miles southwest of the city where two unlimbered pieces of artillery under Berkeley were already in position. Ramseur's men quickly formed and double-quicked to Imboden's aid.[136] An impatient Early galloped down the road to find them, while Berkeley's artillery continued to fire at the onrushing Federals. Suddenly encountering the gunners, Old Jube imme-

---

133. *Ibid.*, Vol. XL, Pt. 2, p. 662, and Vol. XXXVII, Pt. 1, pp. 764–65; Early, *Last Year of the War*, 42–43; Early, *Memoirs*. 373–74; Davis, *Breckinridge*, 442; Vandiver, *Jubal's Raid*, 37, 40–41.

134. Early, *Last Year of the War*, 42–43; Martin F. Schmitt, ed., "An Interview with General Jubal A. Early in 1889," *JSH*, XI (1945), 554.

135. Early, *Memoirs*, 374; Humphreys Autobiography, III, 326–27.

136. Moore, "General Hunter's Raid," 189–90.

diately ordered them to deploy and advance, much to their relief.[137] Ramseur's two brigades, fanning out, rapidly established a new line across Salem Pike, approximately a mile and a half from the one on College Hill. Additional guns rapidly came to Berkeley's support. Two each of Lurty's and Douthat's batteries, plus some from King's battalion, now positioned themselves at the redoubt.[138]

Now possessing a more formidable force, the Southerners repulsed a Federal attempt to flank their position. The arrival of Ramseur's other brigade and part of Gordon's division allowed them to mount a counteroffensive. They attacked ferociously and successfully forced Crook's men back. The Federals were frustrated by their failure to break the Southern line, and the skirmish ended with an artillery duel as night fell. Ramseur's men positioned themselves on the right of the line, while those of Gordon's division held the left. For the troopers of the 8th Virginia Cavalry, the sight of Gordon's men was a relief. As Second Lieutenant James D. Sedinger recounted, after fighting the Federals all the way to Lynchburg, "We was very glad to see the infantry in line of battle ready to fight Hunter."[139]

A lesser Federal threat had developed early that afternoon on Forest Road, north of Imboden's position on the Salem Pike. Duffié, proceeding cautiously along the road, threatened his right flank, and Imboden sent McCausland's brigade and a section of artillery there to check any further advance.[140] The road, narrow and with dense woods on both sides, was not suitable terrain for effective use of cavalry. McCausland's men, along with a portion of infantry under Wharton, positioned themselves in a wooded area. By 1:30 P.M. Duffié's men reached them. In an ensuing two-hour skirmish the dismounted Federals succeeded in driving the Southerners back a "short distance," but with the eruption of fighting around the Quaker meetinghouse, the Confederates gradually fell back to within five miles of the city. At Clay's Mills, Duffié halted his division and rested in battle formation until the following morning.[141]

The fighting on both fronts ended for the night. While Hunter rested

137. Blackford, "Jubal Early," 296; J. C. Featherson, "Gen. Jubal Anderson Early," CV, XXVI (1918), 430.

138. Blackford, "Campaign and Battle of Lynchburg," 289–90.

139. Sedinger, Diary of a Border Ranger, 16; Vandiver, Jubal's Raid, 38–40.

140. OR, Vol. XXXVII, Pt. 1, pp. 159–60.

141. Ibid., 141.

pleasantly at the Hutter farm, however, Early had much to do. Back in Lynchburg he carefully questioned Dr. J. J. Terrell, a local physician, about the countryside and its roads. Confronting Hunter's army, estimated at eighteen thousand, without his artillery and wagons and with the remainder of his men still not fully up, he knew that his position remained extremely precarious. He could probably muster up only some seven thousand troops to hold the Federals at bay in the morning. His line from the Forest Road to the Salem Pike remained thin at best, but at least it appeared stronger. The main Federal thrust, he hoped, would come with Crook's and Averell's men, and McCausland's troopers and Wharton's unit would face only a diversionary tactic and could hold Duffié in check. Therefore, it became essential for Early's men to throw up earthworks to strengthen their lines and buy time to allow the remainder of the II Corps to arrive. An attack on Crook's and Averell's positions would have to wait, for Early "did not feel justified in attacking him until I could do so with fair prospect of success."[142] Instead, he in effect invited the Federals to attack him.[143]

Early shrewdly employed an additional stratagem to create an illusion of growing Confederate power and provide additional time for his remaining troops to come up. While Southerners strengthened their breastworks during the night, they cheered as new men joined and replaced others.[144] The 51st Virginia "marched & countermarched all night," and in the morning they found themselves "within 100 yds" of where they had started the previous evening.[145] A yard engine with several cars, making as much noise as possible, ran in and out of the city on the South Side Railroad to create the impression of an influx of reinforcements.[146] The "repeated cheers and the beating of drums" easily strengthened the mirage. For the residents of Lynchburg "it was a delightful sound to hear their cheers during the night as they passed out to the lines."[147]

142. Early, *Memoirs*, 375.

143. Early, *Last Year of the War*, 44; Vandiver, *Jubal's Raid*, 40–43; Sutton, *History of Second Regiment*, 129; J. J. Terrell, An Address: Delivered before the Garland Camp C.V. at their Thanksgiving Banquet, 1907, 4, JML.

144. *OR*, Vol. XXXVII, Pt. 1, p. 99.

145. Manarin, ed., "Diary of Woolwine," 438.

146. Blackford, "Campaign and Battle of Lynchburg," 289; The Campaign of Lynchburg, [1], n.d., Daniel Collection.

147. Blackford, comp., *Letters from Lee's Army*, 263.

The noise had an unsettling effect on Hunter's army. For the men of the 34th Massachusetts, the rumbling of trains and "the loud hurrahs of the men in the enemy's lines" indicated reinforcements.[148] Hunter also heard the increasing sounds of activity, and he too presumed that it meant "the arrival of large bodies of troops." Reports by that evening had convinced him that "all Confederate forces in the Valley and West Virginia were concentrated at Lynchburg under Breckinridge's command." He estimated the growing Southern army "at from 10,000 to 15,000 men, well supplied with artillery, and protected by strong works." The continuing noise of trains deepened his suspicions. Lacking any intelligence as to whether Lee had detached additional troops, he became cautious as he prepared to give battle the next day.[149]

Around 9 P.M., Federal cornet bands broke out with the "Star-Spangled Banner." Confederates quickly responded with "Dixie." Patriotic tunes soon alternated until the Federals struck up "Home, Sweet Home." Quickly, Southern bands joined in the tune. Both sides, singing in "a chorus of voices that fairly shook the grand old hills," ended the exchange in musical harmony. "As the last strain died away the troops . . . once more sunk to rest," Lieutenant James Abraham noted, "hundreds of them to dream of home, sweet home they were destined never more to see."[150] As Colonel O'Ferrall lay down to rest, he foresaw "that the next day would bring a battle, in the result of which we had no doubt. We had an abiding faith in the ability of 'Old Jube.'"[151]

148. Lincoln, *Thirty-fourth Massachusetts*, 310.
149. *OR*, Vol. XXXVII, Pt. 1, p. 99.
150. Benson, comp., *With the Army*, 51.
151. O'Ferrall, *Forty Years of Active Service*, 106–107.

10

Debacle

For Major General David Hunter, June 18 would involve more than just a trial of arms; it would be fundamentally a test of will. Unfortunately for the Federals, Crook's fears expressed at Staunton proved to be fully justified: delays and the circuitous route had allowed the advantage to shift to the Confederates. Ammunition and stores were now running low, and Hunter found himself operating in hostile territory far from his base with no supporting supply lines. Hunter's failure of judgment, the skirmishing with McCausland, and a lack of aggressiveness allowed Lee the opportunity to reinforce Lynchburg. Despite his overwhelming superiority, Hunter became cautious in the face of Southern reinforcements.

As the Federals formed a battle line, measuring some three miles from Forest Road to roughly three-quarters of a mile across the Salem Pike, the topography of the southwestern approach to Lynchburg posed numerous challenges. The countryside, as the Lynchburg *Virginian* characterized it, consisted of "a succession of hills, gorges, and streams. The former are broken and precipitous, and in many places thick woods intervene to break the view." As Major Comly noted, "The fighting at Lynchburg was all done in a wilderness of underbrush where we could not see the sun."[1] Despite a hostile terrain favorable to the defender, Hunter possessed only two choices, and both carried risks: attack or retreat.

1. Lynchburg *Virginian*, June 22, 1864; Extracts from Comly Diary, June 18, 1864.

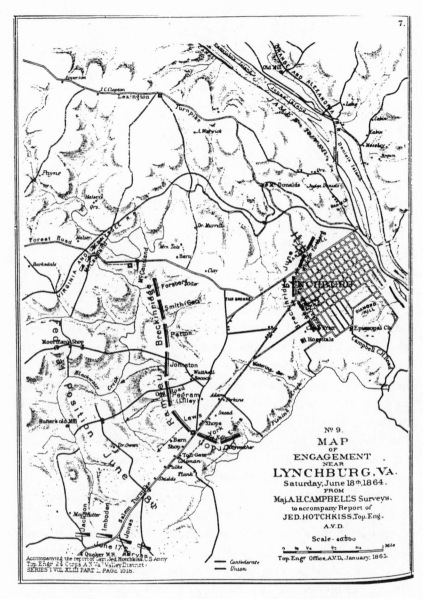

Nº 9.
MAP
OF
ENGAGEMENT
NEAR
LYNCHBURG, VA.
Saturday, June 18th, 1864.
FROM
Maj. A.H. CAMPBELL'S Surveys,
to accompany Report of
JED. HOTCHKISS, Top. Eng.,
A.V.D.

Scale = 40.000

0   ⅛   ¼   ½   ¾   Mile

Top. Engr Office, A.V.D., January, 1865.

Accompanying the report of Capt. Jed Hotchkiss, C.S Army
Top. Engr 2d Corps A N Va Valley District
SERIES 1 VOL XLIII PART 1, PAGE 1015.

—— Confederate
—— Union

Lynchburg Area, Detail from New York *Herald* Map Accompanying Story
on Hunter's Attack

Early's galvanizing energy had toughened and lifted Confederate fighting morale. With little sleep, the Southern commander rose at 2 A.M. to supervise the refinement of his lines. Yet a serious concern remained. Despite the continuous shuttling of trains back and forth from Charlottesville, not all of his troops were up. Hope that they would arrive by daybreak faded. It would not be until late in the day that the remainder finally reached him. Anxious, Early fully expected Hunter to attack after dawn.[2]

Yet Hunter hesitated. Instead of attacking, he cautiously probed Southern lines, believing that he faced a concentration of forces from West Virginia and the Valley under the command of Breckinridge. He estimated the Confederate force—actually only some 7,000 strong by the night of June 17—at between 10,000 and 15,000, "well supplied with artillery, and protected by strong works." Initially he had been unsure if the reinforcements were from Lee's army, but the rumble of trains, the cheers, and the bugles and drums made him increasingly suspicious.[3]

Taking the initiative around sunrise, Confederate batteries on the Salem Pike began shelling Federal positions. Noting their accuracy, Captain Du Pont turned to Hunter and remarked, "General, this is the work of some new artillery. The people with whom we have been dealing could never have made such good practice." Hunter merely dismissed it as "nonsense," for he still assumed that the only guns in Lynchburg were those he had faced at Piedmont.[4] Determined to discover the strength of the Southern force, he advanced skirmishers up the pike to the tollgate. Ramseur's men opened up with a brisk fire of musketry and an occasional burst of artillery.[5]

Behind his skirmishers, Hunter massed his two infantry divisions with Du Pont's artillery "in commanding positions" in the center. He placed Averell's cavalry in reserve. Observing the redoubts guarding the main road, he also took note of the rifle pits and abatis supporting them and Confederate activity in strengthening their fortifications. Believing that the redoubts were too strong for an assault, he decided to find a weak point along the Southern line where he "might push with my infantry, passing

2. McDonald, ed., *Make Me a Map*, 212; Vandiver, *Jubal's Raid*, 42–43.

3. *OR*, Vol. XXXVII, Pt. 1, p. 99; Vandiver, *Jubal's Raid*, 40.

4. Du Pont, *Campaign of 1864*, 76–77; Lincoln, *Thirty-fourth Massachusetts*, 312; Wildes, *One Hundred and Sixteenth Ohio*, 108; Ellis Diary, June 18, 1864; Thomson, "Lynchburg Campaign," 134.

5. *OR*, Vol. XXXVII, Pt. 1, p. 99.

between the main redoubts."[6] In addition he sent Colonel Powell with two squadrons of cavalry, reinforced with a brigade of infantry and two guns, toward the Campbell Court House Road on his extreme right to create a demonstration there.[7] Meanwhile, he ordered Duffié to "attack resolutely" on the Forest Road. Hunter decided to apply pressure at three points, thus gaining a measure of the Confederates' strength and compelling them to weaken one of the positions.[8]

Unfortunately for Hunter, he had lost contact with Duffié during the night. The previous afternoon, Duffié had encountered McCausland's and Wharton's men and driven the Southerners back a short distance. During the night he had attempted to communicate with Hunter but failed. The rough terrain between the Salem Pike and the Forest Road isolated him from the main column. Receiving no orders, Duffié on the following morning, and on his own initiative, began advancing slowly along the road. Around 9 A.M. his troopers ran into McCausland's skirmishers again. As Duffié's men approached the Virginia and Tennessee Railroad bridge over Ivy Creek, resistance stiffened. A section of Captain Douthat's battery with two 3-inch rifles, positioned near the old soapstone quarry, covered the bridge. In a bold attack, the Federals managed to drive the Southerners back from the bridge before they could completely destroy it. Meantime, a messenger from Averell reached Duffié around 10:30 A.M. with an order to attack "the enemy vigorously." He also promised aid.[9]

Dividing his division into three columns, one moving on the road while the other two operated on either side, Duffié renewed his advance. Soon his skirmishers again met stiff resistance from the Southerners, this time positioned behind makeshift rail barricades. Pressing forward, they drove the Confederates out and forced them across Backwater Creek, within a half mile of their fortifications and two miles from the city. There Duffié's men faced a more formidable barrier. The creek, a narrow stream with steep banks and a marshy surrounding terrain, provided an excellent moat for the Confederates. Strong fortifications guarded the bridge, and as Duffié's cavalry approached, two sections of Douthat's battery opened

6. *Ibid.*, 100.

7. Rawling, *First Regiment Virginia*, 183; Lang, *Loyal West Virginia*, 190.

8. Vandiver, *Jubal's Raid*, 44.

9. *OR*, Vol. XXXVII, Pt. 1, pp. 141–42, 159–60; Blackford, "Campaign and Battle of Lynchburg," 285; "The Battle of Lynchburg," Beaumont W. Whitaker Collection; Markham, *Botetourt Artillery*, 61.

with a withering fire. Countering, Duffié ordered up his section of artillery to pour a "destructive fire" to silence them "twice in succession."[10]

Meanwhile, Duffié ordered his skirmishers to advance. On the left the 1st New York (Lincoln) Cavalry briskly moved forward. As they crossed the stream, two squadrons of the 20th Pennsylvania Cavalry rushed toward the bridge. Unknown to the Federals and hidden in woods near the bridge, a detachment of infantry waited. Suddenly they opened fire and repulsed the attack. Despite a limited success in the crossing on the left, the demonstrations against McCausland's line convinced Duffié that he was facing "numbers much superior to my own." In addition, Duffié observed "a heavy cloud of dust" in the distance on his left and feared that a large cavalry force was moving to flank his position. He ordered Colonel Wynkoop to send two squadrons to intercept them. Suddenly, as the colonel's men moved to repulse the flanking movement, Duffié discovered that the Confederates also threatened to overlap his right. Quickly he dispatched a regiment from Colonel R. F. Taylor's 1st Brigade to block them.[11]

Duffié hurriedly sent a courier to Hunter to inform him of the action in his front. Despite having twice attacked the Southerners and driven them back into their fortifications, he maintained that "His force is much superior to mine. All my force is engaged."[12] Then, around 5 P.M., a sudden Confederate assault further alarmed him as the entire Southern line opened up on his men with artillery and other arms. The fire forced Duffié's skirmishers to retreat back across Backwater Creek. From his position, Duffié also observed the accelerating activity behind Southern lines. He could see reinforcements moving down a hill and heard "the whistle of the cars . . . and the playing of bands of music." He believed that the new troops of Rodes's division were heading toward his front.[13]

Duffié failed to recognized the weakness and deception in the Southern line. In marching and countermarching his men, Wharton artfully created the illusion of strength. As Frank Vandiver notes, "Their brilliant bluff saved Early's right," and as Captain Charles M. Blackford pointed out, Early was unable to spare any men from his front, so with "a vigorous assault on the line through Judge Daniel's Rivermont farm," Hunter "could have marched directly into Lynchburg and burned the railroad

10. OR, Vol. XXXVII, Pt. 1, p. 142.
11. *Ibid.*
12. *Ibid.*, 650.
13. *Ibid.*, 142, 649–50.

bridges without successful resistance."[14] Duffié's fears became momentarily compounded when he received a dispatch from Averell around 7
P.M. ordering him "to make a general advance." Moments later, however,
another message informed him that the army was about to retreat and that
instructions would soon follow. They never did.[15]

Duffié's performance, despite his initiative, was hardly stellar. Early's
right flank was saved by McCausland's and Wharton's force, which was
roughly half the size of Duffié's. Wharton's two infantry brigades were
small, and McCausland's cavalry remained badly worn by its constant
movements and skirmishing from the previous ten days. Worse, Duffié, in
conveying his fear of rapidly growing Confederate strength, had an unsettling impact on Hunter. His earlier dispatch, warning that "all my force is
engaged. The enemy is now attempting to turn my right," arrived at headquarters at a most unpropitious moment. Crook and Sullivan had just
learned from captured prisoners that Early's corps, in part or whole, was
there. Duffié's dispatch reinforced Hunter's perception that "the enemy
had concentrated a force of at least double the numerical strength of
mine." Yet the message undoubtedly became only a contributing factor,
for a number of Hunter's staff had little regard for Duffié's ability. Later,
around 5 P.M., when Duffié sent another message reporting that the
enemy was "falling back into Lynchburg," it excited Averell, but Strother
"did not give the slightest credit to the news."[16]

In contrast to the rapidly unfolding action on Forest Road, the skirmishing on Salem Pike initially lacked intensity. The exchange of musket
fire and occasional artillery salvos occupied the troops during the morning
hours. Hunter merely reconnoitered the Confederate line, hoping to find
a weak point. He moved Crook's division with Carlin's battery farther to
the right to probe the Confederate left, hoping to flank the Southerners
and "enter Lynchburg by the rear."[17] Meanwhile, Sullivan's and Thoburn's men, watching Early's lines, became increasingly worried about the
growing Confederate presence there. When Strother talked to the two officers, Sullivan expressed concern that he was "sustaining himself with difficulty." Both indicated that they would advance if ordered, but Sullivan

14. Vandiver, *Jubal's Raid*, 49; Blackford, "Campaign and Battle of Lynchburg," 291.

15. *OR*, Vol. XXXVII, Pt. 1, pp. 142–43.

16. Blackford, "Campaign and Battle of Lynchburg," 290–91; Vandiver, *Jubal's Raid*,
49; *OR*, Vol. XXXVII, Pt. 1, pp. 100, 650; Eby, ed., *Virginia Yankee*, 266.

17. Extracts from Comly Diary, June 18, 1864.

"felt assured that it would end in disaster." They asked Strother to present their views to headquarters. Displeased by the report, Hunter now hesitated to signal an advance.[18]

Federal caution surprised Early, who had expected an assault that morning. Colonel Powell did succeed in challenging Imboden's men at Campbell Court House, only to abort the movement. After the Federals threatened to fire on the town, the Confederates agreed to evacuate the village. But as Powell drove the Southerners back toward Lynchburg, a courier arrived from Averell ordering him to return to headquarters. In suspending the pursuit, Powell would not overtake Hunter's fleeing army until near daybreak the next morning at New London.[19]

Meanwhile, around 1 P.M. the initiative shifted to Early. He decided to probe Union positions on the Salem Pike. As the Federals tested his flanks, Southern batteries opened fire on Hunter's center. Soon Ramseur's and Gordon's men, catching the Federals by surprise, left their works and, with the Rebel yell echoing down their line, attacked. The fighting, complicated by the rough terrain and dense underbrush, became intense on the left. Shocked by the charge, Federal skirmishers broke and headed for the rear. Colonel George Wells's men twice attempted to stop the onslaught but failed. The 116th Ohio, shifting behind to support their battery, soon found skirmishers retreating in disorderly fashion through their lines. Hunter and his staff, stunned by the "violent and sudden" charge, rapidly mounted their horses and with swords drawn rushed to rally Sullivan's men "with shouts and vituperation." In a burst of hyperbole, Strother later attributed the reestablishment of order "to the lionlike bearing of the commander."[20] Major Comly, more cynically, described Hunter on that day as one who "always makes a splendid appearance four miles from the field."[21] Wells's brigade, lying on the crest of a hill, prepared a surprise of their own to stop the oncoming Southerners. Rising, they fired a volley and then charged. With the advantage of descending in their favor, they broke Ramseur's advance and sent his men scurrying back in wild confusion to their fortifications.[22]

18. OR, Vol. XXXVII, Pt. 1, pp. 99–100, 121; Eby, ed., *Virginia Yankee*, 265; Du Pont, *Campaign of 1864*, 78.

19. Lang, *Loyal West Virginia*, 190.

20. Eby, ed., *Virginia Yankee*, 265.

21. Extracts from Comly Diary, June 18, 1864.

22. Lincoln, *Thirty-fourth Massachusetts*, 312–13.

The 116th Ohio, reinforced by the 5th West Virginia from Crook's division, began "clambering over" the Southerners as they pushed them back to their well-entrenched second line. Desperately the Federals assaulted the position in hope that additional reinforcements would arrive, while Chapman's, Lowry's, and Lurty's batteries delivered "such a storm of grape and canister" that they forced them to fall back to the first line of works.[23] Repulsed, the men of the 1st Brigade continued to fight until the fire from a large Southern contingent on their left struck them. Then they retired to their original position. As William Patterson observed, "It was rash to go so far, but showed courage."[24]

Sounds of the fierce fighting by Wells's men on the left quickly alerted Thoburn. With an increasing Southern concentration there, the 18th Connecticut quietly shifted leftward to provide greater support for a platoon of Snow's Maryland battery, positioned between the two brigades. There they formed four lines to defend the guns. Twice the Confederates failed to take them.[25] Meanwhile, on the right, the 12th West Virginia, massed in five close lines in the woods, watched Southern preparations to "sally out." After an artillery barrage, Ramseur's men charged across the open ground toward them. The West Virginians opened fire with "a steady and continuous roaring of musketry" which broke the Southern line before it was halfway across the field. They quickly "skedaddled" back into their fortifications.[26]

Hunter, already apprehensive over a possible attack, had meanwhile sent an aide to Crook ordering him to return to reinforce Sullivan. Crook, finding it impractical to attempt a flanking movement, on his own initiative had started to return to the center before receiving Hunter's order. The courier told Crook that the Southerners were massing for an attack there. Immediately he marched his men off at double-quick to strengthen Sullivan.[27] Just as he began positioning them, Gordon's men sallied forth. From the southeastern side of Salem Pike they swarmed out of the woods "leaping over their defenses . . . with terrific yells" and charged across the

23. OR, Vol. XXXVII, Pt. 1, pp. 100, 123–24; Wildes, *One Hundred and Sixteenth Ohio*, 108–109; Humphreys, *Lynchburg Campaign*, 67.

24. Patterson Diary, June 18, 1864.

25. Walker, *Eighteenth Connecticut*, 255; Lynch, *Civil War Diary*, 79.

26. Hewitt, *Twelfth West Virginia*, 146–47.

27. OR, Vol. XXXVII, Pt. 1, pp. 100, 121; Baggs Journal, June 18, 1864; Journal of 23rd Ohio, June 18, 1864; Wellsburg (W. Va.) *Herald*, July 8, 1864.

field toward Du Pont's guns stretched across the pike. Well positioned at close intervals, the batteries faced open terrain. On their left the land gently sloped toward the Southern deployments. On the right, thick woods concealed much of Gordon's force. Fully confident that his gunners could repel any frontal assault, Du Pont saw his batteries open fire "with a roar" and "with terrible effect" as the Confederates charged, effectively halting them. The guns then delivered an enfilading fire that aided Sullivan in checking Ramseur's advance on the left. The return of Carlin's battery now gave additional strength to the center.[28] The thunder of the cannons and roar of muskets impressed Chaplain Windsor of the 91st Ohio, who "was never so moved before, never realized the majesty and grandeur of battle till then."[29]

As the Southerners wavered and finally halted, the Federals "with a cheer" drove them back into and beyond their fortifications.[30] On the right the 54th Pennsylvania, moving down the slope over rough terrain, suddenly discovered a line concealed by weeds in a ditch. Charging the Southerners, they drove them back in confusion. A second charge, despite an intense fire which accounted for the highest casualties for the regiment, sent the Confederates reeling backwards.[31] After half an hour of fierce skirmishing, Hunter and his staff breathed more easily. Strother noted that the "cheers of our men indicated the enemy was checked." A "continued cheering from the front told us the enemy had been routed and driven back into his works." Despite overlapping the Confederate line, however, Crook's men could not hold their position.[32]

Though Early's assault failed, it succeeded in its purpose. Captured soldiers interrogated that afternoon at Hunter's headquarters confirmed not only the arrival of reinforcements but the presence of Old Jube and the veteran II Corps. The continuing noise of arrivals and the cheers in the late afternoon lent credibility to their claims.[33] In the minds of Hunter's staff, Early's army grew to some thirty thousand ready to defend Lynch-

28. Du Pont, *Campaign of 1864*, 77–79; H. A. Du Pont to H. F. Brewerton, Aug. 10, 1895, Lyman Walter Vere Kennon Papers, DU; Thomson, "Lynchburg Campaign," 134; Lincoln, *Thirty-fourth Massachusetts*, 312.

29. Windsor, "Letter from 91st Ohio," Athens (Ohio) *Messenger*, July 21, 1864.

30. Wellsburg (W. Va.) *Herald*, July 8, 1864.

31. OR, Vol. XXXVII, Pt. 1, pp. 132–33.

32. Eby, ed., *Virginia Yankee*, 265–66; Extracts from Comly Diary, June 18, 1864.

33. OR, Vol. XXXVII, Pt. 1, p. 100.

burg.[34] They knew that their "position was critical and . . . that we must get out if possible." As they discussed their options, Crook remained "cool and matter of fact." Averell "was excited and angry," telling Strother that "I would give my head this night if we could have taken Lynchburg." But the only question that remained was the matter of retreat.[35] Hunter, against his will and despite his persistent belief that Lee would not reinforce the city, ordered his trains to begin a withdrawal toward Buford Gap.[36]

With the Army of West Virginia some 250 miles from its base, the stock of ammunition and other items rapidly depleting, and the presumably superior Confederate force, fears grew for the Federals' safety.[37] The previous evening, Sullivan had warned Hunter that his troops were down to their last rations. The general laconically replied, "Tell them there is plenty of food in Lynchburg." The problem was not a lack of beef, for the army had collected sufficient quantities along the way, but the shortage of items such as corn, sugar, and coffee. McCausland's inhibiting tactics had seriously curbed foraging parties from gathering enough corn and grain for making bread.[38]

The depletion of ammunition presented a more immediate and serious problem. Hunter feared that his troops "had scarcely enough of ammunition left to sustain another well contested battle."[39] The shortage would not only endanger any effort to fend off a major assault by Early but posed risks for a retreat as well. As Captain Du Pont summed up, "It was quite evident that in the event of our supplies of food or ammunition becoming exhausted, the larger part of our command could not hope to escape capture and that we would lose our trains and artillery."[40]

That afternoon, Hunter feared that Early might realize their plight and launch another assault. Five hours remained before nightfall, but no attack came. That evening the general and his staff ate their mess at Hutter's farmhouse in melancholy silence. At its conclusion they conferred in

34. Strother, "Operations in West Virginia," 487.

35. Eby, ed., *Virginia Yankee*, 266; Strother, "Operations in West Virginia," 486–87; O'Reilly, *Baked Meats*, 348; Schmitt, ed., *George Crook*, 118.

36. Du Pont, *Campaign of 1864*, 79–80.

37. Strother, "Operations in West Virginia," 487.

38. O'Reilly, *Baked Meats*, 347–48.

39. OR, Vol. XXXVII, Pt. 1, p. 100.

40. Du Pont, *Campaign of 1864*, 83.

locked rooms and then, intentionally misleading Hutter, excused themselves by suggesting that they were "going to the front." The decision remained a secret until after dusk and after the trains were well on their way.[41] Meanwhile, Hunter kept up "a bold front." To the relief of the Federals, even though sporadic skirmishing continued, Early attempted no serious assaults. Strother believed that "the rough handling they got in their attack no doubt made them cautious."[42] The Confederates, however, were merely biding their time.

Leaving the area was not simple for Duffié and his men. Preparatory to a withdrawal, word quietly passed down the line to pull back after dark. Meanwhile, selected skirmishers moved into advanced positions to keep up a fire on the Confederates as a cover. After waiting until 10 P.M., Duffié began to retreat down Forest Road on his own initiative. After moving some three miles, he halted and formed a battle line, hoping to determine if the Southerners intended to pursue. Concerned, he again attempted to contact headquarters and sent Captain Ricker for instructions. Ricker, unable to find Hunter, returned to report the absence of the army. With that disturbing information, Duffié continued to fall back down the road until he crossed over to the Salem Pike at New London. Finally, after marching all night, he reached Hunter's rear guard four miles from Liberty and personally reported to the general.[43]

Hunter's decision to retreat would be a fateful one. Up until the afternoon of June 18 he had militarily dominated western Virginia. Success at Lynchburg would have crippled Lee's ability to fend off Grant. But now the Army of West Virginia, rather than destroying the Army of Northern Virginia's support system and threatening its western flank, found itself in danger of being badly mauled or even captured. Hunter's failure of will surprised many. Gordon found it "incomprehensible" that "the small force under Early seemed to have filled Hunter with sudden panic."[44] For the Federals, as a correspondent to the Cincinnati *Gazette* noted, "It was galling . . . to retire thus in the guise of retreat before the men they had so often overcome and routed."[45]

Inspiring Early's prudence on the afternoon of June 18 was not, as

41. Lynchburg *Virginian*, June 21, 1864.
42. Eby, ed., *Virginia Yankee*, 266.
43. OR, Vol. XXXVII, Pt. 1, p. 143; McIhenny Diary, June 18, 1864.
44. Gordon, *Reminiscences*, 300.
45. Cincinnati *Gazette* in Wellsburg (W. Va.) *Herald*, July 8, 1864.

Strother believed, the "rough handling" his men had received, but rather the fact that some of his troops and artillery were still en route to Lynchburg. Hunter's army, numerically superior, remained a dangerous adversary.[46] Yet with the Federal army apparently in disarray and vulnerable to an aggressive move, Early's subordinates expected the general to order another assault. Gordon feared that "the 'Yanks' would be gone by morning" and wanted to attack that evening.[47] Generals Ramseur and Ransom reconnoitered the Federal right and reported that "it could be most advantageously assailed."[48] Lee, rushing to the defense of Petersburg against severe pressure from Grant, urgently wired Early on the eighteenth, asking him to "strike as quick as you can and if circumstances authorize, carry out the original plan, or move upon Petersburg without delay."[49]

Tempting as an attack was for someone of Early's pugnacious nature, caution remained much more in order. Failure would threaten not only his own army but Lee's as well, and "I did not feel justified in attacking him until I could do so with a fair prospect of success."[50] Old Jube needed time to consolidate and ready his troops before taking the initiative. His men, worn by the long march, required rest. Elzey and Ransom needed to be briefed before they assumed their commands. Now that all the infantry had arrived, Early began making preparations to take the offensive at daybreak.[51] He issued orders for troops to cook rations and "be ready to move early in the morning."[52] That night the men strengthened their works while a council of war mapped the strategy for taking the offensive. Early consulted Dr. Terrell about the roads and countryside. He expected to use Gordon's division to flank the Federal right as the remainder of his army pressed Hunter's front.[53]

Meanwhile, Hunter began quietly falling back in preparation for a general retreat. To conceal his move, he ordered a line of pickets, positioned

46. Early, *Last Year of the War*, 44.

47. John O. Casler, *Four Years in the Stonewall Brigade* (Guthrie, Okla., 1893), 225.

48. William R. Cox, "Major-General Stephen D. Ramseur: His Life and Character," *SHSP*, XVIII (1890), 243.

49. Lee to Early, June 18, 1864, Telegram Book, 239, Lee's Headquarters Papers.

50. Early, *Last Year of the War*, 44.

51. Humphreys Diary, June 18, 1864.

52. Worsham, *One of Jackson's Foot Cavalry*, 229.

53. Early, *Campbell Chronicles*, 248; J. J. Terrell Letter (3), Beaumont W. Whitaker Collection; Vandiver, *Jubal's Raid*, 53.

close to the Southern line, to remain there and continue pressing it until midnight. Officers permitted no fires and, as the troops pulled out, cautioned them not to make any noise that might alert the Confederates.[54] The 18th Connecticut, detailed to act as a rear guard, held their position until the army was "well under way." Corporal Lynch noted somberly that "we are a sick, tired, discouraged lot of Yankee soldiers," well aware that "our duty is a very dangerous one."[55] Some units, such as Company B of the 12th West Virginia, received no orders. On his own initiative, First Lieutenant David Powell lead his men at double-quick for nearly a mile until they ran into cavalry. Informed that their unit was well ahead of them, they hurried on. It was not until the next day around noon that they finally caught up with their regiment.[56]

Major Halpine, supposing that the flurry of activity concealed the army's true purpose, assumed that the Federal troops believed "firmly that they were to enter Lynchburg as conquerors if it cost them a week's steady fighting."[57] At first the movement fooled the men of the 34th Massachusetts, who believed they were heading for Lynchburg. However, within ten minutes they "saw enough to satisfy us that we were retreating." The moment came as a depressing one to Private William Stark, who thought "we had an awful large army and nothing could stand before it."[58] Many could not understand the decision and attributed it to Hunter's "timid and vacillating" nature.[59]

Despite efforts to conceal the withdrawal, shortly after midnight its noise drew Early's attention. Initially he remained unsure whether Hunter was "retreating, or moving so as to attack Lynchburg on the south where it was vulnerable." Early had no desire to make a fatal blunder and waited until daybreak, for despite preparations the previous day his troops remained unprepared for an extended pursuit. At daybreak the Southern skirmish line discovered Hunter's absence, and the II Corps, galvanized by the news, rapidly began the pursuit.[60] The Richmond *Daily Dispatch* re-

54. OR, Vol. XXXVII, Pt. 1, p. 100; Lincoln, *Thirty-fourth Massachusetts*, 313; O'Reilly, *Baked Meats*, 357–58.

55. Lynch, *Civil War Diary*, 80.

56. Powell Memoir, 77.

57. O'Reilly, *Baked Meats*, 348.

58. Stark, "Great Skedaddle," 86.

59. Benson, comp., *With the Army*, 52.

60. Early, *Last Year of the War*, 44–45; Joseph Lambeth Diary, June 19, 1864, VHS;

ported with satisfaction that the Federals "were not only falling back, but on a precipitate retreat, almost reaching confusion."[61]

By sunrise the Federals were well on their way toward the Blue Ridge. Only the dead and some 117 seriously wounded, quartered in Hutter's barn, remained.[62] Continuing to try to conceal his retreat, Hunter ordered a skirmish line of scouts to attempt a ruse. Dismounting, they struck at the advancing Southerners, but as soon as the Confederates discovered the nature of their unit, the scouts skedaddled.[63] The pursuit would require hard and determined marching if Early was to catch his fleeing adversary. Unfortunately, necessity had forced his troops to leave behind commissary trains, along with ambulances, artillery, and officers' horses. Dr. Abram Miller of the 25th Virginia, without his horse, "had to foot it."[64]

Yet Early was determined to catch Hunter, so much so that he seemed to give little thought to his own safety.[65] The II Corps moved on the Salem Pike, while Elzey, now in command of Breckinridge's brigade, marched along Forest Road with Ransom's cavalry to his right. Early hoped to strike Hunter at Liberty or, if not there, at the Peaks of Otter.[66] Signs of his speedy retreat littered the countryside. Guns, swords, and knapsacks lay strewn along the road. Scores of horses and mules that had given out lay where the Federals had shot them.[67] "The road," Private Richard W. Waldrop observed, "is marked by evidence of a hasty flight—knapsacks, guns, cooking vessels &c. being scattered in all directions."[68] Major Henry Kyd Douglas saw "ransacked houses, crying women, clothes from the bed chambers and wardrobes of ladies, carried along on bayonets and dragged in the road, the garments of little children, and here and there a burning house" along the path of Hunter's retreat. "Vengeance

---

Worsham, *One of Jackson's Foot Cavalry*, 229; Bradwell, "First of Valley Campaign," 230–31.

61. Richmond *Daily Dispatch*, June 21, 1864.

62. Houck, *Confederate Surgeon*, 76, 78.

63. Montgomery, *Blazer*, 20.

64. Miller to Julia, June 22, 1864, 24, Letters of Miller; Nichols, *Soldier's Story*, 166.

65. Goode, *Recollections*, 63.

66. Early, *Last Year of the War*, 45.

67. William Bayless Tull, W. B. Tull's War Story [typescript], Chap. 5, W-FCHS; Baltimore *Sun*, June 28, 1864; Lynchburg *Republican* in Richmond *Whig*, June 24, 1864; Baltimore *Sun*, June 28, 1864.

68. Richard W. Waldrop Diary, June 19, 1864, Waldrop Papers, SHC.

ought not be left entirely to the Lord," Douglas reflected.[69] An outraged Louisiana colonel, after examining one atrocity, charged his men: "Catch the dogs and give them the bayonet. I charge you, take no prisoners." Soon the Confederates began picking up stragglers.[70] "Some," as Petre Jenning of Bryan's battery observed, "stopped & give themselves up."[71]

Fatigue began to take a heavy toll on the retreating Federals. Some from sheer exhaustion dropped by the wayside; others fell asleep on their horses. According to Major Comly, the men of the 23rd Ohio "had had no sleep for two days and nights, and scarcely anything to eat." He watched men "dropping down frequently, asleep, in the road," only to be awakened to continue the march.[72] Blacks, carrying large loads of provisions, flocked to the retreating army and shared their foodstuffs. Often they pointed out to foragers where provisions lay hidden.[73] In the hurried march, William Patterson's unit stopped one morning only "long enough to eat had we anything to eat, but we were almost entirely destitute."[74] Between June 14 and June 28 the men of the 34th Massachusetts survived on eight ounces of flour each, plus small allowances of coffee and sugar and, for the entire regiment, a barrel of meat per day.[75] Captain Hastings felt "pursued by a more formidable foe who was decimating our rank and destroying our command."[76]

But their pursuers were suffering too. For the men of the 25th Virginia, rations gave out by the evening of June 19, leaving them with nothing to eat on the march the following day. Hunger and physical exhaustion slowed their pursuit.[77] The men of the 61st Georgia at least enjoyed seeing that "the Colonels, majors and doctors were all tramping like we privates, and they soon had sore and skinned feet—yes, some of them straggled."[78]

69. Douglas, *I Rode with Stonewall*, 290.

70. Tull's War Story, Chap. 5.

71. Jenning Diary, June 19, 1864; Stark, "Great Skedaddle," 87.

72. Extracts from Comly Diary, entry under June 18, 1864; Journal of 23rd Ohio, June 19, 1864; Keyes, *History of the 123d Ohio*, 68.

73. Wildes, *One Hundred and Sixteenth Ohio*, 112.

74. Patterson Diary, June 19, 1864.

75. *Annual Report of the Adjutant-General, of the Commonwealth of Massachusetts* (Boston, 1865), 793; Lincoln, *Thirty-fourth Massachusetts*, 314.

76. Hastings Autobiography, June 27, 1864, XII, 19.

77. Miller to Julia, June 22, 1864, Letters of Miller, 24; Lambeth Diary, June 20, 1864.

78. Nichols, *Soldier's Story*, 166.

For Private Bradwell, these days were "the beginning of some of our hardest marching during the war."[79]

When Early reached New London at 9:30 A.M. on the nineteenth, he
wired the welcome news to Lee: "Last evening the enemy assaulted my
lines in front of Lynchburg & was repulsed by the part of my command
which was up." He told Lee that before he could attack Hunter that morning, the Federals began "retreating in confusion." He assured him that he
was pursuing them, adding, "If the cavalry does its duty we will destroy
him."[80] Unquestionably, Early was frustrated with the cavalry's performance by the end of the first day. He had hoped to catch the Federals at Liberty or the Peaks of Otter. Imboden's brigade, sent to the Confederate left
the previous day, had remained on the Campbell Court House Road. Early
had wanted Imboden to move rapidly toward Liberty, but his dispatch
failed to arrive in time for its timely execution. McCausland's performance was even more frustrating for Early. Taking a wrong road, McCausland's troopers did not reach Liberty until just after dark.[81]

Averell's troopers, stopping to camp on the edge of Liberty for the
night, rested about a mile and a half behind the infantry. As the Southerners approached, Averell, anticipating an attack, immediately sent a request to Crook for infantry support. Crook refused, saying that his men
"had marched all night and day" and urgently needed rest. Crook believed
that "nothing but the enemy's cavalry could have had time to reach Liberty, and also that our cavalry was superior in numbers to theirs." Only a
serious threat from the enemy would "warrant the harassing of my tired
men."[82]

Southern sharpshooters broke Crook's confidence as they began firing
on Schoonmaker's brigade. The 8th Ohio, two companies of the 14th
Pennsylvania, and part of the 34th Ohio Mounted Infantry attempted to
stop them. The Southerners charged as Averell's men positioned themselves behind a stone wall. Fearing envelopment on their flanks by superior numbers, the Federals soon retreated.[83] Falling back a short distance,

79. Bradwell, "Cold Harbor, Lynchburg, Valley Campaign," 139.

80. Early to Lee, June 19, 1864, Venable Papers; OR, Vol. XXXVII, Pt. 1, p. 160; Blackford, "Campaign and Battle of Lynchburg," 302.

81. Early, Last Year of the War, 45; Early, Memoirs, 376; Humphreys, Lynchburg Campaign, 70.

82. OR, Vol. XXXVII, Pt. 1, pp. 121, 148.

83. Zeller, Reminiscences, June 19, 1864, 16.

they poured a fusillade on the charging Southerners to check them temporarily. Then again falling back, they repeated their actions, but as Private Stark noted, the Southerners "whacked our Cavalry badly and drove
them through Liberty."[84] Suffering severe losses, Averell fell back behind
Crook. For Averell, the encounter was an embarrassing one. In his official
report he cited the shortage of ammunition as the reason for his hasty retreat. Halpine, estimating that the infantry was down to twelve rounds of
ammunition, observed that one cavalry brigade was without any. When a
soldier fell wounded or dead, an inevitable scramble for his cartridge box
ensued.[85]

At his headquarters between Liberty and Buford Gap, Hunter heard the
gunfire just as he began eating his dinner. Alarmed that the firing seemed
"so rapid and approaching so near," he interrupted his mess and, with his
staff, went to investigate.[86] Crook quickly deployed his men into battle
formation to challenge any serious threat. The termination of the fighting
offered his men only a brief respite, for soon he had hundreds of them
chopping trees and tearing down fences until midnight. Crook's purposes
were twofold: the noise would screen and conceal the movement of the
wagon trains, and the obstructions would slow the progress of the pursuing
Southerners.[87] With nightfall, the men of the 31st Georgia could see in
the distance the "thousands of camp fires of the enemy; but it was then
too late to make an attack."[88] By midnight the army again picked up the
march west "in full moon shining gloriously."[89]

Hunter's staff regarded the army's "position to be critical"; as Strother
observed, "all agreed that we must get out if possible."[90] Yet Hunter at
times manifested a surprising sense of unreality during the retreat. Undoubtedly age as well as physical and emotional fatigue unsettled his full
grasp of affairs at times. As Averell's command moved between the Big

84. *Ibid.*; Benson, comp., *With the Army*, 52; O'Ferrall, *Forty Years of Active Service*,
107–108; Lang, *Loyal West Virginia*, 377–78; Stark, "Great Skedaddle," 87.

85. *OR*, Vol. XXXVII, Pt. 1, p. 148; O'Reilly, *Baked Meats*, 361–62.

86. Eby, ed., *Virginia Yankee*, 267.

87. *OR*, Vol. XXXVII, Pt. 1, p. 148; Stark, "Great Skedaddle," 87; "General Hunter's
Expedition," 530; Sutton, *Second Regiment West Virginia*, 130; Baltimore *Sun*, June 28,
1864.

88. Bradwell, "First of Valley Campaign," 231.

89. Eby, ed., *Virginia Yankee*, 267.

90. *Ibid.*, 266.

and Little Otter Rivers on June 19, Hunter ordered him to undertake an expedition against Danville and the Richmond and Danville Railroad in order to free Union prisoners held in that city.[91] Considering the distance, especially with the cavalry short on ammunition, the plan was bizarre and Averell reacted "with a gesture of violent dissatisfaction."[92] At Liberty, however, Hunter wisely suspended the mission.[93]

The general's behavior occasionally perplexed Captain Du Pont even more. On the nineteenth, after an all-night march, the captain stopped his artillery at 4:30 A.M. for an hour's sleep. Awakening, he inquired about orders but found none. Alarmed, he went to see Hunter. He found him just as he was "making his morning ablutions outside of his tent" and "a little dazed." When Du Pont told him that he lacked any directives, the general casually replied, "I think we ought to get away by nine o'clock or thereabouts." Horrified by "his failure to grasp the almost desperate situation of our command," Du Pont informed him that the Southern skirmish line would probably be pressing them no later than "a quarter past eight" and tried to convince him that "our men, knowing that they have but little ammunition and less food won't stand five minutes, so greatly are they demoralized by hunger and exhaustion." Finally realizing "the gravity of the situation," Hunter responded, "Well, we shall have to get off soon after seven."[94]

While the failure to capture Lynchburg had shattered Hunter's "long and persistently" held view that Lee would not reinforce the city,[95] the necessity of retreat destroyed his confidence in a number of his subordinates. He later lashed out at Averell, claiming that "I . . . should certainly have taken it [Lynchburg] if it had not been for the stupidity and conceit of that fellow Averell, who unfortunately joined me at Staunton, and of whom I unfortunately had, at the time, a very high opinion, and trusted him when I should not have done so."[96] Duffié's failure to cut the Orange and Alexandria Railroad created doubts not only about his ability but about his character as well. Hunter came to have utter contempt for Sulli-

91. *OR*, Vol. XXXVII, Pt. 1, pp. 651–52.
92. Eby, ed., *Virginia Yankee*, 267.
93. *OR*, Vol. XXXVII, pt. 1, p. 148
94. Du Pont, *Campaign of 1864*, 83–85.
95. *Ibid.*, 79–80.
96. *OR*, Vol. XXXVII, Pt. 2, p. 366.

van, considering him "not worth one cent." A number of lesser officers, including Lieutenant Meigs, were also recipients of the general's scorn.

In contrast, Crook rose in the commander's esteem. Crook later wrote in his autobiography that "Gen. Hunter had no confidence in the rest of the command. . . . [He] had gotten so now that he would do nothing without first consulting me." [97] And Hunter was not the only one to hold Crook in high esteem. According to a correspondent from the Cincinnati *Commercial*, "Had it not been for General Crook our retreat from Lynchburg would have been a complete rout and terrible disaster." [98]

The route of retreat posed a major question for Hunter. The choice became either to move back into West Virginia or to retire down the Shenandoah Valley. With ammunition and other supplies increasingly short, a move down the Valley—it would probably take them fifteen days to reach a base of supplies—would seriously endanger the Army of West Virginia and allow Early to operate on his flank and rear. A general engagement, he feared, would deplete the army's ammunition. A staff officer, later writing to the New York *World*, commented that such a route "would have resulted, inevitably, in the annihilation, or capture of his whole command." [99] An escape through West Virginia offered the safest route. Hunter expected to find a million rations at Meadow Bluff. As Strother noted, "The move into the mountains was necessary to disembarras ourselves of the enemy's cavalry." [100] In opting to pass through the Blue Ridge by the road through Buford Gap instead of returning by way of the Peaks of Otter, Hunter gained the option of moving toward Salem, Fincastle, or Buchanan.

For Early to have any chance of intercepting or trapping the Federals, he had to learn what route they planned to take. When Hunter took the road toward Buford's Depot on the night of June 19, it was clear that he did not plan to go by way of the Peaks of Otter, but Early still could not be sure of the opposing army's ultimate direction. Despite his uncertainty, he decided on a strategy designed to block any move that might swing northward toward Fincastle or Buchanan. Therefore, he dispatched Ransom's

97. Blackford, "Campaign and Battle of Lynchburg," 304; Schmitt, ed., *George Crook*, 118.

98. Cincinnati *Commercial* quoted in Morgantown (W. Va.) *Weekly Post*, Aug. 20, 1864.

99. New York *World*, quoted in Washington *Daily Morning Chronicle*, July 26, 1864.

100. Strother, "Operations in West Virginia," 487.

cavalry to move across the Peaks of Otter.[101] Strategically, not only would the troopers block an advance in that direction, but they would nicely form a pincer movement with which to strike at Hunter's army.

When Early reached Buford's Depot on June 20, he generally understood what Hunter's route would be. Southern scouts spotted the Federal rear guard as they moved into the Blue Ridge on the road leading to Salem. Early wired Richmond that Hunter "is probably trying to get off by the way of Lewisburg."[102] He immediately sent a courier toward Buchanan to redirect Ransom toward Salem. Accomplishing that, the courier was then "to ride all night" to Fincastle, where another courier would alert Confederate forces in the region. Then proceeding on to Salem, he was to wire other units to blockade the mountain roads leading to Lewisburg.[103]

Meanwhile, Duffié's cavalry had secured Buford Gap. After a hard march the infantry arrived there on the morning of June 20, while Southern units followed in close pursuit. Catching up to the Federal rear around noon, a section of Bryan's battery began to shell them. Crook's men rapidly formed a battle line on the mountain. As Gordon's division approached on the left, Rodes's men moved on the right to flank them. They sent their men up the mountainside, but the rugged terrain proved to be a major obstacle. Strategically placed batteries on the commanding heights of the Gap effectively deterred any serious assault on the Union line. After lying in line until 9 P.M., the Federals again picked up the march for the night.[104]

Averell and Crook reported the assault to Hunter. Crook, who had captured and interrogated a Confederate soldier who identified himself as part of Rodes's division, learned from the prisoner that "his division had taken a by-road to come in our flanks." Crook feared that Rodes now either occupied a position in his front or posed a threat to one of his flanks, and "in either case I felt certain of disaster."[105] Adding to the general ap-

101. Early, *Last Year of the War*, 45; Humphreys, *Lynchburg Campaign*, 70; Cox, "Stephen D. Ramseur," 243.

102. Early to Lee, June 21, 1864, Venable Papers; OR, Vol. LI, Pt. 2, p. 1025.

103. Early, *Memoirs*, 376–77; Allen Diary, June 20, 1864.

104. OR, Vol. XXXVII, Pt. 1, p. 101; Jenning Diary, June 20, 1864; Humphreys Diary, June 20, 1864; Humphreys Autobiography, III, 331; Early, *Last Year of the War*, 45–46; McDonald, ed., *Make Me a Map*, 212; Opie, *Rebel Cavalryman*, 240–43.

105. Schmitt, ed., *George Crook*, 118–19.

prehension, scouts reported to Averell that a large contingent of cavalry had passed them moving north toward the Peaks of Otter.[106]

Another danger came with the temporary breakdown of leadership by Hunter on the evening of June 20. Fatigue and stress had taken a toll on the sixty-two-year-old general. Captain Du Pont, searching for him in order to receive instructions, finally found him lying ill on a couch in a small cottage. He impressed upon the general the necessity of resuming the march quickly; "otherwise we could not hope to escape a great disaster." With Halpine, his adjutant general, also ill, Hunter authorized Du Pont to issue orders on his behalf. The captain began to serve as a liaison between the division commanders. At 7:30 P.M. he went to Crook's headquarters to confer with him, quickly working out a schedule of timing and the line of march toward Big Lick and Salem. With those decisions made, Du Pont hurried to inform Sullivan, then went on to the headquarters of the cavalry divisions to instruct them to follow in the rear, behind the artillery. After four hours of intense activity, Du Pont returned to inform Hunter of their plans. The general merely said "Very well" and returned "to his couch."[107] After the therapeutic rest had "restored his pristine vigor," Hunter at last, as Du Pont observed, "fully appreciate[d] the gravity of the situation."[108]

On the march again on the afternoon of June 20, the Federals continued to burn railroad stations and property along their route. On one occasion Hunter personally supervised two companies in the destruction of a water tower and a pile of wood. With great expertise, his men, whenever they stopped to rest for a few minutes, heaped fences and ties on the track and then lit the pile. After destroying a bridge, they delighted in running captured railroad cars into the gaping ravine as they torched the surrounding buildings. That evening, as Strother observed, "Burning bridges and railroad stations lighted our way."[109]

106. OR, Vol. XXXVII, Pt. 1, p. 148.

107. Du Pont, *Campaign of 1864*, 85–87.

108. *Ibid.*, 88.

109. Eby, ed., *Virginia Yankee*, 268; Keyes, *History of the 123d Ohio*, 68; Mastin Diary, June 21, 1864; Lynch, *Civil War Diary*, 81; Stark, "Great Skedaddle," 87; Deedie Kagey, *When Past Is Prologue: A History of Roanoke County* (Roanoke, 1988), 201–202, 204. In the September 7, 1864, Richmond *Sentinel*, R. L. Owens, president of the Virginia and Tennessee Railroad, gave testimony to Hunter's extensive devastation of the rail line during May and June. Only three depots between Wytheville and Lynchburg, some 135 miles of rail,

As the Federals continued their flight, provisions grew more and more scarce. Even the officers had little to eat except "a little hard bread and fresh beef, the latter doled out in half-rations."[110] Private Stark observed that some of the men were "completely exhausted and had no control of themselves."[111] When the army reached Salem the men were "dragging our weary bodies along, nearly exhausted, unconscious of danger." With such privation, foraging became a dire necessity, and few houses or gardens remained untouched. Soldiers told a local farmer that "they were short of rations, & authorized to impress whenever it could be found."[112]

Earlier on June 20, Hunter intended to break the army's retreat at Bonsack's Station, for as Strother observed, the cavalry looked "very much used up and demoralized."[113] Troopers stole new mounts from farmers in the area, telling them that "they were more obliged to have them."[114] As Hunter attempted to rest by lying on the floor of "a humble house," a courier from Averell roused him at 2 P.M. with the news that Southern units were threatening his rear guard in force. Half an hour later, Crook reported being pressed on both flanks. Immediately Hunter ordered the resumption of the march, much "to the cruel disappointment of many who had hoped for a night's rest."[115]

The wagon trains, escorted by Duffié's men, immediately headed for Salem. Part of Crook's 2nd Brigade with carbines went ahead to the town. On arriving there, Captain William Speers and his troopers charged into the town and cleared it of the two Southern cavalry companies then occupying it.[116] Finally, at sunrise on June 21, Hunter's main column reached the town. Again they attempted to rest, but cannon fire and unwarranted reports that "Crook was cut off" shattered that hope. Hunter hurried his troops along, excitedly "thump[ing] some of them with his fist."[117] The

---

had escaped destruction. All the bridges from Lynchburg to Salem and between Dublin and Christiansburg were burned. Owens estimated the cost to the railroad at some $600,000. It took the company some sixty days to restore the line.

110. Rawling, *First Regiment Virginia*, 185.

111. Stark, "Great Skedaddle," 87.

112. Rawling, *First Regiment Virginia*, 85; David H. Plaine file #4188, microfiche 2717, RG 233, SCCP.

113. Eby, ed., *Virginia Yankee*, 267.

114. J. C. Stover file #14147, microfiche 507, RG 233, SCCP.

115. Eby, ed., *Virginia Yankee*, 268.

116. Elwood, *Old Ringgold Cavalry*, 198; Farrar, *Twenty-Second Pennsylvania*, 247.

117. Thomson, "Lynchburg Campaign," 135; Farrar, *Twenty-Second Pennsylvania*, 246.

trains hurried through Salem toward Catawba Mountain on the New Castle Road.[118]

Fortunately for Hunter, a Confederate blunder allowed him to gain valuable time. A courier carrying verbal orders for Rodes to assume the advance on the morning of June 21 failed to reach him in time. Consequently, Rodes's men did not pick up the march until after daybreak. Early's troops, without understanding the reason, also waited. Some assumed that the Federals still occupied their front and that a move was underway to flank them in the rear. The lapse seriously stalled the resumption of the pursuit. As Sergeant Milton Humphreys noted, if not for a "blockhead" of a messenger, the army "could at any time have been put in motion in less than ten minutes."[119] As the Federals took the Lewisburg Road, Early now was certain of Hunter's destination.[120]

Early's order to redirect Ransom's cavalry toward Salem netted more success. Ransom's troopers, marching all night, crossed the Peaks of Otter after "a hot & forced march" and then moved up Stone Pike toward Salem. Near a gorge known as Hanging Rock, McCausland's brigade overtook Hunter's rear column on the morning of June 21.[121] Duffié's cavalry, preceding Du Pont's artillery and wagon train, had supposedly picketed all the roads intersecting with their route of march. Believing the road secure, Duffié "sent back word that all was clear."[122] With that the wagon train, under heavy guard, followed by the less protected artillery, moved into the pass. Unfortunately for the Federals, the road passed through a narrow gorge, and the cavalry had failed to cover one intersecting road. Their negligence provided McCausland with a golden opportunity.[123]

Spotting the artillery and wagon train, McCausland immediately sent word to Ransom to ask for permission to attack. Ransom preferred to wait until the infantry came up and ordered a delay. Meanwhile, Du Pont's gunners discovered the Southern presence. McCausland now begged Ran-

---

118. Du Pont, *Campaign of 1864*, 87.

119. Humphreys, *Lynchburg Campaign*, 70–71; Diary of W. W. Old, Jubal Early Papers, LC; Cox, "Stephen D. Ramseur," 243–44.

120. Early to Lee, June 21, 1864, Venable Papers; Early, *Last Year of the War*, 46.

121. McCausland to Blackford, n.d., 1, Daniel Collection; Feamaster Diary, June 20–21, 1864.

122. Stark, "Great Skedaddle," 88.

123. *OR*, Vol. XXXVII, Pt. 1, p. 149; Du Pont, *Campaign of 1864*, 87–88; O'Reilly, *Baked Meats*, 364–65.

som to order an attack, and after another delay the returning courier told him that Ransom, who was ill, was turning command over to him. Lieutenant Berkeley, without permission, opened fire with one of his guns on the Federals. Simultaneously, McCausland and sixty of his men charged Snow's and Carlin's batteries and wagons.[124] Colonel Waddell remembered "that awful sight when Gen. McCausland rushed down the mountain road and destroyed our artillery." Killing the unhitched horses by hitting them "in the head with sharp axes . . . [they] blew up the caissons, while some of the cannoneers were still on them. The sights were knocked off the cannons . . . and spokes of the wheels cut."[125] Exploding ammunition wagons created dangerous piles blocking the road.

Schoonmaker's cavalry brigade heard the firing as they approached the Gap. Suddenly a shell exploded fifty yards in their front. Captain Gilmor ordered, "Draw saber and charge the ——— thing before they can reload." Their appearance merely mitigated the disaster. The mass of wreckage and exploding wagons resulted in the death a number of Crook's men as they attempted to pass through the gorge.[126] Beaten off by Schoonmaker's cavalry, McCausland's troopers left "horses . . . still living, and wallowing in the water, still hitched, with harness on; the creek was running red with bloody water."[127] Du Pont was forced to abandon and spike eight guns. As Colonel Lincoln wrote, *"Some one had evidently blundered!"*[128]

Despite the damage inflicted on Du Pont's artillery, McCausland's attack failed to delay the Federal flight. By the time Rodes's division appeared, it was too late. "Had an attack been made when we first reach their rear," McCausland believed, "Hunter would have either lost his entire train or been compelled to fight Early a pitch battle."[129] Hunter was furious. To Strother it seemed "as if we are getting into an ugly position, artillery gone and cavalry worthless."[130] Duffié's men, pushing on to secure

124. McCausland to Blackford, n.d., 1–2, Daniel Collection; Humphreys, *Lynchburg Campaign*, 71–72; Jenning Diary, June 21, 1864; Whitaker, "Hunter's Coming," 36; Driver, *Staunton Artillery—McClanahan's Battery*, 99.

125. J. N. Waddell to editor of *National Tribune* [clipping], Waddell Collection; "General Hunter's Expedition," 529.

126. Benson, comp., *With the Army*, 53.

127. Waddell to *National Tribune*; Stark, "Great Skedaddle," 88.

128. Du Pont, *Campaign of 1864*, 88; OR, Vol. XXXVII, Pt. 1, p. 160; Lincoln, *Thirty-fourth Massachusetts*, 315.

129. McCausland to Blackford, n.d., 3, Daniel Collection.

130. Eby, ed., *Virginia Yankee*, 268–69.

the Catawba Mountain Gap, prepared to clear it of any Confederates there. On reaching the gap they easily drove off the small unit and removed numerous obstructions. McCausland's men continued to press them until the Federals reached the Catawba Valley, but on the following morning an "ambuscade" by Hayes's brigade ended that pursuit and any further molestation of the Army of West Virginia.[131]

Reports and rumors of Southern movements continued to haunt Hunter's commanders. On the evening of June 21, Averell's advanced cavalry units, reaching within seven miles of New Castle, met with no opposition, but a report of a force of "twenty thousand" advancing through Fincastle and Covington caused "great anxiety among the officers of the staff." For Strother, "this day's march was considered the crisis of our retreat." The lack of Southern activity was felt "as an evil omen." In need of accurate intelligence, Strother persuaded Hunter to stop at New Castle until the situation clarified itself. There the general considered various contingency plans. Crook proposed that if attacked, the army should shift directions and move toward the Virginia and Tennessee Railroad and then on toward Tennessee. Strother advanced a more audacious and extremely dangerous plan of dashing along a route through Fincastle to Buchanan, over the Blue Ridge to Charlottesville, and then northward toward Harpers Ferry. He believed that the move would surprise the Southerners if they occupied either Covington or Salem. However, for Crook the proposal was "too rash and impracticable." For the moment, Crook's plan won out, but Strother did persuade Hunter to remain at New Castle overnight.[132]

The next morning, an incoming scout allayed any fears of a large Confederate force passing through Fincastle. He reported that only a cavalry brigade and two mounted infantry regiments occupied that region. Less fearful, Hunter decided to continue on the Sweet Springs Road toward Lewisburg, "fighting anything that molests us." Arriving at Sweet Springs, he stopped, rested, and took advantage of its facilities for the night. With little fear of a Southern attack, the general held a conference of his commanders to select the best route for the army to travel. Three plans emerged. Strother proposed using a road in the Warm Springs Valley,

131. *OR*, Vol. XXXVII, Pt. 1, p. 101, 143; David Powell Memoirs, 80.

132. Eby, ed., *Virginia Yankee*, 270–71; O'Reilly, *Baked Meats*, 363; *OR*, Vol. XXXVII, Pt. 1, p. 149.

which ran parallel to the Shenandoah Valley and which would take them northward through Franklin and Moorefield to New Creek. The virtue of the route, the colonel argued, was that if Early were to move down the Valley to strike at the Baltimore and Ohio Railroad, Hunter could join with Sigel in repulsing him. A second proposal was to move through Beverly. Hunter, considering the nature of the country and the condition of the army, rejected both plans as impractical. Crook's new recommendation, on the other hand, presented a practical and safe solution. He proposed to use the shortest route through Lewisburg to reach the army's supply depots at Meadow Bluff, a march of three days, then continue on to Gauley Bridge and Charleston. The logic of Crook's plan was compelling for an army "disorganized by fatigue," low in morale, and near starvation. The mountain route also offered better opportunities to deal with Early's cavalry if they attempted to snipe at the army's rear. [133]

Continuing to live off the country, the Federals wearily marched through West Virginia. On June 27, the Lynchburg *Virginian* lashed out at them: "We sincerely hope, however, that if their territory is again invaded, it will be with fire and sword. We do not want to see our troops turn thieves and robbers, despoiling ladies of their jewelry and committing all kinds of petty larceny, but we wish them to apply the torch to all public property, and appropriate all private property belonging to Union men to the public use." [134] In less than three months, Chambersburg, Pennsylvania, would suffer retaliation from McCausland's men on orders from Jubal Early.

The long pursuit and hard marching had nearly exhausted Early's army, although General Grimes was surprised that so "very little straggling and very little complaining" occurred. Food remained very scarce, and Rodes's men suffered "nearly three days without any rations." [135] In surveying the desolate countryside that Hunter had just passed through, Early believed that "there was a limit to the endurance even of Confederate soldiers." Given his cavalry's inability to combat the enemy, he concluded that a similar attempt by his army could well result in disaster. Actually, Hunter's route pleased Early, who "knew he could not stop short of the Kanawha River, and [that] he was, therefore, disposed of for some time." [136]

133. *OR*, Vol. XXXVII, Pt. 1, pp. 101–102; Eby, ed., *Virginia Yankee*, 272–73; Strother, "Operations in West Virginia," 487–88.

134. Lynchburg *Virginian*, June 27, 1864.

135. Cowper, comp., *Letters of General Grimes*, 56; Old Diary, June 21, 1864; Beavans Books, June 20, 1864, II, 72; Leonidas Polk to wife, June 1864, Polk Papers.

136. Early, *Memoirs*, 379; Lambeth Diary, June 22, 1864.

Hunter's retreat into West Virginia nicely uncovered the Shenandoah Valley. On June 22, Early readied his army to strike down the Valley into western Maryland to threaten Washington in an attempt to relieve pressure on Lee at Petersburg. Just as important, the absence of a Federal army in the Shenandoah ensured Southern control over this important granary and supplier of foodstuffs during the critical growing and harvesting season. Hunter's debacle temporarily frustrated Grant's grand design of depriving Lee of a major source of necessary sustenance in maintaining the Army of Northern Virginia. The Richmond *Examiner*, despite its disappointment over the lack of a sufficient force in the Valley to trap Hunter, expressed delight that "in any event, however, we may be sure that one wheel is off Grant's chariot, and one important part of the campaign against Richmond utterly defeated."[137] The failure to take Lynchburg also marked the end to any major military movements in West Virginia for the remainder of the war.[138]

Early's initial instructions made the destruction of Hunter's army his primary objective. However, they also provided that if successful, he was to move down the Valley, cross the Potomac River either above Harpers Ferry or near Leesburg, push into western Maryland, and then threaten Washington. On June 15, Lee had told Davis that Early's troops "would make us more secure here [in Richmond], but success in the Valley would relieve our difficulties that at present press heavily upon us." Lee, facing Grant's move on Petersburg, wired Early at Lynchburg on the eighteenth to strike at the Federal army as soon as he could and "if circumstances authorize, carry out the original plan, or move upon Petersburg without delay."[139] As Early's pursuit of Hunter ended on the twenty-second, Lee again submitted to Early's judgment the matter of his moving down the Valley and striking into western Maryland. Yet he tempered his hope with a concern over whether the condition of Early's troops "would permit the expedition across the Potomac to be carried out."[140]

Despite his disappointment that Hunter had escaped without being "much punished, except by the demoralization of his troops and the loss of

137. Richmond *Examiner*, June 20, 1864.

138. John Alexander Williams, *West Virginia: A History* (New York, 1984), 73.

139. Lee to Early, June 18, 1864, Lee's Headquarters Papers, Telegraph Book, 239; Freeman, ed., *Lee's Dispatches*, 239–40; Dowdey and Manarin, eds., *Papers of Lee*, 782–83, 791; Early, *Last Year of the War*, 40; Early, *Memoirs*, 371,

140. Lee to Early, June 26, 1864, Lee's Headquarters Papers, Telegraph Book; Early, *Last Year of the War*, 48.

some artillery," Lee wanted the move. Surprised at Hunter's route of retreat, Lee noted that it left the Valley "open for General Early's advance
into Maryland." If Early returned to Lee, the Federals could easily reorganize and equip another raid, which would again require the II Corps's return to the Valley. An advance down the Shenandoah would instead draw
"Hunter after him." [141]

Unsurprisingly, Early "determined to take the responsibility to con-
tinu[e]" the advance into the Valley. [142] A week earlier, in the aftermath of
Trevillian's Station, he had refused to approve a proposed cavalry expedition into Maryland by Colonel Bradley T. Johnson for the purpose of creating confusion and a diversion there. He had told the colonel, "I'm going
to Lynchburg and as soon as I smash up Mr. Hunter's little tea party, I'm
going to Washington myself." [143] Significantly, his decision not only resulted in a threat to the Federal capital in July but would also keep Union
armies on the defensive in western Virginia until the Battle of Winchester
on September 19. Disappointed yet still optimistic, General Ramseur
wrote his wife from Staunton: "We have had the hardest march of the war.
Couldn't catch Hunter but we hope yet to strike the Yanks a heavy
blow." [144] On June 23, after a short respite, Stonewall Jackson's veteran II
Corps again moved down the familiar Valley Pike toward Winchester and
the Potomac River.

141. OR, Vol. XXXVII, Pt. 1, pp. 766–67, 769–70; Dowdey and Manarin, eds., *Papers
of Lee*, 806–807.

142. Early, *Memoirs*, 381.

143. Bradley T. Johnson, "My Ride Around Baltimore in Eighteen Hundred and Sixty-
Four," *SHSP*, XXX (1902), 216.

144. Stephen Ramseur to wife, June 20, 1864, Stephen Dodson Ramseur Papers, SHC.

BIBLIOGRAPHY

PRIMARY SOURCES

Manuscripts

Cincinnati Historical Society
Thomson, James. Papers.

Duke University, William R. Perkins Library, Durham, North Carolina
Kennon, Lyman Walter Vere. Papers.
Rodgers, Robert Smith. Papers.
Tavenner, Cabell, and Alexander Scott Withers Tavenner. Papers.

The John Handley Library, Winchester–Frederick County Historical Society and Handley Archives, Winchester, Virginia
Chase, Julia. War Time Diary of Miss Julia Chase, 1861–1864.
Jenning, Petre. Diary, April 1864–July 1864.
Kite, O. H. Diary, 1864. Marjorie Copenhaver Collection.
Lee, Mrs. Hugh. Diary, March 1862–November 1865. Mrs. Hugh Lee Collection.
Miller, Abram Schultz. Letters, 1861–1864. James Miller Collection.
Sperry, Kate S. Diary. Transcribed by Lenoir Hunt as "Surrender? Never Surrender!"
Tull, William Bayliss. Memoirs, W. B. Tull's War Story. W. B. Tull War Papers.
Wayland, Anna Kegley. Diary Journal, 1847–1865. John Wayland Collection.

Jones Memorial Library, Lynchburg, Virginia
Cleland, Janet. Diary.
Sommerville, Henry C. Diary.
Terrell, J. J. Battle of Lynchburg: An Address.
Whitaker, Beaumont W. Collection.

Kegley Library, Wytheville Community College, Wytheville, Virginia
Kohlier, Wm. Description, History, and Recollections of the Lead Mines.

Library of Congress
Early, Jubal. Papers.
Feamaster, Thomas. Family Papers.
Lincoln, Abraham. Papers.
Patton, George S., Jr. Papers.
Stanton, Edwin McMasters. Papers.

Marshall University, James E. Morrow Library, Huntington, West Virginia
Sigel, Franz, to Kellian V. Whaley, March 15, 1864. Letter.

Maryland Historical Society, Baltimore, Maryland
Bradwell, J. G. Recollections of Civil War, J. G. Bradwell Papers.
Clarke. Papers.
Gilmor, Harry. Papers.
Letters Sent by the Baltimore & Ohio Railroad, 1859–1867.

Museum of the Confederacy, Richmond, Virginia
Imboden, J. D. Battle of Piedmont, Virginia. Fought on Sunday, June 5th, 1864,
    Account Taken Directly from Original Letter of General J. D. Imboden to Col.
    I. Marshall McCue, Dated, October 1st, 1883.
Johnston, J. Stoddard. Papers.

National Archives
Record Group 56, General Records of the Department of Treasury, Record Group
    217, Records of the U.S. General Accounting Office, Allowed Case Files of the
    Southern Claims Commission.
Record Group 233, Records of the U.S. House of Representatives, Barred and Dis-
    allowed Claims of the Southern Claims Commission, Microfiche.
Records of the Commissioners of Claims [Southern Claims Commission, 1871–
    1880], Microfilm Publication 87, 14 Rolls.
Records of the Department of West Virginia.

Ohio Historical Society, Columbus
Booth, John T. Papers.
Comly, James M. Notebooks, 1862–1864.
Newton, William S. Civil War Letters.
Staley, Josiah. Civil War Letters.

Ohio University, Athens, Ohio
Brown Family Collection

Rutherford B. Hayes Presidential Center Library, Fremont, Ohio
Clugston, John McNulty. Diary.
Comly, James M. Papers.
Journal of the 23rd Regiment, Ohio Volunteer Infantry.
Hastings, Russell. Papers.
Hayes, Rutherford B. Papers.
Stiarwalt, Andrew, Sr. Diary.

Shenandoah County Library, Edinburg, Virginia
Pitman, Levi. Extracts from the Diaries of Levi Pitman of Mt. Olive, Shenandoah
    Co., Va., 1845–1892

U.S. Military History Institute, Carlisle, Pennsylvania
Artman, Albert. Diary.
Davis, Edward. Diary.
Leigh, Lewis. Collection.
McIhenny, William. Diary.
Mulligan, James W. Letters.
Powell, David. Memoirs.
Tall, William Allen. Letters.
Weed, John W. Memoir.
Wright, Albert G. Diary, George A. Fluhr Collection.
Zeller, Benjamin F. Collection.

University of North Carolina, Chapel Hill, Southern Historical Collection
Beavans, William. Diary, William Beavans Books.
Bennette, J. Kelly. Papers.
Clark, Carrie H. Papers.
Green, James E. Diary.
Guerrant, Edward O. Diary.
Paris, John. Papers.
Patterson, William. Diary.
Pendleton, William N. Papers.
Polk, Leonidas Lafayette. Papers.
Ramseur, Stephen Dodson. Papers.
Ransom, Robert. Papers.
Venable, Charles. Papers.
Whitaker, Cary. Diaries.

Withers, C. A. Four Years in Active Service.
Woolfolk, Richard. Diary, Waldrop Papers.

University of Virginia, Charlottesville
Allen, Eva Honey. Diary, 1864–1865.
Berkeley Family of Staunton, Virginia. Papers.
Daniel, John W. Collection.
Emerson Family. Papers.
Harrison, Matthella Page. Diary, 1862–1864.
Humphreys, Milton Wylie. Autobiography (Memoirs).
Humphreys, Milton Wylie. Diary from March 1862 to the End of the War.
Imboden, Frank. Letters.
Imboden, John D. Papers.
Lee, Claude Marshall. Papers.
Neil, Alexander. Letters.
Nolan Family. Papers.
Peyton, George Quintus. Diary, 1864.
Peyton, John W. Diary.
Waddell, Joseph Addison. Diary, 1855–1865.
Williams, B. F. Journal: Crook's Raid.

Virginia Historical Society, Richmond
Bowen, Frederick Fillison. Papers.
Cloyd Family of Montgomery County and Pulaski County. Papers.
Davis, Creed Thomas. Diary, May 4, 1864–February 19, 1865.
Early, Jubal. Papers.
Gibson Family. Papers.
Goddard, Charles Austin. Papers.
Guerrant, William Gibson. Diary.
Hannah Family. Papers.
Lambeth, Joseph Harrison. Diary.
Latrobe, Osmun. Diary.
Lee's Headquarters Papers. Letter Book, 1864.
Meyers, Gustavus Adolphus. Papers.
Perry, Thornton Tayloe. Collection.
Smith, Sara (Henderson). Papers.

Virginia Military Institute, Lexington
Gatewood, Andrew. Collection.
McCausland, John. Biographical File.
New Market Battle File.
Patton, George S. Biographical File.

Superintendent Correspondence: Letters Received.
Superintendent Letter Book: Outgoing Correspondence.

Virginia Polytechnic Institute and State University, Blacksburg
Board of Director's Minutes, August 1864, Virginia and Tennessee Railroad Company Records.

Virginia State Library and Archives, Richmond
Smith, Governor William. Letters Received, Governor's Office, Executive Department, May–September, 1864.

Washington and Lee University, Lexington, Virginia
Bruce, Sallie White. Memoirs.
Davidson, Albert. Correspondence.
Hunter's Raid File.
McCausland, John. Letter.
Reader, Frank S. Diary.
Washington College: Records of Board of Trustees, Feb. 21, 1845–Sept. 1873.
Washington College Trustees' Papers.

West Virginia Archives and History Library, Charleston
Sedinger, James D. Diary of a Border Ranger, Co. E, 8th Va. Cavalry.
Waddell, J. N. Collection.

West Virginia University, West Virginia and Regional History Collection, Morgantown
Cracraft, J. W. Journal, Roy Bird Cook Collection.
Curtis, William B. Papers.
Ellis, James F. Diary, Roy Bird Cook Collection.
Campbell, Jacob. Diary, Jacob Campbell Papers.
Frost, Ephraim W. Letters, H. E. Matheny Collection.
Goudy, William M. Diary, Civil War Diaries Collection.
Mastin, John. Diary. Roy Bird Cook Collection.
Matheny, H. E. Collection.
Young, John Valley. Papers, Roy Bird Cook Collection.

Western Reserve Historical Society, Cleveland, Ohio
Sigel, Franz. Papers, 1861–1902, MS 3123.

Newspapers

Athens (Ohio) *Messenger*
Baltimore *American and Commercial Advertiser*

Baltimore *Sun*
Charlottesville (Va.) *Daily Chronicle*
Cincinnati *Daily Commercial*
Cincinnati *Daily Gazette*
Clarksburg (W. Va.) *National Telegraph*
Cumberland (Md.) *Alleganian*
Lexington (Va.) *Gazette*
Lynchburg (Va.) *Virginian*
Morgantown (W. Va.) *Weekly Post*
New York *Herald*
Point Pleasant (W. Va.) *Weekly Register*
Richmond (Va.) *Daily Dispatch*
Richmond (Va.) *Sentinel*
Richmond (Va.) *Whig*
Staunton (Va.) *Spectator*
Staunton (Va.) *Spectator and Vindicator*
Washington (D.C.) *Daily Morning Chronicle*
Wellsburg (W. Va.) *Herald*
Wheeling (W. Va.) *Daily Intelligencer*

Books

Alexander, John H. *Mosby's Men*. New York, 1907.

Allan, Elizabeth Preston. *The Life and Letters of Margaret Junkin Preston*. Boston, 1903.

Annual Report of the Adjutant-General, of the Commonwealth of Massachusetts. Boston, 1865.

Barrett, John G., and Robert K. Turner Jr., eds. *Letters of a New Market Cadet: Beverly Standard*. Chapel Hill, 1961.

Barton, Randolph. *Recollections, 1861–1865*. Baltimore, 1913.

Basler, Roy P., ed. *The Collected Works of Abraham Lincoln*. 11 vols. New Brunswick, 1953.

Beach, William H. *The First New York (Lincoln) Cavalry*. New York, 1902.

Beale, Howard K., ed. *The Diary of Edward Bates, 1859–1866*. Washington, 1933.
———. *Diary of Gideon Welles*. 3 vols. New York, 1960.

Benson, Evelyn Abraham, comp. *With the Army of West Virginia, 1861–1864: Reminiscences and Letters of Lt. James Abraham*. Publication No. 1 of the Abraham Archives. Typescript. Lancaster, Pa., 1974.

Beymer, William Gilmore. *On Hazardous Service*. New York, 1912.

Blackford, Susan Leigh, comp. *Letters from Lee's Army*. New York, 1962.

Blackford, W. W. *War Years with Jeb Stuart*. Baton Rouge, 1993.

Boley, Henry. *Lexington in Old Virginia*. Richmond, 1936.

Bourke, John G. *On the Border with Crook*. New York, 1902.

Brooks, Noah. *Washington, D.C., in Lincoln's Time*. Edited by Herbert Mitgang. New York, 1962.

Buck, William P., ed. *Sad Earth, Sweet Heaven: The Diary of Rebecca Buck*. Birmingham, Ala., 1973.

Casler, John O. *Four Years in the Stonewall Brigade*. Guthrie, Okla., 1893.

Clark, Walter, ed. *Histories of the Several Regiments and Battalions from North Carolina in the Great War, 1861–'65*. 5 vols. Goldsboro, N.C., 1901.

Clark, Willene B., ed. *Valleys of the Shadow: The Memoir of Confederate Captain Reuben G. Clark, Company I, 59th Tennessee Mounted Infantry*. Knoxville, 1994.

Colt, Margaretta Barton. *Defend the Valley: A Shenandoah Family in the Civil War*. New York, 1994.

Cooke, John Esten. *Wearing of the Gray*. New York, 1867.

Cowper, Pulaski. *Extracts of Letters of Major-General Bryan Grimes to His Wife*. Edited by Gary W. Gallagher. Wilmington, N.C., 1986.

Cox, Jacob Dolson. *Military Reminiscences of the Civil War*. 2 vols. New York, 1900.

Crist, Lynda Lasswell, et al., eds. *The Papers of Jefferson Davis*. 9 vols. Baton Rouge, 1971–.

Davis, William J. *The Partisan Rangers of the Confederate States Army*. Louisville, 1904.

Dawson, Francis W. *Reminiscences of Confederate Service, 1861–1865*. Edited by Bell I. Wiley. Baton Rouge, 1980.

DeButts, Mary Custis Lee, ed. *Growing Up in the 1850s: The Journal of Agnes Lee*. Chapel Hill, 1984.

Dennett, Tyler, ed. *Lincoln and the Civil War in the Diaries and Letters of John Hay*. New York, 1939.

Donald, David, ed. *Inside Lincoln's Cabinet: The Civil War Diaries of Salmon P. Chase*. New York, 1954.

Douglas, Henry Kyd. *I Rode with Stonewall*. Chapel Hill, 1940.

Dowdey, Clifford, and Louis H. Manarin, eds. *The Wartime Papers of R. E. Lee*. Boston, 1961.

Drickamer, Lee C., and Karen D. Drickamer, eds. *Fort Lyon to Harpers Ferry*. Shippensburg, Pa., 1987.

Duke, Basil W. *History of Morgan's Cavalry*. Cincinnati, 1867.

———. *Reminiscences of General Basil W. Duke, C.S.A.* Garden City, N.Y., 1911.

Du Pont, Henry A. *The Campaign of 1864 in the Valley of Virginia and the Expedition to Lynchburg*. New York, 1925.

Durkin, Joseph T., S.J., ed. *Confederate Chaplain: A War Journal of Rev. James B. Sheeran, C.SS.R.* Milwaukee, 1960.

Early, Jubal A. *Jubal Early's Memoirs: Autobiographical Sketch and Narrative of the War Between the States.* Baltimore, 1989.

———. *A Memoir of the Last Year of the War for Independence.* Lynchburg, 1867.

Eby, Cecil D. Jr., ed. *The Old South Illustrated by Porte Crayon: David Hunter Strother.* Chapel Hill, 1959.

———. *A Virginia Yankee in the Civil War: The Diaries of David Hunter Strother.* Chapel Hill, 1961.

Eckert, Edward K., and Nicholas J. Amato, eds. *Ten Years in the Saddle: Memoir of William Woods Averell, 1851–1862.* San Rafael, Calif., 1978.

Egan, Michael. *The Flying, Gray-Haired Yank.* N.p. [Edgewood Publishing Company], 1888.

Elwood, John W. *Elwood's Stories of the Old Ringgold Cavalry, 1847–1865.* Coal Center, Pa., 1914.

Farrar, Samuel Clarke. *The Twenty-Second Pennsylvania Cavalry and the Ringgold Battalion, 1861–1865.* Akron, 1911.

Finerty, John F. *War-Path and Bivouac: The Big Horn and Yellowstone Expedition.* Edited by Milo Milton Quaife. Chicago, 1955.

Ford, Worthington Chauncey, ed. *A Cycle of Adams Letters, 1861–1865.* 2 vols. Boston, 1920.

Freeman, Douglas Southall, ed. *Lee's Dispatches.* Baton Rouge, 1994.

Gilmor, Harry. *Four Years in the Saddle.* New York, 1866.

Goode, John. *Recollections of a Lifetime.* New York, 1906.

Gordon, John B. *Reminiscences of the Civil War.* New York, 1903.

Grant, U. S. *Personal Memoirs of U. S. Grant.* 2 vols. New York, 1885–86.

Gurowski, Adam. *Diary from March 4, 1861, to November 12, 1862.* Boston, 1862.

Haas, Ralph. *Dear Esther: The Civil War Letters of Private Aungier Dobbs.* Edited by Philip Ensley. Apollo, Pa., 1991.

Hamlin, Percy Gatling, ed. *The Making of a Soldier: Letters of General R. S. Ewell.* Richmond, 1935.

Harrisonburg, Virginia: Diary of a Citizen. Berryville, Va., n.d.

Hay, John. *Letters of John Hay and Extracts from Diary.* 2 vols. New York, 1969.

Hayes, John B., ed. *Samuel Francis Du Pont: A Selection from His Civil War Letters.* 3 vols. Ithaca, 1969.

Hewitt, William. *History of the Twelfth West Virginia Volunteer Infantry.* N.p. [Twelfth West Virginia Infantry Association], 1892.

Higginson, Thomas Wentworth. *Army Life in a Black Regiment.* Boston, 1870.

Hildebrand, John R., ed. *A Mennonite Journal, 1862–1865.* Shippensburg, Pa., 1996.

Hoge, John Milton. *A Journal by John Milton Hoge, 1862–5: Containing Some of the Most Particular Incidents That Occurred During His Enlistment as a Soldier in the Confederate Army, Written by Himself, at Guest Station, Wise Co., Va., August, 1865.* Edited by Mary Hoge Bruce. Cincinnati, 1961.

Houck, Peter W., ed. *Confederate Surgeon: The Personal Recollections of E. A. Craighill.* Lynchburg, 1989.

Humphreys, Milton W. *A History of the Lynchburg Campaign.* Charlottesville, 1924.

———. *Military Operations, 1861–1864: Fayetteville, West Virginia, and the Lynchburg Campaign.* Fayetteville, W. Va., 1926.

Hunter, David. *Report of the Military Services of Gen. David Hunter, U.S.A.* New York, 1873.

Johannsen, Robert W., ed. *The Letters of Stephen A. Douglas.* Urbana, 1961.

Johnson, Adam R. *The Partisan Rangers of the Confederate States Army.* Edited by William J. Davis. Louisville, 1904.

Johnson, Robert Underwood, and Clarence Clough Buel, eds. *Battles and Leaders of the Civil War.* 4 vols. New York, 1888.

Jones, J. B. *A Rebel War Clerk's Diary.* Philadelphia, 1866.

Kennedy, Joseph C. G., comp. *Population of the United States in 1860: Compiled from the Original Returns of the Eighth Census.* Washington, 1864.

Keyes, C. M., ed. *The Military History of the 123d Regiment Ohio Volunteer Infantry.* Sandusky, Ohio, 1874.

Lang, Theodore F. *Loyal West Virginia from 1861 to 1865.* Baltimore, 1895.

Lee, Susan P., ed. *Memoirs of William Nelson Pendleton.* Philadelphia, 1893.

Lincoln, William S. *Life with the Thirty-fourth Massachusetts Infantry in the War of the Rebellion.* Worcester, Mass., 1879.

Lindsley, John Berrien, ed. *The Military Annals of Tennessee.* Nashville, 1886.

Lynch, Charles H. *The Civil War Diary 1862–1865.* Privately Printed, 1915.

McClellan, H. B. *I Rode with Jeb Stuart.* Edited by Burke Davis. Bloomington, 1958.

McDonald, Archie P., ed. *Make Me a Map of the Valley.* Dallas, 1973.

McDonald, Cornelia. *A Diary with Reminiscences of the War and Refugee Life in the Shenandoah Valley, 1860–1865.* Nashville, 1935.

McDonald, William N. *A History of the Laurel Brigade.* Edited by Bushrod C. Washington. N.p. [Published by Mrs. Kate S. McDonald], 1907.

[McGuire, Judith White]. *Diary of a Southern Refugee, During the War.* New York, 1867.

McKim, Randolph H. *A Soldier's Recollections.* Washington, D.C., 1983.

Marshall, Jessie Ames, ed. *Private and Official Correspondence of Gen. Benjamin F. Butler.* 5 vols. N.p. [privately printed], 1917.

Martin, Robert Hugh. *A Boy of Old Shenandoah.* Edited by Carolyn Martin Rutherford. Parsons, W. Va., 1977.

Meade, Edwin B., ed. *Memoirs: Early Life and Civil War Days of Captain Edwin E. Bouldin.* Danville, Va., 1968.

Meade, George G., and George G. Meade, Jr. *The Life and Letters of George Gor-*

don Meade, Major General United States Army. Edited by George G. Meade III.
2 vols. New York, 1913.

The Medical and Surgical History of the War of the Rebellion. Washington, 1875.

Mitchell, Adele H., ed. The Letters of Major General James E. B. Stuart. N.p. [The Stuart-Mosby Historical Society], 1990.

Montgomery, Asbe. An Account of R. R. Blazer and His Scouts. Marietta, Ohio, 1865.

Moore, Edward A. The Story of a Cannoneer Under Stonewall Jackson. Freeport, N.Y., 1971.

Moore, Frank, ed. The Rebellion Record: A Diary of American Events. 11 vols. New York, 1867–68.

Mosby, John S. The Memoirs of Colonel John S. Mosby. Edited by Charles Wells Russell. 1917. Rpr. Bloomington, 1959.

Mosgrove, George Dallas. Kentucky Cavaliers. Edited by Bell Irvin Wiley. Jackson, Tenn., 1957.

Munson, John W. Reminiscences of a Mosby Guerrilla. Washington, D.C., 1983.

Neese, George M. Three Years in the Confederate Horse Artillery. New York, 1911.

Newcomer, C. Armour. Cole's Cavalry; or, Three Years in the Saddle. Baltimore, 1895.

Nichols, Clifton M. A Summer Campaign in the Shenandoah Valley in 1864. Springfield, Ohio, 1899.

Nichols, G. W. A Soldier's Story of His Regiment. Kennesaw, Ga., 1961.

Nicolay, John G., and John Hay. Abraham Lincoln: A History. 10 vols. New York, 1914.

Niven, John, et al., eds. The Salmon P. Chase Papers. Kent, Ohio, 1993.

Nivens, Allan, ed. A Diary of Battle: The Personal Journals of Colonel Charles S. Wainwright, 1861–1865. New York, 1962.

Norton, Chauncey S. "The Red Neck Ties"; or, History of the Fifteenth New York Volunteer Cavalry. Ithaca, 1891.

O'Ferrall, Charles T. Forty Years of Active Service. New York, 1904.

Opie, John N. A Rebel Cavalryman. Chicago, 1899.

O'Reilly, Miles. Baked Meats of the Funeral. New York, 1866.

Poague, William Thomas. Gunner with Stonewall: Reminiscences of William Thomas Poague. Edited by Monroe F. Cockrell. Wilmington, N.C., 1957.

Pollard, Edward A. The Last Year of the War. New York, 1866.

"Poore, Ben: Perley," comp. The Political Register and Congressional Directory. Boston, 1878.

Porter, Horace. Campaigning with Grant. New York, 1897.

Preliminary Report on the Eighth Census, 1860. Washington, D.C., 1862.

Quarles, Garland R., et al., eds. Diaries, Letters, and Recollections of the War Between the States. Winchester, Va., 1955.

Rawling, C. J. *History of the First Regiment Virginia Infantry*. Philadelphia, 1887.

Reader, Frank S. *History of the Fifth West Virginia Cavalry*. New Brighton, Pa., 1890.

Reid, Whitelaw. *A Radical View: The "Agate" Dispatches of Whitelaw Reid, 1861–1865*. Edited by James G. Smart. Memphis, 1976.

Report of the Board of Visitors of the Virginia Military Institute. N.p., July 1864.

Robertson, George F. *A Small Boy's Recollections of the Civil War*. Charlotte, N.C., 1932.

Robertson, Margaret Briscoe Stuart. *My Childhood Recollections of the War*. N.p., n.d.

Robertson, Mary D., ed. *Lucy Breckinridge of Grove Hill: The Journal of a Virginia Girl, 1862–1864*. Kent, Ohio, 1979.

Rowland, Dunbar. *Jefferson Davis, Constitutionalist: His Letters, Papers, and Speeches*. 10 vols. Jackson, Miss., 1923.

Runge, William H., ed. *Four Years in the Confederate Artillery: The Diary of Private Henry Robinson Berkeley*. Chapel Hill, 1961.

Scarborough, William Kauffman, ed. *The Diary of Edmund Ruffin*. Baton Rouge, 1976.

Schmitt, Martin F., ed. *General George Crook: His Autobiography*. Norman, Okla., 1986.

Schuckers, Jacob W. *The Life and Public Services of Salmon Portland Chase*. New York, 1874.

Schurz, Carl. *Reminiscences of Carl Schurz*. 3 vols. New York, 1907.

Schwaab, Eugene L., ed. *Travels in the Old South*. 2 vols. Lexington, Ky., 1973.

Schwartz, Gerald, ed. *A Woman Doctor's Civil War: Esther Hill Hawks' Diary*. Columbia, S.C., 1984.

Scott, John. *Partisan Life with Col. John S. Mosby*. New York, 1867.

Sears, Stephen W., ed. *The Civil War Papers of George B. McClellan*. New York, 1988.

Sheridan, Philip H. *Personal Memoirs of P. H. Sheridan*. New York, 1888.

Simon, John Y., ed. *The Papers of Ulysses S. Grant*. 20 vols. Carbondale, 1967–.

Smith, Theodore Clarke. *The Life and Letters of James Abram Garfield*. 2 vols. New Haven, 1925.

Sorrel, G. Moxley. *Recollections of a Confederate Staff Officer*. Edited by Bell Irvin Wiley. Wilmington, N.C., 1987.

Stephens, Robert Grier Jr., ed. *Intrepid Warrior: Clement Anselm Evans, Confederate General from Georgia*. Dayton, Ohio, 1992.

Stevenson, James H. *"Boots and Saddles": A History of the First Volunteer Cavalry of the War*. Harrisburg, Pa., 1879.

Storey, Henry Wilson. *History of Cambria County, Pennsylvania*. 3 vols. New York, 1907.

Sutton, Joseph J. *History of the Second Regiment: West Virginia Cavalry Volunteers.* Portsmouth, Ohio, 1892.

Swiger, Elizabeth Davis, ed. *Civil War Letters and Diary of Joshua Winters.* Parsons, W. Va., 1991.

Sypher, J. R. *History of the Pennsylvania Reserve Corps.* Lancaster, Pa., 1865.

Taylor, Walter H. *Four Years with General Lee.* Edited by James I. Roberston, Jr. Bloomington, 1962.

Thayer, William Roscoe. *The Life and Letters of John Hay.* 2 vols. Boston, 1915.

Thirty-Eighth Annual Report of the President and Directors to the Stockholders of the Baltimore and Ohio Railroad Co. Baltimore, n.d.

Tower, R. Lockwood, ed. *Lee's Adjutant: The Wartime Letters of Colonel Walter Herron Taylor, 1862–1865.* Columbia, S.C., 1995.

Turner, Charles W., ed. *The Diary of Henry Boswell Jones of Brownsburg (1842–1871).* Verona, Va., 1979.

―――. *My Dear Emma. (War Letters of Col. James K. Edmondson, 1861–1865).* Verona, Va., 1978.

U.S. War Department, *Atlas to Accompany the Official Records of the Union and Confederate Armies.* Washington, D.C., 1891–95: Rpr. Gettysburg, 1978.

U.S. War Department. *The War of the Rebellion: A Compilation of the Official Records of the Union and Confederate Armies.* 128 vols. Washington, D.C., 1880–1901.

Valley News Echo: Monthly Civil War Newspaper. Hagerstown, Md., 1965.

Vandiver, Frank E., ed. *The Civil War Diary of General Josiah Gorgas.* University, Ala., 1947.

Walker, William C. *History of the Eighteenth Regiment Connecticut Volunteers in the War for the Union.* Norwich, Conn., 1885.

Ward, J. E. D. *Twelfth Ohio Volunteer Infantry.* Ripley, Ohio, 1864.

Wildes, Thomas F. *Record of the One Hundred and Sixteenth Regiment Ohio Infantry Volunteers in the War of Rebellion.* Sandusky, Ohio, 1884.

Williams, Charles Richard, ed. *Diary and Letters of Rutherford Birchard Hayes.* 4 vols. Columbus, Ohio, 1922.

Williams, Edward B., ed. *Rebel Brothers: The Civil War Letters of the Truehearts.* College Station, Tex., 1995.

Williamson, James J. *Mosby's Rangers.* New York, 1909.

Windsor, A. H. *History of the Ninety-First Regiment, O.V.I.* Cincinnati, 1865.

Wintz, William D., ed. *Civil War Memoirs of Two Rebel Sisters.* Charleston, W. Va., 1989.

Wise, Jennings Cropper. *The Long Arm of Lee.* Lincoln, Nebr., 1991.

Wise, John S. *Battle of New Market, Va., May 15, 1864: An Address.* Lexington, Va., 1882.

―――. *The End of an Era.* Boston, 1899.

Woodward, E. M. *History of the Third Pennsylvania Reserve*. Trenton, N.J., 1883.

Worsham, John H. *One of Jackson's Foot Cavalry*. New York, 1912.

Younger, Edward, ed. *Inside the Confederate Government: The Diary of Robert Garlick Hill Kean*. New York, 1957.

Articles

Anderson, John T. "General Hunter in the Valley: John T. Anderson to J. D. Imboden, April 2, 1877." *Tyler's Quarterly Historical and Genealogical Magazine*, XII (1931), 197–98.

Arthur, E. C. "The Dublin Raid." *Ohio Soldier* II (Jan. 5), 321–23; (Jan. 19), 337–39; (Feb. 2), 353–55; (Feb. 16), 370–71; (March 2), 386–87; (March 16), 402; (March 30), 418–19; (April 13, 1889), 433–37.

"Battle of New Market, Va., Again." *Southern Historical Society Papers*, XXXV (1907), 231–34.

Blackford, Charles M. "The Campaign and Battle of Lynchburg." *Southern Historical Society Papers*, XXX (1902), 279–314.

Bouldin, E. E. "Charlotte Cavalry." *Southern Historical Society Papers*, XXVII (1900), 71–81.

Bradwell, I. G. "Cold Harbor, Lynchburg, Valley Campaign, etc., 1864." *Confederate Veteran*, XXVIII (1920), 138–39.

———. "First of Valley Campaign by General Early." *Confederate Veteran*, XIX (1911), 230–31.

Broun, Thomas L. "Cloyd's Mountain Battle." *Southern Historical Society Papers*, XXXVII (1909), 349–50.

———. "Reminiscences of Maj. Thomas L. Broun." *Confederate Veteran*, IX (1901), 229–30.

Bruce, D. H. "The Battle of New Market." *Southern Historical Society Papers*, XXXV (1907), 155–58, and *Confederate Veteran*, XV (1907), 553–54.

Buchanan, Charles Warner. "Who Fired the First Gun at New Market?" *Confederate Veteran*, XVII (1909), 237.

Caperton, Mary Carr, "A Girl's Recollection of War." *Confederate Veteran*, XXXV (1927), 378–79.

Colley, Thomas W. "Brig. Gen. William E. Jones." *Confederate Veteran*, XI (1903), 266–67.

"Concerning V.M.I. Cadets at New Market." *Confederate Veteran*, XX (1912), 100.

Conway, Wm. B. "Talks with General J. A. Early." *Southern Historical Society Papers*, XXX (1902), 250–55.

Cox, William R. "Major-General Stephen D. Ramseur: His Life and Character." *Southern Historical Society Papers*, XVIII (1890), 217–60.

Crowninshield, Benjamin W. "Cedar Creek." In *Papers of the Military Historical Society of Massachusetts* (Boston, 1907), VI, 155–81.

Daniel, John W. "General Jubal A. Early." *Southern Historical Society Papers*, XXII (1897), 281–32.

Dayton, J. L. Henry. "First Tennessee Cavalry at Piedmont." *Confederate Veteran*, XXII (1914), 397.

"Diary of Robert E. Park." *Southern Historical Society Papers*, I (1876), 370–86.

Early, J. A. "Didn't Want a Pardon." *Southern Historical Society Papers*, XXIV (1896), 176–82.

Eby, Cecil D. Jr., ed. "With Sigel at New Market: The Diary of Colonel D. H. Strother." *Civil War History*, VI (1960), 73–83.

Evans, Thomas J. "Capture the Flag." *Kepi* (Dec. 1983–Jan. 1984), 14–17.

"An Eye Witness Account of the Battle of Lynchburg by Porte Crayon." *Iron Worker*, XXIV (1960), 26–33.

Featherston, J. C. "Gen. Jubal Anderson Early." *Confederate Veteran*, XXVI (1918), 430–32.

"Field Letters from Stuart's Headquarters." *Southern Historical Society Papers*, III (1877), 190–94.

Gatch, Thomas B. "Recollections of New Market." *Confederate Veteran*, XXXIV (1926), 210–12.

"Gen. John Echols." *Confederate Veteran*, IV (1896), 316–17.

"General Hunter in the Valley." *Tyler's Quarterly Historical and Genealogical Magazine*, XII (1921), 197–98.

Greenwalth, Bruce S., ed. "Life Behind Confederate Lines in Virginia: The Correspondence of James D. Davidson." *Civil War History*, XVI (1970), 205–26.

Greer, George H. T. "Riding with Early: An Aide's Diary." *Civil War Times Illustrated*, XVII (1978), 30–35.

Grim, E. C. "Tender Memories of the V.M.I. Cadets." *Confederate Veteran*, XXXIV (1926), 212–13.

"Gunner at New Market, Va." *Confederate Veteran*, XXVI (1918), 191.

Harris, Jasper W. "Sixty-Second Virginia at New Market." *Confederate Veteran*, XVI (1908), 461–62.

Henry, J. L. "First Tennessee Cavalry at Piedmont." *Confederate Veteran*, XII (1914), 397.

Hilldrup, Robert Leroy. "The Romance of a Man in Gray Including the Love Letters of Captain James S. Perry, Forty-Five Virginia Infantry Regiment, C.S.A." *West Virginia History*, XXII (1961), 166–83.

Howard, John Clarke. "Recollections of New Market." *Confederate Veteran*, XXXIV (1926), 57–59.

Humphreys, Milton W. "The Battle of Cloyd's Farm." *Confederate Veteran*, XVII (1909), 598–99.

———. "Rejoinder to Capt. D. H. Bruce on the Battle of New Market." *Confederate Veteran*, XVI (1908), 572–73.

"Hunter's Raid, 1864." *Southern Historical Society Papers*, XXXVI (1908), 95–103.

Huntington, J. N. Potts, "Who Fired the First Gun at New Market?" *Confederate Veteran*, XVII (1909), 453.

Imboden, F. M. "Gen. G. C. Wharton." *Confederate Veteran*, XIV (1906), 392.

Imboden, John D. "Fire, Sword, and the Halter." In *The Annals of the War Written by Leading Participants North and South*, edited by Alexander K. McClure. Philadelphia, 1879, pp. 169–83.

———. "The Battle of New Market, Va., May 15th, 1864." In *Battles and Leaders of the Civil War*, edited by Robert Underwood Johnson and Clarence Clough Buel. 4 vols. New York, 1884–1888.

———. "The Battle of Piedmont." *Confederate Veteran*, XXXI (1923), 459–61, and XXXII (1924), 18–20.

Johnson, Bradley T. "My Ride Around Baltimore in Eighteen Hundred and Sixty-Four." *Southern Historical Society Papers*, XXX (1902), 215–25.

Johnston, J. Stoddard. "Sketches of Operations of General John C. Breckinridge." *Southern Historical Society Papers*, VII (1879), No. 1, pp. 257–62, and No. 2, pp. 317–23.

"Lee's High Estimate of General Imboden." *Confederate Veteran*, XXIX (1921), 420–21.

Levin, Alexandra Lee. "'Why have you burned my house?': Henrietta Lee and the Burning of Bedford." *Virginia Cavalcade* (1978), 84–95.

Long, A. L. "General Early's Valley Campaign." *Southern Historical Society Papers*, III (1877), 112–22, and XVIII (1890), 80–91.

Manarin, Louis H., ed. "Civil War Diary of Rufus J. Woolwine." *Virginia Magazine of History and Biography*, LXXI (1963), 416–48.

Mauzy, Richard. "Vandalism by General Hunter, 1864." *Augusta Historical Bulletin*, XIV (1978), 50–55.

M'Chesney, James. "Scouting on Hunter's Raid to Lynchburg, Va." *Confederate Veteran*, XXVIII (1920), 173–76.

Moore, J. Scott. "General Hunter's Raid." *Southern Historical Society Papers*, XXVII (1899), 179–91.

Morton, Howard, "What a Federal Soldier Wrote of the V.M.I. Cadets at New Market." *Southern Historical Society Papers*, XXXVI (1908), 283–84.

Neilson, T. H. "The Sixty-Second Virginia—New Market." *Confederate Veteran*, XVI (1908), 60–61.

Nelson, B. F. "A Boy in the Confederate Cavalry." *Confederate Veteran*, XXXVI (1928), 374–76.

"New Market Campaign, May, 1864." *Confederate Veteran*, XX (1912), 392.

Parsons, J. W. "Capture of Battery at New Market." *Confederate Veteran*, XVII (1909), 119.

Peerce, John. "Capture of a Railroad Train." *Southern Bivouac*, II (1884), 352–55.

Plecker, A. H. "Who Saved Lynchburg from Hunter's Raid?" *Confederate Veteran*, XXX (1922), 372–73.

Potts, J. N. "Who Fired the First Gun at New Market?" *Confederate Veteran*, XVII (1909), 453.

"Proceedings of First Confederate Congress." *Southern Historical Society Papers*, XLV (1925).

"Recollections of Jubal Early." *Century Magazine*, LXX (1905), 311–13.

"Reminiscences of Maj. Thomas L. Broun." *Confederate Veterans*, IX (1901), 229–30.

Robinson, W. P. "The Battle of Cloyd's Farm." *Confederate Veteran*, XXXIII (1925), 97–100.

Sager, Carl. "A Boy in the Confederate Cavalry." *Confederate Veteran*, XXXVI (1928), 374–76.

Schmitt, Martin F., ed. "An Interview with General Jubal A. Early in 1889." *Journal of Southern History*, XI (1945), 547–63.

Setchell, George Case, "A Sergeant's View of the Battle of Piedmont." *Civil War Times Illustrated*, II (1963), 42–47.

Shank, S. T. "A Gunner at New Market, Va." *Confederate Veteran*, XXVI (1916), 191.

"Shelling of Lexington, Va." *Confederate Veteran*, XXXII (1924), 378–79.

Showell, Margaret Letcher, "Ex-Governor Letcher's Home." *Southern Historical Society Papers*, XVIII (1890), 393–97.

Smith, George H. "More of the Battle of New Market." *Confederate Veterans*, XVI (1908), 569–72.

Stark, William B. "The Great Skedaddle." *Atlantic Monthly*, CLXII (1938), 86–94.

[Strother, David Hunter]. "Virginia Illustrated." *Harper's New Monthly Magazine*, X (1855), 1–25, 289–310, and XI (1855), 288–311.

———. "A Winter in the South." *Harper's New Monthly Magazine*, XV (1857), 435–51.

Thomson, James A. "The Lynchburg Campaign, June, 1864." In *G.A.R. War Papers*. Cincinnati, n.d., I, 121–47.

Turner, Charles W., ed. "General David Hunter's Sack of Lexington, Virginia, June 10–14, 1864: An Account by Rose Page Pendleton." *Virginia Magazine of History and Biography*, LXXXIII (1975), 173–83.

Turner, Edward Raymond. "The Battle of New Market." *Confederate Veterans*, XX (1912), 71–75.

"Vandalism by General Hunter, 1864." *Augusta Historical Bulletin*, XIV (1978), 50–55.

Vandiver, Frank E., ed. "Proceedings of the Second Confederate Congress." *Southern Historical Society Papers*, LI (1958).

"Visiting Battlefield of Piedmont." *Confederate Veteran*, XI (1903), 40.

Warner, Charles, "Who Fired the First Gun at New Market?" *Confederate Veteran*, XVII (1900), 237.

Washington, Bushrod C. "Henry D. Beall." *Confederate Veteran*, XII (1904), 399–400.

Wharton, J. U. H. "Gen. G. C. Wharton." *Confederate Veteran*, XIV (1906), 318–19.

———. "Maj. Gen. Gabriel C. Wharton." *Confederate Veteran*, VIII (1900), 320.

"When Hutter's House was Hunter's House." *Iron Worker*, X (1947), No. 3, pp. 1–6.

Whitaker, B. W. "Hunter's Coming! A Rebel's Experiences in Hunter's Raid on Lynchburg." *Virginia Country's Civil War Quarterly*, VI (1986), 30–36.

Wilson, Edward S. "The Lynchburg Campaign." In *Sketches of War History, 1861–1865*, edited by W. H. Chamberlin, 133–46. Cincinnati, 1896.

Wilson, R. B. "The Dublin Raid." In *G.A.R. War Papers*. Cincinnati, n.d., I, 92–120.

Wise, Henry A. "The Cadets at New Market, Va." *Confederate Veterans*, XX (1912), 361–62.

Wise, John S. "The West Point of the Confederacy." *Century Illustrated Monthly Magazine*, XXXVII (1888–89), 461–71.

Young, Bennett H. "John Cabell Breckinridge." *Confederate Veteran*, XIII (1905), 257–61.

Secondary Sources

Books

Armstrong, Joan Tracy. *History of Smyth County, Virginia*. Marion, Va., 1968.

Barred and Disallowed Case Files of the Southern Claims Commission, 1871–1880. Washington, D.C., 1987.

Bates, Samuel P. *History of Pennsylvania Volunteers, 1861–5*. 5 vols. Harrisburg, 1869.

Bennett, Charles W. Jr. *"Four Years with the Fifty-Fourth": The Military History of Franklin Bennett, 54th Pennsylvania Volunteer Regiment, 1861–1865*. Typescript. Richmond, 1985.

Black, Robert C. III. *The Railroads of the Confederacy*. Chapel Hill, 1952.

Bogue, Allan G. *The Congressman's Civil War*. New York, 1989.

Boney, F. N. *John Letcher of Virginia*. University, Ala., 1966.

Bonnell, John C. Jr. *Sabres in the Shenandoah: The 21st New York Cavalry, 1863–1866*. Shippensburg, Pa., 1996.

Brice, Marshall Moore. *Conquest of a Valley*. Verona, Va., 1965.

Bushong, Millard K. *Old Jube: A Biography of General Jubal A. Early*. Boyce, Va., 1961.

Catton, Bruce. *Grant Moves South*. Boston, 1961.

———. *Grant Takes Command*. Boston, 1968.

Cavanaugh, Michael. *The Otey, Ringgold, and Davidson Virginia Artillery*. Lynchburg, 1993.

Christian, W. Asbury. *Lynchburg and Its People*. Lynchburg, 1900.

Cleaves, Freeman. *Meade of Gettysburg*. Norman, Okla., 1960.

Connelly, Thomas Lawrence, and Archer Jones. *The Politics of Command*. Baton Rouge, 1973.

Cooling, Benjamin Franklin. *Jubal Early's Raid on Washington, 1864*. Baltimore, 1989.

Cornish, Dudley Taylor. *The Sable Arm: Black Troops in the Union Army, 1861–1865*. Lawrence, 1987.

Coulling, Mary Price. *Margaret Junkin Preston: A Biography*. Winston-Salem, 1993.

Couper, William. *History of the Shenandoah Valley*. 2 vols. New York, 1952.

———. *One Hundred Years at V.M.I.* 3 vols. Richmond, 1939.

———. *The V.M.I. New Market Cadets*. Charlottesville, 1933.

Cresap, Bernarr. *Appomattox Commander: The Story of General E. O. C. Ord*. San Diego, 1981.

Cunningham, Horace H. *Doctors in Gray*. Baton Rouge, 1993.

Daniel, W. Harrison. *Bedford County, Virginia, 1840–1860: The History of an Upper Piedmont County in the Late Antebellum Era*. Bedford, Va., 1985.

Davis, James. *51st Virginia Infantry*. Lynchburg, 1984.

Davis, William C. *The Battle of New Market*. Garden City, N.Y., 1975.

———. *Breckinridge: Statesman, Soldier, Symbol*. Baton Rouge, 1974.

Delauter, Roger U. Jr. *18th Virginia Cavalry*. Lynchburg, 1985.

———. *McNeill's Rangers*. Lynchburg, 1986.

———. *Winchester in the Civil War*. Lynchburg, 1992.

Dew, Charles B. *Ironmaker to the Confederacy: Joseph R. Anderson and the Tredegar Iron Works*. New Haven, 1966.

Dickinson, Jack L. *8th Virginia Cavalry*. Lynchburg, 1986.

———. *Jenkins of Greenbottom: A Civil War Saga*. Charleston, W. Va., 1988.

———. *16th Virginia Cavalry*. Lynchburg, 1989.

Driver, Robert J. Jr. *14th Virginia Cavalry*. Lynchburg, 1988.

————. *52d Virginia Infantry.* Lynchburg, 1986.

————. *Lexington and Rockbridge County in the Civil War.* Lynchburg, 1989.

————. *The Staunton Artillery—McClanahan's Battery.* Lynchburg, 1988.

Early, R. H. *Campbell Chronicles and Family Sketches.* Lynchburg, 1927.

Eby, Cecil D. Jr. *"Porte Crayon": The Life of David Hunter Strother.* Chapel Hill, 1960.

Eisenschiml, Otto. *The Celebrated Case of Fitz John Porter.* Indianapolis, 1950.

Engle, Stephen D. *Yankee Dutchman: The Life of Franz Sigel.* Fayetteville, Ark., 1993.

Evans, Clement A., ed. *Confederate Military History.* 12 vols. Atlanta, 1899.

Foote, Shelby. *The Civil War: A Narrative.* 3 vols. New York, 1974.

Freeman, Douglas Southall. *Lee's Lieutenants: A Study in Command.* 3 vols. New York, 1946–50.

————. *R. E. Lee: A Biography.* 4 vols. New York, 1935.

Fulwiler, Harry, Jr. *Buchanan, Virginia: Gateway to the Southwest.* Radford, Va., 1980.

Gallagher, Gary W., ed. *Struggle for the Shenandoah: Essays on the 1864 Valley Campaign.* Kent, Ohio, 1991.

Givens, Lula Porterfield. *Christiansburg, Montgomery County, Virginia: In the Heart of the Alleghenies.* Christiansburg, Va., 1981.

Goldsborough, W. W. *The Maryland Line in the Confederate Army.* 1869. Rpr. Gaithersburg, Md., 1987.

Hagerman, Edward. *The American Civil War and the Origins of Modern Warfare.* Bloomington, 1988.

Hale, Laura Virginia, and Stanley S. Phillips. *History of the Forty-Ninth Virginia Infantry C.S.A.: "Extra Billy Smith's Boys."* Lynchburg, 1981.

Hallock, Judith Lee. *Braxton Bragg and Confederate Defeat.* Tuscaloosa, Ala., 1991.

Hanchett, William. *Irish: Charles G. Halpine in Civil War America.* Syracuse, 1970.

Hildreth, Arthur. *A Brief History of New Market and Vicinity.* New Market, Va., 1964.

Holland, Cecil Fletcher. *Morgan and His Raiders.* New York, 1942.

Horner, Harlan Hoyt. *Lincoln and Greeley.* Urbana, 1953.

Houck, Peter W. *A Prototype of a Confederate Hospital Center in Lynchburg, Virginia.* Lynchburg, 1986.

Howard, Victor B. *Religion and the Radical Republican Movement, 1860–1870.* Lexington, Ky., 1990.

Howe, Daniel Dunbar. *Lovely Mount Tavern—The Birth of a City.* Boyce, Va., 1963.

Johnson, Patricia Givens. *The United States Army Invades the New River Valley, May 1864.* Christiansburg, Va., 1986.

Johnston, Angus James II. *Virginia Railroads in the Civil War.* Chapel Hill, 1961.

Johnston, David E. *A History of Middle New River Settlements and Contiguous Territory.* Huntington, W. Va., 1906.

Jones, Archer. *The Politics of Command.* Baton Rouge, 1973.

Jones, Virgil Carrington. *Gray Ghosts and Rebel Raiders.* McLean, Va., 1984.

Kagey, Deedie. *When Past Is Prologue: A History of Roanoke County.* Roanoke, 1988.

Kegley, Mary B. *Wythe County, Virginia: A Bicentennial History.* Wytheville, Va., 1989.

Kellogg, Sanford Cobb. *The Shenandoah Valley and Virginia, 1861 to 1865.* New York, 1903.

Kent, William B. *A History of Saltville, Virginia.* Radford, Va., 1955.

Klingberg, Frank W. *The Southern Claims Commission.* New York, 1978.

Lambert, Dobbie Edward. *Grumble: The W. E. Jones Brigade of 1863–1864.* Wahiawa, Hawaii, 1992.

Livermore, Thomas L. *Numbers and Losses in the Civil War.* Bloomington, 1957.

Longacre, Edward G. *Mounted Raids of the Civil War.* London, 1975.

Lonn, Ella. *Salt As a Factor in the Confederacy.* University, Ala., 1965.

Lowry, Terry. *22nd Virginia Infantry.* Lynchburg, 1988.

———. *26th Battalion Virginia Infantry.* Lynchburg, 1991.

McKinney, Tim. *The Civil War in Fayette County, West Virginia.* Charleston, W. Va., 1988.

McManus, Howard Rollins. *The Battle of Cloyds Mountain: The Virginia and Tennessee Railroad Raid, April 29–May 19, 1864.* Lynchburg, 1989.

MacMaster, Richard K. *Augusta County History, 1865–1950.* Staunton, Va., 1987.

Markham, Jerald H. *The Botetourt Artillery.* Lynchburg, 1986.

Marvel, William. *Southwest Virginia in the Civil War: The Battles for Saltville.* Lynchburg, 1992.

Massey, Mary Elizabeth. *Refugee Life in the Confederacy.* Baton Rouge, 1964.

Maxwell, Hu, and H. L. Swisher. *History of Hampshire County, West Virginia: From Its Earliest Settlement to the Present.* Morgantown, W. Va., 1897.

Middleton, Norwood C. *Salem: A Virginia Chronicle.* Salem, Va., 1986.

Miller, Edward A., Jr. *Lincoln's Abolitionist General: The Biography of David Hunter.* Columbia, S.C., 1997.

Mills, Gary B. *Southern Loyalists in the Civil War: The Southern Claims Commission.* Baltimore, 1994.

Moore, George Ellis. *A Banner in the Hills: West Virginia's Statehood.* New York, 1963.

Morris, George S., and Susan L. Foutz. *Lynchburg in the Civil War.* Lynchburg, 1984.

Morton, Frederic. *The Story of Winchester.* Strasburg, Va., 1925.

Morton, Oren F. *A History of Rockbridge County Virginia.* Staunton, Va., 1920.

Nicolay, John G., and John Hay. *Abraham Lincoln: A History.* 10 vols. New York, 1914.

Noe, Kenneth W. *Southwest Virginia's Railroad: Modernization and the Sectional Crisis.* Urbana, 1994.

Norris, J. E., ed. *History of the Lower Shenandoah Valley.* Chicago, 1890.

Olson, John E. *21st Virginia Cavalry.* Lynchburg, 1989.

Osborne, Charles C. *Jubal: The Life and Times of General Jubal A. Early, C.S.A.* Chapel Hill, 1992.

Patchan, Scott C. *The Forgotten Fury: The Battle of Piedmont, Virginia.* Fredericksburg, Va., 1996.

Patterson, Gerard A. *Rebels from West Point.* New York, 1987.

Pauley, Michael J. *Unreconstructed Rebel: The Life of General John McCausland C.S.A.* Charleston, W. Va., 1993.

Pendleton, Wm. C. *The History of Tazewell County and Southwest Virginia, 1748–1920.* Richmond, 1920.

Peyton, J. Lewis. *History of Augusta County, Virginia.* Staunton, Va., 1882.

Phillips, David L., and Rebecca L. Hill. *Tiger John: The Rebel Who Burned Chambersburg.* Leesburg, Va., 1993.

Phillips, Edward H. *The Lower Shenandoah Valley in the Civil War.* Lynchburg, 1993.

Pond, George E. *The Shenandoah Valley in 1864.* New York, 1883.

Pratt, Fletcher. *Stanton: Lincoln's Secretary of War.* New York, 1953.

Quarles, Garland R. *Occupied Winchester, 1861–1865.* Winchester, Va., 1991.

Ramage, James A. *Rebel Raider: The Life of General John Hunt Morgan.* Lexington, Va., 1986.

Ramsdell, Charles W., *Behind the Lines in the Southern Confederacy.* Baton Rouge, 1944.

Rawls, Walton, ed. *Great Civil War Heroes and Their Battles.* New York, 1985.

Reed, Rowena. *Combined Operations in the Civil War.* Annapolis, 1978.

Reid, Whitelaw. *Ohio in the War.* Cincinnati, 1868.

Robertson, James I. Jr. *The Stonewall Brigade.* Baton Rouge, 1963.

Rose, Willie Lee. *Rehearsal for Reconstruction: The Port Royal Experiment.* New York, 1967.

Schuckers, J. W. *The Life and Public Services of Salmon Portland Chase.* New York, 1874.

Scott, J. L. *Lowry's, Bryan's, and Chapman's Batteries of Virginia Artillery.* Lynchburg, 1988.

———. *23rd Battalion Virginia Infantry.* Lynchburg, 1991.

Scruggs, Philip Lightfoot. *The History of Lynchburg, Virginia, 1786–1946.* Lynchburg, n.d.

Sifakis, Stewart. *Who Was Who in the Civil War.* New York, 1988.

Smith, Conway Howard. *Land That Is Pulaski County.* Pulaski, Va., 1981.

Smith, Francis H. *The Virginia Military Institute: Its Building and Rebuilding.* Lynchburg, 1912.

Smith, George H. *The Positions and Movements of the Troops in the Battle of New Market.* Los Angeles, 1913.

Smith, Theodore Clarke. *The Life and Letters of James Abram Garfield.* 2 vols. New Haven, 1925.

Starr, Stephen Z. *The Union Cavalry in the Civil War.* 3 vols. Baton Rouge, 1979–85.

Strickler, Harry M. *A Short History of Page County, Virginia.* Harrisonburg, Va., 1985.

Stutler, Boyd B. *West Virginia in the Civil War.* Charleston, W. Va., 1963.

Thomas, Benjamin P., and Harold M. Hyman. *Stanton: The Life and Times of Lincoln's Secretary of War.* New York, 1962.

Trefousse, Hans L. *The Radical Republicans.* Baton Rouge, 1975.

Turner, Edward Raymond. *The New Market Campaign, May 1864.* Richmond, 1912.

Turner, George Edgar. *Victory Rode the Rails.* Indianapolis, 1953.

Utley, Robert M. *Frontier Regulars.* New York, 1973.

Vandiver, Frank E. *Jubal's Raid.* New York, 1960.

———. *Rebel Brass: The Confederate Command System.* Baton Rouge, 1956.

Waddell, Jos. A. *Annals of Augusta County, Virginia.* Harrisonburg, Va., 1979.

Walker, Gary C. *The War in Southwest Virginia.* Roanoke, 1985.

Warner, Ezra J. *Generals in Blue: Lives of the Union Commanders.* Baton Rouge, 1964.

———. *Generals in Gray: Lives of the Confederate Commanders.* Baton Rouge, 1965.

Warner, Ezra J., and W. Buck Yearns. *Biographical Register of the Confederate Congress.* Baton Rouge, 1975.

Wayland, John W. *A History of Rockingham County, Virginia.* Dayton, Va., 1912.

———. *A History of Shenandoah County, Virginia.* Strasburg, Va., 1969.

Weaver, Jeffrey C. *22nd Virginia Cavalry.* Lynchburg, 1991.

Wellman, Manly Wade. *Rebel Boast: First at Bethel—Last at Appomattox.* New York, 1956.

Wert, Jeffry D. *Mosby's Rangers.* New York, 1990.

Williams, John Alexander. *West Virginia: A History.* New York, 1984.

Williams, T. Harry. *Hayes of the Twenty-Third: The Civil War Volunteer Officer.* New York, 1965.

———. *Lincoln and His Generals.* New York, 1952.

———. *Lincoln and the Radicals.* Madison, Wisc., 1941.

Wilson, James Grant, and John Fiske, eds. *Appleton's Cyclopaedia of American Biography.* 6 vols. New York, 1888.

Wilson, James Harrison. *The Life of John A. Rawlins*. New York, 1916.

Wise, Henry A. *Drawing Out the Man: The V.M.I. Story*. Charlottesville, 1978.

Wise, Jennings Cropper. *The Long Arm of Lee*. Lincoln, Nebr., 1991.

———. *The Military History of the Virginia Military Institute from 1839 to 1865*. Lynchburg, 1915.

Wittke, Carl. *Refugees of the Revolution*. Westport, Conn., 1970.

Woodward, Harold R. Jr. *Defender of the Valley: Brigadier General John Daniel Imboden C.S.A.* Berryville, Va. 1996.

Woodworth, Steven E. *Jefferson Davis and His Generals: The Failure of Confederate Command in the West*. Lawrence, Kans., 1990.

Zucker, A. E., ed. *The Forty-Eighters*. New York, 1967.

Articles

Abbot, Hariland Harris. "General John D. Imboden." *West Virginia History*, XXI (1960), 88–122.

Barclay, W. Houston. "Rockbridge Goes to War." *Proceedings of Rockbridge Historical Society*, VI (1966), 9–14.

Boney, F. N. "John Letcher: Pragmatic Confederate Patriot." In *The Governors of Virginia, 1869–1978*, edited by Edward Younger. Charlottesville, 1982.

Brice, Marshall Moore. "Augusta County During the Civil War." *Augusta Historical Bulletin*, I, no. 2, pp. 5–19.

Bright, Simeon Miller. "The McNeill Rangers: A Study in Confederate Guerrilla Warfare." *West Virginia History*, XII (1951), 338–87.

Brown, James Earl. "Life of Brigadier General John McCausland." *West Virginia History*, IV (1943), 239–93.

"Col. Francis Lee Smith." *Confederate Veteran*, XXVI (1918), 83–84.

"Col. George M. Edgar." *Confederate Veteran*, XII (1914), 85.

Cook, Roy Bird. "Albert Gallatin Jenkins—A Confederate Portrait." *West Virginia Review*, XI (1934), 225–27.

———. "Charleston and the Civil War." *West Virginia Review*, XI (1934), 322–24, 337.

———. "The Civil War Comes to Charleston." *West Virginia History*, XXIII (1962), 153–67.

Cox, William R. "Major-General Stephen D. Ramseur: His Life and Character." *Southern Historical Society Papers*, XVIII (1890), 217–60.

Craighill, Edley. "Lynchburg, Virginia, in the War Between the States." *Iron Worker*, XXIV, 2 (1960), 1–13.

Daniel, W. Harrison. "Old Lynchburg College, 1855–1869." *Virginia Magazine of History and Biography*, LXXXVIII (1980), 446–77.

Davis, James A. "The 51st Regiment, Virginia Volunteers, 1861–1865." *West Virginia History*, XXIX (1968), 178–202.

Davis, William C. "'Jubilee': General Jubal A. Early." *Civil War Times Illustrated,* IX (1970), 5–11, 43–48.

Donnelly, Ralph W. "The Confederate Lead Mines of Wythe County, Va." *Civil War History,* V (1959), 402–14.

Donnelly, Shirley. "General 'Tiger John' McCausland: The Man Who Burned Chambersburg." *West Virginia History,* XXIII (1962), 139–45.

Dooley, Edwin L., Jr. "Lexington in the 1860 Census." *Proceedings of the Rockbridge Historical Society,* IX (1975–79), 189–96.

Duncan, Richard R. "The Raid on Piedmont and the Crippling of Franz Sigel in the Shenandoah Valley." *West Virginia History,* LV (1996), 25–36.

Eby, Cecil D. Jr. "David Hunter: Villain of the Valley." *Proceedings of the Rockbridge Historical Society,* VI (1966), 87–92.

———. "David Hunter: Villain of the Valley: The Sack of the Virginia Military Institute." *Iron Worker* (Spring 1964), 1–9.

Eskew, Garnett Laidlaw. "They Called Him 'Town Burner.'" *West Virginia Review,* XVI (1938), 40–43, 61–63.

Feis, William B. "A Union Military Intelligence Failure: Jubal Early's Raid, June 12–July 14, 1864." *Civil War History,* XXXVI (1990), 209–25.

Fordney, Chris. "A Town Embattled." *Civil War Times Illustrated,* XXXIV (1996), 30–36, 70.

Gallagher, Gary W. "The Army of Northern Virginia in May 1864: A Crisis of High Command." *Civil War History,* XXXVI (1990), 101–18.

Gerhardt, E. Alvin Jr. "The Battle of Lynchburg, June 17–18, 1864." *Lynchburg Historical Society and Museum Papers,* VIII, No. 3, pp. 1–10.

"'Grumble' Jones: A Personality Profile." *Civil War Times Illustrated,* VII (1968), 35–41.

Hawke, George. "History of Once-Important Mount Torry Furnace Traced." *Augusta Historical Bulletin,* XIV (1978), 33–37.

Henderson, Catherine. "The Man Who Never Knew Defeat." *Civil War Times Illustrated,* XXIII (1984), 36–45.

Hess, Earl J. "Sigel's Resignation: A Study in German-Americanism and the Civil War." *Civil War History,* XXVI (1980), 5–17.

Hilldrup, Robert Leroy. "The Romance of a Man in Gray, Including the Love Letters of Captain James S. Perry, Forty-Fifth Virginia Infantry Regiment, C.S.A." *West Virginia History,* XXII (1961), 177–83.

Johnson, Flora Smith. "The Civil War Record of Albert Gallatin Jenkins, C.S.A." *West Virginia History,* VIII (1947), 392–404.

Kelley, Joseph Crockett, Sr. "Cove Brick Presbyterian Church." *Wythe County Historical Review* (1979), No. 15, pp. 30–34.

Kennon, L. W. V. "The Valley Campaign of 1864." *Confederate Veteran,* XXVI (1918), 517–23.

Kimball, William J. "The 'Outrageous Bungling at Piedmont.'" *Civil War Times Illustrated*, V (1967), 40–46.

Kincaid, Mary Elizabeth. "Fayetteville, West Virginia, During the Civil War." *West Virginia History*, XIV (1953), 339–64.

Longacre, Edward G. "A Profile of Major General David Hunter." *Civil War Times Illustrated*, XVI (1978), 4–9, 38–43.

McManus, Howard R. "Cloyd's Mountain." *Civil War Times Illustrated*, XVIII (1980), 20–29.

Neely, Mark E. Jr. "Was the Civil War a Total War?" *Civil War History*, XXXVII (1991), 5–28.

Pauley, Michael. "They Called Him 'Tiger John,'" *Blue and Gray*, I (1984), 12–17.

Porter, Charles H. "Operations of Generals Sigel and Hunter in the Shenandoah Valley, May and June, 1864." In Vol. VI, pp. 61–82, *Papers of the Military Historical Society of Massachusetts*. 14 Vols. Boston, 1881–1914.

Reid, Brian Holden. "Another Look at Grant's Crossing of the James, 1864." *Civil War History*, XXXIX (1993), 291–316.

Richardson, Hila Appleton. "Raleigh County, West Virginia in the Civil War." *West Virginia History*, X (1949), 283–98.

Robertson, James I. Jr. "The War in Words." *Civil War Times Illustrated* (May, 1977), 48.

Ruffner, Kevin Conley. "'More Trouble Than a Brigade': Harry Gilmor's 2nd Maryland Cavalry in the Shenandoah Valley." *Maryland Historical Magazine*, LXXXIX (1994), 389–411.

Saunders, Harold R. "The Early History and Development of Princeton, West Virginia." *West Virginia History*, XX (1959), 80–119.

Schenck, Robert C. "Major-General David Hunter." *Magazine of American History*, XVII (1887), 138–52.

Turner, Charles W. "The Virginia Central Railroad at War, 1861–1865." *Journal of Southern History*, XII (1946), 510–33.

———. "The Virginia Southwestern Railroad System at War, 1861–1865." *North Carolina Historical Review*, XXIV (1947), 467–84.

Turner, Edward Raymond. "The Battle of New Market." *Confederate Veteran*, XX (1912), 71–75.

Wilson, James A. "51st Virginia Regiment." *West Virginia History*, XXIX (1968), 178–202.

Theses and Dissertations

Bouldin, Mary Jane. "Lynchburg, Virginia: A City in War, 1861–1865." M.A. thesis, East Carolina University, 1976.

Morris, George Graham. "Confederate Lynchburg, 1861–1865." M.A. thesis, Virginia Polytechnic Institute and State University, 1977.

Smith, Everhard H. III. "The General and the Valley: Union Leadership During the Threat to Washington in 1864." Ph.D. dissertation, University of North Carolina, Chapel Hill, 1977.

Index